Trade Policy Issues and Empirical Analysis

A National Bureau
of Economic Research
Conference Report

Trade Policy Issues and Empirical Analysis

Edited by Robert E. Baldwin

 The University of Chicago Press

Chicago and London

ROBERT E. BALDWIN is the Hilldale Professor of Economics at
the University of Wisconsin–Madison, a research associate of the
National Bureau of Economic Research, and director of the
NBER's trade relations project.

The University of Chicago Press, Chicago 60637
The University of Chicago Press, Ltd., London
© 1988 by the National Bureau of Economic Research
All rights reserved. Published 1988
Printed in the United States of America
97 96 95 94 93 92 91 90 89 88   5 4 3 2 1

Library of Congress Cataloging-in-Publication Data

Trade policy issues and empirical analysis / edited by Robert E.
Baldwin.
    p. cm. — (A National Bureau of Economic Research
conference report)
  Papers from a conference held by the National Bureau of
Economic Research in Cambridge, Mass., Feb. 13–14, 1987.
  Includes indexes.
  ISBN 0–226–03607–3
  1. Commercial policy—Congresses.   2. Commercial policy—
Econometric models—Congresses.   I. Baldwin, Robert E.
II. National Bureau of Economic Research.   III. Series:
Conference report (National Bureau of Economic Research)
HF1411.T7133 1988
382′ .3—dc19   88–10346
                                                                            CIP

Since this volume is a record of conference proceedings, it has been exempted from the rules governing critical review of manuscripts by the Board of Directors of the National Bureau (resolution adopted 8 June 1948, as revised 21 November 1949 and 20 April 1968).

Contents

Preface

This volume is the result of a conference held by the National Bureau of Economic Research in Cambridge, Massachusetts, on February 13–14, 1987. I would like to thank Kirsten Foss and Ilana Hardesty of the NBER for the efficient manner in which they handled the conference arrangements and Anne Spillane and Mark Fitz-Patrick of the NBER for ensuring that the papers and comments were in the appropriate form for submission to the University of Chicago Press.

Funding for the conference was provided by The Ford Foundation; I am especially grateful to Tom Bayard of The Ford Foundation for his suggestions on issues to analyze and possible authors and commentators. I should also like to thank Nancy Klatt of the University of Wisconsin for editorial assistance.

Robert E. Baldwin

1 Introduction

Robert E. Baldwin

1.1 New Analytical Developments and the Need for Empirical Analyses

Increased interest in U.S. trade policy, stimulated by such factors as the massive U.S. trade deficit, a belief that intervention by foreign governments in international markets has given other countries a competitive edge over the United States, and concern about the increase in protection among industrial countries, has led to major analytical developments in international economics in recent years. The most important of these is the so-called new trade theory that emphasizes imperfect competition and increasing returns to scale in contrast to the traditional assumptions of perfect competition and constant returns. With this new framework it is possible to show that governments can sometimes "create" comparative advantages for their countries by exploiting market imperfections and scale economies. Furthermore, by introducing appropriate trade taxes or subsidies, governments can sometimes raise domestic welfare by shifting excess oligopolistic profits from foreign to domestic firms.

Another major development is the broadening of the scope of international economics to include the study of the political and economic factors shaping trade policy decisions by governments. By modeling the public choice process, economists are able to better understand not only why it is often very difficult politically to introduce trade measures that they believe will raise national welfare but why policies that they think will reduce national welfare are sometimes implemented.

Robert E. Baldwin is Hilldale Professor of Economics at the University of Wisconsin–Madison, a research associate of the National Bureau of Economic Research, and director of NBER's trade relations project.

As is the case with the traditional competitive framework, a wide range of economic outcomes is possible in both imperfectly competitive and public choice models. Which outcomes are most likely under various conditions can only be determined by careful empirical, institutional, and historical analyses of relevant cases and events. Unfortunately, such studies do not exist in sufficient numbers to draw many general conclusions, due to the long-standing lack of interest by economists in trade policy matters and the newness of the imperfectly competitive and public choice approaches. The purpose of this volume is to help correct this state of affairs by analyzing various trade policy issues not only theoretically but in empirical, institutional, and historical terms. It contains the papers presented at a National Bureau of Economic Research conference on Trade Policy Issues and Empirical Analysis, which took place in Cambridge, Massachusetts, on February 13–14, 1987. Most of the comments of the discussants of the papers are also included. The conference was one of a series being held as part of NBER's trade relations project, which is financed by the Ford Foundation.

The volume is divided into four parts. The four chapters in part I, "Measuring Trade Policy Effects under Imperfectly Competitive Market Conditions," empirically assess the economic impact of various trade policies introduced in industries where the "new" trade theory seems to apply. Part II, "Measuring the Economic Effects of Protection," contains two chapters that attempt to isolate the effects of protection from the influences of the many other economic changes that accompany actual periods of protection and one chapter that examines how the effects of exogenous changes in economic conditions vary depending on the form of protection. The chapter in part III, "Determining the Relationship between Foreign Direct Investment and Exports," provides new empirical evidence on the issue of the effect of foreign production by a country's firms on the home country's exports. In part IV, "Assessing U.S. Bilateral Trade Policy Disputes," two key bilateral issues are analyzed, namely, recent U.S.-Japanese trade tensions and the incident involving the threat of the imposition of countervailing duties by the United States on Canadian softwood lumber. The latter chapter adopts an explicit political economy framework.

1.2   Measuring Trade Policy Effects under Imperfect Competition

The first chapter in part I, "Empirics of Taxes on Differentiated Products: The Case of Tariffs in the U.S. Automobile Industry," by James Levinsohn, focuses on the trade and domestic production effects of imposing a tariff on a subset of a group of differentiated products, in particular, automobiles imported from only one country or only small cars rather than all cars. To deal with the problem of estimating own- and cross-price elasticities of demand for over a hundred different models of available cars, most of which are available for only a few years, Levinsohn adopts a Lancasterian characteristic approach to determine which multidimensionally differentiated automobiles closely compete with each other, that is, which are neighbors. This technique makes the estimation problem tractable, since the cross-price effects of non-neighbors are assumed to be zero.

The resulting list of neighbors for the various models is quite reasonable and the derived demand elasticities are both reasonable and statistically significant. Levinsohn's calculations indicate, for example, that a 1 percent increase in the price of imported Japanese automobiles leads to a .187 percent rise in the demand for domestically produced autos and a .393 percent and .300 percent rise in the demand for imported German and Swedish cars, respectively. In contrast, he estimates that a 1 percent rise in the price of all imported cars would stimulate a .367 percent increase in U.S. auto production.

Richard Baldwin and Paul Krugman empirically model international competition in the market for large commercial jet aircraft in chapter 3, "Industrial Policy and International Competition in Wide-Bodied Jet Aircraft." The aircraft industry is technology-intensive, involving large initial development expenses as periodic fundamental breakthroughs in design are made. There are significant reductions in production costs as experience with new technology is gained. A special feature of the medium-range, wide-bodied aircraft sector on which the authors focus is that one of the two suppliers, Airbus, is a consortium jointly owned and heavily subsidized by four European governments. The authors' main aims, using the simulation model they develop, are to reproduce the competitive conflict between Airbus and the U.S. supplier of such aircraft, Boeing, and to estimate the magnitude of the actual subsidy received by Airbus and its effect on welfare in the United States, Europe, and the rest of the world.

The authors model international competition between Boeing and Airbus as a Cournot duopoly situation in which the willingness of European governments to subsidize Airbus enables this firm to use a zero discount rate in calculating its optimum output path, in contrast to a 5 percent rate for Boeing. Relying on various industry studies for estimates of initial setup costs, the elasticity of the learning curve, the price elasticity of demand for the aircraft, and other needed parameters, Baldwin and Krugman first calibrate the model to a base period in which the price of the aircraft and the market shares of the two producers are known and then simulate the behavior of prices and market shares thereafter. They also simulate a scenario in which the European countries do not subsidize production and Boeing is the only producer throughout the period. Their basic result is that the subsidized entry of Airbus cost Europe about $1.5 billion and reduced Boeing's potential profits significantly. The early market entry of the aircraft due to the existence of Airbus also brought significant consumer benefits to all, although not enough to offset the loss in producer surplus in the United States.

In chapter 4, "Strategic Models, Market Structure, and State Trading: An Application to Agriculture," Marie Thursby considers the optimum role for government trade policy in a situation in which two countries, one represented by a marketing board that maximizes joint producer returns and the other by one or more private firms that maximize profits, compete in exporting a homogeneous agricultural product to a third country. Both countries consume the product themselves but do not export to each other's domestic market. This framework fits the stylized role of Canada and the United States in the world wheat market.

Thursby finds that optimal trade policy differs depending on whether the marketing agent maximizes producer returns or profits only if the government with the marketing board regulates the domestic price of the commodity. In particular, an export tax might be the optimal policy for the government of the country with a regulated marketing board, whereas an export subsidy is always the optimal policy for a government when the country's exports are controlled by a private, profit-maximizing monopolist. If the private export industry is composed of more than one firm, however, an export tax also might be optimal for this government.

Using the ability to price-discriminate between export and domestic markets as an indicator of market power, Thursby empirically analyzes the relationship between differences in U.S. export and domestic prices of grains and volumes of U.S. exports of these commodities (a positive relationship indicates the existence of market power); she concludes that, except in the case of wheat, there is no evidence of the exercise of monopoly power by U.S. exporters. This suggests that the appropriate strategic grains policy for the U.S. government would be export taxes.

Surprisingly little work has been done in applying the "new" trade theory to developing countries. Yet, as Dani Rodrik points out in chapter 5, "Imperfect Competition, Scale Economies, and Trade Policy in Developing Countries," available evidence on concentration ratios and scale economies suggests that the imperfect competition framework is even more germane for developing countries than developed economies.

Rodrik first develops a general equilibrium framework for assessing the benefits and losses from partial trade liberalization by developing countries in which he shows the potential clash between pulling resources out of protected sectors and expanding firm output in industries with significant scale economies. He then simulates the effect of liberalizing imports in three typical developing-country industries, automobiles, tires, and electrical appliances, in order to assess the relative importance of these two conflicting forces. His conclusion is that the levels of protection observed in the manufacturing sectors of most developing countries greatly exceed any that can be justified by the presence of imperfect competition. He stresses, however, that the optimal pattern of liberalization under imperfectly competitive conditions is likely to be quite different from what one might anticipate on the basis of intuition deriving from the competitive paradigm.

1.3 Measuring the Economic Effects of Protection

In measuring differences in the degree of openness among countries, economists are hampered by the difficulty of quantifying the many nontariff trade barriers presently restricting international trade. Edward Leamer in chapter 6, "Measures of Openness," which is the first essay in part II, tries to overcome this problem by using data on supplies of productive resources and distances to markets to explain the observed degree of a country's openness and then by taking the difference between the degree of openness predicted by the model and the actual degree of openness as a measure of the effects of a country's trade barriers.

Utilizing 1982 trade data for 183 three-digit Standard International Trade Classification (SITC) commodities covering sixty-five countries, he estimates both a factor-analytic model with resources treated as unobserved variables and a model with measured values for the resources. The factor-analytic model fits the observed data quite well, and an examination by country of the commodities contributing the most to the absolute residuals suggests that they can be explained by reasons other than trade barriers. Rather than concluding that trade barriers are not an important impediment to openness, Leamer concludes that the technique itself is seriously flawed because only peculiarities in a country's trade in comparison with the trade of others can give rise to the result that barriers are important. For example, if all countries protect to the same degree, the technique will not pick up any of the restrictive effects of these barriers.

The model based on measured values for resources is not open to the same criticism, but its relatively poor fit suggests that there are important omitted variables. An examination of the individual items contributing the most to the residuals reinforces the view that omitted variables are the major explanation why most items appear on the list. Leamer, consequently, is pessimistic about the ability of residual techniques to capture the effects of trade barriers on the degree of openness among countries.

Chapter 7, by Robert Baldwin and Richard Green, "The Effects of Protection on Domestic Output," attempts to measure the degree to which import protection stimulates domestic output and employment levels in the protected industries. After reviewing various theoretical reasons why protection may be less effective than policymakers might expect, the authors review reports of the International Trade Commission (ITC) evaluating industry requests for the extension of import protection and then undertake an econometric analysis of the effectiveness of protection.

The ITC documents several instances where protection has been undermined because of various unanticipated responses by suppliers and consumers. Country-specific protection granted the color television and nonrubber footwear industries, for example, was rendered ineffective by an increase in imports from noncontrolled suppliers. Quality upgrading, modifications in the product in order to qualify for a different tariff classification, and shifts by consumers to substitute products have also caused protection to be ineffective in various cases.

Using data for five industries at the four-digit SITC level over the period 1972–82, the econometric analysis utilizes a vector autogression model to test the hypothesis that a change in the level of protection does not "Granger cause" a change in the level of domestic output. In only one industry, footwear, are the results inconsistent with this hypothesis.

Rather than assessing the effects of different forms of protection introduced because of an increase in imports, Val Lambson, in chapter 8, "Trade Restraints, Intermediate Goods, and World Market Conditions," explores the effects of changes in economic conditions once protective policies are in place. In particular, using a general equilibrium model with intermediate goods, he contrasts the effects of a change in a country's terms of trade on domestic prices, factor use, and consumption when protection is provided, alternatively, by tariffs, by quotas, and by domestic content requirements in either physical or value terms.

Lambson finds that world and domestic prices of inputs move together when a tariff is in place, whereas under a quota a change in the world input price has no effect on its domestic price. With a domestic content requirement expressed in physical terms, the two prices are negatively correlated. The sign of the relationship when the domestic content requirement is stated in value terms is ambiguous. Lambson illustrates the possible magnitude of these various effects with a simple simulation exercise.

1.4 Measuring the Effects of Foreign Direct Investment on Exports

As Magnus Blomström, Robert Lipsey, and Ksenia Kulchycky note in chapter 9, "U.S. and Swedish Direct Investment and Exports," which makes up part III of the volume, the effect of the foreign production associated with foreign direct investment on the investing country's exports is still not fully settled, despite a considerable amount of previous empirical research. Policy proposals to hinder foreign investment out of concern that domestic jobs are lost by the substitution of foreign production for domestic production are still frequently put forth. A difficulty with all empirical studies of this issue is the likelihood that the variables determining investment and affiliate production in a country are the same ones determining trade flows. The authors attempt to overcome this simultaneity problem by using changes in exports rather than export levels, since it seems likely that the most troublesome unaccounted-for factors simultaneously influencing investment and exports do not determine changes in exports.

Blomström, Lipsey, and Kulchycky find that the higher the level of Swedish affiliate production in a country, the higher the level of Swedish exports to that country and that industry. Their results based on U.S. data are more mixed, however. At the most disaggregated industry level there is a preponderance of positive relationships between affiliate net sales and U.S. exports, but there are a few negative relationships, implying some substitution between affiliate production and U.S. exports.

1.5 Assessing U.S. Bilateral Trade Policy Disputes

In "United States–Japan Economic Relations," chapter 10 in part IV, Rachel McCulloch reexamines the main sources of economic friction between the United States and Japan and evaluates their significance in affecting current and future relations between the two countries. She concludes that the major source of friction, the huge Japanese export surplus with the United States, has been caused by a mismatch of macroeconomic policies and conditions in the two countries, in particular, U.S. fiscal policies that have produced the large federal budget deficit, the increased attractiveness of U.S. investments to foreigners coupled with the reduced appeal of foreign investments to Americans, and the liberalization of Japanese restrictions on capital outflows.

As McCulloch points out, the econometric evidence on whether Japan's low import share, especially in manufacturing, is due to trade barriers is conflicting. Some investigators of this issue find that Japan's trade is adequately explained by the same basic determinants that explain the trade of other countries; others find the opposite result, which they attribute to hidden import barriers. Even the latter group agrees, however, that removing the barriers is unlikely to have a major effect in reducing the overall trade imbalance.

McCulloch notes that the catch-up phase in Japan's technological knowledge has been completed and that, as the United States and Japan continue to become more similar in terms of technology base, capital, and labor skills, intra-industry trade is likely to grow significantly. She argues that sectoral trade conflicts will continue, however, as the two countries pursue different approaches to phasing out declining industries and nurturing new ones.

The final, very interesting chapter in the volume is by Joseph Kalt. As the title, "The Political Economy of Protectionism: Tariffs and Retaliation in the Timber Industry," indicates, Kalt uses a public choice perspective to analyze a major trade dispute between Canada and the United States. The incident involved preliminary findings, by the U.S. Commerce Department and the International Trade Commission, that Canada was subsidizing exports of softwood timber and that this was causing material injury to U.S. softwood lumber producers. It was highly likely that these findings would be confirmed in the final decisions of these organizations and that a 15 percent countervailing duty against Canadian softwood lumber exports would be imposed. But after high-level political efforts to contain the dispute, Canada agreed to impose a 15 percent duty on softwood lumber exports to the United States in return for the U.S. lumber industry's dropping the case.

Kalt finds that the actions of the U.S. lumber industry fit the "capture" theory of policy-making very well. The industry was able to organize effectively, produce well-reasoned technical and legal documents for the relevant government agencies, and enlist congressional support for its appeals to the White House. The Canadian lumber industry and the Canadian government objected vigorously to the pending imposition of countervailing duties but eventually accepted the export tax compromise, a solution that, by Kalt's calculations, actually increases Canada's national welfare on balance. He finds the paths that protectionism took in this case to be sobering. The United States was not pursuing a strategic policy to improve welfare but was pushed into protection by powerful domestic political interests and then had to find a way to halt the threat of a trade war by appeasing the affected foreign country.

I Measuring Trade Policy Effects under Imperfectly Competitive Market Conditions

2 Empirics of Taxes on Differentiated Products: The Case of Tariffs in the U.S. Automobile Industry

James Levinsohn

Recent theoretical advances in the industrial organization literature have provided insight into modeling the demand for differentiated products. Lancaster (1979) introduced and developed what he termed the "characteristics approach" to modeling the demand for differentiated products, while Dixit and Stiglitz (1977) pioneered what has come to be known as the "love of variety" approach to the subject. Both approaches have been applied to international trade theory. The result has been a heightened awareness of the role that product differentiation plays in trade theory. This work is presented in Helpman and Krugman (1985).

There have thus far been relatively few empirical applications of the new theories of trade. In this chapter, I present a new technique for econometrically estimating the demand for differentiated products. I adopt a Lancasterian approach to product differentiation and use theoretical results from this approach to solve several empirical problems. I then apply the technique to the demand for automobiles.

The estimates derived from this method allow me to analyze various trade and industrial policies for the U.S. automobile industry. For example, what would be the effect of a tariff applied only to Japanese imports on the total automobile import demand? Would domestically produced auto sales replace the Japanese imports or might German and Swedish imports rise, leaving total imports relatively constant? Some economists have argued for a tariff on all small foreign cars. Such a tax does not discriminate by country of origin and hence is not

James Levinsohn is assistant professor in the Department of Economics at the University of Michigan, Ann Arbor.

inconsistent with General Agreement on Tariffs and Trade (GATT) rules. As small foreign cars became more costly, would domestic car sales rise substantially or would the United States just trade imports of small cars for imports of larger cars? Optimal industrial policy toward the U.S. auto industry may involve subsidies to domestic producers, thereby possibly lowering the price of domestic autos.[1] Or perhaps government policy may involve subsidizing only one producer (e.g., Chrysler). What effects would these policies have on demand for different types of foreign and domestic automobiles?

All of these questions are, in a formal sense, quite similar. Each considers the effect of a tax placed on a subset of a group of differentiated products. Parameters needed to answer questions such as those posed above are own-price and appropriately defined cross-price elasticities of demand. Any analysis of the taxation of differentiated products must estimate (or use existing estimates of) these demand elasticities. The approach developed in this chapter provides a utility-consistent technique for deriving these elasticities. While I apply the methodology to issues of trade and industrial policy in the U.S. automobile industry, I believe that the general approach will have wider application. The methodology could, for example, be used to estimate demand elasticities in other differentiated products industries such as microcomputers, audio-video equipment, lumber, and steel. All of these industries have been the subject of recent trade policy debate.

This chapter is a first attempt at solving some of the empirical issues associated with the analysis of taxation of differentiated products. While the chapter provides some answers, it also raises a number of micro-economic and econometric issues for future research.

In section 2.1, I provide a brief critical review of the literature. Section 2.2 develops the methodology that is then applied in section 2.3. Using the demand system estimated in section 2.3, section 2.4 addresses many of the policy concerns posed in this introduction. Section 2.5 concludes with a brief summary.

2.1   A Brief Summary of the Literature

In theory, estimating the demand system for a set of differentiated products is no different than estimating a demand system for several homogeneous products. A typical estimated equation in such a system would regress quantity of a good demanded on its own price, the prices of the other differentiated or homogeneous products, and several other variables such as income and personal and demographic characteristics. Food is a good example of a set of differentiated products whose demand functions are nicely estimated by standard techniques. Recent work based on Deaton and Muellbauer's almost-ideal demand system provides excellent examples of this approach.[2]

For many sets of differentiated products, though, standard techniques are inapplicable. In the case of automobiles, there are over one hundred models available and few models are available for more than four consecutive years. The standard techniques would imply a system of, say, one hundred equations with ninety-nine cross-price effects. With so few years of data, the system is not estimable with any degree of accuracy. In the case of video cassette recorders or microcomputers, technology changes so quickly that no more than two or three years' data are likely to be available.

Several approaches to these problems have been taken in the empirical literature. Almost all have been applied to the automobile industry—at least partly because data are relatively plentiful. I accordingly focus on this body of research.

The easiest way around the problems posed by product differentiation is to ignore the issue. Not surprisingly, this was the approach first adopted. Work by Suits in 1958 used time series of total quantity of autos sold, average auto price, and real disposable income to arrive at aggregate demand elasticities. While it is surely unfair to judge the econometric methods of thirty years ago by the standards permitted by today's computing technology, Suits's approach is incapable of addressing the issues raised in this chapter's introduction. Surprisingly, research as recent as Toder (1978) uses elasticities imputed in part from Suits's original work when analyzing current automobile trade and industrial policy. Tarr and Morkre (1984) and Dixit (1987) in turn use elasticities derived from Toder.

Time-series techniques, even modern ones, are not applicable to investigating the effects of trade policy in the U.S. automobile industry because both products and tastes have changed significantly over the period of estimation (approximately the last twenty years). A 1965 Toyota is not the same car as a 1985 Toyota. As Toyotas change, the meaning of a single (constant) elasticity of demand for Toyotas becomes unclear. Tastes for autos and the characteristics that comprise them have also changed. While it may be theoretically possible to control for the reputation effects and network externalities that are responsible for this shift of tastes, it is not easy to do so in practice.

The most recent comprehensive study of the U.S. demand for automobiles is reported in Toder's (with Cardell and Burton) *Trade Policy and the U.S. Automobile Industry.* In that book, demand elasticities are estimated using three methodologies. Because most studies of the welfare effects of trade policy in the auto industry have used elasticity estimates from Toder, it is worthwhile taking a close look at these alternative approaches. Each is discussed in turn.

Toder's first approach is a time-series analysis. This work is more sophisticated than earlier work in that it introduces hedonic price indexes. Toder estimates the following regression:

$$ln\left(\frac{F}{D}\right) = \alpha_0 + \alpha_1 \, 1n\left(\frac{P_f}{P_d}\right) + \alpha_2\bar{Z},$$

where F/D is the foreign domestic auto sales ratio. P_f/P_d is the ratio of foreign to domestic hedonic prices. $\bar{Z}$ is a vector of exogenous variables.

The estimation uses annual data from 1960 to 1974. Estimates of α_1 ranged from -0.9 to -1.7, depending on the Z vector. The coefficient α_1 is the elasticity of substitution in demand. Using the estimate of α_1 and older estimates of total market demand elasticities, conventional price elasticities of demand can be derived.

There are at least four problems with this approach. First, as mentioned above, tastes seem to have changed over time, since casual empiricism suggests that a foreign car in 1960 was viewed very differently from one in 1974. As tastes vary over time, the economic relevance of the estimates of the elasticity of substitution in demand is called into question. Second, older estimates of the total market elasticity of demand are required to convert Toder's results into standard price elasticities of demand. While Toder used hedonic price indexes, the older studies did not. As cars are not homogeneous products, it is unclear exactly what the results of the older studies by Suits and others mean. Also, the older studies were conducted before auto imports were an empirically relevant phenomenon. Using these older out-of-sample market elasticities to derive the standard elasticities of demand may yield very misleading results. Third, even if the time series would yield accurate estimates, the agglomeration of all foreign cars prevents the analysis of taxes applied to only a subset of foreign autos. Fourth, regressing relative demands on relative hedonic prices does not follow from either a Lancasterian or Dixit-Stiglitz model of product differentiation. The choice of using relative demands and relative prices of domestic and foreign goods allows Toder, like all his predecessors, to estimate a single equation instead of a complete demand system. Toder's implicit assumption that an otherwise homogeneous good is differentiated only by country of origin is termed the Armington assumption. This assumption makes little sense from a consumer theory viewpoint unless there is some basis for supposing that goods are homogoeneous within countries but not across countries. Toder's first approach is, then, a utility inconsistent approach to modeling demand for differentiated products.

Toder's second method employed a cross-sectional approach to the demand-estimation problem. Toder used transport costs to introduce cross-sectional price variation. The units of observation were each of the continental United States. Here the regression estimated was

$$\frac{F}{D} = \alpha_0 + \alpha_1\left(\frac{P_f}{P_d}\right) + \alpha_2 PC2029 + \alpha_3 PCI + \alpha_4 PGAS,$$

where F/D is the ratio of foreign to domestic new car sales, P_f/P_d is the ratio of *delivered* foreign to domestic list prices, $PC2029$ is the percentage of population between ages 20 and 29, and $PGAS$ is the price of gasoline.

While the problems of time-varying parameters are not present in this cross-sectional approach, this method still relies on previously derived market elasticities to construct conventional price elasticities of demand. The cross-sectional methodology yielded generally unsatisfactory results. This is not surprising, since one might suspect that variables other than transport costs, gasoline costs, per capita income, and the percentage of the population in their twenty's explain why foreign cars are more predominant in New Jersey or California than they are in Michigan or Indiana.

Toder's third approach is by far the most innovative. Although computationally complex, the intuition behind this methodology—termed a hedonic market share model—is straightforward.

The model requires only one year's data on sales, list prices, and characteristics of automobiles. Let $\{\alpha_n^i\}$ be the set of marginal rates of substitution between N characteristics and price. Toder posits a lognormal distribution of $\{\alpha^i\}$ across consumers. Next, he estimates coefficients, β, which form a vector of sufficient statistics for the probability distribution of the α's. Let S be the vector of actual shares of auto sales by model. He next chooses β to maximize the likelihood of observing S. In brief, the technique selects statistics describing a distribution of consumer's utility functions that reproduce as nearly as possible the actual market shares observed.

Toder then applies the estimated taste distribution to a new set of available models (differing from the old set by price) to generate a new market share distribution. In this sense, the model simulates the relevant elasticities. Unlike the previous two approaches, the hedonic market share model can, in principle, predict market share elasticities for any subset of models. In practice, only an elasticity of substitution in demand between all foreign and all domestic cars is estimated. This yielded coefficients of -2.3 and -2.1, depending on the price increase simulated.

There are at least three major problems with this approach, the first two being interrelated.

1. The model is computationally quite difficult. Toder uses five characteristic variables to estimate the taste distribution. Calculating the maximum likelihood estimates for β requires a fifth-order numerical integration between each iteration of the likelihood function maximization. The cost of such computational techniques can be prohibitive. Also, some experts at numerical analysis question the accuracy of such a high-order integration of a complicated distribution function.

2. More importantly, this technique does not yield standard errors. For policy analysis, point estimates without standard errors are of limited use. Without the standard errors, it is impossible to know whether and how well the data fit the model.

3. The results of this technique hinge critically on the choice of the distribution function of tastes. Toder used a log-normal distribution. The choice of the distribution function is completely arbitrary, yet possibly key to the results. While all nonrobust estimation methods are subject to this critique, the problem is compounded here by the lack of standard errors of the estimates. Without the standard errors, it is especially difficult to ascertain whether the distribution function of tastes chosen fits the model.

Bresnahan (1981) also models the demand for automobiles. Using sophisticated econometric techniques, he accounts for product differentiation and avoids the pitfalls of time-series analysis. His goal, though, is more ambitious than just a model of automobile demand, as he focuses on the issue of departures from marginal cost pricing in the automobile industry. Because he looks at a broader range of issues than just the demand side of the model, his results are not disaggregated enough to analyze the questions posed in the introduction of this chapter. While he does not estimate elasticities per se, estimated parameters can be manipulated to give an industry demand elasticity (a proportionate change of all prices) of .25 and an elasticity for the *average* product (one price changes and all others are constant) of 3.2. Bresnahan is forthright about the restrictive assumptions that he requires on the demand side of his model. The most serious of these is the assumption that the density of consumer tastes is uniform (as opposed to Toder's log-normal assumption). Bresnahan's methodology also is computationally complex, and, like Toder's hedonic market share model, it does not yield estimates of standard errors. Bresnahan, though, approximates the variances of parameter estimates in four ways. Although variances depend on the approximation used, this does give some feel for how well the data fit the model. In short, Bresnahan's method is carefully developed, but it is not suitable for addressing the types of issues raised in the introduction of this chapter.

Finally, a number of studies of automobile demand investigate whether a car is purchased at all, and if so, how many are purchased. These studies are fairly common in mode-of-transportation studies. Methods used range from simple logit to multinomial logit to multinomial probit. A technically sophisticated example of this approach is found in Train (1986).[3] These studies ask a set of questions that are for the most part only tangentially related to questions about the demand effect of taxes on differentiated products. As such, their results are not very useful to the issues with which I am concerned.[4]

2.2 Methodology

In this section, I explain my approach to the estimation of demand for differentiated products. This is done in two steps. In step 1, the demand function to be estimated is derived. I avoid many of the pitfalls of previous approaches by relying on results from Lancasterian consumer theory. In step 2, I explain how the insights offered by Lancasterian consumer theory are empirically implemented.

Step 1: I avoid the problems associated with time-series analysis by using only three years of data—1983 through 1985.[5] Three years of time-series data, though, leaves few degrees of freedom. The much-needed additional price-quantity variation is introduced by using a cross section of (the same) 100 models of automobiles for each year. The data are a time-series cross section, or panel, consisting of 300 observations.[6]

While using panel data instead of only time-series introduces additional price-quantity variation, it also poses some problems. It may be wrong to regress quantity on price since, across observations, the good is not the same. I address these problems using results from the characteristics approach to product differentiation.

In the Lancasterian model of product differentiation, a good is represented by its bundle of characteristics. Different models of the good contain different bundles of these characteristics. With this view of product differentiation, as tastes vary across consumers, demands for a model, given its price, will vary with the model's characteristics bundle. Because products are identified by their bundle of characteristics, it is appropriate to control for the cross-sectional variation in models by including in the demand function those characteristics that differentiate models.[7]

Lancaster hence posits that the quantity demanded of a model depends on its own price and characteristics and on the price and characteristics of competing models. In log-linear form, this implies

$$ln\ Q_{it} = \alpha_0 + \alpha_1 ln\ P_{it} + \alpha_2 ln\ \bar{P}_{jt} + \beta' X_{it} + \Gamma' X_{jt},$$

where Q_{it} is the quantity demanded of model i in year t, P_{it} is the price of model i in year t, $\bar{P}_{jt}$ is the vector of prices of substitutes to a model with sales Q_{it}, X_{it} is a characteristics vector of model i in year t, and X_{jt} is a characteristics vector of model j in year t.

I posit that the above model may be subject to country-of-origin specific errors, and hence use a fixed effects model.[8] Allowing also for time-dependent shifts of demand gives

(1A) $ln\ Q_{it} = \alpha_0 + \alpha_1 ln\ P_{it} + \alpha_2 ln\ \bar{P}_{jt} + \beta' X_{it} + \Gamma' X_{jt}$

$\quad\quad\quad + \alpha_3 JAPAN_i + \alpha_4 GERMAN_i + \alpha_5 SWEDE_i + \alpha'_6\ T_t,$

where $JAPAN_i = 1$ if model i is Japanese, $GERMAN_i = 1$ if model i is German, $SWEDE_i = 1$ if model i is Swedish, and T_t is a time dummy for year t. Equation (1A) is consistent with a Lancasterian approach to consumer demand for autos.

Somewhat surprisingly, Lancaster's work does not discuss the hedonic price literature, which posits that the price of a good is a linear combination of the implicit prices of the attributes of the good. Thus in equation (1A), X_{it} would be highly collinear with P_{it}. An analogous relationship holds for X_{jt} and P_{jt}. According to the hedonic approach, the price of a good already contains information about the qualities of the good. Hence, estimating equation (1A) merely introduces severe multicollinearity. Instead, the hedonic hypothesis argues in favor of estimating the following demand function.

$$(1B) \quad ln\ Q_{it} = \alpha_1 + \alpha_2 ln\ P_{it} + \alpha_2 ln\ \bar{P}_{jt} + \alpha_3 JAPAN_i$$
$$+ \alpha_4 GERMAN_i + \alpha_5 SWEDE_i + \alpha_6' T_t.$$

I econometrically consider both equations (1A) and (1B). In doing so, I assume the consumer takes as given all independent variables.

The functional form of the demand function should follow from the density of consumers over characteristics space. Formally, demand for a model is given by integrating the density of consumers over the neighborhood of the model. Making the link between distribution of consumers and functional form of demand is a difficult question that I do not address. Rather, I consider equations (1A) and (1B) as convenient statistical approximations of demand.

In standard consumer theory, with 100 models, 99 models could serve as substitutes for model i, and thus 99 prices would appear in $\bar{P}_{jt}$. This would imply 9,900 cross-price terms to be estimated in the standard demand system. This is not feasible with only three years of data. Again, I rely on the theory of product differentiation to, in effect, place many zero restrictions on the vector α_2.

The earliest work on product differentiation by Hotelling (1929) arranged products along a line. In figure 2.1, model B competes for customers with models A and C but not with any other models.

Here, models A and C are termed "neighbors" of model B, whereas the other models (D, E, etc.) were not. Were there 100 models arranged along the spectrum, this setup would imply 97 zero restrictions on the vector α_2 for good B. Only the price of B and the prices of its neighbors, A and C, would enter the demand function for B.

Fig. 2.1   Hotelling product differentiation

Lancaster extends the Hotelling model to allow products to differ across more than one dimension. Lancaster posits that each good is a bundle of several characteristics. In this case, if there are n products, each product may have up to $n-1$ neighbors and all have at least one neighbor.[9] I rely on the Lancasterian approach to product differentiation to determine endogenously which products compete with each other for consumers. This, in turn, allows me to place zero restrictions on α_2 in a utility-consistent manner.

Step 2: Empirically determining the neighbors for each product is complicated by the fact that while characteristics of the goods are observed, individual consumer tastes over these characteristics are not. I adopt an approach to this problem that is based in part on a methodology developed by Feenstra (1986).[10]

The first task in any Lancasterian model is to define the metric in characteristics space that is to be used to determine how far apart any two products are. To this end, let $x = (x_1, x_2, \ldots, x_n) > 0$ be a vector of physical characteristics that differ across models and X^n be the n-dimensional space in which products are differentiated. Let $\Theta = (\Theta_1, \Theta_2, \ldots, \Theta_n)$ represent the vector of taste parameters for a particular individual.

I assume that all individuals have the same form of utility function, namely, CES, but that individuals differ in their vector of tastes Θ. Then, an individual's utility is given by[11]

(2) $$U(x,\Theta) = \sum_{i=1}^{n} \Theta_i x_i^{\delta}.$$

The parameter δ is related to the elasticity of substitution between characteristics, σ, that is,

$$\sigma = \frac{1}{\delta - 1}.$$

The twin constraints of utility increasing in x and concavity of utility in x imply $\sigma \in (0, -1)$. This range of σ is perhaps overly restrictive for the case of substitutability of auto characteristics. In order to permit $\sigma \in (0, -\infty)$, I take a Box-Cox transformation of equation (2). This yields

$$U(x,\Theta) = \sum_{i=1}^{n} \Theta_i \tilde{x}_i^{\delta},$$

where $\tilde{x}_i^{\delta} = (x_i^{\delta} - 1)/\delta$, 0 not equal to $\delta < 1$,

and $\tilde{x}_i^{\delta} = \ln x_i$, if $\delta = 0$.

As I will be working with the case of less than perfect substitutability between characteristics, I will, for notational simplicity, henceforth use the (still CES) utility function:

(3) $$U(x,\Theta) = \sum_{i=1}^{n} \Theta_i \, (x_i^\delta - 1)/\delta.$$

The price of a model depends on its characteristics. I specify the functional form for $P(x)$. In particular,

(4) $$P(x) = \exp(\alpha + \beta'x),$$

where $\alpha > 0$ and $\beta = (\beta_1, \beta_2, \ldots, \beta_n) > 0$ are parameters.

Denoting the homogeneous numeraire good by N and exogenous income by Y, the consumer's problem is to

(5) $$\max_{x,N} \; U(x,\Theta) + N$$

subject to $P(x) + N \leq Y$. The additively separable form of the utility function in equation (5) and the linearity in N imply that the optimal choice of auto characteristics is independent of income. The first-order conditions for equation (5) imply

(6) $$\Theta_i x_i^{\delta-1} = \beta_i \exp(\beta'x + \alpha)$$

at an optimum x^*.

Equation (6) can be solved for the unobservable taste parameters in terms of observables. As in Feenstra (1986), it proves useful to do so. This yields

(7) $$\Theta_i = (x_i^*)^{1-\delta} \, \beta_i \exp(\beta'x^* + \alpha).$$

I next define a consumer surplus function $S(x,x^*) = U(x,x^*) - p(x)$. This function gives the surplus associated with a model having characteristics vector x if the consumer's optimal choice is described by x^*.

Simple substitution gives

(8) $$S(x,x^*) = \exp(\beta'x^* + \alpha) \, \Sigma \left[\frac{B_i}{\delta} \right] (x_i^*b)^{1-\delta} \, (x_i^\delta - 1)$$
$$- \exp(\beta'x + \alpha).$$

It is easy to verify that S is maximized when $x = x^*$. This surplus function will serve as the metric for measuring distance in characteristics space.

Having defined the metric, I turn now to the task of using this metric to determine which products compete with one another, that is, which are neighbors. While there are many models of automobiles, and hence many available bundles of characteristics, there is not a continuum of products available on the market. Thus, a consumer may find that her optimal model, x^*, does not exist in the market. In this case, the consumer receives less surplus than she would if x^* had been available. In figure 2.2, I illustrate an iso-surplus contour for a typical consumer for the case of two characteristics. In the figure, $S(x,x^*)$ is constant along any contour and $S(x,x^*)$ decreases as one moves away from x^*. Thus, the consumer whose optimal characteristics bundle is x^* is indifferent between point A which entails slightly more horsepower and less weight and point B which gives relatively much more horsepower and a heavier auto.

Two models A and B would be neighbors if there is any consumer who is indifferent between A and B who prefers these two to all other models. Graphically, in figure 2.2, A and B would *not* be neighbors if there existed a model such as C.

Different consumers may have different ideal models. Because of this, there are many iso-surplus contours that will pass through any two models. In figure 2.3, individual 1 has an optimal choice of x^*_1, and A and B lie on the same iso-surplus contour—S_1. Another consumer, individual 2, has an optimal choice of x^*_2. For this consumer, A and B also lie on the same iso-surplus contour (S_2). The analogous story applies to consumer 3 whose optimal choice is x^*_3.

An ideal algorithm for determining neighbors would proceed in steps. For every possible pair of models in the sample, one would conduct a detailed grid search in characteristics space. At every point in the grid search, one would pose the following question: Is the consumer whose ideal model is this point in characteristics space indifferent to the two potential neighbors? If the answer is no, move on to the next point on the grid and repeat the question. If the answer is yes, ask if any of the other ninety-eight models in the sample give higher surplus than the

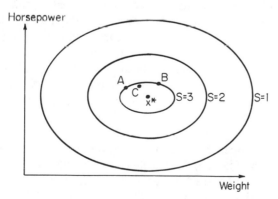

Fig. 2.2   Iso-surplus contours

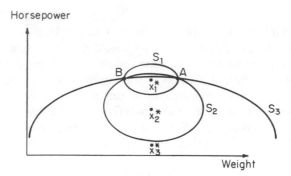

Fig. 2.3   An example of many consumers indifferent to two models
A and B

pair being considered. If the answer here is no, the pair of potential
neighbors are indeed neighbors.

This algorithm will determine which multidimensionally differentiated products are neighbors. Unfortunately, the algorithm is computationally infeasible for the case of automobiles. This is because I
find that at least five characteristics are necessary to adequately account
for differentiation between autos. The algorithm described above, then,
would require many five-dimensional grid searches entailing many calculations at each point in each search. This is too expensive on a
mainframe computer and too time-consuming on an advanced personal
computer.

I refine the above definition of neighbors. (Two models were neighbors, it will be recalled, if there existed a consumer indifferent between
them and who preferred them to all other available models.) Amending
this definition allows me to derive a computationally feasible method for
determining neighbors to each model in my sample. I take the *smallest*
iso-surplus contour containing the potential neighbors as the basis for
comparison. In figure 2.3, this is S_1—the surplus that consumer 1 ob-
tains. This is akin to saying that it is the preferences of the consumer
whose optimal bundle is most similar to the potential neighbors that, on
the margin, matter. In figure 2.3, then, when I ask if A and B are neighbors, I use the preferences of consumer 1 and then look for a point such
as C that lies within S_1. If a point such as C exists, A and B are not
neighbors. This method is economically sound if it will always be the
case that if consumer 1 has a model preferred to A and B, so will all
other consumers. There are examples in which this will not be true, and
this issue will be discussed in detail. First, though, it is convenient to
state a working definition of "neighbors."

Definition: Models A and B are considered neighbors if, for the smallest iso-surplus contour containing both of them,

$$S(x_a, x^*) [= S (x_b, x^*)] > S(x_c, x^*) \text{ for all models } c.$$

This is, I believe, an economically intuitive and computationally straightforward definition of neighbors. It is not a perfect definition for at least two reasons. I discuss each in turn.

The first problem with the definition concerns identifying the x^* that defines the highest surplus associated with indifference between models A and B. Recall that x^* is a consumer's optimal choice of characteristics and as such is not observed. I posit that x^* is the midpoint of a line drawn between two potential neighbors, A and B, where the surplus function provides the metric. Since a model is represented by a vector of its characteristics, I find x^* by varying Ω from 0 to 1 until $x^* = \Omega x_A + (1 - \Omega) x_B$ and $S(x_A, x^*) = S(x_B, x^*)$. If iso-surplus contours were proper ellipsoids, the x^* defined in the above linear fashion would indeed identify the smallest iso-surplus contour containing A and B. Insofar as the iso-surplus contours defined by equation (8) are not proper ellipses, defining x^* as the midsurplus point on the line between points A and B may not yield the smallest contour containing A and B.

There are two possible responses to this critique. First, the iso-surplus contours defined by equation (8) are, in fact, not too different from ellipses for the case of automobiles. Iso-surplus contours derived from data are drawn in weight-horsepower space in figure 2.4. Due to

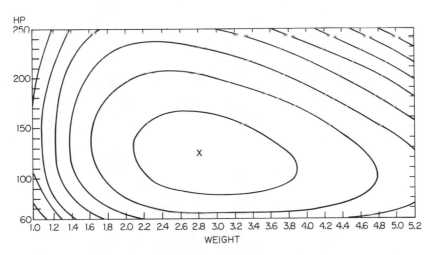

Fig. 2.4   Iso-surplus contours with Box-Cox CES utility and log-linear hedonic price function (weight versus HP)

the symmetry of equation (8), contours are similarly shaped in the shape of any two characteristics. Second, if x^* was poorly defined by drawing a line between A and B, one would expect the method to yield nonsensical sets of neighbors. I show in the next section that this is not the case.[12]

A second problem is that this definition of neighbors, which uses the smallest iso-surplus contour as the basis for comparison, may falsely reject potential neighbors. This is demonstrated in figure 2.5.

Suppose there are only three models, A, B, and C. My definition of neighbors rules out A and B as potential neighbors, since the iso-surplus contour drawn is the smallest containing A and B, and C is preferred to A and B. Yet for a consumer whose optimum is $x^{*\prime}$, A and B are neighbors. My method for determining neighbors, though, will never account for the preferences of a consumer with an optimal choice of $x^{*\prime}$ in figure 2.5. Because I find the optimum bundle by drawing a line between two models, and do so for all pairs in the sample, I will never account for the preferences of a consumer whose optimum bundle lies outside the outermost envelope of available models. The preferences of these consumers are ignored. In figure 2.5, this envelope is defined by the triangle ABC—an area that does not include $x^{*\prime}$.

For the automobile market, this problem is not likely to be an empirically important one because, in a market with as many models as the auto market, it is unlikely that there are many consumers whose ideal lies outside this outer envelope. Were this the case, one would expect such profitable market niches to be readily filled.

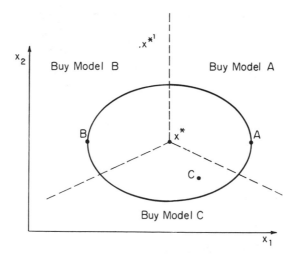

Fig. 2.5   An example of preferences for which the model will not account

The algorithm for finding neighbors, then, is as follows.

Step 1: Find x^* such that $S(x_1,x^*) = S(x_2,x^*)$ using the above-described linear method.

Step 2: See if there exists a model j not equal to 1,2 such that $S(x_1,x^*) < S(x_j,x^*)$. Models 1 and 2 are neighbors if no such j exists in the sample.

Step 3: Repeat the above two steps for all possible pairs in the sample. This algorithm ensures that if 1 is a neighbor of 2, then 2 is a neighbor of 1. If 3 is a neighbor to 2, though, it need not be a neighbor to (2's neighbor) 1. The number of neighbors a model has depends on its characteristics and the characteristics of the other models in the sample. The actual number of neighbors for each model is endogenous and will differ across models.

This procedure yields the neighbor(s) to every model in the sample. I use these neighbors as the elements of P_{jt} in the demand equation (1). Conversely, models that are not neighbors are assumed to have no cross-price effect in equation (1).

This concludes the description of the methodology. In this section, I have explained how I use results from a Lancasterian model of product differentiation to derive an estimable demand function. The resulting demand function circumvents many of the myriad problems that plagued earlier attempts to estimate the demand for differentiated products—specifically automobiles.

2.3 Data and Results

The data set comprises almost all automobile models sold in the calendar years 1983–85. Specialty models with annual sales of under 4000 were excluded (e.g., Ferrari and Rolls Royce). Models not produced for all of each of the three years were also deleted. This allows me to avoid the problems that would be posed by a model that is introduced in October and hence has very low annual sales for the calendar (as opposed to model) year. A similar, though less severe, problem would exist for models withdrawn after October. Models included in the sample are given in table 2.1. Each model/year observation consists of the following variables for the base model: (1) sales by Nameplate, (2) suggested retail list price, (3) wheelbase, (4) length, (5) width, (6) height, (7) weight, (8) headroom, (9) legroom, (10) number of engine cylinders, (11) engine displacement, (12) fuel injection or carburation, (13) manual or automatic transmission, (14) power or manual steering, (15) power or manual brakes, (16) air conditioning as standard, (17) horsepower (HP), (18) turning radius, and (19) country of origin. All data were collected from annual issues of *Automotive News Market Data Book.*

Table 2.1   **Models Used in the Sample**

Toyota Tercel	Saab 900 S	Buick Skyhawk
Toyota Corolla	Saab 900 Turbo	Buick Skylark
Toyota Celica	Porsche 944	Buick Century
Toyota Camry	Porsche 911	Buick Regal
Toyota Cressida	Isuzu I-mark	Buick LeSabre
Toyota Supra	Isuzu Impulse	Buick Electra
Nissan Sentra	Peugeot 505	Buick Riveria
Nissan Maxima	American Motors Alliance	Cadillac Cimarron
Nissan 300zx	American Motors Eagle	Cadillac Seville
Nissan 200SX	Plymouth Horizon	Cadillac DeVille
Nissan Stanza	Plymouth Turismo	Cadillac ElDorado
Nissan Pulsar	Plymouth Reliant	Chevrolet Chevette
Honda Accord	Plymouth GF	Chevrolet Cavalier
Honda Civic1.5S	Plymouth LeBaron	Chevrolet Citation
Mazda 626	Plymouth NewYorker/5thAvenue	Chevrolet Camaro
Mazda RX-7	Dodge Omni	Chevrolet Celebrity
Mazda GLC	Dodge Charger	Chevrolet Corvette
Subaru DL/GL	Dodge Aries	Chevrolet MonteCarlo
Chry/Ply Colt	Dodge Dodge600	Chevrolet Chevrolet
Volvo DL	Dodge Diplomat	Oldsmobile Firenza
Volvo 760 GLE	Ford EXP	Oldsmobile Cutlass/Sierra
VW Jetta	Ford Escort	Oldsmobile Cutlass/Supreme
VW Quantum	Ford Mustang	Oldsmobile Olds88
BMW 320/318	Ford T-Bird	Oldsmobile Olds98
BMW 530/528	Ford LTD	Oldsmobile Toronado
BMW 733	Ford CrownVictoria	Pontiac 1000
Mercedes 300D	Mercury Lynx	Pontiac Sunbird
Mercedes 300SD	Mercury Cougar/XR7	Pontiac Firebird
Mercedes 190E	Mercury Capri	Pontiac 6000
Audi 5000	Mercury Marquis	Pontiac Bonneville
Audi 4000	Mercury GrandMarquis	Pontiac GrandPrix
Mitsubishi Tredia	Lincoln Continental	Volkswagen Rabbit
Mitsubishi Cordia	Lincoln MarkVii	
Mitsubishi Starion	Lincoln Lincoln	

Some variables of economic significance are absent from the above list. In particular, data on the incomes of consumers and on the actual transaction prices are not available. The suggested list price of the base model for P_{it} is used.[13] This introduces systematic bias insofar as some models consistently sell for more or less than list price. For some Japanese models, this may have been the case in my sample.[14]

Neighbors are computed for the 1984 models. I assume that product characteristics do not change so much that neighbors change over the sample period; I will relax and test this assumption in future work. Indeed, computing neighbors for each year provides an alternative test of Feenstra's (1985) upgrading results. Here, differential upgrading would take the form of changing neighborhoods over time.

I begin by estimating the hedonic price equation $P(x)$. Like most researchers before me,[15] I find that the functional form of $P(x)$ that best fits the data is equation (4):[16]

$$P(x) = \exp(\alpha + \beta'x).$$

I find that a linear combination of the following five characteristics accounts for almost 90 percent of the variation of $P(x)$—weight, horsepower, and dummies for power steering, air conditioning, and foreign made. Dummy variables take the value of 2 if a car is foreign and if air and power steering are standard, and a value of 1 otherwise. This differs from the usual 1-0 convention because some dummies are raised to negative powers. The only effect of this change is to alter the constant term in the hedonic regression. Numerical experiments show that this has no effect on the determination of neighbors. I estimate the log of equation (4) to give

(9) $\ln P = .215 + .209$ Weight $+ .0045$ HP
          (.123)   (.056)   (.0009)
          $+ .1261$ PS $+ .4703$ Air $+ .161$ Foreign.
          (.052)   (.050)   (.044)

Standard errors are in parentheses. 100 observations. $R_2 = .885$.

It is useful to view dummy variables here as proxies for various degrees of luxury and/or quality. Hence an optimal choice of characteristics, x^*, may involve .5 units of air conditioning. This just means that the consumer would prefer less luxury than is imposed by the all-or-nothing choice of air conditioning but more than is afforded by a no-air model. The coefficients in equation (9) are used to parameterize the surplus function of equation (8). While the coefficients are subject to measurement error, their very small standard errors argue that neglecting this error is unlikely to be an empirically relevant omission.

The only remaining unknown in the surplus function is the parameter δ which is related to the degree of concavity of the utility function. Recall that the elasticity of substitution, $\sigma = 1/(\delta - 1)$. This parameter is not identifiable with the data available. Following Feenstra (1986), I posit many different values for δ and replicate the entire methodology from the beginning for each of these. Fortunately, I find that the choice of δ over a wide range of plausible values does not affect the qualitative results. I consider values of $\delta = .5, -1, -3, -6,$ and -8. Only at values of -8 and below do results change substantially. That is, the choice of neighbors is mostly unaffected until $\delta = -8$. At -8, neighbors become much more numerous and, to a degree, counterintuitive.

Once δ has been specified, I compute neighbors for every model using the 1984 data.[17] The results for δ = −3 are given in table 2.2. Table 2.2, for example, tells us that the neighbors of the Honda Accord, model 13, are the Toyota Camry, Nissan Stanza, Mazda 626, Mitsubishi Tredia and Cordia, Chevrolet Cavalier, and Pontiac Sunbird. An intuitive way of interpreting table 2.2 is to note that it answers the question, What other autos did the consumer consider before she decided to purchase the one actually selected?

Table 2.2   Neighbors of Models (δ = −3)

Model No.	Model Name	No. of Neighbors	Model Nos. of Neighbors								
1	Toyota Tercel	6	17	18	19	42	44	80			
2	Corolla	2	18	39							
3	Celica	4	4	10	16	45					
4	Camry	8	3	11	13	15	45	52	81	82	
5	Cressida	4	6	21	37	67					
6	Supra	3	5	9	37						
7	Nissan Sentra	4	12	17	19	100					
8	Maxima	3	25	29	36						
9	300zx	3	6	26	38						
10	200SX	8	3	11	16	20	24	31	41	53	
11	Stanza	5	4	10	12	31	53				
12	Pulsar	8	7	11	17	18	22	23	31	100	
13	Honda Accord	5	4	15	32	33	81				
14	Civic 1.5S	1	100								
15	Mazda 626	9	4	13	23	32	57	69	81	82	88
16	RX-7	4	3	10	20	34					
17	GLC	7	7	12	1	18	19	56	100		
18	Subaru DL/GL	8	2	12	17	1	22	51	61	94	
19	Chry/Ply Colt	3	7	17	1						
20	Volvo DL	10	10	16	24	30	34	35	41	54	62 98
21	760 GLE	4	5	25	27	37					
22	VW Jetta	6	12	18	39	55	61	100			
23	Quantum	5	12	15	31	40	76				
24	BMW 320/318	6	10	20	31	35	40	76			
25	530/528	4	8	21	27	92					
26	733	5	9	28	38	68	85				
27	Mercedes 300D	8	21	25	28	74	75	79	92	93	
28	300SD	5	26	27	74	77	78				
29	190E	2	8	35							
30	Audi 5000	3	20	35	40						
31	4000	6	10	11	12	23	24	76			
32	Mitsubishi Tredia	5	13	15	33	81	95				
33	Cordia	3	13	32	39						
34	Starion	6	16	20	36	54	60	62			
35	Saab 900 S	4	20	24	29	30					
36	900 Turbo	3	8	34	37						

Table 2.2   (continued)

Model No.	Model Name	No. of Neighbors	Model Nos. of Neighbors							
37	Porsche 944	4	5	6	21	36				
38	911	3	9	26	85					
39	Isuzu I-mark	4	2	22	33	55				
40	Impulse	5	23	24	30	41	76			
41	Peugeot 505	7	10	20	40	43	59	83	98	
42	Alliance	2	1	80						
43	Eagle	5	41	59	76	87	99			
44	Horizon	3	1	50	94					
45	Turismo	4	3	4	46	53				
46	Reliant	3	4	45	52					
47	Plymouth GF	7	20	34	49	54	73	91	92	
48	LeBaron	5	10	53	70	76	84			
49	NewYorker/5thAvenue	5	47	60	73	75	92			
50	Omni	3	44	1	51					
51	Charger	2	18	50						
52	Aries	4	4	46	53	82				
53	Dodge600	6	10	11	45	48	52	70		
54	Diplomat	7	20	34	47	58	73	91	92	
55	EXP	4	22	39	61	95				
56	Escort	5	17	18	22	61	80			
57	Mustang	5	15	63	70	71	82			
58	T-Bird	6	20	34	54	62	92	98		
59	LTD	3	41	43	64					
60	CrownVictoria	6	34	49	65	67	75	92		
61	Lynx	7	17	18	22	55	56	80	94	
62	Cougar/XR7	4	20	34	58	92				
63	Capri	3	3	57	71					
64	Marquis	3	59	76	83					
65	GrandMarquis	3	60	67	75					
66	Continental	4	7	68	77	79				
67	MarkVii	4	5	65	66	79				
68	Lincoln	4	26	66	78	85				
69	Skyhawk	5	15	32	81	88	95			
70	Skylark	6	48	53	57	71	82	84		
71	Century	5	57	63	70	84	89			
72	Regal	4	41	76	86	98				
73	LeSabre	3	47	49	91					
74	Electra	5	27	28	77	79	93			
75	Riviera	5	27	49	65	92	93			
76	Cimarron	11	23	24	31	40	43	48	83	92 96 97 98
77	Seville	5	28	66	74	78	79			
78	Cadillac DV	3	28	68	77					
79	ElDorado	7	27	28	66	67	74	77	93	
80	Chevette	5	42	56	61	1	94			
81	Cavalier	6	4	13	15	32	69	82		
82	Citation	6	4	15	52	57	70	81		
83	Camaro	5	41	64	76	96	98			
84	Celebrity	5	48	70	71	76	89			

Table 2.2   (continued)

Model No.	Model Name	No. of Neighbors	Model Nos. of Neighbors					
85	Corvette	3	26	38	68			
86	MonteCarlo	5	20	41	72	76	90	
87	Chevrolet	4	43	91	92	99		
88	Firenza	3	15	69	70	95		
89	Cutlass/Sierra	3	71	84	97			
90	Cutlass/Supreme	5	41	43	76	86	99	
91	Olds88	4	54	73	87	92		
92	Olds98	8	25	27	49	54	58	60 75 76
93	Toronado	4	27	74	75	79		
94	1000	5	18	44	61	80	1	
95	Sunbird	5	15	32	55	69	88	
96	Firebird	3	76	83	97			
97	6000	3	76	89	96			
98	Bonneville	6	20	41	58	72	76	83
99	GrandPrix	4	41	43	87	90		
100	Rabbit	5	7	12	14	17	22	

In addition to varying δ, another type of sensitivity test was conducted in calculating neighbors. Because iso-surplus contours are not perfect ellipses, the linear method of finding the optimal model x^* is, as noted above, only an approximation. I used another approximation and retested for neighbors. This other approximation was based on finding x^* such that consumers whose ideal models were A and B were equally dissatisfied with x^*. This approximation yielded the same qualitative results as the linear approximation of x^*.

The next step in the methodology is to estimate the demand functions given in equations (1A) and (1B). Models have, on average, about 6 neighbors. With 100 models, this implies 600 cross-price terms to be estimated. While this is certainly an improvement over the previous 9,900 terms, the demand functions are still not accurately estimable with only 300 observations. I take the mean price of neighbors as the observation for P_{jt}. Similarly, I take the mean characteristics of neighbors as the observation for X_{jt}. Because the demand functions use the log of P_{jt}, it matters that the average of the logs is not the log of the averages. Numerical experiments show that this approximation does not affect results. There are other specifications for P_{jt}. Recall that the estimated demand equation is just a convenient statistical representation. Perhaps P_{jt} should be the average price of neighbors weighted by their sales. This representation of P_{jt} yields the same qualitative results, but standard errors on the parameters in the demand function are larger.

I estimate equations (1A) and (1B) using ordinary least squares (OLS). Because equation (1B) is nested within equation (1A), a straightforward F-test is used to test which specification should be used. That is, I test to see if own and neighbors' mean characteristics are jointly statistically significant.[18] For all values of δ tested, the data cannot reject the hypothesis that own and neighbors' characteristics are jointly insignificant.

The existence of multicollinearity in equation (1A) is confirmed by collinearity diagnostics following the approach of Belsley, Kuh, and Welsch (1980). Singular-value decomposition analysis indicates multicollinearity. The SVD analysis does not indicate that the data matrix is so ill conditioned as to suggest numerical error in the estimates. Due to the multicollinearity in equation (1A), estimated standard errors are inflated. This biases the F-test toward rejecting joint statistical significance of own and neighbors' mean characteristics. I nonetheless accept the results of the F-tests and use equation (1B) as the demand function in the analysis that follows. Table 2.7 presents the results of using instead equation (1A). As the collinearity diagnostics indicated, results are very similar to those obtained using equation (1B) (and given in table 2.4), except that standard errors are inflated.

OLS estimates of equation (1B) are presented in table 2.3. In table 2.3, equation 1 presents estimates of the demand function excluding any

Table 2.3   Estimated Automobile Demand Functions

Equation	(1)	(2) δ = .5	(3) δ = −1.0	(4) δ = −3.0	(5) δ = −6.0	(6) δ = −8.0
CONSTANT	6.085	5.814	6.087	6.041	6.004	5.772
	(.278)	(.276)	(.277)	(.270)	(.267)	(.411)
LOGLIST	−.7942	−1.814	−1.333	−2.076	−2.271	−.912
	(.119)	(.254)	(.319)	(.313)	(.311)	(.165)
LOGPN		1.112	.522	1.250	1.444	.237
		(.246)	(.287)	(.284)	(.282)	(.290)
D84	.114	.111	.118	.122	.120	.108
	(.116)	(.113)	(.116)	(.113)	(.112)	(.116)
D85	.1672	.161	.173	.178	.179	.155
	(.117)	(.113)	(.116)	(.113)	(.112)	(.117)
SWEDE	−1.321	−1.350	−1.316	−1.228	−1.181	−1.302
	(.253)	(.245)	(.252)	(.246)	(.244)	(.254)
JAPAN	−.554	−.607	−.570	−.578	−.594	−.529
	(.117)	(.113)	(.116)	(.113)	(.112)	(.119)
GERMAN	−1.01	−.615	−.843	−.537	−.424	−.928
	(.117)	(.183)	(.189)	(.193)	(.196)	(.183)
R^2	.3954	.4349	.4022	.4330	.4450	.3976

Notes: Standard errors in parentheses. Dependent variable is LOGSALE. Variable definitions: LOGSALE = log of sales in 1000s; LOGLIST = log of the list price in $1000s; LOGPN = log of the average price of the neighbors in $000; D84 = 1 if the year is 1984, 0 otherwise; D85 = 1 if the year is 1985, 0 otherwise; SWEDE = 1 if the car is Swedish, 0 otherwise; JAPAN = 1 if the car is Japanese, 0 otherwise; and GERMAN = 1 if the car is German, 0 otherwise.

cross-price effects. This equation is roughly a panel data version of the older time-series studies that neglected cross-price effects. Equation 1 gives a highly significant total market elasticity of demand of $-.794$. This estimate is in line with existing, older estimates. Equation 1, though, is misspecified, as cross-price effects are omitted.

Equations 2–6 in table 2.3 give estimates when the demand function includes the price of neighbors, hence allowing for the possibility of substitution. Varying δ from .5 to -6 affects the significance of the parameters on own and neighbors' price, but the point estimates are fairly constant. (Recall that the choice of δ only enters the demand function via its effect on the determination of the set of neighbors.) For $\delta = .5$, -1, -3 and -6, the coefficient on the neighbors' price is highly significant. For these values of δ, the coefficient on own price is somewhat stable across equations and is highly significant.

For values of δ between -1 and -6, the total market elasticity $(\alpha_1 + \alpha_2)$ varies from $-.81$ to $-.83$, all of which are statistically significant at the 90 percent level. As theory would lead one to expect, allowing for substitutability leads to a more elastic own-price elasticity. This is evidenced by own-price elasticities (α_1) greater in absolute value than the coefficient of $-.794$ in equation 1.

In sum, the "neighbors" approach to restricting the dimensionality of the demand function in conjunction with a short panel of data seems to fit the data remarkably well. I have completed some sensitivity analyses in the spirit of Leamer (1985). These ad hoc specification tests include using other hedonic characteristics to control for cross-sectional variation. The results have been exceptionally robust to such tests.

2.4   On the Empirics of Taxation Schemes for Differentiated Products

The methodology by which the demand functions in table 2.3 were derived was based on Lancasterian consumer theory. That theory tells us that not all differentiated products need be substitutes. It also tells us to group products according to their characteristics and not only, as the Armington assumption implies, according to their country of origin.[19] The elasticities that are estimated in the equations of table 2.3, then, are the relevant ones from the vantage point of consumer theory.

Trade policy, though, typically taxes a good based on its country of origin. The analysis of trade policy issues requires trade elasticities. I derive these elasticities from the estimates of the demand system provided in sections 2.2 and 2.3. This is accomplished by perturbing the system on whatever margin trade policy operates to simulate the elasticity relevant to the study of trade taxes. This approach is more likely to give valid elasticities than direct estimation of import demand equations (see, for example Leamer and Stern 1970) because it is based on a utility-consistent framework for demand.

Suppose, for example, that policymakers wish to know how the demand for domestic autos changes when a tariff is applied to *all* auto imports. To derive this elasticity, I increase the price of all foreign cars by one percent—my proxy for a small change. This increases the demand for models of domestic autos that have as neighbors some foreign model. Summing the new demand for all domestic autos gives the information needed to construct the relevant elasticity.

This approach requires a caveat. I have nothing to say about the effect of large taxes. This is because the estimated demand system is only a local representation of demand. The system may behave quite differently at a point far from the initial situation. This is a standard warning in the empirical tax analysis literature. Also, here, large taxes may change the neighbors of a model. I assume that the taxes I consider are small enough that neighbors do not change. Preliminary numerical experiments indicate that this is indeed the case for the one percent price changes I consider.

In table 2.4, I give a wide variety of elasticities corresponding to various policy scenarios. For each elasticity, I also give its standard error. This statistic is computable given the variance-covariance matrix of the estimates of the initial demand equation. These elasticities all are simulated using the demand equation 4 found in table 2.3. That is, δ from

Table 2.4	Elasticities of Demand by Country of Origin Using Equation (1B) $(\delta = -3)$				
	Quantity Change				
Price Change	Domestic Autos	All Imports	Japanese Imports	German Imports	Swedish Imports
All domestic	−1.187	.225	.213	.258	.076
	(.146)	(.051)	(.048)	(.058)	(.017)
All foreign	.367	−1.045	−1.030	−1.078	−.897
	(.084)	(.129)	(.128)	(.132)	(.118)
Japanese	.187	−.663	−1.43	.393	.300
	(.042)	(.081)	(.187)	(.089)	(.068)
German	.112	−.279	.317	−1.717	.745
	(.025)	(.036)	(.072)	(.240)	(.169)
Swedish	.024	−.064	.071	.247	−1.971
	(.005)	(.011)	(.016)	(.056)	(.292)
All foreign weighing < 2300 lbs.	.096	−.376	−.550	−.199	0.0
	(.021)	(.046)	(.067)	(.025)	—

Note: Standard errors in parentheses.

the utility function is set to -3. I take this as a central case for expositional purposes. Tables 2.5–2.7 present the same elasticities when the entire methodology is conducted using other values of δ. Those tables show that results remain qualitatively similar for a range of δ's.

Table 2.4 is easily interpreted. The table shows, for example, that the elasticity of demand for domestically produced automobiles with respect to the price of Japanese autos is .187. That is, a one percent increase in the price of all Japanese cars (via a tariff, perhaps) yields a .187 percent increase in demand for domestically produced autos. Were such a price increase applied to all imported autos, demand for domestically produced autos would rise instead by .367 percent. This example illustrates an error present in earlier studies of U.S.-Japanese auto trade policy. These studies used an imputed elasticity of demand for domestic autos with respect to a *foreign* price change because there were no estimates available of elasticities of domestic demand with respect to a change in only the Japanese price. Table 2.4 tells us that this error leads one to believe that demand for domestic autos is *twice* as responsive to a small tariff on Japanese cars as is actually the case. The difference arises due to substitution by American consumers away from Japanese cars toward other foreign cars not affected by the trade policy. These results serve as another indication of the ineffectiveness of selective protection.

Suppose that the purpose of trade or industrial policy in the U.S. automobile industry is to increase demand for domestically produced autos. Table 2.4 shows that a tax on all imports has less than half the effect on domestic demand that an equal subsidy on domestic models would have (.367 versus -1.187). (Consequences for government revenue are, of course, quite different.) An increase in a tariff on Swedish autos has very little effect on domestic demand; the relevant elasticity is .034. This is because most of the neighbors to Swedish autos are also foreign.

Suppose that the purpose of trade taxes is to reduce imports from a specific country. Then table 2.4 shows that a tax on only Swedish cars reduces Swedish imports by relatively less than the same tariff on German autos. Swedish cars are the most elastically demanded import, followed by German models, then Japanese models (-1.97 versus -1.71 versus -1.43). This is because Japanese models have many Japanese neighbors, while this is not the case for Swedish models. Indeed, most neighbors to Swedish models are German, as evidenced by the relatively high cross-price elasticities between German and Swedish autos.

Perhaps contrary to prior beliefs, a tax on all imports would have roughly the same relative impact on Japanese, German, and Swedish producers.

Some economists have argued for a tax on all small foreign cars instead of a tax on Japanese autos. Such a tax would not discriminate on the basis of country of origin and is viewed more kindly by GATT. I arbitrarily define small cars to be those weighing under 2,300 pounds. (For purposes of comparison, a Toyota Tercel weighs 1,985 lbs., a Honda Accord 2,187 lbs., and a Saab 900 2,612 lbs.) While such a broadly based tax might make the U.S. trade representative's job easier, the policy is only half (.096 versus .187) as effective at increasing demand for domestically produced autos as a direct tax on all imports. Swedish producers are totally unaffected by such a tax since no Swedish export to the United States weighs less than 2,300 pounds (there is a reason Volvos are so safe), and no Swedish car has a neighbor weighing less than 2,300 pounds.

It is possible to investigate the effects of various other trade and industrial policies using table 2.4. The above scenarios provide only a beginning.

2.5 Summary

This chapter has developed a new methodology for investigating empirically the effects of taxes on differentiated products. The approach adopted a Lancasterian, utility-consistent view of product differentiation. Using this approach, I calculated which multidimensionally differentiated products were neighbors. This information proved a useful basis for decreasing the dimensionality of the demand-estimation problem. Using a panel of one hundred automobile models over three years, a demand function was estimated. This yielded quite reasonable and statistically significant demand elasticities.

Recognizing that tax policy often acts on a different margin than consumer theory, the demand elasticities necessary for tax policy analyses were simulated. This provided the first estimated set of such elasticities. These elasticities provide some insight into a number of possible policy scenarios.

The methodology developed in this chapter provides ample opportunities for Leamer-type ad hoc specification tests. Results using different elasticities of substitution are presented in tables 2.5–2.7. These results appear robust.

The elasticities estimated and given in table 2.4 are well suited to simulation analyses of strategic trade and industrial policies concerning the U.S. automobile industry. This is the subject of ongoing research.

Table 2.5   **Elasticities of Demand by Country of Origin Using Equation (1B) ($\delta = -1$)**

Price Change	Quantity Change				
	Domestic Autos	All Imports	Japanese Imports	German Imports	Swedish Imports
All domestic	−.967	.112	.122	.100	.053
	(.154)	(.062)	(.067)	(.055)	(.029)
All foreign	.162	−.918	−.928	−.906	−.859
	(.089)	(.137)	(.140)	(.134)	(.124)
Japanese	.086	−.559	−1.080	.147	.108
	(.047)	(.089)	(.198)	(.081)	(.059)
German	.042	−.259	.120	−1.173	.343
	(.023)	(.037)	(.066)	(.241)	(.189)
Swedish	.015	−.078	.026	.101	−1.326
	(.008)	(.011)	(.014)	(.056)	(.318)
All foreign weighing < 2300 lbs.	.051	−.338	−.491	−.188	0.0
	(.028)	(.052)	(.076)	(.028)	—

Note: Standard errors in parentheses.

Table 2.6   **Elasticities of Demand by Country of Origin Using Equation (1B) ($\delta = -6$)**

Price Change	Quantity Change				
	Domestic Autos	All Imports	Japanese Imports	German Imports	Swedish Imports
All domestic	−1.247	.239	.231	.267	.100
	(.083)	(.046)	(.045)	(.052)	(.019)
All foreign	.426	−1.060	−1.052	−1.088	−.922
	(.145)	(.125)	(.125)	(.128)	(.117)
Japanese	.226	−.709	−1.568	.466	.361
	(.044)	(.082)	(.190)	(.091)	(.070)
German	.124	−.243	.427	−1.849	.821
	(.024)	(.035)	(.083)	(.236)	(.160)
Swedish	.026	−.074	.071	.269	−2.144
	(.005)	(.010)	(.014)	(.052)	(.288)
All foreign weighing < 2300 lbs.	.119	−.390	−.581	−.189	0.0
	(.023)	(.045)	(.067)	(.024)	—

Note: Standard errors in parentheses.

Table 2.7   **Elasticities of Demand by Country of Origin Using Equation (1A)**
($\delta = -3$)

Price Change	Quantity Change				
	Domestic Autos	All Imports	Japanese Imports	German Imports	Swedish Imports
All domestic	−1.412	.201	.191	.230	.067
	(.533)	(.103)	(.584)	(.118)	(.034)
All foreign	.328	−1.285	−1.275	−1.314	−1.152
	(.168)	(.580)	(.098)	(.569)	(.633)
Japanese	.167	−.793	−1.636	.352	.268
	(.085)	(.309)	(.046)	(.180)	(.137)
German	.100	−.358	.284	−1.886	.666
	(.056)	(.195)	(.145)	(.405)	(.342)
Swedish	.021	−.091	.064	.221	−2.113
	(.011)	(.068)	(.033)	(.113)	(.385)
All foreign weighing < 2300 lbs.	.086	−.462	−.672	−.250	0.0
	(.044)	(.206)	(.293)	(.124)	—

Note: Standard errors in parentheses.

Notes

The author is grateful to Angus Deaton, Avinash Dixit, Rob Feenstra, Gene Grossman, Whitney Newey, and Duncan Thomas for helpful comments and suggestions, as well as to the Sloan Foundation and the National Bureau of Economic Research for financial support.
1. See Dixit 1987, which argues this point.
2. See, for example, Deaton and Muellbauer 1980.
3. Other simpler examples of this type of methodology are Johnson 1978 and Cragg and Uhler 1970.
4. Demand for automobiles is the most prevalent example of modeling the demand-differentiated products. I am unaware of any modeling approach for other differentiated products that is not mentioned in this section of the chapter.
5. This is the most recent data available until April 1987.
6. Note that this differs from the usual panel in which goods are the same, but demand is across consumers and over time. Here, the consumers are assumed the same, but goods differ across models, and these models are tracked over time.
7. Actually, it is sufficient to include in the regression those characteristics of which a linear combination accounts for the product differentiation.
8. All foreign models except the Peugeot 505 are produced by either Japan, Germany, or Sweden.
9. This differs from the Dixit-Stiglitz approach to product differentiation. There, all products are neighbors.

10. The approach I use to find neighbors when products are multi-dimensionally differentiated benefited greatly from discussions with Rob Feenstra. I am very grateful for his many helpful suggestions.

Recent theoretical work by Caplin and Nalebuff (1986) has also addressed the issue of determining neighbors to a good when products are multi-dimensionally differentiated. They show that if preferences can be represented by a utility function that is Cobb-Douglas in product characteristics and income, there exists a straightforward way of finding neighbors. Using the unit simplex in Cobb-Douglas parameter space, they show that a hyperplane divides all consumers who prefer good x to good y from those who prefer y to x. Because sets of consumers who prefer one model to another (that is, the model's neighborhood) are defined by hyperplanes, finding neighbors is a tractable problem. The tractability comes from the functional form of the utility function. While this is an elegant result, it is not applicable to the automobile market because the utility function that permits the tractability of the problem also implies that all consumers purchase the same value of the most preferred model but differ in quantities purchased. For big-ticket items such as automobiles, this is just not the case.

11. This function over characteristics is sometimes referred to in the literature as a subutility function.

12. While this line of reasoning has strong Bayesian overtones, I do not know another way of getting a feel for the validity of a new methodology. This is another reason why the auto industry is a good candidate to which to apply a new methodology. If my methodology were first applied to lumber and I found clear pine-2 to be a neighbor to grade 3 birch, few economists would have any idea of how well neighbors are defined.

13. This is also the practice adopted by Feenstra 1985. In that paper, he puts forth the argument that for national welfare considerations, dealer markups represent an intracountry transfer.

14. Implicit discounts due to selectively applied low financing rates have also been ignored due to lack of data.

15. The most recent examples are Feenstra 1985 and 1986. Griliches 1971 is a much earlier example.

16. I also estimate this function without logarithms. This functional form yielded a loss of about .20 in the R^2.

17. This procedure is programmed in IBM Profortran for implementation on IBM-compatible personal computers.

18. Throughout this chapter, *statistically significant* means statistically significant from zero at the 90 percent confidence level unless stated otherwise.

Because *FOREIGN* is a near-linear combination of *SWEDE, JAPAN,* and *GERMAN*—the fixed effects, I do not include *FOREIGN* in equation (1A) as an own characteristic.

19. Indeed, demand estimation according to the Armington assumption, using my data set, yields statistically insignificant and nonsensical demand elasticities.

References

Automotive news market data book. Various annual issues. Chicago: Crain Communications.

Belsley, D. A., E. Kuh, and R. E. Welsch. 1980. *Regression diagnostics.* New York: John Wiley.

Bresnahan, T. 1981. Departures from marginal-cost pricing in the American automobile industry. *Journal of Econometrics* 17:201–27.

Caplin, A., and B. Nalebuff. 1986. Multi-dimensional product differentiation and price competition. Mimeo. Princeton University.

Cragg, J., and R. Uhler. 1970. The demand for automobiles. *Canadian Journal of Economics* 3:386–406.

Daganzo, Carlos. 1979. *Multinomial probit: The theory and its applications to demand forecasting*. New York: Academic Press.

Deaton A., and J. Muellbauer. 1980. An almost ideal demand system. *American Economic Review* 70:312–26.

Dixit, A. In press. Optimal trade and industrial policies for the U.S. automobile industry. In R. Feenstra, ed., *Empirical methods for international trade*. Cambridge: MIT Press.

Dixit, A., and J. Stiglitz. 1977. Monopolistic competition and optimum product diversity. *American Economic Review* 67:297–308.

Feenstra, R. 1985. Quality change under trade restraint: Theory and evidence from Japanese autos. Columbia University Department of Economics Paper No. 298.

———. 1987. Gains from trade in differentiated products: Japanese compact trucks. In R. Feenstra, ed., *Empirical methods for international trade*. Cambridge: MIT Press.

Griliches, Z. 1971. Hedonic price indices for automobiles. In Z. Griliches, ed., *Price indexes and quality changes*, 55–87. Cambridge: Harvard University Press.

Helpman, E., and P. Krugman. 1985. *Market structure and foreign trade: Increasing returns, imperfect competition, and the international economy*. Cambridge: MIT Press.

Hotelling, H. 1929. Stability in competition. *Economic Journal* 39:41–57.

Johnson, T. 1978. A cross-section analysis of the demand for new and used automobiles in the United States. *Economic Inquiry* 16:531–48.

Krugman, P. 1980. Scale economics, product differentiation, and the pattern of trade. *American Economic Review* 70:950–59.

Lancaster, Kelvin. 1979. *Variety, equity, and efficiency*. New York: Columbia University Press.

Leamer, E. 1984. Model choice and specification analysis. In Z. Griliches and M. Intriligator, eds., *Handbook of econometrics*, 1:285–330. Amsterdam: North-Holland.

———. 1985. Sensitivity analyses would help. *American Economic Review* 75:308–13.

Leamer, E., and R. Stern. 1970. *Quantitative international economics*. New York: Aldine.

Ohta, M., and Z. Griliches. 1975. Automobile prices revisited: Extensions of the hedonic hypothesis. In N. E. Terleckj, ed., *Household production and consumption*, 325–98. New York: Columbia University Press.

Salop, Steven. 1979. Monopolistic competition with outside goods. *Bell Journal of Economics* 10(1):141–56.

Suits, D. 1958. The demand for automobiles in the United States, 1929–1956. *Review of Economics and Statistics* 40:273–80.

———. 1961. Exploring alternative formulations of automobile demand. *Review of Economics and Statistics* 43:66–69.

Tarr, D. G., and M. E. Morkre, 1984. *Aggregate costs to the United States of tariffs and quotas on imports*. Bureau of Economics Staff Report. Washington, D.C.: Federal Trade Commission.

Toder, E., with N. Cardell and E. Burton. 1978. *Trade policy and the U.S. automobile industry.* New York: Praeger.

Train, K. 1986. *Qualitative choice analysis: Theory, econometrics, and an application to automobile demand.* Cambridge: MIT Press.

Comment   Raymond Riezman

The trade policy issue addressed in this chapter is how the existence of differentiated products alters our approach to trade policy. Levinsohn outlines a procedure for estimating elasticities for different models of automobiles purchased, but not necessarily produced, in the United States. The Lancasterian characteristics approach is used to reduce the number of cross elasticities considered, thereby making these estimates tractable.

The estimates are then used to conduct a number of interesting policy experiments. For example, if the goal of policy is to increase demand for domestically produced autos, a direct production subsidy is roughly twice as effective as a tariff. This result is an empirical verification of the theme that emerges from the domestic distortions literature, namely, that a policy should be focused as directly as possible at the source of the problem. This finding goes beyond the usual one in which direct subsidies are superior to tariffs because they involve fewer distortions. Here, we also have to worry about the neighbor effects, that is, the extent to which protection increases demand for domestically produced autos depends on whether the banned imports are neighbors of domestically produced autos or other imports.

Generally, it seems that the effectiveness of any trade policy is dependent on what is a neighbor to the good to which the policy is applied. For example, if the goal is to increase domestic production, then taxing imports will work only to the extent that domestic products are neighbors to the imports. If the goal is to reduce the trade deficit, taxing Japanese imports works if these imports are neighbors to U.S.-produced products but will not work if their neighbors are other imported goods. This chapter provides us with a methodology to empirically determine which goods are neighbors.

The basic equation to be estimated (1A) has quantity of a particular model in a certain year as the dependent variable. Independent variables are own price, own characteristics, charactcristics and prices of all other models in all other years, time and country dummies. A re-

Raymond Riezman is associate professor of economics at the University of Iowa.

stricted version (1B) which eliminates direct effects of the characteristics is also estimated.

Estimating equation (1A) directly is not tractable. A procedure is developed to eliminate many cross-characteristic effects. First, a Lancasterian utility function is defined. A surplus function is defined which determines a metric in characteristic space. Given this metric, a procedure is outlined to determine which models are neighbors. Non-neighbor models are assumed to have zero cross effects. Once neighbors are determined, equations (1A) and (1B) are estimated. I found the discussion of this procedure difficult to follow. It is particularly puzzling to understand how the heterogeneous tastes are aggregated. Another result needing elaboration is that equation (1B) performs as well as equation (1A).

While it is true, as the author states, that all of these estimates are for "small changes" in tariffs, an interesting extension would be to do simulations to see how the estimates change for finite changes in tariffs. It appears that these estimates would be robust until neighbor relationships start to change. It would be of interest to know how much tariffs can change without substantially altering neighbors. This extension is important since ultimately, the usefulness of this methodology depends on being able to extend the results to finite changes in tariffs.

Data are available on average transaction prices, from consumer publications. It is important to get this information because casual observation suggests that biases exist, namely, Japanese cars sell at list or above, while U.S. autos sell at discounts up to 15 percent.

This chapter has relevance for the Baldwin-Green essay (chap. 7, in this volume) which is concerned with why protection does not always stimulate domestic production. The effect on domestic production of any protectionist policy depends on which goods are neighbors to the protected goods.

Since Levinsohn is concerned with the demand side only, there is little discussion about the industry structure. However, if the industry is competitive it seems that existing methods would work for an appropriately defined characteristic space. If the industry is not competitive, this needs some discussion since there is no general characterization of equilibrium in this kind of model and identification problems seem serious because these noncompetitive firms presumably react to things, such as taste changes, that are causing the demand to change.

Sometimes work such as this is misinterpreted as advocating or encouraging the use of protection. Such a view is quite misguided in this case. In the short run, policymakers operate under many political and institutional constraints. Policy studies such as this one are useful for helping policymakers optimize under the given constraints. Of course, we should also be thinking about long-run issues, but there still is a place for analysis that is useful for current policy problems.

Comment   James E. Anderson

This chapter attempts a significant step forward in the estimation of detailed cross-price effects in a demand system for a differentiated products industry. Such cross effects are badly needed for policy analysis, yet very difficult to obtain. One problem is that for an industry with many models, the number of cross effects outruns any possible econometric effort to catch them. James Levinsohn's answer is to develop a method for imposing zero restrictions that is not purely a priori. I think the technique is clever and will undoubtedly be used in future related work. The possible objections to it have been anticipated and discussed by Levinsohn. The zero restrictions are then used to implement a standard type of aggregate demand system estimation. It is here that Levinsohn runs into some significant difficulties.

I have two sets of comments; one on the paper written and one on the paper I think the author should attempt to write. The latter is of course unfair, but I am going to do it anyway, because the problems I raise are significant and tend to vitiate the type of conclusion possible based on the current research strategy. Essentially they involve trying to model the supply side of the auto market.

Below, I critique Levinsohn's demand analysis and then make a case for a simultaneous attempt to model the supply side.

Critique of the Demand Study

Even leaving aside the identification issues of the next part, it is doubtful that Levinsohn's study has pinned down a stable and accurate demand system. I see two major flaws—the failure to treat aggregation issues and the failure to consider the time dimension of the demand for a durable good. I also have one minor comment.

Aggregation

The first flaw concerns aggregation. An aggregate price elasticity set is econometrically estimated, and its values depend on both the underlying utility structure and the aggregation structure. The author develops only the former. The problem is that a great deal of the "action" in determining the elasticities is in the latter. I have little confidence that the estimated elasticities will be accurate when considering policy-induced perturbations.

The difficulty is clearest with the aggregate price elasticity of demand for autos as a group, implied by Levinsohn's estimated set. The underlying consumer theory models an agent who will buy either zero or

James E. Anderson is professor of economics at Boston College.

one automobile. Levinsohn's price elasticity of demand for autos is zero everywhere but at the jump point, where it is undefined. So also in the aggregate: if all consumers are located on one or the other side of the jump point, the elasticity of demand is zero. In the sample data, price movements evidently push some consumers across the jump point, allowing a nonzero elasticity. But all the action is in the distribution of consumers. Without an aggregation theory, there is no way to know how accurate the estimated elasticity is.

Turning to the estimated cross-price elasticities that are the main focus of the chapter, the same difficulty exists. The consumer theory of Levinsohn's program (5) does not define any cross-price effects in autos The analog to the usual elasticities is the elasticity of demand for a characteristic with respect to a marginal cost p_x. Each model bundles together a given quantity for each characteristic. A rise in the price of a model (proportionately raising all p_x), given an interior solution in program (5), should induce a jump to a new model: an undefined cross-price effect. Realistically, not all possible models are offered, so program (5) has further constraints on it. This means that the effect of a rise in price of model j may not induce a jump in demand for its close substitute model k: a zero elasticity. Aggregation again has all the action in averaging together the two effects. Without a structure for aggregation, there can be little confidence in the results.

The Time Dimension

The second flaw in the demand study is a failure to treat the time dimension of the demand for autos. There are three aspects of this to consider. First, durability and frequency-of-repair data are available and belong in the list of characteristics. There is ample evidence that consumers care about such properties and that manufacturers attempt to respond.

Second, the demand for a durable good must be modeled in an intertemporal setting. This will have a number of implications. For example, initial stocks of autos may be important (do not necessarily disappear into a wealth term). Second, a well-known effect of a rise in the price of a durable is that it shifts up the duration of use. There have been significant changes in the average vintage of U.S. autos in the past fifteen years. Also, such data vary by model. There is no easy way to stuff such phenomena into the author's static model. Presumably a start is for the taste for durability to rise with price, imposing a nonlinearity on program (5), but it is better to confront the problem.

Third, it seems to me that the closest substitute to the cars an agent might buy may often be the car he already owns. There are two aspects to this. First, the choice in program (5) and in the demand system also includes use of the depreciated current auto. Second, knowledge of characteristics is imperfect, and the currently owned auto is the best source of information on the potential new auto from the same source. Manufacturers and dealers certainly act on that belief in their efforts to build and maintain brand loyalty. This suggests another role for the existing stock of autos in demand estimation, standing in for reputational effects.

Minor Comment

The author's technique for identifying close substitutes is the major contribution of the chapter. It would be useful to check this technique with the results of market survey research. One concern of that literature is also the identification of close substitutes, proceeding on the basis of sampling techniques.

The Case for a Supply-Side Model

A basic assumption of the study is that the supply side of the auto market offers a technically fixed price-quality mix to consumers. See program (5), where $p(x)$ is given. Simultaneous equations bias arises when this is not true. Also, policy conclusions based on a tariff levied assuming an unchanging supply side will be falsified by shifts in manufacturers' behavior.

It is idle to complain about identification problems in the absence of a demonstration that they are significant and that feasible methods exist for remedying the situation. The evidence is that for autos these issues are highly significant. Folk wisdom has it that Japanese manufacturers shifted their quality mix in response to the VERs (Voluntary Export Restraints). Robert Feenstra has done some work along these lines suggesting that a large portion of the rise in price was in fact explained by the shift in quality.

It is more dubious whether feasible methods exist for estimating the full structure. Sherwin Rosen (1974) has a full treatment of the structure of perfectly competitive differentiated product markets and some suggestions for estimation. He comments that the problem of monopolistically competitive markets, with discrete differences in brands, is significantly more difficult. I suggest that the sort of cleverness and willingness to heroically simplify that is visible in the author's technique for identifying close substitutes should also be spent on the simultaneous system problem.

Reference

Rosen, Sherwin. 1974. Hedonic prices and implicit markets: Product differentiation in pure competition. *Journal of Political Economy,* 82(1):34–55.

3 Industrial Policy and International Competition in Wide-Bodied Jet Aircraft

Richard Baldwin and Paul Krugman

The international market for large commercial jet aircraft is about as far as one can get from the standard trade theory paradigm of static constant returns and price-taking competition. It is an industry in which the survival of firms depends on periodic introduction of new families of aircraft, and the introduction of a new family is marked by massive dynamic scale economies. A huge initial expenditure on development is followed by a steep learning curve at the level of the firm, a curve that industry experts believe lasts throughout the product cycle. The fixed cost and the dynamic increasing returns introduced by learning ensures that this is an industry in which only a few firms can profitably exist. In the world market there are only three significant manufacturers of airframes for jets that seat more than one hundred passengers. It is arguable that in the absence of government support there would be only one.

For those who work on the "new" trade theory that emphasizes increasing returns, dynamics, and imperfect competition, these economic characteristics would in and of themselves make aircraft a natural target for study. An additional reason for interest in the aircraft industry, however, is that the industry is the center of a policy conflict between the United States and Europe. Aircraft production is widely

Richard Baldwin is assistant professor of economics at Columbia University's Graduate School of Business and a faculty research fellow at the National Bureau of Economic Research. Paul Krugman is professor of economics at the Massachusetts Institute of Technology and a research associate of the National Bureau of Economic Research.

The authors would like to acknowledge comments and suggestions of Cathy Mann, Eric Fisher, Victor Norman, and Ray Riezman. Richard Baldwin gratefully acknowledges financial support from the Wenner-Gren Center Foundation and the Institute for International Economics.

regarded as a "strategic" industry and has long been a target of industrial policy in Europe. In the late 1970s this policy for the first time achieved some commercial success, when Airbus Industrie, a four-nation European consortium, began to achieve a significant market share with its A300 family of large, medium-range jets. Since then, accusations have flown and tension has risen.

The U.S. dominance of the world aircraft industry is one of the few remnants of the United States' vanishing technological superiority, so a challenge in this area is particularly irksome. Both U.S. manufacturers and U.S. government officials have charged that Airbus has bought market share only with the help of government subsidy. On the other side, the Europeans deny that the government loans supporting Airbus represent a subsidy; they argue that the governments expect to be repaid in full, and they charge in return that U.S. manufacturers receive de facto support from military procurement.

This chapter takes a preliminary look at international competition in the market for large commercial jet aircraft, viewing the competition in terms of the recent style of trade modeling that emphasizes imperfect competition and increasing returns. We develop a simulation model that roughly reproduces the conflict between the United States and Europe in medium-range, wide-bodied transports. The focus is on two questions: How large is the effective European subsidy, and what have been the welfare effects of this subsidy on the United States, Europe, and the rest of the world?

The chapter is in six sections. Section 3.1 presents some background on the industry. Section 3.2 presents a preliminary analytic overview of the welfare issues raised by European targeting. Section 3.3 lays out the analytics of the simulation model; section 3.4 then describes the calibration of the model to data and its solution. Finally, section 3.5 discusses the conclusions and possible future work.

3.1 Technology, Competition, and Cost

The production of aircraft is a technology-intensive industry. That is, relative to other products, a large part of the cost of producing an airplane is the cost of creating the technology embodied in its design and manufacturing. This cost is incurred both directly, in the form of research and development (R&D) expenses, and indirectly, by the acceptance of losses during the initial phase of the learning curve in the expectation that costs will fall with experience.

Like other technology-intensive industries, aircraft is characterized by a distinct product cycle. At intervals, fundamental breakthroughs in design are made, and manufacturers introduce new families of aircraft to take advantage of these breakthroughs. In between, production costs are reduced through experience, and relatively minor modifications of existing aircraft are undertaken to suit them more precisely to market demand.

Table 3.1 shows the deliveries of large passenger aircraft by manufacturers since the introduction of the first commercially viable jets in the late 1950s. The product cycle is clear-cut. In the late 1950s, turbofan jets, the Boeing 707, and the McDonnell-Douglas DC-8 were introduced and remained strong sellers until the early 1970s. In the mid-1960s, somewhat larger aircraft, the roughly 150-seat 727 and DC-9, were introduced. At the end of the 1960s came the "jumbo jets," wide-bodied aircraft (two aisles)—the Boeing 747 and the McDonnell-Douglas DC-10. Finally, at the end of the 1970s came wide-bodied medium-range jets, the Airbus A300 and the Boeing 767.

The important point is that in contrast to other technology-intensive industries, such as semiconductors, the product cycles in aircraft are quite long. A few 707s are still being produced for military use. While such a long product life is exceptional, the life of a successful airframe is something like twenty years. The counterpart is that each time a new generation is being developed, companies must essentially stake their survival on a successful design.

Once an aircraft has been developed, average cost falls steeply as cumulative production mounts, both because the R&D can be spread over a larger base and because production costs fall with the learning curve. Figure 3.1 presents estimates of costs for the hypothetical new aircraft, as calculated by the U.S. Commerce Department in cooperation with McDonnell-Douglas.

3.1.1 Demand and Competition

Aircraft are capital goods that are one of several inputs into the production of passenger service. The existence of different air routes creates a demand for aircraft with different characteristics and thereby supports a limited Lancasterian differentiation among aircraft. To minimize costs, airlines typically own a mixture of airplanes. Currently there are fourteen types of large turbojets operating in the world air carrier fleet.

The composition of the mix depends primarily on the types of air routes the airline flies. Due to both physical and organizational considerations, a plane will have lower operating costs per passenger the larger it is (because large planes are more fuel-efficient per seat but still need only the same size cockpit crew) and the shorter the planned range (because less space and weight are allocated to fuel storage). Nonetheless, certain routes require long-range planes and some routes

Table 3.1   **Deliveries of Large Passenger Aircraft**

	1958	'59	'60	'61	'62	'63	'64	'65	'66	'67	'68	'69	'70
707	8	77	91	80	68	34	38	61	83	118	111	59	19
727						6	95	111	135	155	160	115	54
737										4	105	114	37
747												4	92
DC-8		21	91	42	22	19	20	31	32	41	102	85	33
DC-9/MD-80								5	69	152	203	121	54
DC-10													
L-1011													
880/990			14	33	33	16	4	2					
757													
767													
U.S. Manufacturers Subtotal	8	98	196	156	122	75	157	210	319	470	681	498	289
Comet	7	19	20	14	13	2	2	1		1			
Caravelle		18	39	39	35	23	22	18	18	21	14	11	9
Trident							12	18	11	1	11	9	2
VC-10							14	11	7	10	9	2	1
BAC-111								34	46	20	26	40	22
F-28												9	11
Mercure													
A300													
A310													
BAe 146													
VFW-614													
Concorde													
Non-U.S. Manufacturers Subtotal	7	37	59	53	48	25	50	74	82	53	60	71	45
Total	15	135	255	209	170	100	207	284	401	523	741	569	334

are more cheaply serviced by small planes that fly full than by large, half-empty planes. Thus roughly speaking, aircraft are differentiated in a two-dimensional space of range versus number of passengers.

Table 3.2 presents some characteristics of wide-body aircraft now in production. The main point to notice in the table is that not all wide-bodied aircraft are close substitutes. The four-engine Boeing 747 is a monster compared with the other aircraft, both in terms of size and range; essentially there is nothing else like it. The three-engine DC-10 is considerably smaller and shorter-range; it is also at this point almost out of production (see below). Still smaller and shorter-range are the

Table 3.1   (continued)

'71	'72	'73	'74	'75	'76	'77	'78	'79	'80	'81	'82	'83	'84	Total
10	4	11	21	7	9	8	13	6	3	6	8	8	8	969
33	41	92	91	91	61	67	118	136	131	97	26	11	8	1834
29	22	23	55	51	41	25	40	77	92	111	95	82	67	1070
69	30	30	22	21	27	20	32	67	73	58	25	23	16	609
13	4													556
44	32	29	48	42	50	22	22	39	23	73	44	50	44	1166
13	52	57	47	43	19	14	18	36	40	23	11	4	2	379
	17	39	41	25	16	11	8	14	24	29	14	6	4	248
														102
											2	25	18	45
											20	55	29	104
211	202	281	325	280	223	167	251	369	386	397	243	264	196	7082
														112
4	5	3												279
13	11	7	4	6	9	7	4							117
														54
12	7	2	4	2		6	3		3	2	2			231
10	13	19	9	20	17	13	11	13	13	13	11	19	17	218
			6	4										10
			4	9	13	16	15	24	40	45	46	21	19	252
												17	29	46
												7	11	18
			1	4	5									10
			1	6	2				3	2				14
39	36	31	27	43	49	49	33	38	59	62	59	64	76	1361
250	238	312	352	323	272	216	284	412	445	450	302	328	272	8443

A300 and the Boeing 767. It is between these two planes that the effective U.S.-European competition has taken place. Thus we do not look at aircraft as an aggregate and count 747s as part of the U.S. market share. On the demand side, the close substitution is between the 767 and the A300.

3.1.2 Government Policy and the State of Competition

At the beginning of the 1970s there were three major U.S. civilian aircraft manufacturers: Boeing, McDonnell-Douglas, and Lockheed. Competitive pressure, however, narrowed the field. McDonnell-Douglas

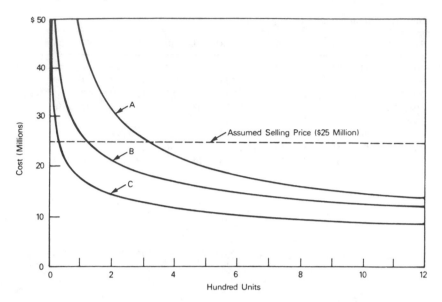

Fig. 3.1   Development and production costs, hypothetical 150-seat transport. *Notes:* A is Total Average Cost = ([Cumulative Production Cost] + [Development Cost])/Number of Units; B is Cumulative Average Production Cost = Cumulative Production Cost/Number of Units; C is Individual Unit Production Cost, calculated using the following learning curves developed in cooperation with Douglas Aircraft company: units 1–10, 71.4 percent; units 11–20, 76.3 percent; units 21–50, 78.2 percent; and units 51 or greater, 81.1 percent. *Source:* Office of Competitive Assessment.

and Lockheed both introduced three-engine wide-bodied jets (the DC-10 and the L-1011) that were close substitutes in a market that apparently was not large enough to support two firms. The result was that both suffered serious losses. Lockheed withdrew from civilian manufacturing altogether. McDonnell-Douglas basically exited the market for wide-bodied aircraft, although it continues to sell substantial numbers of narrow-bodied MD-80s. The production of the DC-10 was actually stopped in 1984; then the company restarted the production line on a limited basis because it can also sell a military version of the same aircraft. If it were not for the presence of Airbus, the manufacture of wide-bodied aircraft would be essentially a Boeing monopoly.

Airbus was founded in 1970. After some reshuffling, it has ended as a consortium jointly owned by the governments of France, Germany, the United Kingdom, and Spain. The mechanics of government support are complex, but in essence Airbus is able to borrow money that it will repay only to the extent that the consortium is profitable. In other

Table 3.2   **Characteristics of Wide-Bodied Aircraft**

Maker/Model	No. of Engines	First Delivered	No. of Seats	Range (No. Miles)
Airbus				
A310	2	1985	212	3100
A300 B2	2	1974	251	1550–1910
A300 B4-100	2	1974	251	3050
A300 B4-200	2	1974	251	3300
A300-600	2	1974	267	3550–3750
Boeing				
767-200	2	1982	216	3300–4000
767-200ER	2	1982	216	5300
767-300	2	1986	261	4000
747	4	1969	330–496	5600–6000
McDonnell-Douglas				
DC-10-10	3	1971	250–380	3300
DC-10-15	3	1971	250–380	3780
DC-10-30	3	1971	250–380	5090
DC-10-40	3	1971	250–380	4995

Source: Economist, June 1, 1985.

words, it is able to finance its investment through what is nominally debt, but what closely resembles equity.

The size of the subsidy provided to the A300 is a matter of dispute for the simple reason that it is not a directly measurable quantity. Airbus is currently producing the A300 and the A310. It has also begun to invest in research and development on the A320. It has lost money consistently since its founding. However, all new aircraft lose money at first—that is the nature of a technology-intensive product, in which investment in knowledge is expensed and therefore appears as an accounting loss. The true test is one of future prospects: can Airbus reasonably be expected to yield a competitive market rate of return? Boeing, not surprisingly, claims that it will not, that the development of the A300 would not have been undertaken under normal commercial evaluation of its prospects. European governments deny this and say that they expect to be fully repaid. Most observers agree with Boeing's assessment, but not necessarily with the large estimates of the size of the implicit subsidy that Boeing has circulated.

One important reason Airbus probably would not have succeeded as a private project is that it has taken a long time to achieve significant commercial sales. As table 3.3 shows, the first deliveries of the A300 took place in 1974, but it was not until 1979 that large sales were made. There followed several years of large sales, which then fell off substantially after Boeing introduced the 767.

Table 3.3 Deliveries of Commercial Aircraft

	1969	'70	'71	'72	'73	'74	'75	'76	'77	'78	'79	'80	'81	'82	'83	'84	'85
A300						4	9	13	16	15	24	40	45	46	21	19	17
767														20	55	29	25
DC10			13	52	57	47	43	19	14	18	36	40	23	11	4	2	n.a.
747	4	92	69	30	30	22	21	27	20	32	67	73	58	25	23	16	24

Source: Economist, June 1, 1985.

3.2 Analytical Welfare Issues

Although competition in the aircraft industry is dynamic in nature, some of the policy aspects can be illustrated with static models. Two models in particular are useful in thinking about the results we derive: a simple model of subsidized entry of a monopolist, and a similarly simple model of subsidized entry of a duopolist.

As a first model for thinking about the effect of the Airbus program, let us disregard the competitive aspect. What would have happened if Airbus's entry had simply been a subsidized entry of a monopolist into a market where no other firms would have produced? This is not entirely irrelevant as a description of the situation. When the A300 was first introduced, it did not face any closely competitive aircraft: it was smaller and shorter-range than the U.S. wide-bodies, larger and cheaper to operate than U.S. narrow-bodies. From 1979 to 1982, in particular, Airbus was clearly filling a market niche that made it in a sense a monopolist.

Figure 3.2 illustrates the position of a monopolist subject to decreasing cost. D is the market demand curve, MR the associated marginal revenue curve, MC the marginal cost curve, and AC the average cost curve. P_m and Q_m are the profit-maximizing price and quantity. As drawn, the monopolist cannot enter profitably. If it were to enter, it would suffer losses equal to the shaded area.

Suppose, now, that a government provides the monopolist with a subsidy sufficiently large to induce entry. Then the shaded area still represents a social loss. Against this, however, must be set the gain in consumer surplus. It is certainly possible that the gain might exceed the loss, so that privately unprofitable entry is socially beneficial.

Where does international trade enter into this story? If there is an integrated world market, all that happens is that the gain in consumer surplus is divided among several countries. Thus if one country subsidizes the entry of a monopolist into an otherwise unprofitable market, the effect will be a gain for all other countries, a possible gain for the world as a whole, and a possible gain for the subsidizing country. It is of course possible that the policy will be beneficial for the world as a whole but not for the subsidizing nation.

Matters become more complex if there is already an incumbent firm. In that case, subsidizing entry will reduce the incumbent firm's profits. If the existing firm is located in a different country from the new firm, the profit shifting can make subsidizing the entry a beggar-thy-neighbor policy.

Much of the strategic trade policy literature has focused on the possibility that a credible commitment by a government to subsidize entry will deter entry by foreign rivals. In this case entry may turn out to be

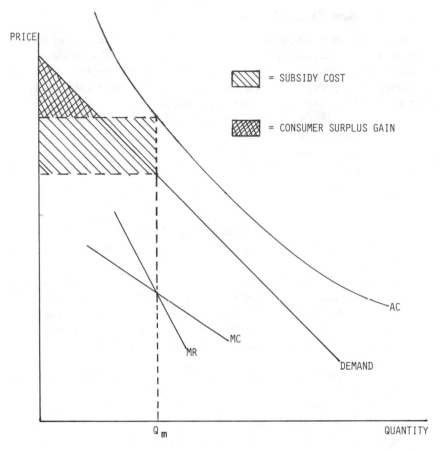

Fig. 3.2   Impact of the subsidized entry of a monopolist

profitable ex post, even though a firm operating without subsidy would not have found it profitable. In the case of the A300, however, it is clear that the Airbus subsidy did not succeed in keeping Boeing out of the market. (The Airbus entry into the 150-seat narrow-bodied market, the A320, may be a different story.) Thus the right model must be one in which entry leads to the formation of a duopoly, in which the subsidized firm has negative profits.

In assessing the effects of this entry, we need to consider first the effect on output and prices. Suppose that after entry, competition takes the form of Cournot quantity-setting. Then we can represent the competition by two firms' reaction functions, as in figure 3.3. In the absence of a government subsidy, output will lie at point A. With a government subsidy, the equilibrium will shift to B, with Airbus's entry causing both a fall in the price and a fall in Boeing's output.

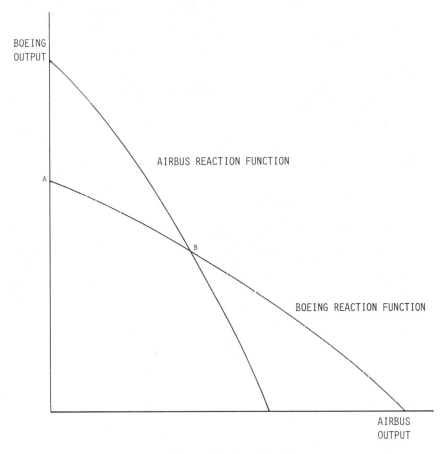

Fig. 3.3   Two possible equilibriums in a Cournot game

To assess the welfare effects in this case, we need to consider three regions: Europe, the United States, and the rest of the world. The effects of the subsidized entry on Europe and the United States are illustrated in figures 3.4 and 3.5.

In figure 3.4 we see the effect of subsidized entry in Europe. The world price is driven down from P_1, the monopoly price, to P_2, the duopoly price. This produces a gain in consumer surplus, illustrated by the shaded area. On the other hand, by assumption, European production, at Q_2, takes place at an average cost that exceeds P_2. This leads to a loss that offsets the consumer gain. As in the case of monopolistic entry, Europe may either gain or lose.

In figure 3.5 we see the effect of Europe's subsidy on the United States. The fall in the price from P_1 to P_2 produces a consumer gain.

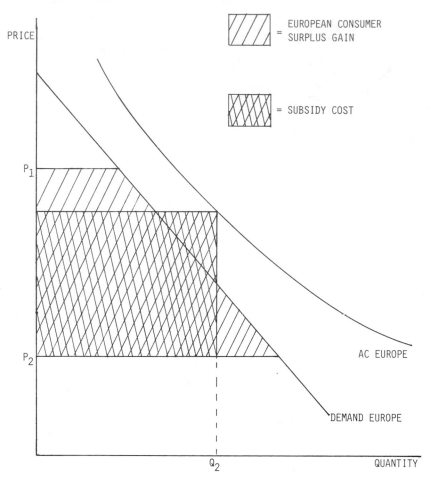

Fig. 3.4   Effect of Airbus entry on European welfare

But there is also a producer loss. This loss consists of two parts. First, at the initial output Q_1, the fall in the price produces a loss. Second, the domestic firm is induced to reduce its output from Q_1 to Q_2. Since even in the duopoly situation marginal cost is less than the price, this output reduction leads to a further loss in profits, also shown in the figure.

In general, the welfare effect on the United States is ambiguous. However, if (as is realistic) the United States remains a net exporter even with subsidized European entry, the net effect is unambiguously negative. The reason is that the conventional terms-of-trade effect— the consumer gain, less the profit loss that would be incurred if output

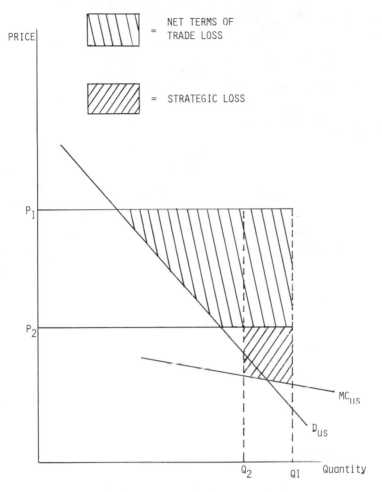

Fig. 3.5   Impact of Airbus entry on U.S. welfare

remained at Q_1—is clearly negative, and to this must be added any negative "strategic" effects, as captured by the decline in Q, even though price remains above marginal cost.

The rest of the world, of course, gains unambiguously from the decline in the price.

To sum up, we see that in a duopoly situation in which the United States remains a net exporter, the effects of subsidized European entry would be unambiguously negative. Europe could gain, but not because the strategic deterrent effect of its subsidy enables it to capture rents; instead, the gains would come on the consumer side.

3.2.1 Putting the Model Together

We have sketched out two models. In the first, Europe is seen as subsidizing the entry of a monopolist into a market where nobody would otherwise produce. This entry benefits everyone except possibly Europe. In the second model, Europe's entry changes a U.S. monopoly into a duopoly. Provided that it is a net exporter even after European entry, the United States must be a net loser. Again Europe can either gain or lose.

Now in actual fact the situation created by Airbus's entry can be viewed as having reproduced each of these situations in turn. When the A300 was first introduced, it did not face close substitutes; thus for several years it might make sense to view Airbus as a new product provided to the world. After 1982 the A300 shared the market with a fairly close substitute, the Boeing 767, of which the United States was a net exporter. Thus the United States was a net gainer during the early years of Airbus's presence, but was a net loser once its own entry into the market had taken place. The overall effect is ambiguous and depends on the relative weight given to the early period versus the later one.

3.3 A Model of Aircraft Competition

To produce a solvable model of competition in aircraft, we abstract from many real-world complications. We focus entirely on the competition between the A300 and the 767, ignoring both the residual presence of McDonnell-Douglas and the linkage between competition in this area and other families of aircraft. Equally important, our treatment of the intertemporal substitutability of aircraft is less than complete. The main focus is on the dynamics of competition that arise from learning by doing and the corresponding strategies of output over time.

3.3.1 Setup of the Model

Aircraft constitute large and lumpy purchases. Since airlines like to have compatible equipment, the usual aircraft sale involves dozens of planes. These planes will usually be built after the order, with the design modified somewhat to the buyer's specifications. Furthermore, aircraft are durable goods. The typical airliner has a service life of twenty years. For these reasons it is typical for each airline to negotiate only once for each model.

Aircraft are not consumed directly but rather constitute one of many inputs into the production of air carrier service. Airlines purchase a variety of planes in order to service their air routes. As discussed above, the composition of a carrier's fleet is chosen to minimize costs. Since planes are durable goods, buying an additional A300 or 767 will affect an airline's profit via a cost-savings effect for the life of the aircraft. In general, the derived demand for A300s and 767s would depend on the price of all large jets as well as the price of jet fuel, staff wages, and so forth. Appealing to tractability, we shall ignore these cross-price effects.

This cost-saving effect of an additional A300 or 767 clearly depends only on the number of such jets in an air carrier's own fleet. However, in principle the A300s and 767s delivered to other carriers would affect profits by increasing the total supply of available passenger seats and therefore the equilibrium passenger fare. This effect, however, is diluted by several factors. The desired number of passenger seats is determined chiefly by the air routes chosen by airlines. This later choice is in turn determined by a host of demand and cost factors. Aircraft constitute between a third and a tenth of the variable costs (this figure is very sensitive to the price of fuel) of operating an air route. Moreover, the stock of planes chosen is affected by the retirement of old aircraft as well as the purchases of the dozen other types of commercial jets currently in production. To simplify the dynamics we shall ignore this revenue effect. We shall assume that an airline's evaluation of the marginal benefits of an A300 or 767 depends only on the number of them in its own fleet.

Formally, we assume that air carriers choose the number of jets to maximize the discounted sum of profits, taking as given the aircraft's price. If the service life of the aircraft is N years, the first-order condition of a typical airline (in the year it actually purchases planes) is

$$\sum_{i=0}^{N-1} [R^i \Pi'_{t+i}(q)] = p_t ,$$

where q is the number of A300s or 767s it buys, R is the discount factor, p_t is the price of the aircraft, and $\Pi'_{t+i}(q)$ is the derivative of the purchaser's profits in year $t+1$ with respect to q. The standard Kuhn-Tucker conditions hold for all other years (notice we have skirted the consideration that leads airlines to buy all at once rather than year by year). We ignore the integer constraint and assume that the two models are perfect substitutes. Assuming for simplicity's sake that "l" airlines purchase each year, the market demand for the planes is

$$(1) \qquad p_t = \sum_{l=0}^{N-1} R^i b(x_t + x_t^*)^{1/E} ,$$

where we have assumed a functional form for $\Pi'_t = \beta(x_t + x_t^*)^{1/E}$, and b equals $\beta l^{1/E}$. The deliveries of Boeing are denoted by x, the deliveries of Airbus by x^*, and the demand elasticity by E.

It is worthwhile to point out two features of this demand relation. First, it has the form of a standard, atemporal demand function with a constant elasticity equal to E. Second, the quantity sold today depends only on today's price, as long as the airlines find it optimal to buy this year rather than next. This last modification will play an important role below.

Turning now to the producers, we assume there are two firms capable of producing a single good (medium-range wide-bodies). To produce the good, each firm must incur a start-up cost F (paid in the first period). Thereafter, the firms' production costs decline with experience according to the standard learning curve specification. Specifically, the direct marginal production costs of Boeing, c, and Airbus, c^*, in period t are

(2) $$c_t = h(K_t)^{-g}, \text{ and } c_t^* = h^*(K_t^*)^{-g},$$

where K_t and K_t^* are cumulative production to date, and g is the elasticity of cost with respect to cumulative output. K_t and K_t^* are related to x and x^* by

(3) $$K_t = K_{t-1} + x_t, \text{ and } K_t^* = K_{t-1}^* + x_t^*.$$

To define the objective function of the aircraft manufacturers, we must address the choice of strategic variables. The standard choices are price and quantity. To some extent Boeing and Airbus are selling differentiated products. This would in principle allow them to compete in a Bertrand fashion, by setting a list price and selling to whoever wants to buy at those prices. But the circumstances of the market mitigate against this. Aircraft purchases are negotiated on an individual basis. These deals include financing, options for future orders, spare parts arrangements, and so forth. In the jargon of the industry, these "green stamps" alter the effective price in such a way that price-setting competition is not really feasible. More practically, to model Bertrand competition between two close, but not perfect, substitutes would require an aggregate cross-price elasticity. To our knowledge such a figure does not exist in the industry literature.

It is a long leap from arguing that price-setting competition is the wrong model to arguing that quantity setting is the right one. In actuality the strategic choice set of Boeing and Airbus probably contains price, quantity, and a wide variety of green stamps. Nonetheless, the Cournot assumption provides a sensible yet simple way to model imperfect competition. Given that we are treating the A300 and the 767 as one homogeneous product, Cournot is a better model than Bertrand.

The objective of firms is to maximize their present value; these are defined as

$$(4) \qquad V = -F + \sum_{t=0}^{T} (P_t - c_t)x_t R^t, \text{ and}$$

$$V^* = -F + \sum_{t=0}^{T} (P_t - c_t^*)x_t^* R^t,$$

where R and R^* are the discount factors of the two firms. We assume that the product cycle has a known length T. After T periods a new technology arrives exogenously and makes this generation of aircraft obsolete.

3.3.2 Profit-Maximizing Behavior

This model is a standard Spence-type (1981) learning curve setup. The major decision that needs to be taken is how sophisticated to make the strategies of the players. In principle, each player should take into account the effect of its current decisions on the future output of the other; that is, current output, because it adds to a firm's stock of experience K, may have a valuable strategic effect in lowering future costs. However, we have chosen (which is perhaps a more realistic option as well) to assume that each firm takes the other's whole output time path as given. This means that the firms do not attempt to act strategically in a dynamic sense, but rather act as monopolists on the residual demand.

In each period the U.S. firm faces a first-order condition of the form

$$(5) \qquad 0 = P_t + x_t(dP_t/dx_t) - c_t - \sum_{i=1}^{T-t} x_{t+i} (dc_{t+i}/dK_{t+i})R^i,$$

where the rightmost term represents the shadow value on experience, that is, the reduction in the present value of future costs that an additional unit of current output brings. Let z_t be this shadow value at time t; then it is straightforward to show that z_t obeys the difference equation

$$(6) \qquad z_t = z_{t-1}/R - x_t (dc_t/dK_t).$$

This equation is tied down at one end by the condition that learning has no value in the last period:

$$(7) \qquad z_t = 0.$$

An exactly parallel set of relationships of course applies to the foreign firm.

We turn next to the determination of output at a point in time. Equation (5) may be rewritten as

$$P_t + x_t(dP_t/dx_t) = c_t + z_t .$$

In a Cournot duopoly with constant elasticity demand, once we have marginal costs, $c_t + z_t$, we can solve for both market shares and the price. In each period t, it can be shown that the market share of the European firm is

$$(8) \qquad s = \frac{1 - m(1 - 1/E)}{(1/E)\,(1+m)},$$

where m is the ratio of $(c_t + z_t)$ to $(c_t^* + z_t^*)$. The market price, in turn, can be determined from the relationship

$$(9) \qquad P_t = \frac{c_t + z_t}{1 - ((1-s)/E)}.$$

From the demand curve (1) and the market share, we can then determine x_t and x_t^*.

Up to this point the durability of the good has had no formal role in the model. As noted above, the demand equation (1) is indistinguishable from a static demand function. A problem with the static formulation arises in trying to reproduce the historical situation. Since Boeing did not enter until 1982, Airbus had a monopoly from 1979 through 1981. With a static demand for aircraft, this quantum change in market structure would lead the model to predict a very large drop in the price between 1981 and 1982. However, since planes are capital goods, air carriers have some ability to shift their demand intertemporally. It is therefore unlikely that any airline would purchase at the high, pre-1982 price.

If an airline finds it more profitable to buy today rather than next year, it must be the case that

$$(10) \qquad \sum_{i=0}^{N-1} R^i\,[\,\Pi_{t+i}(q)] - qp_t > \sum_{i=0}^{N-1} R^i[\,\Pi_{t+i+1}(q)] - qp_{t+1}.$$

This implies that the price cannot fall too fast. Specifically,

$$(11) \qquad p_t - p_{t+1} \le (1/q)\Pi_t(q)(1-R^N).$$

This inequality restricts the rate at which the price falls. As it turns out, this constraint only binds during the Airbus monopoly period.

3.3.3   Solution of the Model

This model can be solved iteratively, using what amounts to the Fair-Taylor method. We used the following procedure.

1. An initial guess is made at the output path. These paths are used to solve for the corresponding sequence of K's and K^*'s.

2. The K's, K^*'s, x_t's, and x_t^*'s are used to construct the sequence of marginal costs for Boeing and Airbus.

3. Given these sequences of marginal costs we can construct the market shares s_t, and $1 - s_t$, the market price series p_t, and therefore the time path of x and x^*.

4. This new series of x_t's and x_t^*'s are fed back into the loop.

The whole process is repeated until it converges. The result is a path of outputs that satisfies the first-order condition for both firms.

3.4   Calibration and Results

We have carried out a simulation of the model described above, with parameters and assumptions designed to resemble the actual competition between Boeing and Airbus in medium-range jet aircraft. We begin by describing the calibration procedure, the base case. Next we examine what our model predicts would have happened if there had been no Airbus program.

3.4.1   Calibration

The first issue that arises in calibrating the model to the aircraft industry is conceptual rather than quantitative: how to represent European industry policy. As we pointed out earlier, the governments backing Airbus have provided loans that could in principle be fully repaid, so they are not a simple subsidy. On the other hand, the loans will be repaid only to the extent of Airbus's profits. Since it seems clear that Airbus is willing to undertake projects that would not appear likely to earn market rates of return, we model the subsidy as equity participation by governments that expect less than the "market" rate of return.

In an industry with a twenty-year product cycle and substantial learning, the discount rate employed by a firm plays a significant role in the choice of its output path. As part of our modeling of the subsidy, we model the Airbus program as one that effectively lowers the discount rate of the European firm to whatever it takes to make entry barely profitable (taking zero as a lower bound). This is conceptually equivalent to calculating the internal rate of return on the A300, and assuming that Airbus chose its output path using this discount rate. We set the Boeing discount rate arbitrarily at 5 percent.

Two parameters of the model are assigned on the basis of industry estimates. Following a survey in the *Economist* (June 1, 1985), we assume the learning curve has an elasticity of .2. That is, a 1 percent increase in cumulative production will decrease direct production costs by .2 percent. From a Commerce Department study (Schlie 1986) we take the initial setup costs as $1.5 billion for both firms.

The price elasticity for wide-bodied medium-range planes poses more problems. We found no direct estimate of this quantity in the existing literature. Moreover, due to the nature of the market, the exact price of planes is difficult to ascertain and rarely reported. It was therefore impossible to directly estimate the elasticity ourselves. What we have done is to use the fact that the demand for commercial aircraft is a derived demand, together with the predictions of the whole model, to get a rough approximation of the price elasticity.

Using aggregate data on U.S. air carriers we estimated the demand elasticity for commercial domestic passenger air service at 2.85. Assuming that aircraft account for a fifth of the marginal cost of providing air services, we can deduce that the derived demand elasticity for all aircraft is .57. However, medium-range wide-bodied planes are only one of several types of jets. Thus we should expect a cross-price effect in addition to the direct effect. That is, a one percent rise in the price of the A300 results in some substitution toward smaller or larger jets, as well as a rise in the marginal costs of providing air services. We arbitrarily guess at a range for this cross-price elasticity. If we assume it is equal to 1.0, then $E = 1.57$; if it equals 2.0, then $E = 2.57$.

There is an additional source of inferences on E. The total profitability of the two firms depends directly on E (due to the markup equation (9)). In simulations calibrated to an E much greater than 2.5, Boeing makes negative profits. Since by all accounts, the 767 is forecasted to be a profitable project, we focus on E's that are less than 2.57. Similarly, simulations calibrated to much less than 1.57 imply an internal rate of return on the A300 in excess of 3.5 percent—and thus might have been a commercially viable project. Since most studies forecast the A300 to have a low or negative rate of return, we limit ourselves to E's greater than 1.57. We take $E = 2$ as the central case.

It is necessary to recognize somewhere the extra cost incurred by Airbus as a result of its slow development. We approximate the cost by assuming that Airbus incurred its development cost in 1974 but was unable to deliver aircraft until 1979. Boeing, in contrast, is assumed to incur its development cost in the same year that 767 deliveries began, 1982. Both planes are assumed to be sold until 1998.

For allocation of consumer surplus to regions, it is necessary to allocate demand. Based on average numbers for the first half of the 1980s, we allocate 41.5 percent of consumer surplus to the United States, 25.9 percent to Europe, and 32.6 percent to the rest of the world.

This still leaves us with three free parameters—the European discount rate and the constant terms in the two learning curves. We carried out a search over parameter values, repeatedly solving the model, so as to choose the values for these parameters that meet the following conditions: nonpositive present value for Airbus; a 1984 price of $50 million corresponding to total sales of forty-eight planes (taken from

Schlie 1986 and the *Economist* survey); and a 1984 Airbus market share of 39.6 percent (also taken from the *Economist*).

To line up the model on these values (for the central case of $E = 2$) required that we set the intercept of the Airbus learning curve 17.2 percent higher that of Boeing. In other words, with equal-length production runs, Airbus's direct production costs would be 17.2 percent higher than Boeing's.

3.4.2   The Base Case

The upper part of table 3.4 shows the results of a solution of the model in the base case where the demand elasticity is taken as 2 and Airbus is given sufficient subsidy to enter the market. Notice that the price falls throughout the product life, but more rapidly before 1982 than after. If it were not for intertemporal substitution on the demand side, the price during the Airbus monopoly phase (1979–82) would be near $100 million, falling to the $50 million range after Boeing's entry. Clearly no airline would purchase a jet in 1981 when it knew that by waiting a year it could save $50 million. This consideration limits the price Airbus can charge in the first three years, as is described by equation (11).

Once both planes are in the market, the price falls very slowly. Despite the presence of substantial discounting by Boeing, the solution is quite close to the constant price path that emerges from learning curve models with no discounting. The slow fall in prices is reassuring since nowhere in the industry literature is there a discussion of a significant price trend. Indeed aircraft industry studies often assume a constant price in evaluating the commercial prospects of a projected aircraft.

The Airbus market share falls through time since it is learning at a lower rate than Boeing. The total deliveries rise slowly as the true marginal cost falls. The simulation predicts total sales of 398 planes for Airbus and 573 planes for Boeing. The figure for Airbus is a bit low compared with other projections, but the Boeing figure is quite near the 600–700 range predicted for the Boeing 767.

Table 3.4 also shows that for $E = 2$, Airbus is simulated to lose money even when it chooses an output path using a zero discount rate. Clearly, Airbus's entry depended on the existence of a subsidy. To calculate the size of the subsidy we need to know the opportunity cost of public funds. Taking this number as 5 percent, the present value of the A300 earnings is a negative 1.471 billion 1974 dollars—a large sum, although not on the scale of the $10–12 billion number sometimes suggested by Boeing.

Boeing's 767, not surprisingly, has a positive present value of $1.02 billion.

Table 3.4 Simulation Results for the Central Case (*E* = 2.0)

	1979	'80	'81	'82	'83	'84	'85	'86	'87	'88	'89	'90	'91	'92	'93	'94	'95	'96	'97	'98
BASE CASE																				
Prices ($ million)	61	58	55	52	51	50	49	49	48	48	48	48	48	47	47	47	47	47	47	47
Airbus share (%)	100	100	100	47	43	40	39	37	36	36	35	34	34	34	33	33	33	33	33	33

Consumer surplus (discounted to 1974)

	Europe	*U.S.*	*RoW*	*Subsidy Cost*
Social discount rate = 3%	5843	9363	7355	1294
= 5%	4487	7190	5648	1471
= 10%	2482	3976	3123	1672
Profits	−836	1020	—	—
Discount rate	0%	5%	—	—
Cumulative production	398	573	—	—

No AIRBUS CASE (Intertemporal demand substitution)

	1979	'80	'81	'82	'83	'84	'85	'86	'87	'88	'89	'90	'91	'92	'93	'94	'95	'96	'97	'98
Prices ($ million)	—	—	—	70	70	69	68	68	67	67	66	66	66	66	66	65	65	65	64	63
Airbus share (%)	0	0	0	0	0	0	0	0	0	0	0	0	0	0	0	0	0	0	0	0

Consumer surplus (discounted to 1974)

	Europe	*U.S.*	*RoW*	*Subsidy Cost*
Social discount rate = 3%	3962	6348	4987	—
Change from base case	(−1881)	(−3015)	(−2368)	—
= 5%	3053	4892	3843	—

	67	68	69	70	70	70	70	70	70	71	71	72	72	73	74	76	78	82	—	—	—
Change from base case = 10%										(−1805)				(−2298)			(−1434)				
Change from base case										2129				2710			1692				
Change from base case										(−944)				(−1266)			(−790)				
Profits															6297						
Change from base case															(5277)						
Discount rate										—				5%							
Cumulative production										—				542							

No Airbus Case (Static demand formulation)

	67	68	69	70	70	70	70	70	70	71	71	72	72	73	74	76	78	82	—	—	—
Prices ($ million)	0	0	0	0	0	0	0	0	0	0	0	0	0	0	0	0	0	0	—	—	—
Airbus share (%)	0	0	0	0	0	0	0	0	0	0	0	0	0	0	0	0	0	0			

Consumer surplus (discounted to 1974)

	Europe	U.S.	RoW	Subsidy Cost
Social discount rate = 3%	2688	4307	3383	—
Change from base case	(−3155)	(−5056)	(−3972)	—
= 5%	1996	3198	2513	—
Change from base case	(−2491)	(−3992)	(−3135)	—
= 10%	1006	1612	1267	
Change from base case	(−1476)	(−2364)	(−1856)	
Profits		4215		
Change from base case		(−3195)		
Discount rate		5%		
Cumulative production		409		

Note: RoW = rest of world.

3.4.3 A World without Airbus

The lower part of table 3.4 shows two scenarios for what would have happened, according to our model, if there had been no government support of Airbus. The scenario at the bottom of table 3.4 (static demand formulation) simulates a Boeing monopoly where Boeing enters in 1982 and there is no intertemporal substitution of demand. That is, the demand curve in 1982 is the same as in the base case despite the fact that there were no sales in the 1979–81 period. In addition to delaying the availability of medium-range wide-bodied jets, the absence of Airbus results in a higher market price. In the monopoly case, Boeing consistently sells the 767 for about 40 percent more than it would in the presence of Airbus competition.

A comparison of this scenario with the base case shows that the primary effect of the Airbus subsidy is redistributive. The subsidy benefits all consumers by several billions of 1974 dollars, hurts Boeing's profits by several billion dollars, and costs European taxpayers about a billion and a half dollars. The net welfare effects are much smaller. On net, the subsidy is calculated to improve European welfare by about a billion 1974 dollars (using the 5 percent social discount rate) and harms the United States by about a half billion dollars. The rest of the world, of course, gains due to lower prices.

3.4.4 Allowing for Intertemporal Substitution

The static demand scenario has some problems. Recall that our examination of static models suggested that in the duopoly case the United States could not gain if it remained a net exporter of aircraft. This suggests that the narrowness of the U.S. loss hinges crucially on the consumer gains during the first three years. As we have formulated the model, the availability of aircraft in 1979–81 provides large consumer benefits. This is not a plausible result. Could it really have been so important that wide-bodied jets be available in 1979 rather than 1982?

In the standard learning curve models, demand is taken to be represented by a relation between current price and current sales. Aircraft, however, are capital goods; there is therefore a possibility of intertemporal substitution, with the consumer delaying purchase to wait for a lower price or availability of a better product. To take account of this possibility we run another—more realistic—simulation, assuming that all of the airlines that would have purchased in the 1979–81 period shift their demand to 1982. This simulation in effect increases the constant term in the 1982 demand function by a factor of 3.

The middle part of table 3.4 presents the results of this simulation (intertemporal demand substitution). Note that, as before, the principal impact of the A300 is redistributive. The A300 improves the welfare of consumers in all regions, reduces the profits of Boeing, and costs European taxpayers approximately $1.5 billion. The difference in consumer surplus with and without Airbus is less drastic although still substantial. On net, Europe loses (except for the low 3 percent discount rate), the United States loses, and the rest of the world gains. Europe is now calculated to have a consumer surplus gain due to Airbus, which is less than the cost of the subsidy by $37 million (for the 5 percent discount rate). For a 3 percent discount rate Europe gains on net from the competitive effect of Airbus by about a half billion dollars. For a 10 percent discount rate, Europe's net loss is almost $.9 billion.

The simulation predicts that Airbus caused a net loss to the United States, but now the net loss is estimated at a much higher $3 billion. The difference lies partly in the fact that U.S. consumers do not gain as much by the existence of Airbus, and partly in the fact that the shifted demand increases the profitability of the Boeing monopoly.

The basic conclusion from table 3.4 is that the subsidized entry of Airbus cost Europe something like $1.5 billion. This expenditure provided large benefits to all consumers, but did substantial harm to Boeing's profits. Overall it seems that the A300 project constituted a beggar-thy-neighbor and beggar-thyself policy for Europe. Allowing for intertemporal substitution of demand, the United States suffered a loss in the sum of producer and consumer surplus for the social discount rates considered. The gain to Europe's consumers outweighs the cost of the subsidy only for a discount rate of 3 percent.

3.4.5   Sensitivity Analysis

So far we have tested the sensitivity of our results only to the social discount rate. We now turn to sensitivity analysis of the demand elasticity. The demand elasticity is crucial since it directly affects all three components of the welfare calculations. Consumer surplus obviously depends on it, as does the profitability of both Airbus and Boeing. This in turn affects our assessment of the size of the subsidy and Boeing's profit loss. Moreover, it is neither estimated independently nor deduced directly from calibration.

The case where $E = 1.57$ seems a reasonable lower bound on the price elasticity. The calculated internal rate of return on the A300 corresponding to this figure is 3.544 percent—a rather high figure. If the demand for wide-bodied medium-range jets were even more inelastic, our simulation would come to the unreasonable result that the A300 would have been undertaken even without government support. Likewise, $E = 2.5$ seems to be a reasonable upper bound, since for this figure the simulation predicts that Boeing barely breaks even on the 767, turning a profit of only $193 million.

Table 3.5   Sensitivity Analysis for Welfare Results

Price Elasticity	Demand Formulation	Social Discount Rate (%)	Region		
			Europe	U.S.	RoW
$E = 1.57$	Intertemporal substitution	3	+	−	+
		5	+	−	+
		10	+	−	+
$E = 2.0$	Intertemporal substitution	3	+	−	+
		5	−	−	+
		10	−	−	+
$E = 2.5$	Intertemporal substitution	3	−	−	+
		5	−	−	+
		10	−	−	+

Note: RoW = rest of world.

Table 3.5 presents the sensitivity analysis on E. The table indicates the net welfare effect of the presence of Airbus for each of three clasticities. A positive sign indicates a net gain; a negative sign a net loss. As is evident, the subsidization of the A300 left the United States worse off for all values of E. Specifically, the loss in Boeing's profits due to the A300 always exceeds the gain to U.S. consumers. Similarly, the welfare impact of the A300 on the rest of the world is unambiguous. This is of course expected since the rest of the world neither earns profits nor pays the subsidy, leaving only the consumer surplus gain.

The question of whether the A300 was a good idea for Europe turns out to be rather sensitive to the price elasticity. For relatively inelastic demand the cost of the subsidy is low and the gains to European consumers are high. For the case of $E = 1.57$ we estimate the subsidy cost as a very low $301 million (using a social discount rate of 5 percent), while the European consumer gain is close to $2 billion. By contrast, for $E = 2.5$ the subsidy is in the $2 billion range while Europe's consumer gain is near $1 billion.

3.5 Conclusion

In this chapter we have examined international competition in wide-bodied aircraft. Given the degree of simplification necessary to produce a tractable model, it is difficult to base policy conclusions on our results. What does emerge from the study is the importance of consumers' welfare in determining the desirability of strategic trade policy. This industry is marked by a large fixed-cost cum learning curve, which would appear to be a ready-made setup for strategic trade policy aimed at capturing pure rents. We find, however, that for Europe as a whole the welfare consequences of Airbus's subsidized entry are dominated not by competition over profits, but by gains in consumer surplus resulting from earlier product introduction and increased competition. While there are many reasons to be skeptical of the precise results, this chapter suggests an important lesson for theoretical I.O. trade models: models that, in the spirit of Brander and Spencer (1981), neglect consumer effects of strategic trade policy, while useful for expositional purposes, are likely to be misleading when applied to real situations in which a sizable fraction of production goes to satisfy domestic demand.

Second, this chapter has brought out just how far from constant returns and perfect competition the industry is. While the aerospace industry appears highly concentrated even in aggregate statistics and is known to be subject to strong increasing returns, it is only when one examines competition at the level of specific products that the decisive role of dynamic economies of scale becomes apparent. The world market in no case supports more than two firms producing aircraft that are close substitutes in demand, and perhaps could only support one without government intervention. Thus Boeing 747s have no close competitors; the A300 coexists with the 767 only because of government support; and when McDonnell-Douglas and Lockheed developed similar craft, the DC-10 and the L-1011, both lost money.

Finally, we should note as a caution that the analysis here focuses on the already existing competition in wide-bodied aircraft. This is not the whole story of the prospective competition. Airbus is about to start delivering the narrow-bodied 150-seat A320. The A320 is intended to meet a new niche (created by the deregulation of the U.S. air carrier industry) for smaller jets to serve as feeders in the hub-and-spoke routing system. Surrounding the A320 is a new set of strategic issues; both Boeing and McDonnell-Douglas have decided not to challenge the A320 directly, but instead to try to leapfrog it by entering a few years later with an improved technology. It is the A320, not the A300, that is the focus of current trade tension.

References

Brander, J., and B. Spencer. 1981. Tariffs and extraction of foreign monopoly rents under potential entry. *Canadian Journal of Economics,* 371–89.

Schlie, T. 1986. A competitive assessment of the U.S. civil aircraft industry. Written for the U.S. Department of Commerce. Boulder, Colo.: Westview Press.

Spence, M. 1981. The learning curve and competition. *Bell Journal of Economics* 12: 49–70.

A survey of the world's aircraft industry. 1985. *The Economist* (June).

Comment   Richard Harris

This chapter is a nice mix of theory and empirical work, and represents the type of analysis we could use a great deal more of in international trade. The chapter draws on some of the authors' earlier work applying the Spence oligopoly learning model to semiconductors. In this instance the application is to commercial wide-bodied aircraft, and in particular to the competition between Boeing and Airbus. It would be difficult to pick an industry for which this model is more appropriate; the industry is close to a pure duopoly, and the overwhelming significance of learning economies that are internal to the firm is well documented.

The first part of the chapter lays out some simple issues of subsidy in static monopoly and oligopoly models. In the duopoly case the authors conclude that there is a welfare loss for the exporting country if entry into a duopoly is subsidized by the importing country. I have no quarrel with this conclusion in the particular model used, but would caution the reader that it is far from general. There are two potential problems, both having to do with the effect of entry deterrence. In the model, the incumbent exporting monopolist has a clear incentive to deter entry. In the commercial aircraft industry the most likely vehicle for deterrence is up-front investment in research and development. R&D costs are a substantial portion of the total costs of any particular aircraft model. It is now well known that the existence of this incentive to invest for deterrence reasons can lead to overinvestment in R&D. In this case the existence of a subsidized potential entrant who can effectively enter with subsidy may reduce this overinvestment, which would be welfare-improving for the country in which the over-investment initially occurred. On the other hand, if the initial situation were one in which entry-deterring investment was not occurring, then the introduction of a subsidized entrant might lead to inefficient R&D races. The net impact in this situation would depend crucially on how consumers gain relative to the inefficiency costs associated with R&D.

On a related topic, the two simple models and the basic dynamic model used later in the core of the chapter all assume that the costs and benefits of R&D are entirely internal to the firm. I believe this is a questionable empirical assumption; the existence of spillovers between firms in the R&D process can reverse many of the conventional conclusions. From the world's point of view, and quite possibly from both countries' point of view, the larger problem could be not enough investment in R&D. It is difficult to balance this traditional concern with issues of entry deterrence, but it is clearly important.

Richard Harris is professor of economics at Queen's University, Kingston, Canada.

The main part of the chapter is concerned with a dynamic duopoly model with scale economies derived from a learning curve. It is worth noting two features of this model. First, the solution concept is one of "open loop" equilibrium; each firm takes the other firm's entire future output sequence as given. The importance of this assumption is that it implies that an increase in output today by firm A will *not* increase market share of A in the future, even though learning induces lower marginal costs to A in the future. An alternative would be a "closed loop" equilibrium concept that would focus on cumulative outputs of the two firms as the natural state variables, and in addition would yield a subgame perfect equilibrium. I would guess that the equilibrium in this alternative model would yield lower prices, larger outputs, and greater consumer surplus because of the additional incentives for each firm to preempt *future* market share via current output decisions. The second feature of the model is that the marginal cost, which marginal revenue is anchored to, is a variant of "long-run" marginal cost, that is, marginal cost after learning has ceased. In a model without discounting, this is exactly true, but it is "approximately" true even in this model. Thus because long-run marginal costs remain remarkably constant, so do prices. This is evident in table 3.4, where price sequences are given both before and after entry. Alternative equilibrium concepts might indeed change this result, and the higher the discount rate the more significant the difference might be.

The empirical section of the chapter calibrates the model to a single year's data. The authors choose as a free parameter the discount rate of Airbus. This parameter is chosen so as to equate the present value of the Airbus net revenue stream to zero. They then argue that because this rate is much lower than the discount rate used by Boeing, Airbus is "subsidized." It seems to me this is an inappropriate procedure for two reasons. First, the welfare results of the model are crucially dependent on this calibration procedure. We have no idea what the extent of any actual subsidy is, nor what is the sensitivity of the results to possible errors in estimating the extent of the subsidy. In the computable general equilibrium (CGE) literature a great deal of effort is put into getting estimates of all relevant policy variables. The calibration procedure of the CGE exercises is used only to scale constants and share parameters on utility and production functions. While subject to measurement problems, the CGE procedure does not bury key assumptions regarding policy variables, which are themselves usually the focus of the analysis. In this model I think it is particularly unfortunate that the discount rate for Airbus was used as the free parameter. With learning effects there is at least the potential that the discount rate could be the key structural parameter in determining the characteristics of equilibrium. On theoretical grounds, the existence of capital cost subsidies does not provide a rationale for discounting cash flows at something different than the market rate if profit maximization is the appropriate objective of the firm. In short, I think it would be much better if the authors used equal discount rates for both firms and introduced the subsidy quite explicitly. Clearly the form of the subsidy would affect the results.

My last comment relates to the assumption in the chapter that Boeing is not subsidized. Non-U.S. observers would think this assumption a bit peculiar, particularly in the case of commercial aircraft. It is commonly argued that the close association of Boeing with the U.S. defense establishment allows security of market size, together with long-term cross subsidization of R&D costs; both are obvious effective subsidies to commercial aircraft development. While no one knows the true extent of such subsidies, nor how they should be treated in international trade policy, as economists we should at least acknowledge that these features of the U.S. market could be a potentially important determinant of international market structure in this and related industries.

Comment   Catherine L. Mann

Richard Baldwin and Paul Krugman's chapter on evaluating the magnitude of the Airbus subsidy arrived on my desk almost concurrently with a news clipping about the tough stance U.S. trade negotiators were taking with the Europeans on the Airbus subsidy issue. Coming on the heels of the "luxury edibles" trade problem, I was certain that I would have to write a memo on the Airbus topic, detailing this most recent trade skirmish between the United States and the European Community (EC). But, as events turned out, with both Boeing and McDonnell-Douglas backing off from their earlier pressure on the U.S. trade negotiators, I didn't need to write the memo. Nevertheless, I found Baldwin and Krugman's essay quite topical and a refreshing departure from the majority of trade theory papers which only infrequently address a real-world issue.

Baldwin and Krugman use Airbus Industrie as an example of a high-technology industry with dramatic dynamic economies of scale. High fixed costs of introducing a new generation of aircraft combine with a significant learning curve in production to lead to steeply downward sloped average cost curves for each family of aircraft. Such an industry structure can support only a few firms. Airbus Industrie, founded in

Catherine L. Mann is an economist in the Office of the Vice-President, Development Economics, and Chief Economist, the World Bank.

1970, is a consortium jointly owned by the governments of France, Germany, Spain, and the United Kingdom. It joins Boeing and Mc-Donnell-Douglas as the major participants on the producer's side of the market for civilian aircraft. Lockheed departed the field in the late 1970s.

Baldwin and Krugman consider one mode of competition in demand for civilian aircraft, that between the Airbus A-300 and the Boeing 767. They argue that these models of aircraft are sufficiently different from other aircraft that they can model this competition as Cournot. Before Boeing introduced the 767, the A-300 had a monopoly over this market segment for wide-bodied jets. After introducing the 767, Boeing shared the market with the A-300 in a Cournot duopoly.

Measuring the welfare consequences of the competition between Boeing and the A-300 involves, in part, weighing the gain to consumer surplus of moving from a monopoly to a duopoly against the loss to producer surplus (in this case, Boeing profits) from causing each producer to move back and up the production and learning curve for this generation of aircraft. Baldwin and Krugman estimate that the gain in consumer surplus outweighs the loss in producer surplus, both overall and for all consuming groups (the EC, the United States, and the rest of the world). That Europe gains overall is striking because the gains are spread over all consumers while Europe alone incurs the subsidy necessary for Airbus to enter the airframe industry.

How to measure this implied subsidy? Baldwin and Krugman choose to estimate the internal rate of return on the A-300. The subsidy is the difference between some measure of normal internal rate of return (set at 5 percent for the other participant, Boeing) and the internal rate of return that makes the present discounted value of Airbus's net earnings on the A-300 just equal to zero. They estimate an internal rate of return of 0.75 percent.

As an exercise in analyzing an industry characterized by dynamic scale economies, and one that exhibits imperfect competition and government intervention, the aircraft industry is a terrific one to examine. However, since a main point of the chapter is to estimate the magnitude of a particular subsidy, and the magnitude of the welfare consequences of such a departure from free trade, it is important to characterize the industry with as much specificity as possible, remaining within the bounds of the parsimony required of international quantitative analysis.

While Baldwin and Krugman have done a relatively good job at introducing the important aspects of the production side of the aircraft industry, I think they need to do a better job on the demand side before we can pay too much attention to the estimates of the magnitude and welfare consequences of Airbus's entry into the airframe industry. I have some suggestions for a richer theoretical formulation of the demand side that cast doubt on the monopoly-duopoly structure of the model. This model suggests that the lifetime of a generation of aircraft may be more related to characteristics of demand than to technological breakthroughs or to the useful life of the aircraft. Moreover, estimating the gains from subsidizing Airbus as the reduction in prices associated with increased competition fails to consider the technological externalities accruing to Europe as farmland gives way to high-technology factories. On the production side, the learning curve occurs not only for a single generation, but for all generations. Finally, from a policy standpoint, it matters whether Airbus will eventually be profitable from this one-time infusion of capital or whether a per unit subsidy will be necessary on all future production.

Operationally, most of my comments can be handled through some sensitivity analysis on the three key parameters. In particular, I suggest that the elasticity of demand for a particular type of airframe is higher, that the Boeing internal rate of return is probably lower, and that the lifetime of a generation may be shorter than the parameter values chosen by Baldwin and Krugman.

Demanders of airframes have a current and projected set of "missions" to which must be applied the existing fleet, new purchases, and purchases from or sales to the secondary market. It would seem that airframes, new and old, contain a vector of attributes designed to match the missions. Age, and the associated trade-off between airframe ownership cost and airframe operating cost, is an obvious attribute. "Brand loyalty" remains an attribute from a maintenance standpoint, although in the new purchases market it apparently has been less important in recent years. Missions can change over the forecast period, either because the specific demander's operational characteristics change (a merger and change of route structure) or because of a more general shift in passenger travel preferences (shuttle flights between cities, or the opening up of certain parts of the country because of economic development there). Because aircraft can be sold to the secondary market (or put back to the manufacturer via "walk-away" leases), the economic life of the airframe to a specific demander may be significantly different from its useful life. Moreover, sufficient change in the industry's route structure (say, because of the move from the direct flight concept to the hub-and-spoke concept) could lead to manufacturers experiencing a significantly different length for the product life-cycle than they had estimated. Finally, developers of airframes and demanders of airframes work together to design new aircraft. Thus, new purchases can be put off until the desired product is ready.

All these factors taken together suggest that it is not appropriate to model the A-300 and 767 as a monopoly-duopoly. First, these wide-bodied aircraft are direct competitors, but indirect competition created by a significant fringe of other aircraft types and by the secondary market restrains prices in the direct competition. Second, in Baldwin and Krugman's comparison simulation (used to measure the changes in welfare associated with the entry of Airbus), Boeing retains a monopoly because Airbus does not enter. We do not know if perhaps McDonnell-Douglas would have entered the market for wide-bodied airframe if Airbus had not. Therefore, I suggest that the parameter for the elasticity of demand is higher (more elastic) than that suggested in the chapter. At minimum, this parameter should receive a fair amount of sensitivity testing. In fact, Baldwin and Krugman note that aircraft are capital goods and that because this aspect is not included in the model, their simulation results unfortunately show that the price of the A-300 is "too high" in the part of the life cycle where it has the monopoly in the base case simulation.

Baldwin and Krugman estimate the magnitude of the subsidy in part by comparing the internal rate of return for Airbus with that of Boeing. Aircraft are not produced in single generations by a new start-up each time. Airbus Industrie may eventually reach a more reasonable rate of return after it has been in business for the forty-odd years of Boeing. Moreover, while it appears clear that the consortium's governments have subsidized Airbus, the relationship between the defense establishment in the United States and the airframe manufacturers here suggests implied subsidies to their operations as well. Whether those subsidies are contained in Baldwin and Krugman's estimate of a 5 percent internal rate of return for Boeing is unclear. (In fact, Europe's threat to examine just this question might have led to Boeing's quieting its demands for a deeper investigation of the Airbus subsidy.) One could argue that even if the subsidy to Airbus were not outweighed by the consumer gains as measured here, there are clear technological (and defense) externalities gained by the birth of Airbus Industrie.

Policy considerations suggest examining in greater detail the characteristics of the subsidy. A subsidy to entry followed by competitive operations has different policy implications than one where the entrant is never competitive. The Baldwin and Krugman estimate suggests that production costs for the A-300 ran about 20 percent higher than those for the 767. Is this a long-run equilibrium difference in production costs caused by having factories spread all over Europe? Will Airbus have to subsidize each airframe design because Airbus chooses to compete against both Boeing and McDonnell-Douglas at different points in the product spectrum, a competition that we are starting to observe in the next generation airframe in the various families? Or does this subsidy represent the one-time cost of gaining credibility for a new airframe producer? I'm not sure that the model currently formulated can handle a question of this type, but as Baldwin and Krugman note, the action in the political arena is no longer about the A-300 but is about the subsequent models in the family.

4 Strategic Models, Market Structure, and State Trading: An Application to Agriculture

Marie Thursby

The purpose of this chapter is to examine the strategic use of trade policy when homogeneous products are competitively produced but their marketing is imperfectly competitive. This type of imperfect competition occurs in agricultural markets when state trading agencies or marketing boards are the sole marketing agents for products. It has also been hypothesized to occur in private trade of some agricultural products, but the extent of the market power of private traders is a highly controversial issue. Since the large USSR purchases of grain in the mid-1970s, the competitiveness of the U.S. grain exporting industry has been highly disputed. Some have argued that high concentration ratios for the largest exporting firms indicate market power (Gilmore 1982), while others argue that arbitrage opportunities and frequent entry and exit of firms indicate a relatively competitive market (Caves 1978; Caves and Pugel 1982; Thompson and Dahl 1979).

This chapter focuses on how the presence of state trading and the competitiveness of private trade affect optimal government policy. By examining a model in which a marketing board and private exporters are Cournot rivals in the world market for a competitively produced good, I show that optimal policy is sensitive to both the manner in which marketing boards operate and the degree of competition in private export trade. The empirical analysis focuses on the importance of state trading in the world wheat market. Since the United States is

Marie Thursby is professor of economics at Purdue University and a research associate of the National Bureau of Economic Research. This chapter was written while the author was visiting the Economics Department at the University of Michigan under the funding of National Science Foundation grants IST-8510068 and RII-8600404.

the major private trader of wheat, I examine the competitiveness of the U.S. grain export sector.

There is a wealth of literature examining the implications of imperfect competition in agricultural markets, but most of it focuses on countries as units with market power and abstracts from issues relating to whether marketing is done by state agencies or trading companies.[1] The only study that examines the impact of marketing institutions on optimal government policy is by Just, Schmitz, and Zilberman (1979). They analyze a model in which a single marketing agent price discriminates between domestic and foreign markets and the government determines policy to maximize the sum of domestic consumer and producer surplus. They show that as long as the government does not regulate the domestic pricing of the agent and can subsidize domestic consumption and production, free trade is the optimal trade policy. This result is the same whether the marketing agent is a board that maximizes producer surplus or a monopoly-monopsonist that maximizes profits. If, however, the government forces a competitive price in the domestic market, it should tax exports of a marketing board and subsidize exports if the agent is a monopoly-monopsonist. The major shortcoming of the analysis is that it ignores the strategic interaction of firms and governments when more than one country exports a product.

The "new" literature on the strategic use of trade policy under imperfect competition has, however, largely ignored the types of imperfect competition that can occur in agricultural markets. Dixit (1984) and Eaton and Grossman (1986) note imperfect competition in distribution as a reason for imperfectly competitive trade, but recent models examining government policy have focused on markets with oligopolistic producers. This is not surprising since the insights of these models are concerned with the potential for a government to shift rents toward its domestic market in industries with positive profits. Agriculture is hardly a high-profit sector!

However, if governments frequently intervene in agricultural markets, and if one way they intervene is by creating state trading agencies, it is worth examining how these institutions affect the strategic use of policy. Marketing boards are common on both the export and import side of agricultural markets; for example, several major exporters of dairy products and grain sell through marketing boards, and major importers of grains, tobacco, and silk purchase through such boards (Hoos 1979; Kostecki 1982). For OECD trade in thirty-four agricultural products for 1976, Kostecki (1982, 26, 286–88) estimates that 28 percent of exports and 27 percent of imports are accounted for by state trading.

It is also clear from the emphasis on agriculture in the current GATT negotiations that government use of trade policy in these markets is not trivial. Table 4.1 presents post–Tokyo Round trade-weighted nom-

Table 4.1   **Nominal Tariff Protection, Post–Tokyo Round (1976) by Sector**

Industry	ISIC	EEC		Japan		U.S.	
		% Level	Rank	% Level	Rank	% Level	Rank
Agriculture, forestry, & fish	1	4.86	12	18.4	2	1.80	17
Food beverages, & tobacco	310	10.1	3	25.4	1	4.70	7
Textiles	321	7.17	8	3.30	12	9.20	2
Wearing apparel	322	13.4	1	13.8	4	22.7	1
Leather products	323	2.01	21	3.00	13	4.20	9
Footwear	324	11.6	2	15.7	3	8.80	3
Wood products	331	2.51	18	0.30	21	1.70	18
Furniture & fixtures	332	5.60	9	5.10	7	4.10	11
Paper & paper products	341	5.37	11	2.10	16	0.20	22
Print & publishing	342	2.06	20	0.10	22	0.70	21
Chemicals	35A	7.95	5	4.80	8	2.40	16
Petrol & related products	35B	1.16	22	2.20	15	1.40	19
Rubber products	355	3.54	17	1.10	18	2.50	14
Nonmetal mining products	36A	3.66	16	0.50	20	5.30	5
Glass & glass products	362	7.70	7	5.10	6	6.20	4
Iron & steel	371	4.67	14	2.80	14	3.60	12
Nonferrous metals	372	2.13	19	1.10	19	0.70	20
Metal products	381	5.46	10	5.20	5	4.80	6
Nonelectric products	382	4.37	15	4.40	10	3.30	13
Electric machinery	383	7.89	6	4.30	11	4.40	8
Transportation equipment	384	7.95	4	1.50	17	2.50	15
Miscellaneous manufacturing	38A	4.67	13	4.60	9	4.20	10
AVERAGE		6.09		8.28		3.59	

Source: Deardorff and Stern 1986, tables 5.7–5.9.
Note: The percentage levels are weighted by own-country imports.

inal tariff protection for twenty-two traded good sectors for the EEC, Japan, and the United States. Note that for the EEC and Japan, the agriculture, and food, beverage, and tobacco sectors are among the four top-ranked sectors. A ranking of export subsidies by sector would be difficult (particularly given the prevalence of indirect subsidies in both manufacturing and agriculture); however, the GATT code regarding export subsidies is more lenient for primary products (other than minerals) than for nonprimary products,[2] so direct export subsidies are more prevalent in agriculture.

The models I examine are based on rivalry of marketing agents and governments of two countries exporting a homogeneous good, presumably agricultural, to a third country. In part, the motivation for the models is the widespread use of export subsidies in agriculture (World Bank 1986; Hillman 1978) and the recent result of Brander and Spencer (1985) that in the presence of imperfect competition, export subsidies may be welfare improving for the country imposing them. It is well understood that producers (in our case, farmers) stand to gain if their governments increase their share of world markets, ceteris paribus. The question of interest in light of the Brander-Spencer analysis is whether export subsidies can be welfare improving given the type of imperfect competition that occurs in agricultural markets.

The models in this chapter are similar to the Brander-Spencer export rivalry model (1985) in that marketing agents play a Nash quantity game given government policies, but the governments can precommit to these policies so as to give their agents a strategic advantage in world markets. There are, however, several important differences between their model and mine: (1) production and marketing in our model are carried out by different agents, and in one of our countries, the marketing agent maximizes joint producer returns rather than profits; (2) there is domestic consumption in each exporting country, and governments can subsidize or tax domestic production and consumption as well as exports; and (3) governments have the option of regulating prices charged to domestic consumers. The first and third of these are important because they are common characteristics of marketing boards and their regulation (Hoos 1979), and the second is particularly important for any model of agricultural trade. For many products domestic consumption is a large portion of total sales, and government intervention in domestic agricultural markets is quite common (Brown 1986; Gardner 1986; Johnson 1973).

These features of the models I consider are critical to the chapter's contribution. A major theoretical contribution of this analysis is to show that even when a good is sold by two marketing agents, an export tax or free trade may be the optimal government policy when the marketing agent maximizes producer returns and is regulated in its domestic price policy. This differs from the Brander-Spencer result that a subsidy is optimal when two profit-maximizing firms sell a homogeneous good in a third market. My results differ from the existing ones in the agricultural economics literature in that I show circumstances in which a marketing board's government would optimally subsidize exports. The latter results hinge on introducing rivalry into the analysis.

The second contribution of the chapter concerns the optimal policy of the government in the country that privately markets the good. A quasi-competitive model of private marketing is constructed to show that when a marketing board and private trading industry with more than a few firms are rivals, it is unlikely that the government of the private trading country should subsidize exports.

Finally, I present evidence on the structure of world trade in wheat to indicate the relevance of the models presented.

4.1 Unregulated Marketing Board and Monopoly-Monopsony

Consider a world in which a homogeneous good is exported by two countries to a third country that does not produce it. Each of the exporting countries consumes the good, but because of restrictions outside the model, they do not import it. One such restriction could be transport cost, which, for simplicity is assumed to be zero here. The good is competitively produced, and producers sell to a distributor or marketing agent rather than directly to consumers. In practice this might occur because of technological features of transportation and marketing services, but, again, I abstract from these here. The competitive producer supply curve is upward sloping.

In each country there is a single marketing agent. In the home country it is a private monopolist and in the foreign exporting country it is a statutory marketing board. In both cases the agent handles all domestic as well as foreign sales to consumers. The essential difference between them is their objective functions. The home monopolist is assumed to maximize profits, while the foreign marketing board maximizes the joint returns of its competitive producers (farmers).[3] Given its objective, the marketing board does not exercise monopsony power, but in the absence of regulation, the monopolist does, since its marginal cost (outlay) for the good is higher than the competitive supply (producer) price.

Throughout this chapter the assumptions about marketing agents comply with stylized facts from the world wheat market, which is the focus of the empirical analysis in section 4.4. Empirical models of wheat trade often treat Canada and the United States as duopolists since, together, they export roughly 60 percent of world wheat exports. All Canadian sales of wheat are through the Canadian Wheat Board, while the United States exports are through private firms. In this section, I assume the private export industry is a domestic monopoly, but in section 4.3 I consider a quasi-competitive export industry since the competitiveness of the United States grain export industry is disputed.

With only two marketing agents, there is no loss of generality in restricting the analysis to a marketing board–private firm rivalry. The policies that would be optimal for the government with a marketing board in this game would carry over (qualitatively) to a game with two marketing boards. The same is true for the government with a monopoly exporter.

As in Brander and Spencer (1985), the marketing agents are assumed to play a Nash quantity game in which they take as given the subsidies and/or taxes levied by their respective governments and the export sales of their rival. The exporting country governments can precommit to their policies so that they play a Stackelberg game against the marketing agents and a Nash game against the rival government. Unlike Brander-Spencer, the governments have three policy instruments at their disposal: a consumption subsidy (tax), a production subsidy (tax), and an export subsidy (tax). All subsidies or taxes are specific. This allows us to compare optimal policies in this government game with those of Just, Schmitz, and Zilberman (1979). Throughout the chapter the analysis is partial equilibrium.

4.1.1   Marketing Agent Equilibrium

Let lowercase variables refer to home country variables and uppercase to corresponding variables in the foreign exporting country. The home country monopolist maximizes profits given by

$$(1) \qquad \pi = [d(y) + r]\, y + [D_m(x + X) + s]\, x \\ - [p(y + x) - v\,](y + x),$$

where y denotes domestic sales, x export sales, $d(\cdot)$ domestic inverse demand, $p(\cdot)$ the competitive home inverse supply (producer price), $D_m(\cdot)$ inverse demand for imports by the third country, and r, s, and v the home government consumption subsidy (tax), export subsidy (tax), and production subsidy (tax), respectively. A positive (negative) value for a policy denotes a subsidy (tax). The marketing board maximizes the joint returns of competitive producers in its country, given by

$$(2) \qquad \Pi = [D(Y) + R]\, Y + [D_m(x + X) + S]X \\ - \int_0^{Y+X} [P(q) - V]\, dq.$$

For simplicity let inverse demand and supply curves be linear and given by $d(y) = a - by$, $D(Y) = A - BY$, $p(\cdot) = f + k(y + x)$, $P(\cdot) = F + K(Y + X)$, and $D_m = a_m - b_m(x + X)$, where a, b, A, B, f, k, F, K, a_m, and b_m are positive. The linearity assumption is consistent with the bulk of empirically estimated agricultural demand and supply equations. Other functional forms would not alter the major points of the chapter, although magnitudes of effects and assumptions required for uniqueness and stability of equilibria would differ.

First-order conditions for the monopolist dictate that marginal revenue in each market equal marginal cost and are given by

$$(3) \quad \partial\pi/\partial y = a + r - 2by - f + v - 2k(x + y) = 0, \text{ and}$$

$$(4) \quad \partial\pi/\partial x = a_m + r - 2b_m x - b_m X - f + v - 2k(x + y) = 0.$$

Second-order conditions are given by $-2(b + k) < 0$, $-2(b_m + k) < 0$, and $4(b + k)(b_m + k) - 4k^2 > 0$. First-order conditions for the marketing board are given by

(5) $\partial\Pi/\partial Y = A + R - 2BY - F + V - K(X + Y) = 0$, and

(6) $\partial\Pi/\partial X = a_m + S - 2b_m X - b_m x - F + V - K(X + Y) = 0$,

with second-order conditions $-(2B + K) < 0$, $-(2b_m + K) < 0$, and $(2B + K)(2b_m + K) - K^2 > 0$. As expected, the essential difference between the monopolist and marketing board's first-order conditions is that the monopolist's marginal cost reflects its monopsony power while the board's marginal cost is the competitive supply price.

For given values of r, v, s, R, V, and S, equations (3)–(6) determine equilibrium consumption and exports of the two exporting countries. A convenient way to describe the equilibrium is in terms of the two reaction functions, $\phi(X)$ and $\Phi(x)$, which are derived by solving equations (3) and (5) for y and Y, substituting into equations (4) and (6), and solving for $x = \phi(X)$ and $X = \Phi(x)$. The reaction functions are

(7) $\phi(X)$
$$= \frac{b(a_m - f + s + v) + k(a_m - a + s - r) - b_m(b + k)X}{2[b_m(b + k) + bk]}, \text{ and}$$

(8) $\Phi(x)$
$$= \frac{2B(a_m - F + S + V) + K(a_m - A + S - R) - b_m(2B + K)x}{2[b_m(2B + K) + BK]},$$

where $\phi'(\Phi(x))\Phi' < 1$ is assumed to ensure uniqueness and stability of the equilibrium. Equilibrium values of exports are (x^*, X^*) such that $\phi(X^*) = x^*$ and $\Phi(x^*) = X^*$, and y^* and Y^* are given by equations (3) and (5) evaluated at x^* and X^*.

4.1.2   Government Policy Choices

Following Just, Schmitz, and Zilberman (1979), I measure each country's welfare by the sum of domestic consumer and producer surplus and net government revenue. Home country welfare is given by

(9) $$w = \int_0^y [a - bq + r]dq - \int_0^{y+x} [f + kq - v]dq$$
$$+ [a_m - b_m(x + X) + s]x - ry - v(x + y) - sx.$$

Recalling that each government plays Stackelberg against marketing agents and Nash against the rival government, the home government is assumed to choose r, v, and s in order to maximize equation (9), given the behavior of agents and fixed foreign policies. First-order conditions for the home government are $\partial w/\partial\tau = 0$ for $\tau = r$, v, and s where

(10) $\partial w/\partial \tau = [a - by^*](\partial y^*/\partial \tau)$
$$- [f + k(y^* + x^*)][(\partial y^*/\partial \tau) + (\partial x^*/\partial \tau)]$$
$$+ [a_m - 2b_m x^* - b_m X^*](\partial x^*/\partial \tau) - b_m x^* \partial X^*/\partial \tau.$$

Using the monopolist's first-order conditions, $\partial w/\partial \tau$ can be written as

(11) $\partial w/\partial \tau = [k(y^* + x^*) - v][(\partial y^*/\partial \tau) + (\partial x^*/\partial \tau)]$
$$+ [by^* - r][\partial y^*/\partial \tau] - [s(\partial x^*/\partial \tau) + b_m x^*(\partial X^*/\partial \tau)].$$

Welfare is maximized for the following choices of r, v, and s,

(12) $r = by^* > 0,$

(13) $v = k(y^* + x^*) > 0,$ and

(14) $s = -b_m x^*(\partial X^*/\partial \tau)/(\partial x^*/\partial \tau) > 0,$

where $(\partial X^*/\partial \tau)/(\partial x^*/\partial \tau) = -b_m(2B + K)/[2(b_m(2B + K) + BK)] = \Phi'(\cdot)$ for any $\tau = r$, v, and s.[4]

While these choices of r, v, and s are not unique, they are the only choices of the three consistent with offsetting each distortion in the model at its source. Any other choices would necessitate targeting the export policy partially toward either the domestic consumption or production distortion.[5] Hence we follow Just, Schmitz, and Zilberman in assuming that each policy is chosen to exactly offset the distortion at its source. To see that this is possible, notice that v, the production subsidy, enters both first-order conditions for the home exporter. If v is chosen according to equation (13), the two first-order conditions are separated, and the consumption subsidy can be used to offset the domestic consumption distortion, while the export subsidy can be used to exercise market power abroad.

The foreign country's welfare, W, is given by an equation analogous to equation (9), with the appropriate substitution of uppercase letters. That government chooses R, V, and S to maximize welfare given the behavior of marketing agents and fixed home country policies. Differentiating W with respect to $\tau = R$, S, and V and substituting from the marketing board's first-order conditions, the first-order conditions for the foreign exporting government can be written as

(15) $\partial W/\partial \tau = -V[(\partial Y^*/\partial \tau) + (\partial X^*/\partial t)]$
$$+ [BY^* - R](\partial Y^*/\partial \tau) - [S(\partial X^*/\partial \tau) + b_m X^*(\partial x^*/\partial \tau)] = 0.$$

Welfare is maximized for

(16) $R = BY^* > 0,$

(17) $V = 0,$ and

(18) $S = -b_m X^* (\partial x^*/\partial \tau)/(\partial X^*/\partial \tau) > 0,$

where $(\partial x^*/\partial \tau)/(-\partial X^*/\partial \tau) = -b_m(b + k)/2[b_m(b + k) + bk] = \phi'(\cdot)$ for $\tau = R, V,$ and S. I maintain the assumption that policies are determined to exactly offset distortions at their source.

The Nash equilibrium for the government policy game is characterized by the first-order conditions for the monopolist and the marketing board, equations (3)–(6), and equations (12)–(14) and (16)–(18). The governments' domestic policies are similar to those of Just, Schmitz, and Zilberman, and the export subsidies are positive as in the Brander-Spencer model without domestic consumption or a marketing board. This is not surprising since I have targeted policies so that export policy need not be adjusted to offset domestic distortions. Domestic policies are determined completely by domestic distortions, so the optimal policies are no different in my model with export rivalry than in Just, Schmitz, and Zilberman's nonstrategic environment. The government of the country with an unregulated monopoly-monopsonist will subsidize domestic consumption and production, and the government of the country with a marketing board need not subsidize production but will subsidize consumption.

The difference in my export policy and Just, Schmitz, and Zilberman's comes from the export rivalry. In Just, Schmitz, and Zilberman's analysis, a single marketing agent supplies the world market. Given the ability to price discriminate, this marketing agent exports the socially optimal quantity. With a Cournot export rivalry, however, each agent's exports are a function of its rival's exports. A government with the ability to precommit to an export subsidy can use that fact to improve its country's welfare, ceteris paribus. Any marketing agent (marketing board or monopolist) will export more with an export subsidy than it would otherwise. This reduces the exports of the foreign rival in equilibrium, hence increasing domestic welfare via an increase in the marketing agent's profits. This is a key feature missing in the Just, Schmitz, and Zilberman analysis.

4.2   Regulated Marketing Board and Monopoly-Monopsony

The literature on strategic trade policy has focused on the impact of governments being able to precommit to tax/subsidy policies. But governments precommit to more than simple tax/subsidy policies. The market structures they permit and their regulation of industry involve a precommitment! In the previous section, I showed that a government precommiting to a statutory marketing board (to eliminate potential exercise of monopsony power against producers) did not affect the policy prescriptions for strategic use of trade policy. In this section, I show that this result is altered when the government with a marketing board regulates the domestic pricing of the board. There are two reasons for doing this. One is to show that regulating the board in the hope of eliminating the need for a consumption subsidy is not as innocuous as it might seem. The second reason is that it is not uncommon for governments to impose such rules on their marketing boards (Hoos 1979).

Consider a game identical to the one in the previous section, with the exception that the marketing board maximizes joint returns of its competitive producers subject to the constraint that domestic inverse demand equals inverse supply, that is, $D(Y) + R = P(Y + X) - V$. The regulated marketing board's first-order conditions are

$$(19) \qquad A + R - BY - F + V - K(Y + X) = 0, \text{ and}$$

$$(20) \quad a_m + S - 2b_m X - b_m x - F + V$$
$$- K(X + Y) + KBY/(B + K) = 0,$$

where use has been made of the constraint in obtaining equation (20). Notice the regulation prevents the marketing board from equating marginal revenue in each market with marginal cost. Moreover, the last term in equation (20) implies that the board will export more than it would in the absence of regulation.

The regulated board's reaction function is derived by solving equation (19) for Y, substituting into equation (20), and solving for $X = \Psi(x)$ given by

$$(21) \qquad \qquad \Psi(x) = (\eta + \mu - \lambda x)/\sigma,$$

where

$$\eta = B(B + 2K)(a_m + S - F + V),$$
$$\mu = K^2(a_m + S - A - R),$$
$$\lambda = b_m(B + K)^2, \text{ and}$$
$$\sigma = 2b_m(B + K)^2 + BK(B + 2K).$$

For given values of r, v, s, R, V, and S, equations (3), (4), (19), and (20) determine equilibrium consumption and exports of the two exporting countries when the marketing board is regulated. Equilibrium exports in this game are given by $(x^\#, X^\#)$ such that $\phi(X^\#) = x^\#$ and $\Psi(x^\#) = X^\#$ and equilibrium values of $y^\#$ and $Y^\#$ are given by equations (3) and (19) evaluated at $x^\#$ and $X^\#$. $\phi'(\Psi(x))\Psi' < 1$ is assumed to ensure uniqueness and stability of the equilibrium.

To determine optimal policies for the foreign exporting government, we differentiate W with respect to $\tau = R$, V, and S and substitute the modified first-order conditions, equations (19) and (20), to obtain

$$(22) \quad \partial W/\partial \tau = -V[(\partial Y^\#/\partial \tau) + (\partial X^\#/\partial \tau)] - R(\partial Y^\#/\partial \tau)$$
$$- [S + KBY^\#/(B + K)](\partial X^\#/\partial \tau) - b_m X^\#(\partial x^\#/\partial \tau).$$

Welfare maximizing policy choices are

(23) $R = V = 0$, and

(24) $S = -KBY^{\#}/(B + K) - b_m X^{\#}(\partial x^{\#}/\partial \tau)/(\partial X^{\#}/\partial \tau)$,

where $(\partial x^{\#}/\partial \tau)/(\partial X^{\#}/\partial \tau) = \phi'(\cdot)$ is independent of the policy tool.

The equilibrium for this policy game is characterized by the first-order conditions for the monopolist and the regulated marketing board, equations (3), (4), (19), and (20), and equations (23), (24), (12)–(14) evaluated at $x^{\#}$, $y^{\#}$, and $X^{\#}$. Qualitatively, the home government policies are not affected by whether or not the board is regulated. However, the optimal trade policy of the foreign exporting government becomes ambiguous when it substitutes domestic price regulation for a consumption subsidy. The optimal policy is a tax if the first term in S dominates, and a subsidy if the second term dominates. The reason a tax might be appropriate is most easily seen in Just, Schmitz, and Zilberman's nonstrategic case. In their model a regulated marketing board would export too much from society's point of view unless it were taxed. This occurs because at the socially optimal level of exports the board could purchase an extra unit of the good at the competitive supply price, increase its domestic price by the increase in the supply price, and sell the extra unit plus the reduction in domestic consumption abroad. The first term in equation (24) reflects the fact that for a given level of home exports, the regulated board will export too much, while the second term reflects the effect of the board's exports on home country exports in equilibrium.

4.3   Quasi-Competitive Home Market

It is well known that optimal policy in oligopolistic trade models is sensitive to the number of firms (Dixit 1984; Salant 1984; Krugman 1987; Cooper and Riezman 1986), and it is natural to expect the same to be true here. The statutory marketing board is a clear barrier to entry in the foreign exporting country,[6] but unless barriers to entry are prohibitive in the home country we might expect more than one marketing agent even if there are economies of scale in distribution. For that reason I examine a quasi-competitive model for the home country.

This exercise is motivated largely because the competitiveness of the U.S. agricultural marketing system has been a controversial issue. In the mid-1970s some sources claimed that the market was essentially monopolistic-monopsonistic, and in response, several government, academic, and private studies have examined the issue empirically. As is seen in section 4.4, even if the U.S. agricultural marketing system is not purely competitive, it is clearly not a pure monopoly-monopsony.

For that reason, it is important to know how sensitive the policy choices are to the number of firms in the home country.

The simplest way to do this would be to increase the number of firms in the previous two games. A more general model and one consistent (in a stylized fashion) with the example of U.S. wheat trade presented in section 4.4 is one that allows two types of home firms: one that exports and one that only markets domestically because of a cost disadvantage. In the limit the model allows the possibility of imperfect competition in the export sector, but exporting firms are unable to exercise monopsony power in the domestic market because of competition with firms marketing the good domestically. In this section I examine optimal policy when the home market is modified to allow for this possibility.

Suppose export marketing involves a distribution cost in addition to the producer price of the good. I abstract from whether this is a transport or information-related cost, and for simplicity we assume it is constant per unit sold. There are $n + h$ firms, the last h of which have a cost disadvantage relative to the first n firms. Distribution cost, per se, in the domestic market remains zero. Profit for the ith firm is given by

$$(25) \quad \pi_i = [a + r - b(y_i + \mathbf{y}_i)]y_i + [a_m + s - b_m(x_i + \mathbf{x}_i + X)]x_i$$
$$- [f - v + k(x_i + \mathbf{x}_i + y_i + \mathbf{y}_i)](y_i + x_i) - c_i x_i,$$

where
$$\mathbf{y}_i = \sum_{j \neq i} y_j$$

and
$$\mathbf{x}_i = \sum_{j \neq i} x_j$$

and c_i is per unit export distribution cost. Firms are differentiated only by this cost parameter, which for simplicity we assume to be low, c_1, or high, c_2. For $i = 1, \ldots, n$, $c_i = c_1$, $y_i = y_1$, and $x_i = x_1$; for $i = n + 1, \ldots, n + h$, $c_i = c_2$, $y_i = y_2$, and $x_i = x_2$.

For high enough values of c_2, $x_2 = 0$, and the relevant first-order conditions are

$$(26) \quad \partial\pi_1/\partial y_1 = a + r - (n + 1)by_1 - hby_2 - f$$
$$+ v - k(n + 1)(y_1 + x_1) - hky_2 = 0,$$

$$(27) \quad \partial\pi_2/\partial y_2 = a + r - (h + 1)by_2 - nby_1 - f$$
$$+ v - k(h + 1)y_2 - nk(y_1 + x_1) = 0, \text{ and}$$

$$(28) \quad \partial\pi_1/\partial x_1 = a_m + s - (n + 1)b_m x_1 - b_m X - f$$
$$+ v - k(n + 1)(x_1 + y_1) - hky_2 - c_1 = 0.$$

The reaction function for a home exporter in this model is derived by solving equations (26) and (27) for y_1, substituting into equation (28), and solving for $x_1 = \phi_1(X)$. Since exporting firms are symmetric, the reaction function for the home country export sector is $n\phi_1(X)$ where

(29) $$\phi_1(X) = (\alpha + \beta - \gamma X)/\delta,$$

where

$$\alpha = b(a_m - f + s + v - c_1),$$

$$\beta = k(a_m - a + s - r - c_1),$$

$$\gamma = b_m(b + k), \text{ and}$$

$$\delta = (n + 1)[b_m(b + k) + bk]/n.$$

Notice that $\phi_1(X)$ differs from $\phi(X)$ only by the subtraction of $c_1(b + k)$ in the numerator and replacement of the number 2 in the denominator by $(n + 1)/n$. Domestic consumption in the home country is $ny_1 + hy_2$ where

(30) $$y_1 = y_2 - kx_1/(b + k).$$

As we might expect, each exporter sells less at home than a typical domestic marketing firm.

As before, the marketing board's reaction function will depend on whether or not it is regulated. Denoting the marketing board's cost to distributing exports by C, its reaction function if it is unregulated is given by subtracting $C(2B + K)$ from the numerator of the expression for $\Phi(x)$ in equation (8). If the board is regulated, its reaction function is given by subtracting $C[B(B + 2K) + K^2]$ from the numerator of the expression for $\Psi(x)$ in equation (21). Notice that because of the way C enters, it does not affect the slope of either marketing board's reaction function.

As before, optimal policies for each government are derived by differentiating the expressions for welfare with respect to policies and substituting from the relevant first-order conditions. The expressions for welfare differ from those in section 4.3 by the subtraction of the distribution cost multiplied by exports. The equilibrium for a game between the home government and the unregulated board is now characterized by equation (29) and the reaction function for the unregulated marketing board incorporating C and the following policies:

(31) $$r = by_1^{**},$$

(32) $$v = k(y_1^{**} + x_1^{**}),$$

(33) $$s = -b_m x_1^{**}(n[1 + \Phi'(\cdot)] - 1),$$

(34) $$R = BY^{**},$$

(35) $$V = 0, \text{ and}$$

(36) $$S = -b_m X^{**} n\phi_1'(\cdot),$$

where superscript ** denotes equilibrium values for this game.

Table 4.2 presents these policies and the policies from the previous games. Notice that qualitatively the foreign exporting government's policies are unaffected by the modification of home market structure. Subsidizing both domestic consumption and exports remains optimal. The home government continues to subsidize both domestic consumption and production, but the optimal export policy is now ambiguous. It is a subsidy, free trade, or a tax as n is less than, equal to, or greater than $1/(1 + \Phi'(\cdot))$. Since $\Phi'(\cdot)$ is independent of any choice variable, this result is independent of the foreign government subsidy or tax policy. In fact, since $\Phi'(\cdot) \in (-.5, 0)$, the existence of two home exporting firms is sufficient for a tax to be optimal.

Now consider the game with $n > 1$ home firms and a regulated marketing board. The policy equilibrium is described by equation (29) and the regulated marketing board reaction function incorporating C and the following policies:

(37) $$r = by^{\#\#}{}_1,$$

(38) $$v = k(y^{\#\#}{}_1 + x^{\#\#}{}_1),$$

(39) $$s = -b_m x_1^{\#\#}(n[1 + \Psi'(\cdot)] - 1),$$

(40) $$R = V = 0, \text{ and}$$

(41) $$S = -b_m X^{\#\#} n\phi_1'(\cdot) - KBY^{\#\#}/(B + K),$$

where superscript $\#\#$ denotes equilibrium values for this game.

Again two exporting firms are enough for an optimal export tax at home. And as before, the invariance of the slope of the board's reaction function with respect to choice variables makes this result independent of foreign policy. As shown in table 4.2, optimal foreign policies are

Table 4.2   **Optimal Government Policy**

Foreign Exporter	Unregulated Marketing Board		Regulated Marketing Board	
Home exporter				
Monopoly-monopsony	$r > 0$	$R > 0$	$r > 0$	$R = V = 0$
	$v > 0$	$V = 0$	$v > 0$	
	$s > 0$	$S > 0$	$s > 0$	$S \gtreqless 0$
Quasi-competitive (two or more exporters)	$r > 0$	$R > 0$	$r > 0$	$R = V = 0$
	$v > 0$	$V = 0$	$v > 0$	
	$s < 0$	$S > 0$	$s < 0$	$S \gtreqless 0$

Notes: Lowercase letters denote home government policies and uppercase denote foreign. $r > 0 \ (< 0)$ denotes specific consumption subsidy (tax); $v > 0 \ (< 0)$ denotes specific production subsidy (tax); and $s > 0 \ (< 0)$ denotes specific export subsidy (tax).

qualitatively the same as those for the regulated board with a home country monopoly-monopsony. Essentially the regulation of domestic price gives the board extra incentive to export, so the optimal export policy is either a lower subsidy than in the unregulated case or a tax.

4.4   World Wheat Trade, State Trading, and Market Structure

Each of the four models examined is characterized by the rivalry of two exporting countries with market power in international trade, where one of the countries exercises its power, in part, through a marketing board. Hence these models would apply to markets dominated by a few countries, at least one of which sells through a marketing board. One such market is the world wheat market. The combined exports of the two largest exporting countries, Canada and the United States, comprise roughly 60 percent of world exports. The combined market share of the top four exporters is approximately 80 percent.[7]

Table 4.3 indicates the portion of world wheat exports either sold or purchased by marketing or state trading agencies for selected periods between 1963 and 1984.[8] The table includes exports of the United States, Canada, EEC, Australia, Argentina, and USSR. Exports of the

Table 4.3   **State Trading in Wheat (percentage of volume of principal exporters accounted for by state traders)**

	1963–67 (%)	1973–77 (%)	1980–84 (%)
1. Private exporters to private importers	5.9	4.4	2.2
2. Private exporters to state importers	51.2	56.6	64.1
3. State exporters to private importers	8.1	4.3	2.2
4. State exporters to state importers	34.8	34.7	31.6
5. Exports by private traders = (1 + 2)	57.1	61.0	66.3
6. Exports by state traders = (3 + 4)	42.9	39.0	33.8
7. Imports by private traders = (1 + 3)	14.0	8.7	4.4
8. Imports by state traders = (2 + 4)	86.0	91.3	95.7
Volume of trade (000 mt)	49,891	60,385	93,339
Total exports (000 mt)	56,397	63,506	97,839

Sources: McCalla and Schmitz 1982, table 3.5, for 1963–77 data; International Wheat Council, various issues, for 1980–84 data.

United States and EEC are private, and after 1963–67 Argentina's exports are private. Canada and Australia sell through marketing boards. The EEC is the only major importer that is private; the Western European countries other than the EEC have state trading agencies for wheat, and the Japanese import through the Japanese Food Agency. Although their market shares are variable, the USSR and People's Republic of China are large importers.

Less than 6 percent of the exports in table 4.3 is sold by private traders to private traders. This trade represents primarily U.S. exports to the EEC and has been declining over time. Percentages in the second row indicate that over half of the exports are sold by private traders to state importers. These percentages reflect mainly U.S. and EEC exports. Rows three and four indicate the exports of state exporters by their destination. Note that the sum of these (given in row six) is roughly a third of total exports. Finally, the sum of imports by state traders ranges between 86 percent and 96 percent.

4.4.1 Imperfectly Competitive Models of World Wheat Trade

Market shares for the major wheat exporters have remained fairly stable over the past twenty years, with the exception that the EEC share of world exports has roughly doubled in the last decade. Because of the large and stable export shares, a number of studies have examined oligopolistic models of the world wheat market (McCalla 1966; Taplin 1969; Alaouze, Watson, and Sturgess 1978; Schmitz et al. 1981; Karp and McCalla 1983; Paarlberg and Abbott 1984; and Kolstad and Burris 1986). These studies have made a variety of assumptions about numbers of rivals and the nature of competition among them.

Perhaps the closest to the models developed here is that of Kolstad and Burris (1986) which is a spatial equilibrium trade model in which producing country governments are Nash quantity competitors who maximize profits and have the ability to price discriminate between domestic and foreign sales. For 1972–73 trade flows, they examine hypotheses of (1) a United States–Canada duopoly, (2) a U.S.-Canada-Australia triopoly, (3) a Japan-EEC duopsony, and (4) perfect competition. They find that the U.S.-Canadian duopoly comes the closest to predicting actual trade for that year.[9]

These results suggest that a game between the U.S. and Canadian governments, with sales agents being the Canadian Wheat Board and U.S. grain exporters, is a useful abstraction. One of the major goals of the Canadian Wheat Board is to maximize producer returns, and it is the sole agent for both domestic and foreign sales of Canadian wheat. Since September 1973, the price it can charge domestically has been regulated (Schmitz and McCalla 1979), so its behavior comes closest to the regulated board in our models. The remaining issue as to which of the models would apply to a U.S.-Canadian duopoly concerns the competitiveness of the U.S. marketing system.

4.4.2 Competitiveness of U.S. Grain Marketing

A 1976 report of the USDA's Farmer Cooperative Service claimed that the six largest grain exporting firms accounted for 90 percent of U.S. exports of grain (USGAO 1982). Estimates of concentration in U.S. grain exporting plus the controversial sales of grain to the USSR in the mid-1970s stimulated a series of studies of the competitiveness of this sector.

Several of these studies were done by the General Accounting Office of the U.S. government. They focused on providing revised estimates of concentration in the export sector (USGAO 1982; Conklin 1982) and on the efficiency of futures markets for grains (Conklin 1982). Table 4.4 presents GAO's estimates of concentration ratios for wheat, corn, soybeans, and all grains. Since many of the same firms that export wheat also trade other grains, we present evidence for other grains as well. Three characteristics are evident. First, the export sector is not as concentrated as the 1976 estimate suggests. The largest four exporters account for 61 percent of export sales for wheat, and one must include the largest twenty firms to account for 90 percent of export sales. Second, the concentration ratios for corn, soybeans, and all grains are lower than for wheat. Finally, concentration ratios for domestic sales are lower still. Caves and Pugel (1982) present similar evidence based on a survey of members of the North American Export Grain Association. Their evidence points to the largest firms handling a majority of "direct" export sales, while many smaller firms purchase grain from farmers to sell domestically or to the largest exporters, who then export it (the latter type of sale being classified as "indirect" exports).

Table 4.4   Concentration Ratios for U.S. Grain Sales

Number of Firms	Export Sales (Marketing Year 1974–75)				Wholesale Sales (Calendar Year 1977)
	Wheat	Corn	Soybeans	All Grains	All Grains
Four largest	61.0%	42.0%	40.5%	48.6%	25.4%
Eight largest	81.7%	63.8%	63.7%	68.6%	38.1%
Twenty largest	89.2%	93.3%	90.8%	90.1%	54.5%

Source: Conklin 1982, 30–33.

High concentration ratios are not necessarily indicative of the exercise of market power. In the short run, firms in a highly concentrated industry have the potential to exercise market power until entry can occur. While the grain export industry is highly concentrated, there has been considerable entry and exit in the industry over the last decade. The number of firms reporting export sales of wheat increased 40 percent between marketing year 1974–75 and 1983–84, and the number of firms exporting corn and soybeans increased 30 percent over the same period.[10] As reported in Caves and Pugel (1982), one of the largest firms exited the industry during that period (Cook).

Evidence of price discrimination by exporting firms in the absence of government subsidies would indicate market power. Except in the limiting case ($n = h = \infty$) of the quasi-competitive model, the analysis in this chapter assumes firms have the ability to price discriminate between the home and foreign market. Although the difference between the export and domestic consumer price in any of the models may be positive or negative, all of the models predict a positive correlation between this difference and export volume for zero or constant distribution cost per unit. With perfect competition and constant distribution cost, export volume and this price difference are unrelated. It is, therefore, possible to test for market power and the ability to price discriminate by testing for a positive relation between export volume and the difference between export and domestic prices.

To prove the ability of firms to price discriminate, one needs data for export and wholesale prices for the same type and grade of exports, net of distribution costs. I have export and wholesale prices for the same grade of wheat for hard red winter (hrw) and dark northern spring (dns) wheat for 1962/63–1983/84. Export and wholesale price data for the same period are also available for corn and soybeans.[11] Unfortunately data for distribution cost are not available, so any analysis of the relation between the export-wholesale price differential and export volume must be interpreted in light of potential effects this cost might have. For example, it would be possible in the framework of the models presented here for the export-domestic consumer price difference to be negatively correlated if there were significant economies of scale in distribution. Caves and Pugel (1982) present evidence of such economies of scale in distribution as part of their explanation for the high concentration of the U.S. grain export industry.

Table 4.5 presents the results of eight regressions of the export-wholesale price differential on export volume. The first four columns describe the results for the period 1962/63–1983/84. Column labels denote the commodity for which the price differential is the dependent variable. All data are yearly, and prices are in real terms. Because the price differential could be affected by shifts in underlying consumer

Table 4.5   **U.S. Export-Wholesale Price Differential**

	1962/63 – 1983/84			
Variables	Wheat (hrw)	Wheat (dns)	Corn	Soybeans
Constant	−0.201	−0.309	−.167	.338
	(−.60)	(−.944)	(−.65)	(.46)
Volume	0.025	0.058*	.0004	.0002
	(.76)	(1.81)	(1.01)	(.08)
Trend	0.014	0.033	.013	−.045
	(.70)	(1.66)	(.55)	(−.61)
Trend*volume	−0.001	−0.003*	−.000	.000
	(−.56)	(−1.83)	(−.58)	(.27)
Number firms	n.a.	n.a.	n.a.	n.a.
Dummy	−0.678**a	−0.846**a	−.383*b	n.a.
	(−6.16)	(−7.85)	(−1.79)	
R^2	0.938	0.958	.175	.03

	1974/75 – 1983/84			
Variables	Wheat (hrw)	Wheat (dns)	Corn	Soybeans
Constant	−.0924**	−0.577**	−1.284	1.44
	(−6.55)	(−3.47)	(−1.67)	(.34)
Volume	0.093**	0.053**	.0004	.001
	(5.41)	(2.61)	(1.44)	(.30)
Trend	0.153**	0.082**	.129	.247
	(6.55)	(2.99)	(1.35)	(.72)
Trend*volume	−0.013**	0.009**	−.000	−.0002
	(−7.05)	(−4.39)	(−1.87)	(−.24)
Number firms	−0.000	0.008	.018	−.065
	(−.03)	(1.88)	(1.92)	(−1.17)
Dummy	n.a.	n.a.	n.a.	n.a.
R^2	.925	.915	.647	.439

Sources: For wheat, export volume and export prices are from International Wheat Council, various issues; wholesale prices are from USDA, various issues of *Wheat Situation* and *Wheat Situation and Outlook*. For corn and soybeans, export prices and volume and wholesale prices are from USDA 1986. All prices are deflated by the consumer price index taken from USDA 1986.

Notes: Export price for hard red winter wheat is for no. 2, 13 percent protein, f.o.b. Gulf. Export price for dark northern spring wheat is the average of f.o.b. Gulf and Pacific prices for 14 percent protein. Wholesale prices for wheat are "prices to millers" for the same types of wheat and protein content. The wholesale price for hard red winter wheat is the Kansas price, and the wholesale price for dark northern spring wheat is the Minnesota price. Export prices for corn and soybeans are f.o.b. Gulf, and wholesale prices are Chicago prices for no. 2 yellow corn and no. 1 yellow soybeans.

aDummy for export subsidy through 1972.

bDummy for demand shift in 1973.

*Significant at 10 percent level.

**Significant at 5 percent level.

demand and producer supply or changes in distribution cost, I include time as a regressor to capture any systematic changes in these excluded variables. Since the relation between the price differential and export volume can be affected by economies of scale in distribution and export volume has grown over time, I also include time multiplied by export volume. Finally, for the years 1962/63–1972/73, the United States subsidized wheat exports, so I include a dummy equal to one in the subsidy years and zero in nonsubsidy years. Neither corn nor soybeans were subsidized; however, corn exports showed a dramatic shift in 1972–73, so a dummy equal to one is included for that and subsequent years.

With the exception of wheat, the explanatory power of these regressions is low. Moreover, the wheat regressions are consistent with the export subsidy being the major determinant of any price differential. The wheat subsidy dummy is the only variable significant at the 5 percent level in any of the regressions. Export volume and trend*volume are significant at the 10 percent level only in the case of dns wheat.

The last four columns in table 4.5 refer to results of a slightly different regression for the period 1974/75–1983/84. For each of the years in the period, data are available for the number of firms reporting export sales. For the same reasons that concentration ratios are a poor measure of market power, the number of firms need not be indicative of either the presence or absence of market power. Nonetheless, there was substantial entry during this period, so I include the number of firms as a regressor. If the industry were purely competitive there should be no relation between the price differential and the number of firms. The dummy variables are not applicable to this period.[12]

Notice first the marked difference between the explanatory power of the wheat regressions and those for the other grains. While the coefficient of export volume is positive in all cases, it is significant at the 5 percent level only for wheat (the significance level for corn is 21 percent). Recalling that the four-firm concentration ratio for wheat is noticeably higher than that for the other two, these results are at least suggestive of the exercise of market power in wheat. In none of the regressions, however, is the coefficient for the number of firms significant.

Note that because the regressions include trend*volume, the partial effects of volume and trend are functions of both their coefficients and the coefficient of trend*volume. Thus for the wheat regressions, I report the partial effects of volume and trend for each year in table 4.6. As expected, in the regressions for 1962/63–1983/84 the partial effects are rarely significant. For 1974/75–1983/84, however, the partial effects of volume and trend are often significant. The partial effect of volume on the price differential is positive until the late 1970s and becomes negative in the 1980s. The partial effect of trend on the differential goes

Table 4.6   **Partial Effects of Export Volume and Trend on U.S. Export-Wholesale Price Differential for Wheat**

Year	Export	t-Statistic	Trend	t-Statistic
1962/63–1983/84 (hrw)				
62	0.024	0.771	0.0079	0.6918
63	0.023	0.778	0.0058	0.5961
64	0.022	0.7851	0.007	0.6657
65	0.021	0.7921	0.0056	0.5882
66	0.02	0.7989	0.0069	0.6601
67	0.019	0.8051	0.0067	0.6518
68	0.018	0.8103	0.0089	0.7088
69	0.017	0.8139	0.0082	0.6986
70	0.016	0.8149	0.007	0.6625
71	0.0149	0.8122	0.008	0.6954
72	0.0139	0.8042	0.0025	0.2557
73	0.0129	0.7891	0.0028	0.2963
74	0.0119	0.7648	0.0038	0.4153
75	0.0109	0.7294	0.0026	0.275
76	0.0099	0.6817	0.0045	0.4918
77	0.0089	0.6216	0.0026	0.2776
78	0.0079	0.5511	0.0023	0.2358
79	0.0069	0.4732	0.0008	0.0696
80	0.0059	0.3921	−0.0013	−0.0969
81	0.0049	0.3116	−0.004	−0.234
82	0.0039	0.2349	−0.0003	0.0213
83	0.0028	0.1639	0.0001	0.0099
1962/63–1983/84 (dns)				
62	0.055 *	1.8015	0.0126	1.1274
63	0.0518*	1.787	0.0058	0.6147
64	0.0486*	1.7694	0.0099	0.9565
65	0.0454*	1.7477	0.0055	0.5811
66	0.0422	1.721	0.0095	0.9248
67	0.039	1.6879	0.0089	0.8792
68	0.0358	1.6467	0.0157	1.281
69	0.0326	1.5954	0.0136	1.1818
70	0.0294	1.5314	0.0097	0.9384
71	0.0262	1.4517	0.0131	1.1551
72	0.023	1.3529	−0.0047	−0.4936
73	0.0198	1.2315	−0.0036	−0.3849
74	0.0166	1.0849	−0.0003	−0.0374
75	0.0134	0.9118	−0.0041	−0.4423
76	0.0102	0.7139	0.0019	0.2143
77	0.007	0.4964	−0.0041	−0.4356
78	0.0038	0.268	−0.0052	−0.5454
79	0.0006	0.039	−0.01	−0.9411
80	−0.0026	−0.1805	−0.0165	−1.2772
81	−0.0058	−0.3828	−0.0251	−1.5085
82	−0.0091	−0.5634	−0.0133	−1.132
83	−0.0123	−0.721	−0.0121	−1.0685

Table 4.6   (continued)

Year	Export	t-Statistic	Trend	t-Statistic
1974/75 – 1983/84 (hrw)				
74	0.0801**	5.088	0.0208**	3.0017
75	0.0674**	4.6792	0.0058	0.9632
76	0.0547**	4.1521	0.0298**	3.8598
77	0.0421**	3.4755	0.006	1.0057
78	0.0294**	2.6225	0.0016	0.2718
79	0.0167	1.5862	− 0.0176**	− 2.9771
80	0.0041	0.4006	− 0.0432**	− 5.6039
81	− 0.0086	− 0.8507	− 0.077 **	− 6.702
82	− 0.0213*	− 2.0551	− 0.0304**	− 4.5808
83	− 0.0339**	− 3.1172	− 0.0257**	− 4.07
1974/75 – 1983/84 (dns)				
74	0.0434*	2.3449	− 0.0146	− 1.7938
75	0.0342	2.0145	− 0.0256**	− 3.6339
76	0.0249	1.6033	− 0.008	− 0.8848
77	0.0156	1.0949	− 0.0254**	− 3.5995
78	0.0063	0.4791	− 0.0287**	− 4.1713
79	− 0.003	− 0.2379	− 0.0428**	− 6.1301
80	− 0.0122	− 1.0217	− 0.0615**	− 6.7732
81	− 0.0215	− 1.8094	− 0.0862**	− 6.3774
82	− 0.0308*	− 2.5288	− 0.0521**	− 6.6736
83	− 0.0401**	− 3.1279	− 0.0487**	− 6.5413

*Significant at the 10 percent level.
**Significant at the 5 percent level.

from positive to negative in the case of hrw wheat, while it is consistently negative for dns wheat.

There are a number of interpretations one could give to the volume and trend results for 1974/75 – 1983/84. One interpretation is that exporting firms have market power and that the trend term reflects economies of scale in distribution. If economies of scale became more important toward the end of the period, the partial effect of volume would become negative over time. Another interpretation is that the industry is relatively competitive, with entry occurring over the period in response to short-run profits of the mid-1970s. The latter interpretation is consistent with evidence of Caves (1978), who found a significant relation between profit margins and volume of sales for all grains for the year 1973–74. For a more extended period, he found a significant relation only for soybeans.

In summary, the evidence presented here is consistent with that of others (Caves 1978; Caves and Pugel 1982; Conklin 1982; and USGAO

1982). Grain exporting is highly concentrated because of economies of scale in distribution, but barriers to entry in U.S. grain marketing are not prohibitive. Large exporting firms may be in a position to exercise market power in the short run, and they may have done so in the mid-1970s. Nonetheless, the industry cannot be characterized as a pure monopoly-monopsony.

This result is important in light of my results in section 4.3. The optimal trade policy for the home government changes from an export subsidy with monopoly-monopsony to an export tax with two exporting firms. Whether or not U.S. exporting firms have market power, it appears that the appropriate government policy to maximize social welfare would be an export tax.

4.5   Concluding Remarks

In this chapter I examined several theoretical models capable of showing how state trading and competition in private export trade affect strategic use of trade policy. Recent literature in this area has focused on oligopolistic industries in which private firms maximize profits and are unregulated. In my analysis, if domestic tax/subsidy policy can be used in conjunction with trade policy, optimal trade policy is qualitatively the same whether an export agent maximizes producer returns or profits. If, however, governments regulate domestic consumer prices, appropriate trade policy may be quite different depending on the marketing agent's objective.[13] I find that the exports of a regulated marketing board might be optimally taxed by its government, whereas a government would optimally subsidize exports of a monopolist exporter.

I also find that when a marketing board and a private export industry composed of one or more firms compete as Cournot rivals, the government of the country with the private industry would subsidize exports only when marketing is done by a monopolist. In light of this result, the empirical analysis of the United States grain industry suggests export subsidies would not be welfare improving from a national point of view. Based on the ability of exporters to price discriminate between domestic and export sales, I find no evidence of the exercise of market power in corn and soybean markets. For the period 1974/75–1983/84, I find limited support for price discrimination in wheat markets. Nonetheless, during this period at least forty-one firms recorded export sales of wheat, so the policy prescription of the theoretical model for this case would be an export tax.

Several issues not addressed here are potentially interesting. First, the importing country in these models also has market power. Brander and Spencer (1984, 1985) have examined optimal policy of an importing country in the face of imperfect competition. Evidence for wheat trade suggests two ways optimal import policy might be approached. Since over 80 percent of wheat imports is purchased by state traders (recall table 4.3), it would be interesting to examine how the objective of the state importing agency affects policies and market outcomes. The other interesting approach would be to allow the importer to produce (and perhaps export) the good. The motivation for this complication comes from the prominent role of the EEC in agricultural markets and trade negotiations. Carter and Schmitz (1979) have examined the EEC's variable levy as an optimal tariff, but it is clear that EEC intervention in agricultural markets comes from more than a simple optimum tariff calculation (Brown 1986; Gardner 1986; Hayes and Schmitz 1986; and Sarris 1986).

Finally, in my models the marketing board maximized joint producer returns and its government maximized social welfare. In practice, marketing boards and governments also have price stability goals. Since it is well known that policy implications in strategic models are sensitive to whether rivals compete in output or price (Eaton and Grossman 1986), one would expect policies to differ if agents competed in prices and if objectives pertained to stability of these prices.

Notes

Thanks are due to Robert Baldwin, Alan Deardorff, Tom Grennes, Richard Jensen, Paul Johnson, Alex McCalla, James Markusen, Steve Salant, Robert Stern, and Jerry Thursby for insightful suggestions, and Aileen Thompson for research assistance.

1. McCalla and Schmitz 1982 and studies in McCalla and Josling 1981 argue that market outcomes will vary depending on the source of the imperfect competition.

2. Export subsidies for primary products are to be avoided when they lead to a more than "equitable" share of the market, whereas countries are not to grant subsidies (either direct or indirect) that lead to export prices below domestic prices in the case of nonprimary products.

3. See Markusen 1984 for an analysis of marketing boards that maximize profits.

4. As shown by Dixit 1984, this choice is equivalent to the government choosing domestic and export sales to maximize welfare. To see this, substitute r, v, and s, given by equations (12)–(14), into equations (3) and (4). The monopolist's first-order conditions are then equivalent to those that would emerge if the government were to choose x and y to maximize equation (9):

$$\delta w/\delta y = a - by - f - k(y + x) = 0, \text{ and}$$
$$\delta w/\delta x = a_m - 2b_m x - b_m [\Phi(x) + x\Phi'(x)] - f - k(y + x) = 0.$$

5. It is, of course, also possible to employ only a production and consumption subsidy/tax, but exposition would be more difficult.

6. I abstract from issues relating to entry of competitive producers. This issue arises because the board is acting to maximize their joint returns. Entry in response to an increase in returns would, in turn, affect the supply curve facing the board in our analysis. In practice, production quotas are used for this purpose, and the reader is referred to Hoos 1979.

7. These percentages were calculated from data in International Wheat Council, *International Wheat Statistics,* and may be off by $+/-$ 2 percent or 3 percent in any year. Nevertheless, the market shares have been relatively stable over the past twenty years.

8. See McCalla and Schmitz 1982, appendix 3, 291–93, for a list of state trading boards and agencies.

9. Essentially there are more nonzero bilateral trade flows for wheat than a perfectly competitive spatial equilibrium model would predict. An alternative approach to predicting these flows would be to treat wheat as a differentiated product (Johnson, Grennes, and Thursby 1979).

10. Information was provided by the Export Sales Reporting Division of the Foreign Agricultural Service. In marketing year 1974–75 there were 41 firms reporting exports of wheat, 56 firms reporting corn exports, and 39 reporting soybean exports. In 1983–84 there were 61 firms reporting exports of wheat, 76 firms reporting corn exports, and 53 reporting soybean exports.

11. Data for wheat are available by protein content, while price data are available only for no. 2 yellow corn and no. 1 yellow soybeans. The difference lies in the fact that, strictly speaking, wheat is not homogeneous and is demanded for different end uses, while corn and soybean are not. See Johnson, Grennes, and Thursby 1979 on this point.

12. It can be argued that credit policies are effective subsidies, but neither my models nor my empirical work incorporate these.

13. If the private monopolist, for example, were regulated in the same manner, a higher export subsidy than otherwise would be optimal.

References

Alaouze, C. M., A. S. Watson, and N. H. Sturgess. 1978. Oligopoly pricing in the world wheat market. *American Journal of Agricultural Economics* 60:173–85.

Brander, J. A., and B. J. Spencer. 1984. Trade warfare: Tariffs and cartels. *Journal of International Economics* 16:227–42.

———. 1985. Export subsidies and international market share rivalry. *Journal of International Economics* 18:83–100.

Brown, D. K. 1986. Agriculture: The interests of the developing countries in in the next round of trade negotiations. Mimeo.

Carter, C., and A. Schmitz. 1979. Import tariffs and price formation in the world wheat market. *American Journal of Agricultural Economics* 61:517–22.

Caves, R. E. 1978. Organization, scale, and performance in the grain trade. *Food Research Institute Studies* 16:107–23.

Caves, R. E., and T. A. Pugel. 1982. New evidence on competition in the grain trade. *Food Research Institute Studies* 18:261–74.

Conklin, N. C. 1982. *An economic analysis of the pricing efficiency and market organization of the U.S. grain export system.* U.S. General Accounting Office, Staff Study GAO/CED-82-61S. Washington, D.C.

Cooper, R., and R. Riezman. 1986. Optimal trade policy with oligopoly. Mimeo.

Deardorff, A. V., and R. M. Stern. 1986. *The Michigan model of world production and trade.* Cambridge: MIT Press.

Dixit, A. K. 1984. International trade policy for oligopolistic industries. *Economic Journal* 94:1–16.

Eaton, J., and G. M. Grossman. 1986. Optimal trade and industrial policy under oligopoly. *Quarterly Journal of Economics* 101:383–406.

Gardner, B. 1986. International competition in agriculture. Mimeo.

Gilmore, R. 1982. *A poor harvest.* New York: Longman.

Hayes, D., and A. Schmitz. 1986. The price and welfare implications of current conflicts between the agricultural policies of the United States and the European community. Mimeo. National Bureau of Economic Research.

Hillman, J. S. 1978. *Nontariff agricultural trade barriers.* Lincoln: University of Nebraska Press.

Hoos, S. 1979. *Agricultural marketing boards: An international perspective.* Cambridge, Mass.: Ballinger.

International Wheat Council. Various issues. *International wheat statistics.* London.

Johnson, D. G. 1973. *World agriculture in disarray.* London: Trade Policy Research Center.

Johnson, P. R., T. Grennes, and M. Thursby. 1979. Trade models with differentiated products. *American Journal of Agricultural Economics* 61:120–27.

Just, R., A. Schmitz, and D. Zilberman. 1979. Price controls and optimal export policies under alternative market structures. *American Economic Review* 69:706–15.

Karp, L. S., and A. F. McCalla. 1983. Dynamic games and international trade: An application to the world corn market. *American Journal of Agricultural Economics* 65:641–56.

Kolstad, C. D., and A. E. Burris. 1986. Imperfectly competitive equilibria in international commodity markets. *American Journal of Agricultural Economics* 68:25–36.

Kostecki, M. M. 1982. State trading in agricultural products by the advanced countries. In M. M. Kostecki, ed., *State trading in international markets.* New York: St. Martin's Press.

Krugman, P. 1987. Strategic sectors and international competition. In R. M. Stern, ed., *U.S. trade policies in a changing world economy.* Cambridge: MIT Press.

McCalla, A. F. 1966. A duopoly model of world wheat pricing. *Journal of Farm Economics* 48:711–27.

McCalla, A. F., and T. E. Josling. 1981. *Imperfect markets in agricultural trade.* Montclair, N.J.: Allanheld, Osmun.

McCalla, A. F., and A. Schmitz. 1982. State trading in grain. In M. M. Kostecki, eds., *State Trading in International Markets.* New York: St. Martin's Press.

Markusen, J. R. 1984. The welfare and allocative effects of export taxes versus marketing boards. *Journal of Development Economics* 14:19–36.

Paarlberg, P. L., and P. C. Abbott. 1984. Towards a countervailing power theory of world wheat trade. In G. G. Storey, A. Schmitz, and A. H. Sarris, eds., *International Agricultural Trade.* London: Westview Press.

Salant, S. W. 1984. Export subsidies as instruments of economic and foreign policy. Rand Working Paper.

Sarris, A. H. 1986. EC-US agricultural trade confrontation. Mimeo.

Schmitz, A., and A. F. McCalla. 1979. The canadian wheat board. In S. Hoos, ed., *Agricultural marketing boards*. Cambridge, Mass.: Ballinger.

Schmitz, A., A. F. McCalla, D. O. Mitchell, and C. Carter. 1981. *Grain export cartels*. Cambridge, Mass.: Ballinger.

Taplin, J. H. E. 1969. Demand in the world wheat market and the export policies of the United States, Canada, and Australia. Ph.D. dissertation, Cornell University, Ithaca.

Thompson, S. R., and R. P. Dahl. 1979. *The economic performance of the U.S. grain exporting industry*. Minneapolis: University of Minnesota Bulletin.

U.S. Department of Agriculture. Economic Research Service. 1986. *Agricultural outlook*. October.

———. Various issues. *Wheat situation*.

———. Various issues. *Wheat situation and outlook*.

U.S. General Accounting Office. 1982. *Market structure and pricing efficiency of U.S. grain export system*. GAO/CED-82-61. Washington, D.C.

World Bank. 1986. *World development report 1986*. New York: Oxford University Press.

Comment   Kala Krishna

This chapter addresses an interesting question about optimal trade policy for agriculture. It focuses on the possible distortions that are created by having monopsonistic buyers, a situation that frequently arises in agriculture, when these buyers are also oligopolistic sellers in the world market. The chapter has two components, a theoretical part and an empirical part. I confine my comments to the theoretical part since my comparative advantage seems to lie in this direction.

The model of the chapter has four agents—the domestic and foreign sellers of the product and the two governments. Each firm sells at home and in a third market, and buys its product from competitive sellers. In addition, Thursby has the two governments setting three variables each—the consumption, production, and export subsidy/tax. Thus the firms have two variables each, the amount to sell at home and the amount to sell on the third market, and each government has three variables to set. The collection of first-order conditions looks formidable. However some clever manipulation yields results on overall optimal policy for the case where firms play a Cournot game and face linear demand and supply functions, and governments precommit to policies.

Kala Krishna is assistant professor of economics at Harvard University and a faculty research fellow of the National Bureau of Economic Research.

The chapter considers two kinds of firms—a monopsonist firm whose objective is to maximize its profits and a marketing board whose objective is to maximize the earnings of its suppliers. This is well worth doing since these are commonly found institutions in agricultural markets.

The chapter also considers the effects of having a regulated board that can only price at marginal cost at home, and of more firms, in sections 4.2 and 4.3. In section 4.2 the optimal policy, when the market is regulated and $c'^*y_x^*$ is small, is that of a subsidy on exports. In section 4.3 Thursby shows that if the number of home firms rises (above two) the optimal policy is to tax exports.

Although the results are suggestive, the weakest point of the chapter is that the results are derived for very special models, those of Cournot quantity-setting behavior with linear demand and supply functions. This approach does not cast enough light on the basic structure of the problem. For example, with a domestic monopsonist, there seem to be three basic roles for policy since welfare equals the sum of net profits of government and producers, consumer surplus and competitive producer's surplus. The first role for policy is to fix the strategic wedge à la Eaton and Grossman (1986) which might be called a strategic distortion. With a Cournot duopoly model this always calls for an export subsidy. The second role is to fix the consumption distortion due to monopoly power in the home market. This calls for a subsidy on domestic consumption as the monopolist sells too little in the home market. The third role is to fix the distortion due to the domestic producer's role as a monopsonist buyer. This causes too little to be produced by the competitive suppliers and creates a production distortion, calling for a production subsidy. However, since a production subsidy/tax is equivalent to an appropriate consumption tax/subsidy and export tax/subsidy combination, only the latter two need be set appropriately.

The first and third distortions call for an export subsidy, while the second for a consumption subsidy in the Cournot case with a home monopsonist. It is not clear that the export subsidy will be optimal if, for example, firms play a price game when the first distortion will call for a tax. Moreover, when there is a producer-surplus-maximizing marketing board, the production distortion would seem to vanish so that the case for an export subsidy would be further weakened. The regulated marketing board can also be similarly interpreted. In this case the consumption distortion would vanish due to regulation so that the case for a consumption subsidy would be weakened. However, the regulation would also affect other distortions as the home market gets linked by the regulation to the third market.

Finally, the result of section 4.3, where the number of firms grows, seems closely related to the existing literature. Having more firms at home creates an externality since each does not count the other's profits and so competition is excessive. A tax on exports is then called for.

It would definitely be worthwhile to pursue this line of research and see whether the results generalize as suggested here. It would, in particular, be desirable to find a targeting principle for oligopolistic markets analogous to the analysis developed by Bhagwati, Ramaswamy, and Srinivasan which has been widely applied in the traditional trade literature. It is to be hoped that such work will be forthcoming since this is such an important area, and especially since agriculture has been relatively free from GATT laws and is an item of some importance in the upcoming Uruguay Round.

References

Eaton, J., and G. M. Grossman. 1986. Optimal trade and industrial policy under oligopoly. *Quarterly Journal of Economics* 101:383–406.

5 Imperfect Competition, Scale Economies, and Trade Policy in Developing Countries

Dani Rodrik

To many policymakers in developing countries, the "new" trade theory, with its emphasis on imperfect competition and returns to scale, must appear as a vindication of sorts. For the recent literature has led to a considerable weakening of the traditional neoclassical presumption against policy intervention in foreign trade.[1] The journals are now filled with examples of governments "creating" comparative advantage by exploiting imperfections in markets for goods and technologies and increasing returns to scale. This new emphasis on the indeterminacy of comparative advantage contrasts starkly with the advice these policymakers have typically received regarding the necessity to specialize in unsophisticated, labor-intensive commodities. Indeed, by focusing on learning effects, the new literature has provided some of the best arguments for infant-industry protection since Alexander Hamilton and Friedrich List. The diehard import substituters may now legitimately wonder if the learning processes so important to the U.S. semiconductor industry (see Baldwin and Krugman 1986) are not equally relevant to a wide spectrum of basic industries in developing countries.[2]

As the last example illustrates, the new literature is also a frustrating reminder to the South that too often ideas become intellectually respectable only when they become congruent with the interests of major Northern countries. Hence it is more than a little ironic that the new trade theory has developed against the backdrop of trade conflicts among *developed* countries, and between the United States and Japan, in particular. Market imperfections of the sort analyzed in this context

Dani Rodrik is assistant professor of public policy at the John F. Kennedy School of Government, Harvard University.

109

would appear to be, if anything, more serious in the developing countries. Yet the new insights have still to penetrate the vast literature on trade policy in *developing* countries.[3] Anne Krueger's (1984) survey of the field, for example, found no applications to developing countries worthy of mention. The predominant approach to trade policy in developing countries remains based on intuition and insights deriving exclusively from models with perfect competition.

In practice, of course, the actual policy debates between import substituters and liberalizers have long been carried outside the confining framework of perfect competition. The import substituters remain suspicious of trade liberalization for reasons, not always well articulated, having to do with technological externalities and scale effects. They fear that resources will be reallocated away from the more modern, capital- and knowledge-intensive sectors with unexploited scale economies. The liberalizers, on the other hand, have long proceeded in syncretic fashion. In their role as academic economists, they typically build models in which perfectly competitive markets guide the allocation of resources along lines of comparative advantage. But in their role as policy advocates, they have been driven by the discouragingly small size of the Harberger triangles their models yield to fortify their arguments by appeal to the procompetitive and beneficial scale effects of more open trade regimes. Hence the great advantage of the new approach: it may bring theory and policy much closer than they have so far stood.

In truth, there are elements in the new theories of trade that give comfort to both camps. In the presence of imperfect competition and increasing returns to scale, trade liberalization is compatible both with a magnification of the welfare gains *and* with welfare losses. It all depends on how the economy is expected to adjust, which in turn depends on the frustrating ambiguities of oligopoly theory. At one extreme, we could imagine that free entry eliminates all excess profits and that liberalization rationalizes industry structure by reducing the number of firms and forcing the remaining ones down their average cost curves. In such a view of the world, the benefits of trade liberalization can easily amount to several times the usual Harberger triangles. Harris's (1984) calculations with such a model of Canada show that industry rationalization reduces manufacturing costs to such an extent that the net outcome is an *expansion* of the manufacturing sector— a sector in which Canada has prima facie a "comparative *dis*advantage." This kind of story suggests a wonderful way to sell trade liberalization to policymakers in developing countries: liberalization may actually help expand the modern sectors! But at the other extreme, we can imagine a world in which the contracting sectors tend to be those with supernormal profits and unexploited industrywide scale economies. The protectionists' fears may then well be justified.

My purpose in this chapter is to chisel away at some of these ambiguities. To do so I limit myself to a relatively narrow question: To what extent does the presence of increasing returns to scale and imperfect competition at home alter the received wisdom on the benefits of trade liberalization in developing countries? My focus is on *domestic* market structures only; I ignore imperfect competition in world markets and its consequences for trade strategies. Neither do I have much to say on product differentiation and consumers' taste for variety. Both of these omissions are serious ones. Developing countries frequently face highly oligopolistic structures in their import and export markets alike. And arguably a major source of benefit from trade liberalization in such countries is the greater availability of imported goods to consumers starved for variety. I have no excuse for these omissions but that of keeping the analysis manageable. I also ignore the possibility of dynamic learning-by-doing effects. Here, it is fair to say that the new literature has added little that is new to the concerns with temporary technological backwardness of the traditional infant-industry literature. The new aspects come into play with strategic interactions among firms, and these form the core of the present chapter.

The plan of the chapter is as follows. Section 5.1 reviews some of the salient aspects of market structure in developing countries, and argues that the concern with imperfect competition and scale economies is, if anything, more germane in developing-country contexts than in developed countries. Section 5.2 develops a general equilibrium framework in which the sources of potential gains/losses from partial trade liberalization can be assessed, and discusses their likely relative importance. Section 5.3 carries out partial-equilibrium numerical simulations for a number of industries (calibrated using Turkish data) to gauge the welfare implications of partial liberalization under alternative assumptions regarding the nature of oligopolistic interactions and the ease of entry/exit. Finally, section 5.4 provides a summary and concluding remarks.

5.1 Market Structure in Developing Countries

How important is imperfect competition in developing countries? Stylized facts and casual empiricism suggest that it is very important indeed. Outside peasant agriculture and some services, perfect competition—or any recognizable semblance thereof—is typically conspicuous by its absence. In a wide range of manufacturing sectors, a few firms tend to dominate and, one assumes, make liberal use of their market power. Of course, the same could be said for the developed countries as well. It appears, however, that imperfect competition is in fact more pervasive in the industrial sectors of the developing countries than of the developed ones.

The evidence at hand is necessarily sketchy. Aside from the usual problems with data availability, conceptual uncertainties abound regarding the appropriate measurement of monopoly power. But for our purposes a less discriminating approach will have to suffice. Table 5.1 contains some comparative figures on average concentration ratios in the industrial sectors of a number of countries. All six developing countries included turn out to have very high four-firm concentration ratios, ranging from an average of 50 percent in Chile (with a 41-sector breakdown) to 73 percent in Mexico (with a 73-industry breakdown). The table includes, for comparison, two developed countries—the United States and France. Significantly, all six developing countries have concentration ratios that exceed the relevant figure for the United States, even though the U.S. average has been calculated at a much greater level of disaggregation of industries and is therefore biased upward relative to those for the other countries. The numbers for France and Pakistan are the most directly comparable since their respective levels of disaggregation are similar: the ratio for Pakistan is more than twice as large as that for France (66 percent versus 28 percent).

To be sure, these concentration ratios ought to be taken with a grain of salt, since on their own they cannot tell us how collusive the behavioral outcomes in particular industries or countries are. The latter also depend on conjectures entertained by individual firms regarding their

Table 5.1   Comparison of Four-Firm Concentration Ratios in Industry

Country	Year	Unweighted Average of Four-Firm Concentration Ratios (%)	Number of Industries
Brazil	1972	72	68
Chile	1979	50	41
India	1968	55	22
Mexico	1972	73	73
Pakistan	1968	66	51
Turkey	1976	67	125
U.S.	1972	40	323
France	1969	28	48

Sources: For Brazil, India, Mexico, and Pakistan: from original sources cited in Leff 1979, table 1; for Chile: Melo and Urata 1986; for Turkey: calculated from Tekeli et al., n.d.; for the U.S.: Scherer 1980, 70; for France: Jacquemin and de Jong 1977, table 2.9.

rivals' actions and on the ease of entry and exit. Nonetheless, these numbers would seem broadly indicative of the extent of imperfect competition. There is by now ample evidence for the developing countries that concentration ratios are positively correlated with the measured level of profits. A survey by Kirkpatrick, Lee, and Nixson (1984, table 3.10) summarizes the findings of sixteen major studies on the concentration-profitability relationship in developing countries. Typically, measures of concentration are found to be a statistically significant determinant of "profitability"—measured as price-cost margins or rates of return on capital—once the appropriate controls are introduced.

Moreover, these concentration ratios probably *under*estimate the extent of market power enjoyed by leading oligopolists. This is so for a number of reasons. First, and most obvious, is the absence of serious antitrust policies in most developing countries. Even where antitrust legislation does exist, its implementation is rarely a serious bar to the actions of firms collusively inclined. Second, developing-country industrial policies have typically been biased toward restricting entry, as investment in many manufacturing sectors are subject to complex licensing and financing arrangements. Newcomers to preferred sectors often benefit from special incentive packages, of which latecomers are deprived. Third, the trade regimes tend to be highly protective—effectively eliminating foreign competition—with a bias toward quantitative restrictions rather than tariffs. As Bhagwati (1965) showed long ago, quotas are conducive to higher levels of price-cost margins domestically than are tariffs that generate an identical volume of imports. Fourth, in many developing countries industrial power is concentrated in the hands of minority ethnic groups, such as the Chinese in Southeast Asia and the Indians in East Africa. The common cultural background of these entrepreneurial groups may well facilitate collusion by providing easy reference to a shared set of norms and focal points, thus reducing the severity of the coordination problem. Fifth, the weakness of capital markets in developing countries means that investment funds are typically internally generated. This too acts as a barrier to entry by outsiders into sectors that are generating supernormal profits. Last but not least, the concentration ratios cited above are biased downward insofar as they do not take into account the predominance of conglomerates that span a large number of industrial, commercial, and financial activities (see Leff 1978). These groups have an anticompetitive effect in at least one respect: the close linkages between incumbent firms and their affiliated banks raise the entry costs to outsiders.

In this connection, two special institutional aspects of market structure in developing countries are particularly noteworthy. The first is that the leading oligopolists frequently coexist with a large fringe of small, competitive firms that are in a subordinate relationship to the former. The fringe is typically made up of suppliers and subcontractors whose manufacturing techniques exhibit constant returns to scale and tend to be labor intensive. Entry into this lower end of the industrial spectrum is relatively free. Several studies, surveyed by Kirkpatrick, Lee, and Nixson (1984, 49–52), provide evidence of the pervasiveness of this sort of dualism in the industrial sectors of the developing countries. Unlike the large firms, which are sheltered from economic misfortunes by their price-cost margins, these small-scale establishments are particularly sensitive to changes in their environment. Competition and relative ease of entry are prima facie evidence of their efficiency.[4] This coexistence of the large with the small has some interesting implications for trade policy, which I discuss briefly later on.

The second feature of importance is that many sectors in developing countries—automobiles, chemicals, energy, and so forth—are inhabited by a mixture of firms with different ownership structures. Public firms compete with private firms, and local firms exist side by side with subsidiaries of multinational corporations.[5] Ownership structure matters in industries that are competitive, but it matters even more in industries that are not. State-owned enterprises typically have objective functions which are a mess to contemplate and in which profitability plays at best a minor role. Their interaction with private firms in the same industries provides an interesting area of study in which the industrial-organization theorist has yet to enter. The behavioral response to trade liberalization in such contexts is anybody's guess. The presence of foreign-owned firms alongside domestic ones, on the other hand, introduces an opportunity for strategic trade policy with which to extract rents from the former. In fact, it could be argued that the performance requirements commonly imposed on the local subsidiaries of multinationals perform precisely this role.[6] In any case, the ultimate destination of excess profits—domestic or foreign—makes a difference in the formulation of desirable policies in the presence of imperfect competition.

This discussion indicates that indexes of concentration leave much to be desired as sufficient statistics for market structure and conduct in developing countries. Yet it also suggests that imperfect competition is important and ought be of concern whenever trade reform is contemplated. What the implications may be for trade liberalization is the subject of the next two sections of the chapter. I now turn briefly to scale economies.

There is practically no direct evidence on the importance of scale economies in specific industrial sectors of the developing countries. The available studies are exclusively for the developed countries (Pratten 1971; Scherer et al. 1975). For most manufacturing activities, these studies are probably indicative for the developing countries as well.

But some caution in extrapolation is warranted insofar as differences in relative factor prices lead to the choice of technologies with different scale characteristics. For concreteness, assume—not too unrealistically—that entrepreneurs treat labor costs as variable cost and capital costs as fixed cost. Then the extent of scale economies is determined completely by the choice regarding the capital intensity of the technique selected, itself presumably determined in part by labor costs relative to capital costs. This line of argument would imply that lower relative labor costs in developing countries tend to diminish the importance of scale economies. There is some evidence for this view. In her study of the automobile components industry in India, Krueger (1975, 68–69) reports that the manufacturers she interviewed did not believe larger scale of output would yield substantial cost savings; many thought that a switch in technology would be necessary before such savings would occur.

With this caveat in mind, what can we say about the importance of scale economies in developing-country markets? The fact that developing countries tend to have small internal markets, combined with the domestic orientation of much of industry, would argue for a significant role for scale economies as yet unexploited. The relatively high concentration rates cited above would go some way in the other direction, but probably not too far along. Conventional wisdom says that in a large number of manufacturing industries, too many firms have typically coexisted behind protective walls, official licensing policies to the contrary, at production levels far below minimum efficient scale. This is consistent with models in which a high level of profitability generated by trade protection leads to excessive entry, driving incumbents up their average cost curves (Horstmann and Markusen 1986). In addition, many government policies—such as the allocation of import licenses on the basis of production capacity—induce excess industrial capacity. At times, industrial policy in developing countries has explicitly promoted the establishment of industries that neither domestic market size nor export prospects quite warranted—the so-called white elephant syndrome.

Among horror stories, perhaps the best known center around the automobile industry. This is one industry in which scale economies are widely believed to be important. Estimates of minimum efficient scale in the industrialized countries vary, but most studies put it in the range of 200,000–300,000 cars (per annum) at the final assembly stage.[7] Even if we discount these numbers for the different circumstances in the developing countries—more labor-intensive techniques, fewer model changes, and so forth—average production runs in these countries are commonly inadequate to reap the full advantages of scale. This can be seen in table 5.2, which provides some evidence on production levels

Table 5.2   The Automobile Industry in Developing Countries

Country	Number of Firms[a]	Number of Basic Models[a]	Average Output per Model (per year)[b]
Argentina	4	6	20,357
Brazil	4	4	182,539
Chile	2	5	1,872
India	4	4	20,807
South Korea	3	3	70,494
Taiwan	6	6	19,783
Turkey	3	3	19,123
Venezuela	4	4	17,731

Source: Automobile International 1986.
Note: This survey excludes models with an output of less than 100 units in 1985.
[a]1985.
[b]1984–85 average for models produced in both years.

in selected developing countries. With the exception of Brazil and South Korea, the countries included have average production runs of around 20,000 (per annum) or below per model. This number can be put into perspective by considering that the average production level for the BMW—hardly one of the highest-volume cars—is larger than 400,000. From the economic standpoint, the question of interest is the magnitude of the cost savings forgone by low-volume production of this sort. The very high level of protection that has to be put in place in order to make these automotive industries financially profitable provides some indirect evidence of these costs.

5.2   A General Framework for Trade Policy Analysis

How do the features discussed in the previous section affect trade policy, and the case for trade liberalization in particular? The answer depends partly on how "structural" these features really are. Clearly, many aspects of market structure summarized above cannot be taken as data. These features will be affected by government policies, among which trade policies are often of key importance. As pointed out above, high levels of protection and reliance on quantitative restrictions have served to solidify oligopolistic structures in the manufacturing sectors of developing countries.[8] Often they have also stimulated inefficient levels of production.

But we should also be aware that the processes behind these market structures need not be neatly symmetric. In the real world, as opposed to our models, well-entrenched patterns of imperfect competition may be quite difficult to remove. An oligopoly engendered by trade protection will not necessarily go away when that protection is removed, especially if trade liberalization is only partial, as it is likely to be. The strength of the reverse linkage between liberalization and competition will depend on the extent of hysteresis of this sort. Here, I avoid these difficult questions and concentrate on relatively small changes in the trade regime. The endogenous changes in market structure likely to follow *partial* trade liberalization are easier to conceptualize and handle.

I proceed in two steps. The first question I ask is the extent to which the presence of these new features alters our conceptions about the desirable patterns of resource reallocation. The second question, analyzed in the next section, is the extent to which imperfect competition hampers, or facilitates as the case may be, these resource-pulls in the wake of trade liberalization.

To answer the first question, it is useful to start with a general formulation. Shunting income distribution issues aside, let the consumer side of our economy be represented by an expenditure function $E(p_1, p_2, \ldots, p_l, W)$, where p_i stands for domestic prices and W is an index of welfare. This function represents the minimum expenditure necessary to attain the level of welfare denoted by W, and its partial derivatives with respect to prices yield in usual fashion the compensated demand functions for the relevant good. Denoting consumption of good i as C_i, we have

$$(1) \qquad\qquad C_i = E_i(\cdot).$$

On the production side we let v_j denote the (fixed) supplies of productive factors and w_j their competitive levels of renumeration. For simplicity, each industry i is assumed to be made up of n_i *identical* firms,[9] with x_i and X_i denoting firm- and industry-level outputs, respectively, in that industry. By construction,

$$(2) \qquad\qquad n_i x_i = X_i$$

for each i. For the moment, we do not have to specify (1) whether n_i is fixed or determined by free entry, and (2) under what conditions of oligopolistic interaction, if any, x_i is determined.

Technological conditions are summarized by *unit* cost functions which we can write generally as $c_i(\mathbf{w}, x_i)$, with $\mathbf{w}$ standing for the vector of factor prices. The inclusion of x_i in $c_i(.)$ leaves open the possibility of increasing returns to scale, in which case $\partial c_i(.)/\partial x_i < 0$.[10] It is helpful to summarize the scale characteristics of technology in each sector by the variable θ_i, representing the ratio of average cost to marginal cost:

$$(3) \qquad\qquad \theta_i = c_i/[\partial(c_i x_i)/\partial x_i].$$

In industries with locally increasing returns to scale, $\theta_i > 1$. Factor markets are assumed to be perfectly competitive. By Shephard's lemma, factor demands per unit of output are given by the partial derivatives of $c_i(.)$ with respect to the relevant factor prices, so that

(4) $$v_j = \Sigma_i X_i [\partial c_i(\cdot)/\partial w_j], \quad \forall j.$$

This equation states that the sum of the sectoral demands for each factor equals its (fixed) supply. I assume full employment throughout.

The trade regime in place is protective, but the form of protection—tariffs or quotas or any combination—need not be specified as yet. Whatever the actual policies, protection will insert a wedge between world prices p^*_i and domestic prices p_i for commodities that are importables. Net imports are in turn given by the difference between consumption and production of each commodity:

(5) $$M_i = C_i - X_i, \quad \forall i.$$

For nontraded goods, $M_i = 0$. Since my focus is on domestic market imperfections only, I take world prices to be exogenous.

An initial equilibrium in this economy can be represented by making use of the equality between national expenditures and national income. Income here is made up of three components: (1) "pure" profits; (2) factor income; and (3) quota rents and/or tariff revenues. Therefore, we can write the income-expenditure equality (in domestic prices) as follows:[11]

(6) $$E(\cdot) = \Sigma_i [p_i - c_i(\cdot)] X_i + \Sigma_j w_j v_j + \Sigma_i (p_i - p_i^*) M_i.$$

The three terms on the right-hand side correspond to the components of income just mentioned. This framework is general in that it allows oligopoly and excess profits (in those sectors where p_i exceeds c_i), increasing return to scale, and diverse forms of protection. Intermediate goods are not taken into account explicitly, but they could by interpreting X_i in the first term on the right-hand side as "net" output. Similarly, foreign ownership can be incorporated into this framework by subtracting from the right-hand side payments to foreigners—both in the form of factor payments and as oligopoly profits that accrue to foreign firms.

Now consider a partial trade reform. What kind of resource reallocations are going to be welfare increasing? The answer can be obtained by taking the total differential of equation (6) around this initial equilibrium. After appropriate substitutions from equations (1) – (5), the exercise yields

(7)
$$E_w dW = \Sigma_i (p_i - p_i^*) dM_i + \Sigma_i (p_i - c_i) dX_i + \Sigma_i n_i c_i [1 - (1/\theta_i)] dx_i.$$
$$\quad\quad\quad\quad (a) \quad\quad\quad\quad\quad\quad (b) \quad\quad\quad\quad\quad (c)$$

This expression gives us the aggregate welfare effect of the general equilibrium changes induced by trade reform (or any other policy for that matter).[12] Since E_W is the inverse of the marginal utility of income, it simply translates the real-income effects on the right-hand side into welfare units. The three effects labeled (a), (b), and (c) each correspond to a particular source of market imperfection. The first of these is the familiar one that relates directly to trade protection: it states that it is desirable to expand imports of commodities that are protected (and conversely to expand exports of commodities subject to trade taxes). The welfare effect of such an expansion will be directly proportional to the magnitude of the protection-induced wedge between the relevant domestic and world price. For small changes, this is the usual source of gains from trade liberalization.

The second term relates to "excess" profits and is relevant in the case of industries in which barriers to entry shield incumbent oligopolists from effective competition. In these industries prices will exceed average costs of production, so $p_i - c_i > 0$. Notice that for trade liberalization to be welfare enhancing on this account, total output in such industries must *increase*. The reasoning is that ceteris paribus a reallocation of resources to sectors in which there are excess profits is desirable. This is a new desideratum, and in fact it creates some conflict with the above. Consider that import-competing sectors, for reasons discussed above, tend to be more oligopolistic than export-oriented ones. Then the effect labeled (a) tells us that the former ought to contract in order to make room for expanded imports, whereas (b) suggests quite the opposite. Which way the scale tips will naturally depend on the relative strength of the excess-profits versus protection-distortion effects. The question can be fully resolved only by empirical analysis.

Fortunately, it is possible to say a bit more. Ignoring (c) for the moment—which amounts to assuming that $c_i(.)$ stands also for *marginal* costs—the terms (a) and (b) can be combined to write equation (7) as

$$(8) \qquad E_W dW = \Sigma_i (p_i - p_i^*) dC_i - \Sigma_i (c_i - p_i^*) dX_i.$$

Hence, in the final analysis the desired output response depends on a comparison of domestic (marginal) costs of production with world prices. As long as domestic (marginal) costs are higher than border prices, it is welfare enhancing to reduce the output of import-competing sectors, *irrespective* of the magnitude of excess profits in those sectors.[13] Provided this condition on costs holds, the presence of imperfect competition per se does not alter the desirability of moving resources out of protected sectors.[14] However, it does affect the size of welfare gains from doing so: as expression (8) shows, the output effects are multiplied by $(c_i - p_i^*)$ rather than $(p_i - p_i^*)$ as in the usual analysis. For protected sectors that are imperfectly competitive, this *reduces* the welfare benefits of contraction by exactly the price-cost margin.

The intuitive explanation is as follows. Think of output in import-competing sectors being subject to two distortions. The first of these is due to trade protection, and its size depends on the margin between domestic and world prices. Taken on its own, this distortion would argue for a reduction in output. The second distortion is the monopoly one and is measured by the margin between domestic prices and costs. It would argue for an expansion of output. Now since both distortions are measured by a metric in the same space, it is conceptually straightforward to figure out which dominates. The answer depends on the relative sizes of c_i and p_i^*. Contraction of output in import-competing sectors remains desirable provided costs of production exceed border prices.

How likely is this condition to hold? In practice, highly protected sectors tend to be indeed high-cost ones. More or less direct evidence on this can be obtained by looking at data on effective rates of protection (ERP) and domestic resource costs (DRC) for specific industries in developing countries. In the presence of intermediate goods, these are the direct analogues of our $(p_i - p_i^*)$ and c_i, respectively. By and large these two indicators tend to be highly correlated with each other. Of course, in the absence of imperfect competition (and of factor-market distortions), the ERP and DRC would be linked by the relation DRC = ERP + 1. But the possibility of differential levels of excess profits across industries de-links the two measures. Table 5.3 presents some evidence of this sort for Turkey. Not surprisingly, the most heavily protected industries—chemicals, iron, and steel—turn out to be also the ones whose costs of production exceed world costs by a wide margin: by a factor of 7 in iron and steel, and by a factor of 35 in chemicals! The rank correlation between effective rates of protection and domestic resource costs for sixty-six subsectors is 0.77. Hence the strong presumption that a contraction of protected sectors will be welfare-enhancing, excess profits or not. The conventional analysis of comparative advantage is unlikely to go too wrong here.

Now return to equation (7). The last term (c) here captures the influence of possible scale effects. In industries with increasing returns to scale, the term in square brackets is going to be positive. For trade liberalization to be welfare increasing on this account, therefore, an expansion of average firm output will be called for. To put the same point differently, trade reform may prove harmful if it leads to a large enough contraction of firm size in industries with returns to scale. If such industries tend to be predominantly the protected ones, the stage is set for another potential conflict in objectives.

Table 5.3   **Structure of Protection and Costs in Turkish Manufacturing, 1981**

Sector	Effective Rate of Protection	Domestic Resource Costs
Food	0.19	1.29
Textiles	0.26	0.85
Leather products	0.62	1.47
Wood and paper products	1.25	3.17
Chemicals	−4.49[a]	35.39
Rubber and plastics	1.25	1.20
Cement and glass	−0.12	0.58
Iron and steel products	5.50	7.48
Nonferrous metals	1.10	1.91
Metal products	0.32	0.94
Machinery	0.67	1.01
Electrical machinery	0.41	0.87
Transport equipment	0.85	1.07
Measuring equipment	−0.19	0.44
Manufacturing total	0.81	1.82

Source: Yagci 1984, tables 4.1 and 5.5.
Note: Rank correlation coefficient between ERP and DRC for 66 subsectors is 0.77.
[a]Indicates negative value added at world prices.

What does the empirical evidence suggest? On a priori grounds, we would expect many sectors such as agriculture, clothing, and light manufactures that are generally the least protected in the developing countries to also rank low in terms of scale economies. Many consumer durables, which tend to be highly protected, have technologies with declining unit costs. Table 5.4 displays data on rates of protection (in Turkey) and scale characteristics (in developed countries) for a sample of industries. These industries were chosen on the basis of availability of information on scale economies and protection jointly, and while there may be some selection bias it is unclear which way it would go. The measure of scale economies used here is the ratio of minimum optimal scale to the size of the corresponding domestic market in the United States and, alternatively, in the EEC. As the discussion in the previous section indicated, the absolute level of these numbers may overstate the importance of scale effects in developing-country markets. Nonetheless, the relative standing of the industries included in table 5.4 would probably remain the same.

The evidence portrayed displays a clear correlation between the extent of scale economies and the level of protection. All the industries classified as low-scale economies have ERPs below 100 percent, among which three (plastic shoes, glass bottles, and cement) have negative

Table 5.4   Relationship between Economies of Scale and Protection

Industry	Minimum Optimal Scale		ERP in Turkey, 1981
	% of U.S. Demand, c. 1967	% of EEC Output, c. 1968	
Low-scale economies			
Shoes (nonrubber)	0.2		−0.52 (plastic)
			0.79 (leather)
Cotton and synthetic fibers	0.2		0.04 (cotton textiles)
Glass bottles	1.5		−0.22
Paints	1.4		0.55
Portland cement	1.7		−0.47 (all cement)
Medium-scale economies			
Auto tires	3.8		1.96
High-scale economies			
Nitrogenous fertilizers		6.0– 7.0	1.46 (all fertilizers)
Washing machines		10.0–11.0	1.19
Automobiles	11.0		2.18
Electric motors	15.0		1.24
Diesel engines	21.0–30.0		1.40

Sources: For economies of scale: Scherer 1980, tables 4.2 and 4.3; Jacquemin and de Jong 1977, table 2.3. For original sources, see the references therein. For ERP measures in Turkey, Yagci 1984, tables B.1 nd C.1.

ERPs. By contrast, all other industries with medium- or high-scale economies have ERPs that exceed 100 percent. This pattern of correlation presents an apparent conflict with the usual policy advice that the developing countries should liberalize their capital- and technology-intensive sectors.

To some extent, the conflict can be alleviated if domestic firms can respond by exporting, or if entry and exit are relatively free. In the case of free exit, a contraction of the protected sectors—as the trade distortion would dictate—would no longer conflict with an expansion of firm-level output in those same sectors, *provided* a sufficient number of firms left the industry. In fact, with industry rationalization of this sort, the benefits of trade reform can be magnified greatly (Harris 1984). I leave a discussion of the likelihood of this outcome to the next section. For the moment, let me underscore the conclusions that (*a*) an expansion of average firm output will be required in industries with important scale economies, and (*b*) many of these industries will be the highly protected ones that traditional comparative-advantage models have suggested ought to contract. In the absence of free exit, the requirement translates into an expansion of the entire industry, and here the conflict is the clearest. Notice that the conflict is also strengthened in the presence of additional scale effects external to firms but internal to the industries concerned. We would then have the additional term $-\Sigma_i X_i (\partial c_i / \partial X_i) dX_i$ on the right-hand side of equation (7), and the presumption that resources should move into protected sectors which also happen to possess unexploited scale opportunities would be stronger.

To conclude this discussion, excess profits per se do not alter much our notions about the desirable direction of resource movements in developing countries. Expansion of imports and contraction of protected sectors continue to remain as worthy objectives, even though the magnitude of gains may be reduced. Hence the presence of domestic oligopolies is not a good argument for why neoclassical prescriptions about comparative advantage ought not be taken seriously. Scale economies are a somewhat different matter. The desirability of expansion of firm output in industries with significant scale economies may clash seriously with the objective of pulling resources out of protected sectors. How important this conflict is in practice can be ascertained only by empirical analysis. A beginning on this is made in the next section.

5.3   The Consequences of Trade Liberalization: Some Simulations

So far the analysis has covered only part of the task set. We still have to worry about the following positive question: What are the resource allocation effects of trade reform under conditions of imperfect competition? In a decentralized economy the government does not have the ability to ensure that the desirable resource-pulls, as outlined above, actually materialize. The effects of policies are mediated through markets, and in our case, through imperfect ones. While the presence of oligopolies might not matter much for the ultimate objectives of trade policy, it may affect critically whether those objectives are attained or not. In other words, what are the signs of dX_i/dt, dx_i/dt, and so forth, where t stands generically for trade policy? Are these expressions "large" or "small"? How do they compare with their better-known counterparts under perfect competition?

It is impossible to provide definite answers to these questions at any acceptable level of theoretical generality. Even abstracting from the usual general equilibrium complications, the resource allocation effects of trade liberalization will depend on (1) the type of the trade restriction (tariff or quota), (2) the nature of oligopolistic interactions (the conjectural variation parameter), and (3) the ease of entry and exit. A recent paper by Buffie and Spiller (1986) analyzing this issue in a partial equilibrium framework shows that the range of theoretical possibilities is unbounded. Practically anything can be made to happen by rigging the model appropriately. Domestic output can increase or decrease, as can the domestic price.

Given that the search for theoretical generality is a dead end, an alternative is to carry out numerical simulations under assumptions that seem realistic and sensible. Then the sensitivity of the outcomes can be ascertained by altering key features. This is essentially the approach that has been taken in a number of recent papers by Dixit (1986), Baldwin and Krugman (1986), and Venables and Smith (1986) that analyze trade policy issues for the developed countries under conditions of imperfect competition. The calculations to follow are in the same spirit. Using Turkish data for three industries, I estimate the resource allocation and welfare effects of a partial liberalization of quota restrictions. For the purpose of this exercise, there is no harm in thinking of Turkey as a "typical" developing country, so that the conclusions will have broader applicability. Somewhat surprisingly, the simulations do yield some general conclusions, despite the multitude of scenarios about firm behavior and entry to be experimented with. Of course, a partial equilibrium approach has all the usual limitations, especially when it is used to shed light on across-the-board trade liberalization. But the simplicity of the framework has the advantage that the implications of alternative assumptions regarding technology, market structure, and conduct are easier to ascertain.

The simulations are based on a simple model of industry behavior. The industry is composed of n firms (assumed to be identical), each of which maximizes profits independently. The first-order conditions for the average firm yield a direct relationship among the price-cost margin, the market share, the conjectural variation parameter, and the market elasticity of demand:

(9) $$(p - c)/p = \eta[1 + v]\epsilon,$$

where η is the market share of each firm $(x/[nx + M])$, v is the firm's conjecture of the output response by the rest of the industry to a unit change in own output, and ϵ is the (positive) inverse elasticity of market demand. I assume that marginal costs (c) are constant. Increasing returns to scale are modeled by assuming a fixed cost of production. Notice that equation (9) is capable of generating a wide array of firm behavior, depending on the magnitude of the conjectural variation parameter v. This parameter will equal 0, -1, and $n - 1$, respectively, for Cournot, competitive, and perfectly collusive behavior.

To put flesh on equation (9), I have used a 1976 survey of the manufacturing industry in Turkey (Tekeli et al., n.d.) which provides data at a fairly disaggregated level on price-cost margins and the number of firms. These data have their share of problems. The price-cost margins, in particular, suffer from two shortcomings. First, they do not include a competitive rate of return on capital. Second, they do not reflect that part of supernormal profits appropriated by workers.[15] Since these two factors go in the opposite direction, I assume, for lack of any better procedure, that they offset each other. With data on $(p - c)/p$ and η at hand, equation (9) leaves us with one degree of freedom. We can either select a demand elasticity and then let v take up the slack between the two sides of the equation, or we can impose a particular conjecture and let the implied elasticity reveal itself. In the simulations to follow I have used both methods. For each industry, three sets of simulations are run. In the first of these, a "reasonable" elasticity of demand for the industry in question is selected. The remaining two assume a particular conjecture on the part of the firms: Cournot and fully collusive, respectively. In the fully collusive case, the conjectural variation parameter is adjusted endogenously when and if the number of firms changes; it remains fixed in the other two cases.

The industries selected are all protected by quantitative restrictions.[16] Domestic consumption equals domestic output (nx) plus the binding level of the quota (M). The consumers are parameterized by assuming a demand function with a constant elasticity, $1/\epsilon$. The inverse demand function is given by

$$(10) \qquad p = k(nx + M)^{-\epsilon},$$

where k is a scaling factor. For a given n, equations (9) and (10) jointly determine p and x as a function of the quota level, among other things. Therefore a no-entry equilibrium can be simulated by solving these two equations. With free entry, a third equation is needed to determine the equilibrium number of firms. This is given by the zero-profit condition. Under our technological assumptions, it can be written as

$$(11) \qquad (p - c)x = F,$$

where F is the fixed cost. In the simulations with free entry, the data on initial levels of the price-cost margin and output are taken to reveal F indirectly. A reduction in profits from one equilibrium to the next is then a signal for firms to exit until a pair of p and x can be found such that the incumbents make nonnegative profits. The integer constraint on the number of firms implies that a substantial level of profits is in fact compatible with free entry, as we shall see.[17]

Aggregate welfare in this framework is the sum of consumers' surplus, profits, and quota rents. Under our assumption of a constant elasticity demand curve, the utility function can be written as $U(C) = [1/(1 - \epsilon)]kC^{1-\epsilon}$, so that consumers' surplus is simply $[\epsilon/(1 - \epsilon)]pC$. Welfare is then given by

$$(12) \qquad \begin{aligned} W &= [\epsilon/(1 - \epsilon)]p(nx + M) \\ &\quad + n\,[(p - c)x - F] + (p - p^*)M. \end{aligned}$$

Data on the wedge between world and domestic prices are taken from Yagci (1984), who provides disaggregated estimates of implied nominal protection coefficients $([p - p^*]/p^*)$.[18]

I present in tables 5.5–5.7 the results of the simulations for three industries: automobiles, tires, and electrical appliances.[19] In each case, the policy experiment considered consists of a relaxation of the quota by an amount corresponding to 10 percent of the base level of consumption. The tables list the outcomes under three sets of assumptions regarding conjectures (or elasticities), and under two polar cases regarding entry.

The first column in each table assumes a demand elasticity of 1.50 for the industry concerned. The second column assumes instead Cournot conjectures and derives the implied market elasticity in the manner explained above. For all three industries, the results listed in these two columns are very similar. This suggests that, under the maintained hypothesis that the true market elasticity is close to 1.50, Cournot

Table 5.5   **Automobile Industry: Simulated Effects of Trade Liberalization**

	Nature of Conjectures		
	"Free"	Cournot	Collusive
Initial parameters			
Price-cost margin ($[p - c] / p$)	0.198	0.198	0.198
Number of firms (n)	3	3	3
Rate of protection ($[p - p^*] / p^*$)	0.63	0.63	0.63
Demand elasticity ($1 / \epsilon$)	1.50	1.40	4.21
Conjectural variation (v)	0.07	0	2.00
No-entry solution			
Change in price (%)	−2.6	−2.6	−2.2
Change in average firm output (%)	−7.2	−7.5	−0.2
Change in welfare (% of base consumption)			
Consumers' surplus	2.7	2.6	2.3
Profits	−3.2	−3.2	−1.9
Subtotal	−0.5	−0.6	0.4
Quota rents	3.2	3.2	3.3
Total	2.6	2.6	3.7
Free-entry solution			
Change in price (%)	7.1	7.2	−2.2
Change in average firm output (%)	14.5	15.3	49.7
Number of firms	2	2	2
Change in welfare (% of base consumption)			
Consumers' surplus	−6.7	−6.9	2.3
Profits	6.1	6.3	3.6
Subtotal	−0.6	−0.6	5.9
Quota rents	5.7	5.8	3.3
Total	5.1	5.2	9.2

Note: Trade liberalization consists of a relaxation of the quota by an amount equivalent to 10 percent of base consumption.

Table 5.6   **Tire Industry: Simulated Effects of Trade Liberalization**

	Nature of Conjectures		
	"Free"	Cournot	Collusive
Initial parameters			
Price-cost margin ($[p - c] / p$)	0.238	0.238	0.238
Number of firms (n)	4	4	4
Rate of protection ($[p - p^*] / p^*$)	0.29	0.29	0.29
Demand elasticity ($1 / \epsilon$)	1.50	1.05	4.20
Conjectural variation (v)	0.43	0	3.00
No-entry solution			
Change in price (%)	−2.9	−2.9	−2.7
Change in average firm output (%)	−5.6	−7.0	−2.2
Change in welfare (% of base consumption)			
Consumers' surplus	3.0	2.9	2.9
Profits	−4.0	−4.3	−2.2
Subtotal	−1.1	−1.4	0.6
Quota rents	2.0	2.0	2.0
Total	0.9	0.6	2.6
Free-entry solution			
Change in price (%)	6.2	6.3	−2.7
Change in average firm output (%)	8.5	11.7	36.2
Number of firms	3	3	3
Change in welfare (% of base consumption)			
Consumers' surplus	−5.9	−6.1	2.9
Profits	6.6	7.4	3.7
Subtotal	0.6	1.3	6.6
Quota rents	2.9	2.9	2.0
Total	3.5	4.1	8.6

Note: See table 5.5.

behavior is not a bad approximation to actual market conduct. The last column, on the other hand, assumes that firms act collusively so that they jointly produce no more than the monopoly level of output. This assumption is consistent with the observed price-cost margins only if the actual demand elasticity is considerably higher than 1.50. In fact, the implied elasticity turns out to be around 4 for autos and tires and 6 for electrical appliances. These are probably too high to take seriously, so there is reason to take the results of the collusive scenario with more than the usual grain of salt.

Irrespective of conjectures and in all three industries, free entry leads to better outcomes in terms of aggregate welfare than no entry. Indeed, trade liberalization turns out to be beneficial under all free-entry scenarios considered here. The main reason is that under free entry the output of the average firm rises as one firm, it turns out in each case, leaves the industry. With a fixed number of firms, by contrast, import

Table 5.7   **Electrical Appliances: Simulated Effects of Trade Liberalization**

	Nature of Conjectures		
	"Free"	Cournot	Collusive
Initial parameters			
Price-cost margin ($[p - c] / p$)	0.164	0.164	0.164
Number of firms (n)	8	8	8
Rate of protection ($[p - p^*] / p^*$)	0.10	0.10	0.10
Demand elasticity ($1 / \epsilon$)	1.50	0.76	6.10
Conjectural variation (v)	0.97	0	7.00
No-entry solution			
Change in price (%)	−1.9	−1.9	−1.7
Change in average firm output (%)	−7.1	−8.5	1.0
Change in welfare (% of base consumption)			
Consumers' surplus	1.9	1.9	1.8
Profits	−2.9	−3.1	−1.5
Subtotal	−1.0	−1.2	0.2
Quota rents	0.7	0.7	0.7
Total	−0.3	−0.5	1.0
Free-entry solution			
Change in price (%)	0.5	0.6	−1.7
Change in average firm output (%)	2.0	2.3	11.5
Number of firms	7	7	7
Change in welfare (% of base consumption)			
Consumers' surplus	−0.5	−0.6	1.8
Profits	0.7	0.9	0.5
Subtotal	0.2	0.3	2.3
Quota rents	1.0	1.0	0.7
Total	1.2	1.2	3.0

Note: See table 5.5.

liberalization translates into typically substantial reductions in average production levels. For reasons discussed earlier, the former outcome adds to the usual welfare gains while the second subtracts from them.

Still, except in the collusive case, the welfare gains under free entry are not significantly higher than what we would expect under perfect competition (see Harris 1984). Had perfect competition prevailed, the gains would approximately equal the increase in imports multiplied by the initial price wedge between domestic and world prices. In autos this amounts to $0.10 \times 0.63 = 6.3$ percent of base consumption, compared to the 5.2 percent calculated here under the Cournot assumption. The other two industries yield similar comparisons. Under the collusive scenario, the gains are indeed much higher: 9.2 percent in autos, for example. The explanation has to do with the much greater expansion of average firm output in this scenario. That in turn is the consequence of the higher demand elasticity implied by collusion: as long as there is some exit, the incumbents can expand considerably with minimal damage to their price-cost margins.

Notice that under free entry the domestic price *rises* in all three industries when conjectures are taken to be "free" or Cournot. This may seem counterintuitive, even though it is a theoretical possibility demonstrated by Buffie and Spiller (1986). In this case, the "perverse" effect is due to the integer constraint on the number of firms. Consider what happens as firms exit. Initially, with the number of firms unchanged, average firm output and price are both lower. This means that at least one firm has to leave the industry. At their existing output levels, the incumbents now make large profits as the price jumps up. The firms respond by increasing output, but with the kind of elasticities assumed here, the domestic price remains higher than its initial level. In the final equilibrium, the incumbents are making sizable profits, but entry is blocked by the fact that a discrete jump in the number of firms by one would yield losses for all. This explains why the free-entry simulations are all distributionally partial to producers as opposed to consumers. Domestic prices would fall eventually as the quantitative restrictions are relaxed further.

The aggregate welfare consequences of liberalization look much less appetizing when entry is blocked. In automobiles and tires, the net benefits tend to be small (under "free" and Cournot conjectures). In electrical appliances, liberalization actually results in some small welfare *losses* on the order of 0.3–0.5 percent of base consumption. It is easy to see why. The nominal protection rate in this industry is the lowest among the three considered here: 10 percent as compared to 63 percent in autos and 29 percent in tires. Hence we expect the gains on conventional grounds to be small in the first place. In addition, the industry's price-cost margin of 0.164—while lowest among all three— implies that its costs of production are well below border prices. In this context, the factors discussed in the previous section come into play in full force. By contrast, the much higher level of protection in the other two industries dominates quantitatively the effects of imperfect competition.

Notice also that in autos and tires what turns the welfare effects positive are the substantial quota rents that accrue postliberalization. These changes in quota rents are positive and substantial because the quotas in the industries selected are excessively restrictive prior to liberalization. This introduces an important caveat to the calculations presented here insofar as rent seeking may dissipate some or all of these gains. For that reason, tables 5.5–5.7 include a subtotal in the welfare calculations which leaves out quota rents. By this measure, liberalization leads to losses in all three industries in the absence of free entry (as well as in autos under free entry).

What general conclusions can be drawn from these simulations? First, the potential for perverse welfare effects appears to be a serious one only when entry and exit are problematic. But, paradoxically, even when exit is free, the primary beneficiaries of trade liberalization can turn out to be the import-competing firms rather than the consumers. Moreover, the availability of gains in the aggregate depends on the government's ability to dispose of quota rents in a manner that does not lead to wasteful rent-seeking activities. Finally, even when entry is not free, liberalization is unlikely to prove welfare worsening in industries where the nominal protection rates exceed, say, 25 percent. If this last conclusion can find support in more general models than I have considered here, it would be an important one indeed. Much of manufacturing in developing countries is protected at levels that far exceed this. The analysis would then provide license for substantial amounts of trade liberalization, with little fear from imperfect competition.

The results also show that the ease of entry/exit is likely to be a more important determinant of outcomes than market conduct as captured by the conjectural variations parameter. This requires that we form some opinion on the likelihood of industry rationalization via market forces. I do not know of any systematic empirical evidence that would help settle this issue. Obviously, in the longest of runs everything is flexible. The question of interest is the extent to which firms are able to move frictionlessly in and out of industries within the relevant time horizon.

In one important respect, the free-entry case almost certainly overstates the ease of exit from affected industries. Taken literally, this scenario implies that whole factories are dismantled, sold piecemeal at full economic value in perfect markets, and ultimately used to enhance the productive capacity of expanding firms in the same sector or in others. While the presence of multiproduct firms will generally help in easing the transition, the costs of bankruptcy and idle capacity are likely to be substantial in developing countries. Formally, this can be modeled by assuming that exiting firms continue to pay a portion of their fixed costs, $(1-\delta)F$. The parameter δ can be interpreted as the resale value of the fixed capital stock as a proportion of its current value. The free-entry simulations above assume that $\delta = 1$, that is, that exiting entrepreneurs can capture the *full* value of their fixed investment in secondary markets. More generally, δ will lie between zero and one. This affects both the exit decisions of firms and the ultimate welfare effects. Now firms will exit when profits fall below the (positive) cost of going out of business, that is, when

(13) $$(p - c)x - F < -(1 - \delta)F,$$

or when

(14) $$(p - c)x - \delta F < 0.$$

This reduces the likelihood of exit as some firms will prefer to run losses rather than incurring the costs of exit.[20] Also, for any given amount of industry rationalization (via exit), social welfare benefits are reduced by $(1 - \delta)F$ times the number of exiting firms. Hence, when exit is costly in this manner, the magnitude of gains from trade liberalization will lie in between the no-entry and free-entry cases above.[21]

Empirically, arguments about the ease of exit could be made either way. For example, the automobile industry of Latin America during the early 1960s provides a case with great fluidity: in Argentina, the number of automakers was reduced from 21 to 13 in no more than four years (1960–64); in Chile, the number went from 20 to 14 within a year (1962–63), jumped to 18 in 1964, and then plunged to 10 in 1966 (Jenkins 1977, 146–48). The skeptic would point out that once these industries became well established, the numbers stayed more or less constant. That was the case for both Mexico and Argentina, whereas in Chile some degree of "rationalization" took place only under the heavy prodding of governments. A study on India by Ghosh (1975) finds considerable amount of entry in new and expanding industries, but very little exit in the traditional sectors. A recent study on Chile by de Melo and Urata (1986) reports substantial exit subsequent to trade liberalization.

Indirect evidence on the prevalence of entry barriers is obtained from the studies already mentioned which document a close positive relationship between concentration ratios and profitability. In the absence of barriers to entry, it would be difficult to provide a rationale for this finding. To be sure, there are few barriers in the informal sectors where capital requirements tend to be small and technology is widely available. But the relative ease of entry and exit in such sectors may present its own problems. The common view seems to be that production in these informal activities is organized efficiently and much more in line with the developing countries' underlying comparative advantage in labor-intensive commodities than in some of the imperfectly competitive sectors. Then, to the extent that oligopolistic firms can pass their troubles on to these small-scale producers, which often act as suppliers or ancillary producers, the resulting mix of exit may be biased against the latter. Very little will be gained from such exit if the informal sector is in fact competitive and efficient.

Finally, notice that protection in the form of quota restrictions acts as a facilitating device for collusion on the part of home firms. In all three industries analyzed here, firms would be forced to resort to marginal cost pricing were the quotas to be transformed into tariffs. This is an important argument for utilizing tariffs in lieu of quotas. But tariffs do not make the problem of imperfect competition go away entirely. First, in industries with substantial scale economies, marginal cost pricing will prove impossible, and the consequent elimination of the home industry may result in welfare losses. Second, even in the absence of declining costs, domestic producers will retain market power as long as imports are an imperfect substitute for their output.

5.4 Concluding Remarks

My purpose in this chapter was to evaluate the received wisdom on the benefits of trade liberalization in developing countries in the presence of imperfect market structures typically prevailing in such contexts. Once imperfect competition enters the picture, any argument one way or the other is naturally subject to all sorts of qualifications. But if one conclusion can be drawn from the analysis it is the following: the levels of protection observed in the manufacturing sectors of most developing countries vastly exceed any that could be justified by the presence of imperfect competition. The case for partial trade liberalization stands up well against the new features considered here.

This though should provide little comfort to those who would analyze trade policy in developing countries in models—or mind-sets—of perfect competition. Oligopolistic markets create new conditions which the policymaker would ignore at his own peril. First, actual welfare gains may obtain under patterns of resource allocation quite different from those anticipated on the basis of intuition deriving from the competitive paradigm. For example, the expansion of certain import-competing sectors may be interpreted as perverse and hence be resisted, whereas it is the source of efficiency benefits. Second, certain sectors with strong scale economies and/or large price-cost margins may still present problems against the background of overall gains. A trade reform package sensitive to this asymmetry will likely prove more successful than one that is not. Finally, the *distributional* consequences of liberalization may diverge considerably from the anticipated pattern, and policymakers who are oblivious to this will be in for some unwelcome surprises. Some of the simulations above revealed, for example, that liberalization may benefit the producers in the protected sector rather than consumers. Also, the nature of industrial dualism discussed above suggests that, to the extent the labor-intensive informal sectors are more sensitive to their economic environment than are the oligopolistic sectors, the distribution of gains along factor lines may prove to be much less favorable to labor than anticipated.

There is something paradoxical about these kinds of considerations. As suggested above, imperfect market structures are frequently the direct consequence of the trade and industrial policies followed by governments in the first place. From this perspective, import substitution policies look doubly bad. Not only do they lead to the usual static inefficiencies, but they also create market structures that, unless quick to evaporate, render the future liberalization of the trade regime more problematic. This raises the possibility that in certain sectors the initial protection and its eventual removal may both prove harmful. Fortunately for the economies concerned, the analysis in this chapter suggests that this paradoxical outcome is unlikely to be the case for more than a few industries.

Appendix

This appendix describes in greater detail the data used in the simulations of section 5.3 and some of the procedures followed.

For the tire and electrical appliances industries, data on price-cost margins, sales, and number of firms were taken from the 1976 survey of Tekeli et al. (n.d.). Since some of the firms included were very small compared to others, I have confined the analysis to the large, oligopolistic part of the industry. The four firms (out of eight) in the tire industry that I consider constitute 96.8 percent of total output. In the electrical appliances industry, eight firms (out of eighteen) constitute 91.5 percent of total output. Since the price-cost margins given in Tekeli et al. are average ones, we might conclude that there is a small downward bias in my use of these numbers for the restricted set of firms. I have been unable to find directly relevant information on quantitative restrictions in these sectors. Prior to the reform of the 1980s, the trade regime was extremely restrictive in both sectors, so I have taken quotas that are completely prohibitive (i.e., no imports) to characterize the base level of protection in each case. The resulting nominal protection coefficients (i.e., the margin between domestic and world prices) are taken from Yagci (1984), which covers the same industries but a smaller sample of firms for 1981. In the simulations, the domestic price is initially taken to be 100, with the demand equation scaled appropriately so as to yield the observed level of domestic sales. The world price p^* and the domestic (marginal) cost can then be calculated with the information at hand.

The same procedures were followed for the automobile industry, with some small changes. Tekeli et al. provide information only on a more aggregate category of "motorized vehicles." I have taken the price-cost margin for this sector to apply to autos as well. Sales figures are the average for 1980–81, taken from *Cumhuriyet* (November 12, 1986, 9). The quota has been taken to equal the average volume of imports during the same two years (data are from International Road Federation 1985). This assumes that the volume of imports allowed in 1976, as a proportion of total consumption, was the same as in 1980–81.

Notes

I am grateful to Diana Edge for research assistance and to the Japanese Corporate Associates Program of the John F. Kennedy School of Government for partial financial support. I thank Robert Baldwin, Chip Bowen, Ed Buffie, Alan Deardorff, Shanta Devarajan, Avinash Dixit, Jaime de Melo, Dwight Perkins, Ray Vernon, and Beth Yarbrough for their helpful comments.

1. For surveys, see Dixit 1984, Grossman and Richardson 1985, Helpman and Krugman 1985, and Venables 1985.

2. Krugman argues that the small size of markets in developing countries diminishes the importance of the "privileged access of domestic firms to the home market . . . [as a] significant strategic asset" (1986, 25). Helleiner replies that the potential for product differentiation, as well as the apparent successful case of Korea, suggests that small markets are not a disadvantage in this respect (1986, 9).

3. Some surveys oriented toward the developing countries have begun to appear, however. See Helleiner 1985, Krugman 1986, and Srinivasan 1986. Krugman suggests that developing countries have not yet received enough attention because "advanced-country issues have temporarily preempted the limited supply of economists working on these issues" (1986, 3).

4. See, however, Little 1987 for a more nuanced argument.

5. For summary data on the importance of state ownership in manufacturing in a number of developing countries, see Dervis and Page 1984, table 2, and Kirkpatrick, Lee, and Nixson 1984, table 3.4. For data on the importance of foreign ownership, see Kirkpatrick, Lee, and Nixson 1984, table 3.2. Evans 1979 provides a stimulating sociological account of the interactions of local, state, and foreign capital in Brazil.

6. This argument is made in Rodrik 1987. On performance requirements generally, see Guisinger 1985.

7. See the summary of the evidence in Owen 1983, table 4.12.

8. See Katrak 1980 for a study on India which shows that, after controlling for capital intensity and concentration levels, protection tends to increase price-cost margins, while import penetration has the opposite effect.

9. This is to simplify the notation only; the model can be easily generalized to encompass asymmetries in firm size.

10. Returns to scale that are *external* to firms but internal to the industry can be handled by inserting X_i in these unit cost functions. I return to this type of scale economies at the end.

11. To keep things simple, I assume that tariff revenue or quota rents are distributed in lump-sum fashion, with no additional distortions thereby engendered.

12. Notice that the terms (b) and (c) can be combined and expressed equivalently as a function of the difference between price and marginal cost and of the number of firms: $\Sigma_i(p_i - MC_i)dX_i + \Sigma_i c_i x_i[(1/\theta_i) - 1] dn_i$.

13. Eldor and Levin 1986 makes a similar point in the context of partial equilibrium models of monopoly and Cournot oligopoly.

14. Notice that in practice this comparison between domestic costs and world prices has to be undertaken using the "equilibrium" exchange rate. To the extent that the current exchange rate is overvalued (because of either preexisting protection or fixed exchange rates), it biases domestic costs (relative to world prices) upward. Many industries not "competitive" in this sense may become so after liberalization.

15. For an empirical examination of this issue in the Turkish context, see Çagatay 1986.

16. The features of the trade regime discussed here are meant to apply to the Turkish economy of the 1970s (as well as to a large number of other developing countries presently). In Turkey, trade liberalization during the 1980s has eliminated the great majority of quotas.

17. I assume, however, that the initial equilibrium is one with zero profits. Otherwise, a reduction in profits need not necessarily require exit.

18. For more information on the data, see the appendix.

19. The simulations were carried out for a larger sample of industries. But unlike the industries that it purports to study, the present approach is one with rapidly decreasing returns to scale, at least with the data at hand. The simulation results presented here are representative of the rest.

20. How these losses are financed is an important matter in practice. In developing countries, as well as in developed ones, bailouts by commercial banks (perhaps affiliated with the firms) or by the state are not uncommon. Where economic rationality prevails, such rescue efforts can be seen as a means of averting the costs of bankruptcy.

21. Since firms do not exit unless it is profitable to do so, welfare gains under this scenario can not lie below the no-entry case.

References

Automobile International. 1986. *World automotive market.* New York: Johnston International Publishers.

Baldwin, Richard, and Paul Krugman. 1986. Market access and international competition. NBER Working Paper No. 1936.

Bhagwati, Jagdish. 1965. On the equivalence of tariffs and quotas. In Robert E. Baldwin, ed., *Trade, growth, and the balance of payments.* Chicago: Rand McNally.

Buffie, Edward F., and Pablo T. Spiller. 1986. Trade liberalization in oligopolistic industries: The quota case. *Journal of International Economics* 20: 65–81.

Çagatay, Fatma Nilufer. 1986. The interindustry structure of wages and markups in Turkish manufacturing. Ph.D. dissertation, Stanford University.

Dervis, Kemal, and John M. Page, Jr. 1984. Industrial policy in developing countries. *Journal of Comparative Economics* 8: 436–51.

Dixit, Avinash K. 1984. International trade policy for oligopolistic industries. *Economic Journal* (supplement), 1–16.

———. 1986. Optimal trade and industrial policies for the U.S. automobile industry. Mimeo.

Eldor, Rafael, and Dan Levin. 1986. Trade liberalization and imperfect competition: A welfare analysis. Mimeo.

Evans, Peter. 1979. *Dependent development: The alliance of multinational, state, and local capital in Brazil.* Princeton: Princeton University Press.

Ghosh, A. 1975. Concentration and growth of Indian industries, 1948–68. *Journal of Industrial Economics* 23: 203–22.

Grossman, Gene M., and J. David Richardson. 1985. *Strategic trade policy: A survey of issues and early analysis.* Special Papers in International Economics No. 15. NJ: Princeton University Press.

Guisinger, Stephen, and Associates. 1985. *Investment incentives and performance requirements.* New York: Praeger.

Harris, Richard. 1984. Applied general equilibrium analysis of small open economies with scale economies and imperfect competition. *American Economic Review* 74: 1016–33.

Helleiner, G. K. 1985. Industrial organization, trade and investment: A selective literature review for developing countries. Mimeo.

———. 1986. Comments on Paul Krugman paper. Mimeo.

Helpman, Elhanan, and Paul Krugman. 1985. *Market structure and foreign trade.* Cambridge: MIT Press.

Horstmann, I., and J. R. Markusen. 1986. Up the average cost curve: Inefficient entry and the new protectionism. *Journal of International Economics* 20: 225–48.

International Road Federation. 1985. *World road statistics 1980–1984.* Geneva: International Road Federation.

Jacquemin, Alexis, and Henry W. de Jong. 1977. *European industrial organization.* New York: John Wiley.

Jenkins, Rhys Owen. 1977. *Dependent industrialization in Latin America: The automotive industry in Argentina, Chile, and Mexico.* New York: Praeger.

Katrak, H. 1980. Industrial structure, foreign trade and price-cost margins in Indian manufacturing industries. *Journal of Development Studies* 17: 62–79.

Kirkpatrick, C. H., N. Lee, and F. I. Nixson. 1984. *Industrial structure and policy in less developed countries.* London: George Allen and Unwin.

Krueger, Anne. 1975. *The benefits and costs of import substitution in India: A microeconomic study.* Minneapolis: University of Minnesota Press.

———. 1984. Trade policies in developing countries. In R. W. Jones and P. B. Kenen, eds., *Handbook of international economics,* vol. 1. Amsterdam: North-Holland.

Krugman, Paul. 1986. New trade theory and the less-developed countries. Mimeo.

Leff, N. H. 1978. Industrial organization and entrepreneurship in the developing countries: The economic groups. *Economic Development and Cultural Change* 26: 661–75.

———. 1979. Monopoly capitalism and public policy in developing countries. *Kyklos* 32: 718–38.

Little, I. M. D. 1987. Small manufacturing enterprises in developing countries. *World Bank Economic Review* 1: 203–35.

Melo, Jaime de, and Shujiro Urata. 1986. The influence of increased foreign competition on industrial concentration and profitability. *International Journal of Industrial Organization* 4: 287–304.

Owen, Nicholas. 1983. *Economies of scale, competitiveness, and trade patterns within the European community.* Oxford: Clarendon Press.

Pratten, C. F. 1971. *Economies of scale in manufacturing industry.* Cambridge University Press.

Rodrik, Dani. 1987. The economics of export-performance requirements. *Quarterly Journal of Economics* 102: 633–50.

Scherer, F. M. 1980. *Industrial market structure and economic performance.* 2d ed. Boston: Houghton-Mifflin.

Scherer, F. M., Alan Beckenstein, Erich Kaufer, and R. Dennis Murphy. 1975. *The economics of multi-plant operation,* Cambridge: Harvard University Press.

Srinivasan, T. N. 1986. Recent theories of imperfect competition and international trade: Any implications for development strategy?" Mimeo.

Tekeli, Ilhan, Selim Ilkin, Ataman Aksoy, and Yakup Kepenek. N.d. *Türkiye' de sanayi kesiminde yoğunlaşma* (Concentration in the manufacturing industry in Turkey) Middle East Technical University, Ankara, Turkey.

Venables, Anthony J. 1985. International trade, trade and industrial policy and imperfect competition: A survey. Center for Economic Policy Research, Discussion Paper No. 74.

Venables, Anthony J., and Alasdair Smith. 1986. Trade and industrial policy under imperfect competition. *Economic Policy: A European Forum,* no. 3.

Yagci, Fahrettin. 1984. Protection and incentives in Turkish manufacturing. World Bank Staff Working Paper No. 660.

Comment   Harry P. Bowen

This chapter analyses the effect of trade liberalization on national welfare under the assumption that domestic markets are imperfectly competitive and that production is subject to economies of scale (EOS). At issue is whether the presence of imperfect markets and EOS imply that the resource reallocations attendant to liberalization could run counter to national interest. A general answer to this question is provided by performing a comparative statics analysis of a change in protection in the context of a general equilibrium model. It is shown that a change in welfare can be decomposed into three components: the usual protection component given by the difference between internal and external prices; an "excess profits" component reflecting imperfect

Harry P. Bowen is assistant professor of economics and international business at the Graduate School of Business, New York University, and a faculty research fellow and Olin Fellow, National Bureau of Economic Research.

competition and given by the difference between price and average cost; and finally a component reflecting economies of scale which depends, among other things, on the level of average firm output. Examination of these components indicates that while the traditional protection component requires output of protected sectors to decrease, the imperfect market and EOS components require an increase in output. Hence, liberalization could decrease welfare if protected sectors are imperfectly competitive and subject to EOS.

Since the presence of imperfectly competitive markets and EOS requires resource movements opposite those of the traditional protection component, the question is then the extent to which these factors are important characteristics of the restricted sectors in developing countries. Using data on Turkey, evidence on the extent of imperfect competition is presented in the form of four-firm concentration ratios and effective rates of protection. Leaving aside the debate over concentration ratios as indicators of market power, the comparison shows a positive correlation between concentration and rate of protection. Likewise, a comparison of minimum efficient scale and the rate of protection also indicates a positive correlation between protection and the extent of scale economies.

Having set the stage for potential conflicts in resource movements, the chapter then presents partial equilibrium simulations of the effects of a partial removal of a quota under alternative assumptions about the nature of oligopolistic interaction and the ease of entry and exit. Overall, the results indicate positive net gains in welfare. However, what is interesting about these simulations is not the net effect on welfare but rather the insight they provide about the distributional effects of liberalization. In particular, the presence of imperfect markets and EOS suggests gains and losses that are usually opposite those suggested by the competitive model, namely, consumers lose while producers gain. Equally interesting, if not also disturbing, is that in many cases the net change in consumer-plus-producer surplus is actually negative so that the net increase in national welfare is due almost entirely to an increase in quota rents. As the chapter notes, the crucial contribution of quota rents to the net increase in welfare is particularly disturbing since one could imagine that these gains could easily be dissipated by rent-seeking activity.

As the above remarks suggest, I think the insight concerning the distributional effects of liberalization under conditions of economies of scale and imperfect markets is one of the major contributions of this chapter. As Rodrik notes, the possibility that distributional effects may run counter to those expected on the basis of the competitive model alerts policymakers to the need to exercise caution in blocking apparently undesirable income effects. Moreover, it underscores that liberalization policies would need to address the potentially damaging effects of rent-seeking activity. In this context, the analysis also raises an issue particularly germane to developing countries. Since a large fraction of import-competing firms in developing countries are foreign-owned, attention needs to be given to the possibility that the welfare gains of producers could be siphoned off through repatriation of profits. This latter possibility suggests that a study of ownership structure in developing countries may show that it has importance over and above its role in shaping oligopolistic behavior.

Although admittedly I am enthusiastic about the distributional effects uncovered by the chapter, there are some troubling aspects of the analysis. First, and as the author admits, the data on price-cost margins do not include returns to capital which we might presume to be higher in developing countries. While this is unlikely to change the conclusion about distributional effects, it does suggest caution in accepting both the magnitude and the sign of the overall welfare effect. Second, the simulations, while admittedly a first pass, are nonetheless partial and not general equilibrium. In consequence, the simulations are potentially misleading about the overall effect of trade liberalization since other sectors of the economy may be subject to greater degrees of imperfect competition and EOS than are the protected sectors. The partial equilibrium analysis also ignores the potentially large benefit on the consumption side that would result from world price declines. Note that international price effects become particularly relevant under conditions of imperfect competition and EOS since such effects act to offset the negative distributional effect on consumers.

Another issue is that admitting EOS into the analysis leads us into the realm of nonconvex economies and the domain of second-best calculations. In this context, the issue of local versus global optima raises concern about the appropriateness of marginal analysis and thus the extent to which conclusions would be altered if a discrete change, as would occur under actual liberalization, were considered. In this regard, it would have been interesting if the author had also examined the case of complete elimination of the quota. Not only would this exercise have been in line with the numerous analyses of liberalization under conditions of perfect competition, but one could imagine that a discrete change would lead to entirely different conclusions about the distributional effects of liberalization. For example, under complete removal, quota rents would necessarily disappear and we might expect industry rationalization to result in at most one firm. The welfare effect of such extreme rationalization would be similar to that found for the collusive case considered in the chapter in which both producers and consumers gain. Of course, the reason for joint gains is that industry rationalization leads to a reduction in domestic price since the mode of oligopolistic interaction is closest to the ideal situation under EOS, namely, a single firm. Note that the potential for joint gains from such extreme rationalization further underscores the need to consider the effect of international price declines. For example, one could imagine the even more extreme case in which domestic production ceases altogether and domestic consumption is entirely satisfied by imports produced by a single "superfirm" which reaps scale advantages commensurate with the size of the world market.

Notwithstanding the above remarks, the analysis in the chapter points to the possibility of net welfare losses from liberalization. But does the apparent prevalence of imperfectly competitive markets in developing countries together with the existence of EOS then suggest that attempts to argue for liberalization may be futile? Stated differently, is the bewildering pattern of potential resource effects so confusing as to make the validity of arguing for liberalization rest on the computation of a detailed general equilibrium model? I think the answer is no, and the basis for this belief comes directly from the analysis presented.

As stated earlier, the chapter decomposes a welfare change into three components: protection, excess profits, and EOS. But, as the author states in a footnote, the latter two components can actually be combined into one component: the difference between world price and domestic marginal costs. This implies that a welfare increase is associated with output decreases in sectors where domestic marginal costs exceed world price, regardless of the extent of excess profits or EOS. This simple statement of desired resource reallocations is reassuring since it coincides with what we are accustomed to arguing on the basis of the standard competitive model—that is, that resource movements should be guided by opportunity costs, and in particular, that the relevant comparison is between domestic and international opportunity costs.

The above remarks indicate that one need only assume that an economy's protected sectors have marginal costs in excess of world prices in order to argue that trade liberalization would imply an increase in welfare. Since under normal circumstances the "need" for protection was precisely because domestic costs exceeded international prices, it would appear safe to assume that liberalization would necessarily lead to the "right" resource reallocations. Sadly, a qualification to this happy state of affairs seems warranted in the case of the developing countries, where rent-seeking activity is widespread. That is, protection may have been granted to shelter excess returns and not to compensate for differences in domestic costs and international prices. Only further study can resolve this issue.

In summary, Dani Rodrik has examined a set of provocative questions about the effects of liberalization, particularly when considered in the context of developing countries. While the model is admittedly restrictive in its scope, the finding of contrary distributional effects underscores the need to explore further the implications of imperfect markets and alternative production structures for traditional policy prescriptions.

Comment   Beth V. Yarbrough

This chapter attempts to address a very important question: What are the implications of the "new" developments in trade theory for the trade policies of developing countries? The question is particularly timely as the early stages of the Uruguay Round of GATT may well determine the degree of involvement of the developing countries in the current liberalization efforts.

One of the things I like most about the chapter is its political savvy and insight. It admits up front that the "new" learning will be used by policymakers as a justification for the import substitution policies they have always followed, a fact that makes this conference—and the work it is meant to encourage—particularly important. Policymakers who have ignored economists' policy recommendations for decades may suddenly begin to use economic justifications for their policies. I sense that we all feel a little uneasy about this; in fact, I think there is almost a tendency to want to have some of the work "classified" as "for economists' eyes only" until we have time to assess the full implications.

In chapter 5 Rodrik asks, "To what extent does the presence of increasing returns to scale and imperfect competition at home alter the received wisdom on the benefits of trade liberalization in developing countries?" He argues that imperfect competition is probably more prevalent in developing than in developed countries. The evidence he uses to support his argument is that four-firm concentration ratios are higher and that there is a positive correlation between concentration and profits. He also argues that economies of scale may be an important consideration even though the labor abundance of many developing countries can lead to the choice of less capital-intensive production technologies, generally less subject to economies of scale.

Given the informal evidence that imperfect competition and economies of scale may be important in developing countries, Rodrik develops a three-term expression for the welfare effects of trade liberalization. The first term captures the traditional efficiency benefits

Beth V. Yarbrough is associate professor of economics at Amherst College.

based on the differential between domestic and world prices. These benefits stem from the contraction of a domestic industry in which the domestic price exceeds the world price.

The second term reflects imperfect competition in terms of price-cost margins. Rodrik claims that, to increase welfare, the output of industries with positive price-cost margins must increase and that this is an "entirely new desideratum." But this is a standard result in the domestic distortions literature. It has been widely recognized for a number of years that a domestic distortion in the form of a monopolized industry can cause a country to overspecialize or even to specialize in production of the "wrong" good under unrestricted trade. The relevant question then becomes whether maintaining protection is the first-best policy response. The traditional domestic distortions literature suggests that it is not and finds policies such as production subsidies generally superior. This chapter does not appear to provide a new theoretical answer. Likewise, the result that the key to determining the welfare effects of production changes lies in the comparison of domestic costs and world prices is not really new. In our conversations, Rodrik has shown that he has some interesting new ideas on the tariff-versus-production subsidy choice from a political economy perspective, but those ideas are not contained in the current chapter. However, the empirical work provides some new insights even if the theoretical results do not.

The third term of Rodrik's formulation introduces the possibility of economies of scale. The chapter emphasizes the conflict between economies of scale and trade liberalization. If liberalization leads to a decline in industry output and there is, for one reason or another, inadequate exit from the industry, then per firm output must decline and average costs rise. To gauge informally the extent of this problem, the chapter looks at the relationship between economies of scale in an industry and the effective rate of protection and finds a positive correlation; that is, highly protected industries, the presumed targets of liberalization efforts, appear to be characterized by substantial economies of scale. The lesson drawn is the existence of an "apparent conflict" between economies of scale and trade liberalization.

The relationship between economies of scale and liberalization highlights the crucial role of the specific policy perspective taken in the chapter. The policy being evaluated is the partial elimination of protection already in place. Given this perspective, call it the ex post policy choice, the conflict between liberalization and economies of scale does exist, by definition.

However, would it not be more useful to draw an ex ante lesson concerning the desirability of instituting import substitution through protectionism? If a developing country enters an industry of comparative disadvantage characterized by extensive economies of scale, high levels of effective protection are going to be required. This type of import substitution and trade liberalization *are* in conflict. But does one want to conclude that the appropriate policy response is to not liberalize trade? This is related to Harry Bowen's comments about the propensity of developing countries to enter industries such as steel. The point is also related to Avinash Dixit's comments on chapter 8. In making ex ante policy decisions, one wants to take account of the possibility of ex post changes in circumstances. One of those possible changes would be future removal of the protection itself.

In the empirical section of the chapter Rodrik asks, "What are the resource allocation effects of trade reform under conditions of imperfect competition?" The simulations suggest that liberalization is beneficial under conditions of free entry and exit. This finding is consistent with recent developments in industrial organization theory that imply that entry restrictions may be a more serious cause for concern than imperfect competition per se. Here it is exit that is crucial. Rodrik makes an important point by highlighting the role of free exit in capturing the benefits from trade liberalization. However, in the chapter he seems to lay the responsibility for lack of exit at the feet of the market. This seems inappropriate given the array of mobility restrictions typical in many developing countries.

Rodrik also tries to make a point about the dualistic structure of industry in developing countries. Many industries are characterized by a few oligopolistic firms along with a competitive fringe. He seems to say that the oligopolistic firms will force their small suppliers and subcontractors out of the market, thereby avoiding the need to exit themselves. This part of the chapter is the least clear and well developed. It seems to tread close to the "exploitation hypothesis" concerning the interaction of large and small firms, a notion that has fallen from favor with most industrial organization theorists.

In summary, I enjoyed reading this chapter. I especially liked its political awareness and its clear, simple approach to well-defined questions. The empirical results pointing to the role of unrestricted exit in achieving gains from trade liberalization are important. These should prove useful in arguments concerning the appropriate form of trade adjustment assistance policies. The major weakness of the chapter is inadequate attention to the distinction between ex ante and ex post policy choices. In other words, I would like to see more emphasis on the role of developing countries' import substitution policies in creating the problems that Rodrik, in this chapter, is endeavoring to understand and solve.

II Measuring the Economic Effects of Protection

6   Measures of Openness

Edward E. Leamer

Which countries are most open to international trade?

Tariff averages have frequently been used to measure the height of trade barriers, but the rise in the relative importance of nontariff barriers has made tariff averages increasingly suspect as overall measures of barriers. Coverage ratios for nontariff barriers, such as those in Nogues, Olechowski, and Winters (1986), are suggestive of the severity of nontariff barriers, but not all nontariff barriers can be measured, and not all barriers are equally restrictive. Furthermore, it is unclear how tariff averages and nontariff coverage ratios should be combined. In selected cases such as Pryor (1966), Sampson and Yeats (1977), and Cline et al. (1978), tariff equivalents of nontariff barriers can be formed by comparing the foreign with the domestic price of goods. But data for forming tariff equivalents are very limited, and tariff equivalents are accurate indicators of the height of barriers only for the competitive case in which the product is standardized and there is no market power.

An alternative approach is to examine trade data for circumstantial evidence of barriers. In the traditional small-country micromodel, trade in particular products is a function of resource supplies, prices of products in international markets, technology, tastes, natural barriers to trade, and artificial barriers. When studying trade patterns for evidence of artificial barriers it is therefore important either to assure that the other determinants of trade are relatively constant or to control statistically for their variability. For example, changes over time of the ratio of imports to domestic consumption (or production) can properly be attributed to changes in artificial barriers only if resource supplies,

Edward E. Leamer is professor of economics at the University of California, Los Angeles.

product prices, technologies, tastes, and natural barriers to trade are adequately constant. Differences among countries in the level and commodity composition of trade can be attributed to barriers if the countries are sufficiently similar in terms of resources, tastes, and natural barriers to trade, or if these effects are otherwise controlled.

The goal of this chapter is to compare the levels of trade barriers of different countries at the same point in time, using trade data as circumstantial evidence. The basic measure of openness is the trade intensity ratio: exports plus imports divided by GNP. Data on the supplies of productive resources are used to remove the component of variability of the trade intensity ratio associated with observable variability in resource supplies. Data on distance to markets are used to remove the component of variability of the trade intensity ratio associated with natural barriers. No attempt is made to supplement these data formally with direct measures of trade barriers such as tariff levels or indicators of nontariff barriers, but the results are assessed to some extent according to how well they reveal the best-known trade barriers.

Import penetration ratios, especially their variability over time, have previously been used to suggest the levels of trade barriers by many authors, including, for example, Balassa and Balassa (1984). In one sense, this chapter is an extension of Saxonhouse's (1983) comment that Japan's low ratio of imports to consumption in manufactures is not due to high protection, but rather to resources suited to manufacturing.

In this chapter I have taken the approach of finding a model that provides an adequate, even convincing, explanation of trade at the three-digit SITC (Standard International Trade Classification, Revision 2) level of disaggregation, and then attributing the estimated residuals of the model to the trade barriers. Implicitly, trade barriers are assumed to be (a) the only important omitted variables and (b) uncorrelated with the included variables. Both of these assumptions are suspicious.

The assumption that the only omitted variables are trade barriers is doubtful. There is of course no formal way to verify this hypothesis. Here I study the patterns of residuals in the hopes that peculiar residuals will suggest important omitted variables. When the model can no longer be criticized for failing to account for significant features of the data, I proceed as if all the remaining variability were attributable to trade barriers. Of course it is a matter of art, not science, when I conclude that there are no further meaningful criticisms.

The assumption that the barriers are uncorrelated with the included variables is clearly violated, possibly in a serious way. The included variables are resources that can otherwise account for trade, and if countries that are similar in their resources adopt similar levels of barriers, the resource variables in the model will soak up some of the effect of the barriers. One might hope that the structure of protection is uncorrelated with the resource variables, but Godek (1986) finds in a sample of fifteen developed countries that the overall level of tariffs in 1974 declined with per capita GNP. The best that can be said is that the measures of openness in this paper account only for those barriers that are uncorrelated with other variables in the model, in particular, uncorrelated with the stage of development.

Though these criticisms are serious, they need to be considered in the proper context. The question is not whether a particular method produces perfect measures of openness, since none will. The real question is which method seems likely to produce the best measures. The alternatives to the measures reported here are either unadjusted trade intensity ratios or averages of directly measured barriers. Measures of openness that use trade intensity ratios without any adjustments can conclude that countries with unusual supplies of resources are the most open, merely because these countries have the highest levels of trade in the absence of any barriers at all. Tariff averages seem like appealing indicators of openness, but these averages make the implicit assumption that import elasticities are the same on all commodities. More importantly, tariffs are no longer very high in comparison with the tariff equivalent of many nontariff barriers. Tariff averages accordingly tell only part of the story, and to be very meaningful they need to be combined with measures of the restrictiveness of nontariff barriers. But the tariff equivalents of nontariff barriers can be difficult to compute, especially for the many nontransparent barriers such as administrative paper work, threats of tariffs, health regulations, and so forth.

The approach I use here employs the trade data implicitly to determine the relative restrictiveness of barriers, which seems essential, but the attribution of the total unexplained component to trade barriers is suspicious for the two reasons discussed above. A better approach might be to include measures of tariff and nontariff barriers in the equation, and to measure their restrictiveness in terms of their contributions to the determination of trade. This seems simple enough, but the data problems and the model construction problems are formidable. At the outset my modest hope is that I can do better than merely use trade intensity ratios as measures of openness.

Section 6.1 of this chapter contains a simple general equilibrium model that serves as a backdrop for the data analysis. This model does indicate that, in the absence of trade barriers, the trade intensity ratio is a measure of the peculiarity of the resource supply vector. But barriers to trade that raise the internal prices of commodities have very complex effects on the trade intensity ratio, and there seems to be no guarantee that the trade intensity ratio declines with increases in tariff barriers.

The model outlined in section 6.1 suggests a very complicated data analysis with variables measured subject to multiplicative measurement errors. For computational ease, I opt instead for the traditional linear regression model as an adequate approximation.

Measures of openness and measures of peculiarity are discussed in section 6.3. The openness measures are (1) the ratio of actual to predicted trade and (2) an adjusted trade intensity ratio that allows for differences in resource supplies. One measure of peculiarity is an R^2 that compares the size of the residuals with the size of the observed trade variances. Another measure of peculiarity is the size of residuals relative to other residuals.

Estimates of a factor-analytic model with the resources treated as unobserved variables are reported in section 6.4. These estimates are computed using a 1982 data set on trade of 183 commodities at the three-digit SITC level of aggregation. This factor-analytic model stands up relatively well to criticism, but its measures of openness are suspicious since the factor-analytic method seems likely to remove most of the effects of barriers.

Results based on a model with measured values for the resources are reported in section 6.5. This estimated model does not survive as well the criticism that there are important omitted variables, and its openness measures have also to be viewed with suspicion. This suspicion can probably only be relieved by combining the trade and resource data with direct measures of trade barriers.

6.1   A Theoretical Model

The difference between the "predicted" and the actual trade intensity ratios will be used as an indicator of the level of trade barriers. Obviously, a carefully formulated model is needed both to determine the conditions under which trade intensity ratios can serve as indicators of trade barriers and also to determine the nature of the adjustments to the trade intensity ratios that are needed to account for determinants of trade other than barriers. A particularly convenient model of the determinants of production and trade is the traditional general equilibrium model with identical homothetic tastes, constant returns to scale, equal numbers of goods and factors, and with sufficient similarities in factor endowments that countries are all in the same cone of diversification. No real commitment is made to this model; it is only a useful starting point for thinking about the problems.

6.1.1   The Trade Intensity Ratio without Trade Barriers

Assume initially that there are no barriers to trade. Then the production side of the model can be summarized by the system of equations:

(1) $$\mathbf{Q} = \mathbf{A}^{-1}\mathbf{V},$$

(2) $$\mathbf{w} = \mathbf{A}'^{-1}\mathbf{p},$$

(3) $$\mathbf{A} = \mathbf{A}(\mathbf{w},t),$$

where $\mathbf{Q}$ is the vector of outputs, $\mathbf{V}$ is the vector of factor supplies, $\mathbf{A}$ is the input-output matrix with fixed elements equal to the amount of a factor used to produce a unit of a good, $\mathbf{p}$ is the vector of (internal) commodity prices, and $\mathbf{w}$ is the vector of factor returns. Equation (1), which translates factor supplies $\mathbf{V}$ into outputs $\mathbf{Q}$, is the inverted form of the factor market equilibrium condition equating the supply of factors $\mathbf{V}$ to the demand for factors $\mathbf{AQ}$. Equation (2), which translates product prices into factor prices, is the inverted form of the zero-profit condition equating product prices $\mathbf{p}$ to production costs $\mathbf{A}'\mathbf{w}$. Equation (3) expresses the dependence of input intensities on factor prices $\mathbf{w}$ and on the state of technology t, $\mathbf{A}(w,t)$ being the cost-minimizing choice of input intensities at time t.

In the absence of barriers to trade, all individuals face the same commodity prices, and if they have identical homothetic tastes, then they consume in the same proportions:

(4) $$\mathbf{C} = s\mathbf{C}_w = s\,\mathbf{A}^{-1}\mathbf{V}_w,$$

where $\mathbf{C}$ is the consumption vector, $\mathbf{C}_w$ is the world consumption vector, $\mathbf{V}_w$ is the vector of world resource supplies, and s is the consumption share. Thus trade is

(5) $$\mathbf{T} = \mathbf{Q} - \mathbf{C} = \mathbf{A}^{-1}\mathbf{V} - s\,\mathbf{A}^{-1}\mathbf{V}_w = \mathbf{A}^{-1}(\mathbf{V} - s\,\mathbf{V}_w).$$

The trade balance condition $\pi'\mathbf{T} = 0$, with π the vector of prices, implies that the consumption share is the ratio of GNP to world GNP:

(6) $$s = \pi'\mathbf{A}^{-1}\mathbf{V}/\pi'\,\mathbf{A}^{-1}\mathbf{V}_w = GNP/GNP_w.$$

Using this value for the consumption share and dividing equation (5) by GNP, we obtain

$$\mathbf{T}/GNP = \mathbf{A}^{-1}([\mathbf{V}/GNP] - [\mathbf{V}_w/GNP_w]).$$

Finally, premultiplying by Π, a diagonal matrix with prices down the diagonal, and using $\mathbf{W}$, a diagonal matrix with wages down the diagonal, we find the trade vector in value terms:

$$\begin{aligned}\Pi\mathbf{T}/GNP &= \Pi\mathbf{A}^{-1}\mathbf{W}^{-1}([\mathbf{WV}/GNP] - [\mathbf{WV}_w/GNP_w]) \\ &= \Theta([\mathbf{WV}/GNP] - [\mathbf{WV}_w/GNP_w]) \\ &= \Theta(\lambda - \lambda_w),\end{aligned}$$

where Θ is the inverse of the matrix of input shares, and $\lambda = \mathbf{WV}/GNP$ is the vector of earnings shares.

The trade intensity ratio (*TIR*) thus becomes a measure of the difference between the vector of earnings shares of the world and the vector of earnings shares of the country:

$$(7) \qquad TIR = |\Pi \, T/GNP| = |\Theta \, (\lambda - \lambda_w)|,$$

where $|T|$ indicates the sum of absolute values of the elements of T, and Π is a diagonal matrix with prices on the diagonal. Thus in this model with no differences in technologies or tastes, and no trade barriers, the trade intensity ratio is a measure of resource distinctiveness. The more unusual is the country's vector of earnings shares, the greater is the trade intensity ratio.

Other Assumptions

This model is based on a long list of suspicious assumptions; consequently there is great concern that some minor changes in the model would imply that the trade intensity ratio is not an indicator of resource peculiarity. Four that come to mind are nontraded goods, intermediate goods, nonproportional consumption, and trade imbalance. The trade intensity ratio might be expected to be high for countries with small nontraded goods sectors, for countries that import great amounts of intermediate inputs, for countries that consume large proportions of certain goods, and for countries that have large trade imbalances. Actually, as is shown in Leamer (1984), the model summarized by equation (5) remains basically intact if it includes some forms of nontraded goods, intermediate inputs, and nonproportional consumption. Trade imbalance, alone, and nonproportional consumption together with nontraded goods alter the model in such a way that the trade intensity ratio is not a good indicator of resource peculiarity. What is essential for the empirical work in this chapter, however, is not that the trade intensity ratio is an indicator of resource peculiarity, but that the trade equations are linear in resources. The residuals can then be attributed to trade barriers.

Nontraded goods and intermediate inputs are discussed separately in Leamer (1984, 23 and 33). Consider here the possibility of both intermediate inputs and nontraded goods. Let Q_t and Q_n stand for vectors of final outputs of traded and nontraded goods respectively. Let the intermediate inputs required to produce X be BX, leaving as final output $Q = (I - B)X$ where B depends on factor prices and technology, $B(w,t)$. The condition for equilibrium in the factor markets is $A_t X_t + A_n X_n = V$. Substituting into this equation the condition $X = (I - B)^{-1}Q \equiv DQ$, we can solve for final output of the traded goods as a function of final output of nontraded goods, $EQ_t = V - FQ_n$, where $E = A_t D_{tt} + A_n D_{nt}$, and $F = A_t D_{tn} + A_n D_{nn}$. Furthermore, assume identical homothetic tastes to obtain $C_t = sQ_{tw}$, and

$\mathbf{C}_n = s\mathbf{Q}_{nw}$, where the w subscript refers to world totals and s is the consumption share. Then the trade equations analogous to equation (5) are

$$\mathbf{ET} = \mathbf{EQ}_t - \mathbf{EC}_t = \mathbf{EQ}_t - s\mathbf{EQ}_{tw} = \mathbf{V} - \mathbf{FQ}_n - s(\mathbf{V}_w - \mathbf{FQ}_{nw})$$
$$= \mathbf{V} - s\mathbf{FQ}_{nw} - s(\mathbf{V}_w - \mathbf{FQ}_{nw}) = \mathbf{V} - s\mathbf{V}_w \ .$$

Thus all that changes when intermediate inputs and nontraded goods are included in the model is that $\mathbf{E}$ replaces $\mathbf{A}$ in equation (5).

Leamer (1984, 39–40) shows that essentially the same conclusion applies if consumption is income-dependent: trade depends linearly on excess factor supplies. But it is not possible to have both income-dependent consumption and nontraded goods since, for example, a preference for nontraded goods at low levels of income would imply that the trade intensity ratio would increase in response to a proportional increase in the supply of all resources.

Trade imbalance will also affect the trade intensity ratio. Let B be the trade surplus, $B = \pi'\mathbf{T}$, and $b = B/\mathrm{GNP}$. Then the net export vector relative to GNP can be written as

$$\Pi\mathbf{T}/GNP = \Theta (\lambda - \lambda_w) + b \, \Theta \, \lambda_w \ .$$

The trade intensity ratio then becomes a function of the trade balance b and attains a minimum in general at some value of balance other than zero.

6.1.2 The Trade Intensity Ratio with Trade Barriers

Trade barriers are another major determinant of trade intensity ratios. To model the effects of trade barriers it is necessary to make assumptions about the elasticities of supply and demand. A convenient way to do that is to use Cobb-Douglas utility functions and Cobb-Douglas production functions. On the consumption side, this amounts to the statement that the budget shares are fixed parameters:

$$(8) \qquad\qquad p_c \, C_c = \alpha_c \, Y,$$

where C_c is consumption of commodity c, p_c is the internal (tariff inclusive) price, α_c is the fixed expenditure share, and Y is total expenditure. In words, the value of consumption is equal to the consumption share times total expenditure. Then using the identity that trade is the difference between production and consumption, we can solve for the trade equations as

$$\mathbf{T} = \mathbf{A}^{-1} \mathbf{V} - \mathbf{P}^{-1} \alpha \, Y,$$

where $\mathbf{P}$ is a diagonal matrix with internal prices on the diagonal.

For purposes of discussion, let us proceed as if all barriers amount to a tax on the international exchange of goods at a preset ad valorem rate. These taxes will conveniently be called "tariffs," though they can represent a wider set of trade impediments. The level of a tariff on commodity c will be denoted by τ_c and the corresponding external price by π_c. Then the internal price of the commodity is[1]

$$p_c = \pi_c (1 + \tau_c).$$

Premultiplying the trade vector by the external prices π and imposing the trade balance condition $0 = \pi'\mathbf{T}$, we can calculate the expenditure level:[2]

(9) $$Y = (\pi'\mathbf{A}^{-1}\mathbf{V})/(\pi'\mathbf{P}^{-1}\alpha) = GNP (1 + \tau.),$$

where GNP is the value of output at world prices $\pi'\mathbf{A}^{-1}\mathbf{V}$, and $\tau.$ is an index of trade barriers overall:

(10) $$(1 + \tau.) = (\Sigma\, \alpha_c /(1 + \tau_c))^{-1}.$$

Incidentally, the summation in this expression extends over all commodities, including export items. For example, if tariffs are uniformly set to τ for all import commodities, then $(1 + \tau.) = (1 + \tau)/\alpha_m$ where α_m is the share of imports in consumption.

Cobb-Douglas (log-linear) production functions and cost minimization imply fixed factor shares: $\theta_{fc} = w_f A_{fc}/p_c$ where θ_{fc} is a technologically fixed parameter, w is the factor return, p is the product price, and A is the input-output ratio. In matrix form this becomes

$$\Theta = \mathbf{W}\,\mathbf{A}\,\mathbf{P}^{-1},$$

where Θ is a matrix of technologically fixed factor shares and where notation indicating the dependence of all of the variables on time is suppressed. Substituting this into equation (1) yields the production relationships

$$\Theta\,\mathbf{P}\,\mathbf{Q} = \mathbf{W}\,\mathbf{V}.$$

In words, the product of the value of output $\mathbf{PQ}$ times the input share Θ is equal to the value of the input $\mathbf{WV}$.

The Stolper-Samuelson mapping of commodity prices into factor prices given this Cobb-Douglas technology can be found by substituting the cost minimization condition for selecting the amount of input f in commodity c, $V_{fc} = \theta_{fc}/w_f$, into the unit *value* isoquants in logarithmic form

$$0 = ln(p_c) + ln\,(\alpha_c) + \Sigma_f\, \theta_{cf}\, ln(V_{fc}) , \; c = 1, 2 \ldots$$

to obtain the system

(11) $$\Theta'ln(\mathbf{w}) = ln(\mathbf{p}) + ln(\mathbf{k}),$$

where $ln(\mathbf{w})$ is a vector of logarithms of factor returns, $ln(\mathbf{p})$ is a vector of logarithms of prices, and $ln(\mathbf{k})$ is a vector of constants. In a more direct notation, the return to factor f as a function of the product prices can be written as

$$w_f = \prod_c (k_c p_c)^{\theta cf},$$

where θ^{cf} is the (c,f) element of the inverse of Θ.

Under these assumptions the trade vector satisfies

(12) $\mathbf{PT} = \Theta^{-1}\,\mathbf{W}\,\mathbf{V} - \alpha\,Y = \Theta^{-1}\,\mathbf{W}\,\mathbf{V} - \alpha\,GNP\,(1 + \tau.),$

where the internal factor prices $\mathbf{W}$ are functions of the product prices according to the log-linear relationship (11). In words, the net export vector evaluated at internal prices is a function of factor supplies evaluated at internal prices and the product of GNP times an index of trade barriers.

Estimates of GNP will usually evaluate output at internal prices. This level of nominal GNP will be denoted by

$$GNP^* = \mathbf{p}'\mathbf{P}^{-1}\,\Theta^{-1}\,\mathbf{W}\,\mathbf{V} = \mathbf{1}'\Theta^{-1}\,\mathbf{W}\,\mathbf{V} = \mathbf{1}'\,\mathbf{W}\,\mathbf{V}.$$

Some of the trade flows are evaluated at external prices and some at internal prices. Trade data collected on an f.o.b. basis would exclude tariff receipts and transportation charges, but would include the effects of various nontariff barriers such as voluntary export restraints and quotas administered by the exporting country. Nonetheless, it is probably a good approximation to assume that the trade flows are evaluated at external prices. The trade intensity ratio accordingly becomes

(13) $TIR = |\Pi\,\mathbf{T}/GNP^*|$
$= |\Pi\mathbf{P}^{-1}\,[\Theta^{-1}\,\lambda - \alpha\,(1 + \tau.)\,(GNP/GNP^*)]|$
$= |(1 + \tau)^{-1}\,[\Theta^{-1}\,\lambda - \alpha\,(1 + \tau.)\,(GNP/GNP^*)]|,$

where λ is the vector of earnings shares and $(1 + \tau)$ is a diagonal matrix with one plus the tariff rate on the diagonal.

From equations (12) and (13) it is clear that the assumptions of constant expenditure shares and constant input shares limit the effects that trade barriers can have if inputs and outputs are evaluated at internal prices. In fact the principal influence of barriers is to alter the internal rewards to factors and the internal valuation of commodities. If commodities and factors are evaluated at internal prices, barriers have their only other effect through the term $(1 + \tau.)(GNP/GNP^*)$.

In the absence of trade barriers, the trade intensity ratio (7) is a measure of the difference in earning shares of the country and the world as a whole. Trade barriers obviously have an influence on the trade intensity ratio, as is apparent from equation (13). The precise effect is however not so transparent. When the trade intensity ratio is used as an indicator of trade barriers, an implicit assumption is made that the ordering of countries by trade intensity replicates the ordering of countries by trade barriers, other things like resources held constant. We need now to inspect equation (13) to determine if this inference is legitimate. One restriction that we might expect equation (13) to satisfy is that the derivative of the trade intensity ratio with respect to any single barrier is negative. This restriction is not a necessary property of equation (13), which is not surprising since complementarities among products could easily lead to greater trade intensity overall as the barrier is raised on a single product. A weaker restriction on the function (13) is that proportional increases in all barriers on imports would necessarily lower the trade intensity ratio. Instinctively, one might appeal to Hicks's theorem on composite commodities, but in this case raising the level of tariffs overall may switch commodities from the import group to the export group, thereby altering the relative prices within the original classes of products. Accordingly, there appears to be no guarantee that this trade intensity ratio decreases as tariffs overall increase. Without this minimal property, the trade intensity ratio is a suspicious indicator of the level of trade barriers, even for otherwise identical countries.

6.1.3   Estimation Issues

Another reason for running this model through its paces is to make decisions about the kind of data analysis that is likely to be most fruitful. Our goal is to use a cross-country data set on resources and trade values to infer trade barriers. To do this we must assume that trade, resources, and barriers satisfy a set of relationships like that in equation (12). In addition, we must assume that the taste and technology parameters are fixed across countries, and that the trade barriers are like random draws from some probability distribution. Then we can estimate the taste and technology parameters from the cross-country data set and attribute the unexplained variability of trade to the trade barriers.

This program is not easily carried out because of the complexity of the restrictions that trade, resources, and trade barriers are likely to satisfy. A typical equation from the system (12) is

$$\pi_{ij}T_{ij} = \{\Sigma_f [\delta_{jf} w_{if} V_{if}/w_{wf}] + \Sigma_f [\gamma_{jf} V_{if} (1 + \tau_{.i})]\}/(1 + \tau_{ij}),$$

where $\pi_{ij}T_{ij}$ is the value of net exports of commodity j by country i, τ_{ij} is the tariff barrier on commodity j in country i, w_{ij} is the internal reward to factor f in country i, V_{if} is the supply of factor f in country i, $\tau_{i.}$ is the tariff average, and δ_{jf} and γ_{jf} are taste and technology parameters. To make clear what is observable and what is unobservable in this relationship, we can rewrite it as

$$(14) \qquad y_{ij} = \Sigma_f \, \delta_f \, x_{if} + \Sigma_f \, \gamma_f \, z_{if} \, ,$$

where y_{ij}, x_{ij}, and z_{ij} are unobservables for which there exist the following proxy variables:

$$(15) \qquad \pi_{ij} T_{ij} = y_{ij}(1 + \tau_{ij}),$$

$$V_{if} = x_{if}(w_{wf}/w_{if}), \text{ and}$$

$$V_{if} = z_{if}(1 + \tau_{.i}),$$

where the terms on the left are observable, and the terms in parentheses are associated with the structure of barriers and are treated as unobservables coming from some suitably selected distribution. The goal would be to use observations on the value of trade and on the supply of resources to infer the unobservable variables reflecting the barriers: $(1 + \tau_{ij})$, (w_{wf}/w_{if}), and $(1 + \tau_{.i})$. This could be called an errors-in-variable model with multiplicative measurement errors. The usual additive measurement error model consists of a linear relationship among true variables χ: $\beta' \chi_i = 0$, together with an additive measurement error process $x_i = \chi_i + \epsilon_i$ where x is the measured variable and ϵ is the measurement error. The model suggested by equation (12) has a linear relationship among the true variables, but a multiplicative measurement process: $\log(x_i) = \log(\chi_i) + \log(\epsilon_i)$. This multiplicative error model is of great interest but it presents formidable estimation problems. A linear approximation ($dxy = xdy + ydx$) to the measurement error process allows a tractable treatment of the problem:

$$(16) \qquad \pi_{ij} T_{ij} = y_{ij}(1 + \bar{\tau}_j) + \bar{y}_j(\tau_{ij} - \bar{\tau}_j),$$

$$V_{if} = x_{if} + \bar{x}_{if}(w_{wf}/w_{if} - 1), \text{ and}$$

$$V_{if} = z_{if}(1 + \bar{\tau}_.) + \bar{z}_f(\tau_{.i} - \bar{\tau}_.),$$

where the bar over the figure denotes the average across countries.

Also for tractability, it is assumed that the cross-country variance of τ_{ij} is so much greater than the variances of (w_{wf}/w_{if}) and $\tau_{.i}$ that the latter may be treated as constants. In words, it is assumed that the cross-commodity structure of barriers varies much more than average barriers. This allows us to take the level of trade as a "dependent" variable and to ignore the "reverse" regression solutions to the usual errors-in-variables models that would have to be studied if the other variables were also measured with error. The model then becomes

(17) $$N_{ij} \equiv \pi_{ij}T_{ij} = \beta_j'V_i + \epsilon_{ij} ,$$

where ϵ_{ij} is attributable to the trade barriers and represents the effect of the difference between this country's tariff structure and the typical or average tariff structure $\epsilon_{ij} = \bar{y}_j(\tau_{ij} - \bar{\tau}_j)$.

After the model is estimated, we may set the estimated residuals to zero to determine the effects of the trade barriers. It is important to understand that this corrects for trade barriers only in the sense of equalizing the levels of the barriers for all countries at roughly the existing cross-country average.

6.2   Trade Intensity Ratios and Intra-Industry Trade Ratios

Trade intensity ratios and intra-industry trade indicators based on the 1982 data set are reported in table 6.1. Commodities have been divided as in Leamer (1984) into three subgroups: (R) resource trade:

Table 6.1   Trade Intensity Ratios and Intra-Industry Trade Ratios, 1982

Country	Trade Intensity				Intra-Industry Trade			
	R	A	M	O	R	A	M	O
Low-income economies								
Pakistan	.04	.04	.10	.19	.18	.14	.18	.17
Bangladesh	.02	.06	.10	.19	.13	.03	.10	.08
Ethiopia	.04	.10	.10	.25	.20	.01	.01	.04
Sri Lanka	.12	.17	.22	.51	.23	.09	.10	.13
French Guiana	.28	.28	.68	1.25	.00	.90	.06	.24
Lower-middle-income economies								
Colombia	.01	.07	.09	.18	.72	.05	.21	.19
Dominican RP	.05	.09	.06	.22	.00	.08	.22	.10
Turkey	.07	.05	.09	.22	.10	.12	.29	.18
Philippines	.07	.06	.10	.24	.02	.23	.70	.37
Peru	.09	.04	.11	.24	.05	.13	.12	.10
El Salvador	.06	.11	.11	.28	.15	.13	.44	.25
Cameroon	.07	.07	.13	.29	.02	.08	.11	.08
Ecuador	.11	.07	.11	.30	.00	.03	.03	.02
Egypt	.06	.10	.14	.30	.20	.10	.05	.10
Thailand	.09	.13	.12	.34	.04	.14	.48	.24
Nicaragua	.06	.15	.15	.36	.05	.08	.11	.09
Indonesia	.22	.04	.12	.38	.18	.15	.06	.14
Morocco	.13	.09	.15	.38	.04	.07	.15	.09
Ivory Coast	.08	.31	.15	.55	.52	.04	.42	.22
Costa Rica	.08	.32	.18	.59	.07	.11	.88	.34
Upper-middle-income economies								
Brazil	.05	.03	.02	.11	.12	.11	.93	.31
Argentina	.02	.09	.05	.17	.15	.05	.74	.28
Yugoslavia	.06	.04	.10	.21	.21	.48	1.37	.84
Greece	.08	.06	.12	.28	.10	.24	.41	.28

Table 6.1 (continued)

Country	Trade Intensity				Intra-Industry Trade			
	R	A	M	O	R	A	M	O
Israel	.08	.07	.19	.35	.04	.23	.97	.58
Panama	.11	.08	.22	.42	.10	.24	.06	.10
Portugal	.11	.11	.20	.43	.14	.22	.65	.40
Trinidad and Tobago	.24	.07	.28	.61	1.01	.18	.16	.51
Hong Kong	.07	.10	.45	.62	.25	.86	1.64	1.35
Malaysia	.18	.23	.23	.66	.37	.15	.80	.45
Jordan	.22	.14	.37	.74	.01	.53	.43	.33
Singapore	.80	.13	.68	1.62	.36	2.37	1.67	1.08
High-income oil exporters								
United Arab Emirates	.02	.03	.22	.27	.15	.38	.24	.25
Oman	.04	.06	.25	.36	.01	.12	.31	.24
Saudi Arabia	.50	.04	.21	.76	.00	.04	.04	.01
Industrial market economies								
U.S.A.	.02	.01	.03	.07	.30	.58	1.44	.92
United Kingdom	.02	.03	.05	.12	2.12	.71	3.53	2.36
France	.05	.02	.04	.12	.39	1.34	4.40	1.98
Spain	.07	.03	.06	.16	.24	.44	1.40	.70
Austria	.05	.04	.08	.18	.28	.78	3.37	1.84
Canada	.04	.06	.07	.19	.80	.37	2.24	1.25
Japan	.07	.02	.11	.20	.04	.16	.33	.21
Germany FR	.05	.02	.12	.21	.54	1.24	1.70	1.34
Australia	.05	.05	.09	.21	.24	.15	.38	.28
Sweden	.06	.06	.10	.23	.67	.32	2.47	1.37
Italy	.07	.04	.11	.23	.44	.47	1.48	.94
Switzerland	.03	.03	.17	.24	.29	.54	1.52	1.19
Denmark	.06	.10	.09	.27	.29	.63	2.18	1.11
Finland	.07	.12	.12	.32	.39	.13	1.43	.67
Norway	.17	.04	.13	.35	.40	.43	1.19	.70
Netherlands	.15	.10	.10	.35	.67	1.21	3.46	1.61
Belgium	.12	.06	.19	.38	1.11	2.22	3.28	2.39
New Zealand	.05	.17	.15	.38	.05	.16	.47	.26
Ireland	.09	.17	.21	.49	.14	.53	2.27	1.21
East European nonmarket economies								
Hungary	.01	.02	.02	.06	.13	.17	1.75	.67
Other								
Bermuda	.06	.10	.23	.40	.00	.00	.17	.10
Fiji	.08	.19	.14	.42	1.06	.18	.66	.53
French Polynesia	.06	.10	.25	.43	.00	.01	.07	.05
Martinique	.08	.14	.28	.51	.32	.24	.08	.16
Guadeloupe	.06	.18	.30	.55	.00	.13	.05	.07
New Caledonia	.17	.08	.30	.55	.00	.05	.03	.02
Cyprus	.10	.15	.31	.57	.34	.43	.36	.37
Iceland	.09	.26	.24	.59	.03	.04	.11	.07
Tonga	.08	.27	.25	.61	−0.00	.02	.11	.05
Brunei	.91	.03	.13	1.07	.00	.05	.11	.02

Notes: Trade intensity $= \Sigma|X-M|/GNP$; intra-industry trade $= [\Sigma(|X|+|M|)/\Sigma|X-M|]-1$. Sorted by overall trade intensity. R = resources; A = agriculture; M = manufacturing; O = overall.

SITC 27, 28, 32–35, 68; (A) agricultural trade: SITC 1–26, 29, 41–43, 63, 64, 94; and (M) manufactured trade: SITC 51–96 except 63, 64, 68, 94. See Leamer (1978, chapter 3) for a full description of these SITC categories. Countries have been sorted first according to the World Bank classification in the *World Development Report* and second by the overall measure of trade intensity. Table 6.2 contains ranks of the trade intensity ratios reported in table 6.1.

The overall trade intensity ratio varies from 6 percent of GNP for Hungary to 108 percent of GNP for Singapore. The upper-middle-income economies and the lower-middle-income economies have generally more intense trade than the industrial market economies. Among the industrial market economies, the United States and the United Kingdom engage in little trade, whereas Belgium, New Zealand, and Ireland have a great deal of trade.

Generally, the trade intensities of resource, agricultural, and manufacturing trade are comparable. Some exceptions apparent in table 6.2 are those countries that have one group with a much higher rank than the other two: Ethiopia, Colombia, and Argentina with relatively intense trade in agricultural products; Spain in resources; Switzerland and the United Arab Emirates (U.A.E.) in manufactures. Some other exceptions are Japan, especially, and Germany F.R. with little agricultural trade. Features like these are suggestive of trade barriers, but

Table 6.2 **Ranks of Trade Intensity Ratios, 1982 ($\Sigma|X - M|/GNP$)**

	R	A	M	O
Low-income economies				
Pakistan	12	17	15	11
Bangladesh	3	28	20	12
Ethiopia	9	42	19	24
Sri Lanka	52	55	48	50
French Guiana	62	63	65	64
Lower-middle-income economies				
Colombia	1	31	12	9
Dominican RP	19	36	8	17
Turkey	36	20	11	18
Philippines	32	24	18	22
Peru	44	16	22	23
El Salvador	24	47	23	28
Cameroon	35	33	34	29
Ecuador	50	30	26	30
Egypt	20	40	35	31
Thailand	46	49	29	33
Nicaragua	23	54	38	38
Indonesia	59	15	27	41
Morocco	54	37	40	42
Ivory Coast	38	64	37	51
Costa Rica	41	65	42	55

Table 6.2 (continued)

	R	A	M	O
Upper-middle-income economies				
Brazil	13	10	2	3
Argentina	6	38	5	7
Yugoslavia	28	13	21	16
Greece	43	26	31	27
Israel	42	29	44	34
Panama	49	35	50	44
Portugal	51	46	45	47
Trinidad and Tobago	61	32	57	58
Hong Kong	29	43	63	59
Malaysia	58	60	52	60
Jordan	60	52	62	61
Singapore	64	50	64	65
High-income oil exporters				
United Arab Emirates	4	7	49	26
Oman	10	22	56	37
Saudi Arabia	63	12	46	62
Industrial market economies				
U.S.A.	5	1	3	2
United Kingdom	7	11	6	4
France	15	5	4	5
Spain	31	9	7	6
Austria	16	14	10	8
Canada	11	25	9	10
Japan	30	3	24	13
Germany FR	14	4	30	14
Australia	17	21	14	15
Sweden	22	27	17	19
Italy	33	19	25	20
Switzerland	8	8	41	21
Denmark	26	44	13	25
Finland	34	48	28	32
Norway	57	18	33	35
Netherlands	55	39	16	36
Belgium	53	23	43	39
New Zealand	18	56	39	40
Ireland	47	57	47	48
East European nonmarket economies				
Hungary	2	2	1	1
Other				
Bermuda	21	41	51	43
Fiji	39	59	36	45
French Polynesia	25	45	55	46
Martinique	37	51	58	49
Guadeloupe	27	58	59	52
New Caledonia	56	34	60	53
Cyprus	48	53	61	54
Iceland	45	61	53	56
Tonga	40	62	54	57
Brunei	65	6	32	63

Notes: Sorted by overall trade dependence. R = resources; A = agriculture; M = manufacturing; O = overall.

the question that we attempt to answer is whether these distinctive trade patterns can be accounted for by peculiarities in resource supplies.

The trade data used in this study are collected at the three-digit SITC level of disaggregation. The measure of trade intensity reported in table 6.1 nets imports from exports at this level of disaggregation:

$$TIR = \Sigma_j \mid X_j - M_j \mid /\text{GNP},$$

where the summation is over the set of commodity classes. At the very lowest level of aggregation, we might expect commodities to be either exported or imported, but not both. But at the level of aggregation that we use, there is a substantial amount of "two-way" trade. If the linear trade model summarized by equation (12) is used as a guide, this netting out of imports from exports is an irrelevant issue of aggregation, since the trade vector can be aggregated without affecting the linearity of the model or the conclusion that the trade intensity ratio is under certain circumstances a measure of resource peculiarity. The only concern is that the trade intensity ratio (13) is a somewhat different measure of peculiarity of resource supplies at each level of aggregation. The one exception to this statement would be if the aggregation were carried to the extreme of a single commodity. Then the trade intensity ratio becomes only the ratio of the overall trade surplus to GNP.

The more traditional measure of trade intensity does not net imports from exports:

$$TIR^* = \Sigma_j \, (\mid X_j \mid + \mid M_j \mid)/\text{GNP}.$$

These two measures, TIR and TIR^*, would be identical if the disaggregation were fine enough that commodities were either exported or imported, but not both. A measure of the difference between these two trade intensity indicators is the intra-industry trade measure also reported in table 6.1:

$$IIT = [\Sigma_j(\mid X_j \mid + \mid M_j \mid)/\Sigma_j \mid X_j - M_j \mid] - 1$$
$$= (TIR^*/TIR) - 1.$$

This IIT measure would be zero if there were no intra-industry trade at this level of disaggregation. A value of one indicates the TIR^* is twice as large as TIR, which is a major discrepancy. Most of the large numbers for this measure of intra-industry trade occur in manufactures, and, partly for that reason, the measures are generally greatest for the industrial market economies with trade relatively concentrated in manufactures. In particular, Belgium and the United Kingdom have large amounts of intra-industry trade. Saudi Arabia, Brunei, New Caledonia, and Ecuador have hardly any.

There are some exceptions to the general rule that the IIT is greatest for the industrial market economies and for manufactures. Singapore and Hong Kong stand out among the nonindustrial market economies with much intra-industry trade. Japan, New Zealand, and Australia, though classified as "industrial market economies," have rather low levels of IIT. Some other exceptions are the large values of IIT of resource trade for Trinidad and Tobago, the United Kingdom, Belgium and Fiji, and agricultural trade for Singapore, France, Germany, the Netherlands, and Belgium.

These measures of intra-industry trade are reported in table 6.1 to suggest a potential defect in the model that is used as a foundation for forming measures of openness. This model uses the assumption of constant returns to scale and does not allow for intra-industry trade except as a consequence entirely of aggregation. One may interpret the IIT numbers in table 6.1 as suggesting that the level of aggregation is "higher" in the manufactures categories, or one may conclude that increasing returns to scale or some other phenomenon is a more significant determinant of trade in manufactures than resources or agriculture. If it is the former, the data analysis now to be discussed proceeds intact. If it is the latter, the data analysis becomes suspect. This issue will arise again when we inspect the residuals, which may also suggest economies of scale or determinants of trade not otherwise accounted for.

6.3   Measures of Openness, Interventions, and Peculiarity

Obviously, trade barriers account for only a small fraction of the variability of the trade intensity ratios. To form sensible measures of openness it is necessary to control for the other major determinants of trade intensity. The model of trade outlined previously can serve as a foundation for controlling for variability in resource supplies and other influences. Let N_{ij} be the value of net exports and $N^{*}_{ij} = \beta_{j}'\mathbf{V}_i$ be the corresponding number "predicted" by the model where $\mathbf{V}$ is the vector of resource supplies and β is a vector of parameters depending on tastes, technologies, and prices. The difference between the actual net trade and the predicted net trade will be indicated by $E_{ij} = N_{ij} - N^{*}_{ij}$, which optimistically reflects the impact of trade barriers on trade.

The measure of openness suggested here is the difference between the actual trade intensity ratio and the trade intensity ratio predicted by the model. A country is said to be "open" if its trade is unusually great compared with the predictions of the model. This measure of openness may either increase or decrease as the residuals E_{ij} increase. Measures of the absolute size of the residuals are also of interest for two reasons. Residuals that are large in absolute value can suggest omitted variables, or they can suggest policy interventions that affect trade either negatively or positively.

6.3.1   Measures of Openness

The measure of openness used in this chapter is the adjusted trade intensity ratio

$$TIR^A{}_i = (\Sigma_j \mid N_{ij} \mid - \Sigma_j \mid N^*{}_{ij} \mid)/\text{GNP}_i \,,$$

where N^* is the trade predicted by the model. This adjusted trade intensity ratio is the actual trade intensity ratio minus the trade intensity ratio predicted by the model. The country-size effect is eliminated here by dividing by GNP.

An alternative measure of openness is the ratio of actual trade to predicted trade:

$$O_i = \Sigma_j \mid N_{ij} \mid / \Sigma_j \mid N^*{}_{ij} \mid.$$

Note that these two measures are related by the expression

$$TIR^A = (O - 1)\, TIR^*,$$

where TIR^* is the predicted trade intensity ratio. These two measures will differ for countries with greatly different levels of predicted trade intensity. The choice between these two measures is not entirely clearcut. The ratio of actual to adjusted trade is analogous to a tariff average that suggests how much trade is deterred by barriers. The adjusted trade intensity ratio is analogous to a measure of welfare loss indicating the percentage of GNP lost as a result of trade barriers. The decision here to use the adjusted trade intensity ratio reflects primarily that our starting point is the trade intensity ratio. Regardless, this discussion usefully emphasizes that there are two different openness concepts. It bears repeating that the adjusted trade intensities studied here should not be expected to give the same ranking of countries when countries have very different levels of trade intensity.

6.3.2   Measures of Peculiarity

The size of the residuals $E_{ij} = N_{ij} - N^*{}_{ij}$ can be used to measure the peculiarity of trade of country i or commodity j. The traditional measures of the quality of the model in explaining the variability of the data are country and commodity R^2's. A country R^2 can be defined in the usual way as

$$R_i^2 = 1 - [\Sigma_j E_{ij}{}^2]/[\Sigma_j(N_{ij} - \bar{N}_i)^2],$$

where $\bar{N}_i = \Sigma_j N_{ij}/J$ is the average trade of country i. If trade were balanced, then the mean would be zero and the country R^2 would measure the size of the squared residuals relative to the size of squared net trade. This R^2 need not be a positive number. The model is estimated across countries for each commodity, and a commodity R^2 is necessarily between zero and one for the usual reasons. But it is possible for trade of a country to be so poorly explained for each commodity that the country R^2 is negative.

We will also need measures of peculiarity of specific observations. A measure of the peculiarity of commodity j in country i is its contribution to the total lack of fit for that country:

$$P_{ij} = E_{ij}/\Sigma_j \mid E_{ij} \mid.$$

This measure uses the absolute residual rather than the squared residual to reduce the effect of extreme values and also to make the measure more comparable with the adjusted trade dependence ratio, which uses absolute values of trade. Summing across countries produces an indicator of the overall peculiarity of commodity j:

$$P_j = \Sigma_i \mid P_{ij} \mid.$$

Generally, these measures will be large for commodities that are important in total trade and that are poorly explained by the model. These numbers differ from R^2's in using absolute, not squared, residuals and also in emphasizing those commodities that are important in total trade.

These measures of peculiarity are intended to stimulate a criticism of the model. There are a variety of reasons net exports might be judged peculiar when the linear Heckscher-Ohlin model is used as a guide. One possibility is the presence of nonlinearities in the data set. Theoretically, nonlinearities are associated with the failure of one or more assumptions on which the model is based. Two especially suspicious assumptions are incomplete specialization and constant returns to scale. Another reason for poor fits is the omission of resources that have a substantial effect on the trade of at least a few countries. A third reason for a peculiar trade structure is unusually high or unusually low barriers to trade, either natural or artificial. The approach taken here is to form measures of peculiarity for countries and commodities in the hopes that they will stimulate successful criticisms of the model, such as the presence of important nonlinearities, or omitted resources. When no further successful criticisms can be made, the residuals will be taken to be entirely a consequence of the structure of trade barriers.

6.3.3   Intervention Rates

The presumption made in calling the adjusted trade intensity ratio a measure of openness is that most policies have the effect of deterring trade and that greater trade is therefore associated with less intervention. But many policies promote trade. An alternative concept is the rate of intervention that measures the extent to which trade is distorted by policy, positively or negatively. Analogous to the two measures of openness, we propose two measures of the rate of intervention for country i:

$$Int_{1i} = (\Sigma_j \mid E_{ij} \mid)/GNP_i \text{, and}$$

$$Int_{2i} = \Sigma_j \mid E_{ij} \mid/\Sigma_j \mid N^*_{ij} \mid.$$

A serious problem with these measures is that they take as a norm the average level of policy intervention, since a country with zero residuals is one with typical trade barriers, not with the absence of trade barriers. The data considered here include no information on actual policy interventions, and it is impossible to estimate the effect of eliminating the interventions that contaminate the data. Another comment is that these intervention rates are merely measures of the size of the residuals and might as well be called measures of peculiarity. The difference is only in the denominator.

6.4   Measures of Peculiarity and Openness using a Factor-Analytic Model

Initially a promising approach is to treat the resources as unobservable parameters and to estimate them jointly with the taste/technology parameters. In the statistics literature the study of this kind of model is called factor analysis. In this literature, one set of unobservables is usually treated as a set of fixed parameters and the other as a set of random variables. These random or "latent variables" are called factors, which should not be confused with our other usage of *factor* to refer to an input into a production process. Unlike the traditional approach, both sets of unobservables will be treated as fixed constants.[3]

My initial impression was that the factor-analytic approach would be useful for two reasons, but on further reflection the approach seems fundamentally flawed. I report these factor-analytic results nonetheless since they contrast in an interesting way with the results from the regression model, and since they identify commodities likely to cause great difficulties for the kind of study that attributes what is unexplained to trade barriers.

In the factor-analytic approach, the resource endowments need not be at all measurable, which seems appealing. The unscaled and scaled models we have discussed are

$$N_{ij} = \boldsymbol{\beta}_j'\mathbf{V}_i + \epsilon_{ij}, \text{ and}$$

$$N_{ij}/GNP_i = (\boldsymbol{\beta}_j'\mathbf{V}_i + \epsilon_{ij})/GNP_i .$$

In the regression analysis in the next section, we treat the taste/technology parameters $\boldsymbol{\beta}$ as unobservables and the resources $\mathbf{V}$ as fully observable. The list of observable resources is rather brief, and there is a strong possibility that there are important omitted variables. In addition, the assumption that resources such as capital, labor, and land could be measured without error is highly doubtful. A factor-analytic approach addresses both of these problems by treating the resources as unobservables that are estimated jointly with the taste/technology parameters by minimizing either the unscaled or scaled sum of squared residuals:

$$\min_{\beta_j, \mathbf{V}_i} \quad \Sigma_{ij}[N_{ij} - \beta_j'\mathbf{V}_i]^2, \text{ and}$$

$$\min_{\beta_j, \mathbf{V}_i} \quad \Sigma_{ij}[(N_{ij} - \beta_j'\mathbf{V}_i)/GNP_i]^2.$$

The fact that there is no need actually to measure the resources $\mathbf{V}$ seems to make the factor-analytic approach very appealing. But there is one minor problem and one major problem that together make the approach questionable. First, by ignoring altogether the measurements of resources, the method is necessarily inefficient in a statistical sense, though certainly more convenient than a treatment that deals properly with the errors in variables issues.

This inefficiency seems minor compared with the more serious short-coming of the factor-analytic approach. Since only trade data are used to infer the existence of barriers, only peculiarities in the structure of trade in comparison with other countries can give rise to the conclusion that barriers are important. Protection schemes used by a sufficient number of countries in the sample will go undetected because the structure of trade of any of these countries would not seem abnormal.

The point that many barriers will go undetected is evident from the theoretical model summarized by equations (14) and (15) which indicate that the variables in the trade equations are the resources valued at internal (local) prices. The factor-analytic estimation would impute values for the explanatory variables that would offer the best overall fits. Theoretically, these are resources evaluated at internal prices. The residual left over from the factor-analytic approach therefore does not include the effects that barriers have on internal factor rewards, or for that matter the overall tariff average τ_i.

In models other than the one summarized in equations (14) and (15), the imputed factors can be expected also to partly reflect the trade barriers. One of the imputed factors may just be the overall level of barriers, another may be the average tariff level on labor-intensive manufactures, and so forth. The assumption necessary to preclude this undesirable outcome is that the effects of the barriers ϵ_{ij} behave like a set of independent random variables with a zero mean and a common variance. Among many other things, this implies that there are no "country effects" and no "commodity effects" in the structure of protection, which seems doubtful.

Of course it is also necessary to make doubtful assumptions when doing the regression analysis with observed resources. In the spirit of this chapter, we cannot discard the factor-analytic approach merely because the method is imperfect, since all methods share that property. The argument, instead, is that the regression analysis is superior to factor analysis because the measures of openness associated with the regression method are likely to be indicative of trade barriers even when the assumptions fail, but the factor-analytic approach seems to produce residuals that are mostly unrelated to barriers.

In the regression approach, the estimated residuals include the components of the variability of (1) trade barriers and (2) unmeasured resources that are uncorrelated with the measured resources. At least we can hope that trade barriers have a substantial effect on these residuals, particularly if the major resources are observed and if the effects of barriers are substantial. This contrasts with the factor-analytic approach in which the residuals will reflect whatever variables do not have a general effect on the structure of trade. These may be partly the "random" component of trade barriers, but are likely to be dominated by unusual resources that affect the trade of a few commodities in a few countries. I am thinking here of the "specific factors" that account for such things as the Swiss export of watches or the Austrian importation of automobiles. More on this below.

Another issue that must be raised in the factor-analytic approach is how to choose the number of factors. I adopt the asymptotic Bayes criterion of Schwartz (1978) and Leamer (1978):

$$\text{Criterion} = -(p/2)ln(n) - ln(\text{maximized likelihood})$$

$$= -(p/2)ln(n) - (n/2)ln(ESS),$$

where n is the number of observations, ESS is the residual sum of squares, and p is the number of parameters, which for this factor-analytic model is equal to the number of commodities times the number of latent factors. This criterion involves a specific form of penalty for the number of parameters and relates to the maximized likelihood function as the adjusted R^2 relates to the unadjusted R^2. This criterion is an asymptotic approximation to the logarithm of the marginal likelihood function from which the posterior odds ratio can be calculated. The approximate posterior odds ratio of one model, H_1, in comparison with another, H_2, is formed by exponentiating the criterion:

$$\text{Posterior Odds } (H_1 : H_2) = \exp [\text{Criterion}(H_1) - \text{Criterion}(H_2)]$$
$$\times \text{Prior Odds}(H_1 : H_2).$$

These posterior odds ratios can sometimes be very extreme when it seems intuitively unlikely that the data admit such sharp inferences. The extreme odds are a consequence of the assumptions that lead up to them, in this case especially the assumption of normality. Normality is always a doubtful assumption, and when it leads to incredible conclusions from a data set, either the conclusions need to be "consumed with a grain of salt" or the data analysis needs to be redone with a wider class of error distributions. Here we will consume with a grain of salt.

These asymptotic Bayes criteria for the unscaled and the scaled models are reported in table 6.3. (The data set for the unscaled model has 182 commodities and 72 countries, comprising a total of $n = 13,104$ observations. Each factor adds $p = 182 + 72 = 254$ parameters. Because of missing GNP data, the scaled model has only 65 countries, making a total of $n = 11,830$ observations. Each factor adds $p = 182 + 65 = 247$ parameters.) The numbers in table 6.3 indicate a sharp preference for nine factors in the unscaled model and a slightly milder preference for seven factors for the scaled model. The scaling might in effect play the role of one of the factors, and it is thus not surprising to lose one factor in the scaled model. Possibly the loss of the other factor is related to the elimination of seven countries without GNP data.

Table 6.4 reports the ranks of the adjusted trade intensity ratios. The last column contains the ranks of the unadjusted trade intensity ratios. A comparison of this column with the adjacent one indicates that the factor-analytic approach makes dramatic adjustment in the trade intensity ratios. French Guiana, Costa Rica, Trinidad and Tobago, Hong Kong, Saudi Arabia, and Iceland, which all have very large ratios of

Table 6.3   **Choice of Number of Factors (criterion defined in text)**

Factors	4	5	6	7	8	9	10
Unscaled model							
ESS	.4428	.32269	.24053	.18741	.14908	.11994	.10132
n	13104	13104	13104	13104	13104	13104	13104
k	1016	1270	1524	1778	2032	2286	2540
Criterion	521	1390	2112	2543	2838	3059	2960
Odds	0.0	0.0	0.0	0.0	0.0	1.00	0.0
Scaled model							
ESS	.238543	.197649	.161047	.13219	.109752	.0929958	.0792891
n	11830	11830	11830	11830	11830	11830	11830
k	988	1235	1482	1729	1976	2223	2470
Criterion	3844	3799	3852	3861	3804	3625	3410
Odds	0.0	0.0	0.0	1.0	0.00	0.0	0.0

Table 6.4   **Ranks of Openness Measures: Adjusted Trade Intensity Ratios**

	Unscaled Model				Scaled Model				Unadjusted
	R	A	M	O	R	A	M	O	O
Low-income economies									
French Guiana	7	24	47	25	1	19	3	3	64
Ethiopia	8	37	14	11	19	13	8	11	24
Pakistan	42	36	51	45	29	31	49	40	11
Sri Lanka	24	58	45	58	15	60	10	42	50
Bangladesh	39	40	48	46	32	49	52	48	12
Lower-middle-income economies									
Costa Rica	1	61	3	8	14	2	5	2	55
Colombia	14	28	11	10	25	10	12	9	9
Ecuador	27	42	16	24	24	16	19	14	30
Indonesia	53	8	6	5	46	15	16	15	41
Cameroon	19	41	35	32	28	17	20	16	29
Ivory Coast	5	64	5	52	9	54	1	19	51
Egypt	29	50	50	51	33	48	14	25	31
Nicaragua	6	48	34	36	22	34	37	29	38
Dominican RP	20	47	23	34	21	45	27	31	17
Peru	63	25	19	39	63	20	22	36	23
Philippines	54	35	32	30	54	37	32	37	22
El Salvador	12	46	41	43	23	43	43	39	28
Turkey	44	34	38	35	40	35	45	41	18
Morocco	64	38	46	53	64	52	38	54	42
Thailand	55	56	40	55	50	58	48	59	33
Upper-middle-income economies									
Hong Kong	2	4	31	3	3	5	15	4	59
Trinidad and Tobago	11	3	2	2	12	9	9	6	58
Panama	22	32	56	50	20	14	30	17	44
Jordan	62	44	65	64	59	27	4	18	61
Brazil	45	26	15	21	45	24	29	23	3
Singapore	13	2	58	4	2	12	60	32	65
Portugal	38	51	28	42	34	47	23	33	47
Greece	46	45	39	44	41	40	33	35	27
Yugoslavia	56	29	43	40	52	38	56	49	16
Malaysia	51	63	9	57	61	64	2	50	60
Israel	47	39	61	59	31	41	61	51	34
Argentina	31	52	12	33	36	57	47	52	7
High-income oil exporters									
Saudi Arabia	25	9	18	9	4	1	6	1	62
Oman	26	10	52	28	8	6	21	8	37
United Arab Emirates	17	6	49	12	17	3	25	10	26
Industrial market economies									
Germany FR	41	17	21	15	35	8	7	7	14
Japan	37	14	25	13	48	11	17	13	13
U.S.A.	40	15	24	14	30	23	39	24	2
France	43	21	27	20	39	25	34	28	5
Sweden	32	20	42	27	42	39	28	30	19
Norway	61	5	20	7	58	22	35	34	35

Table 6.4 (continued)

	Unscaled Model				Scaled Model				Unadjusted
	R	A	M	O	R	A	M	O	O
Spain	50	33	36	31	44	29	44	38	6
United Kingdom	36	22	33	23	37	36	50	43	4
Austria	59	23	44	38	51	32	53	45	8
Australia	60	16	13	19	62	44	41	46	15
Italy	33	13	29	16	43	42	55	47	20
Switzerland	18	7	53	26	26	21	64	53	21
Netherlands	30	27	22	22	53	55	42	55	36
Canada	49	12	26	18	57	51	54	56	10
Denmark	52	49	37	47	49	56	58	60	25
New Zealand	10	55	8	29	47	61	57	62	40
Finland	15	18	7	6	55	59	62	63	32
Belgium	58	31	60	56	60	46	65	64	39
Ireland	57	53	30	49	56	63	63	65	48
East European nonmarket economies									
Hungary	48	19	17	17	38	28	31	27	1
Other									
Iceland	4	62	4	37	18	4	11	5	56
Brunei	3	1	1	1	16	18	13	12	63
Martinique	34	54	63	62	5	33	26	20	49
Guadeloupe	23	60	59	63	6	50	18	21	52
French Polynesia	28	43	57	54	11	26	36	22	46
Bermuda	21	30	54	48	7	30	40	26	43
New Caledonia	65	11	64	60	65	7	51	44	53
Cyprus	35	57	62	61	27	53	59	57	54
Fiji	9	59	10	41	13	62	46	58	45
Tonga	16	65	55	65	10	65	24	61	57

Notes: Seven factors in the scaled model, nine in the unscaled model. R = resource; A = agriculture; M = manufacturing; O = overall. Sorted by overall measure, scaled model.

trade to GNP, after adjustment are judged to be relatively closed countries. The United States, Hungary, and Brazil, which have low ratios of trade to GNP, after adjustment are judged to be moderately open.

Table 6.5 contains the R^2's by country. Do not be alarmed by negative R^2's, which are compatible with the method of estimation. Both the scaled model and the unscaled model fit the data rather well by conventional standards. The scaled model seems to do a bit better overall, but somewhat worse for the larger countries. This finding is not surprising since the scaled model deals with a heteroskedasticity problem that is likely to be present. Trade in resource products is very well explained but trade in agricultural products is often poorly explained. Among the industrial market economies, New Zealand stands out for

Table 6.5   **Country R^2**

	Unscaled Model				Scaled Model			
	R	A	M	O	R	A	M	O
Low-income economies								
Bangladesh	.94	.19	.05	.26	.97	.08	.09	.25
Ethiopia	.96	.20	.44	.45	.99	.61	.68	.73
French Guiana	.97	−1.03	.13	.75	.99	.79	.93	.97
Pakistan	.99	−.05	.41	.73	.99	−.05	.37	.73
Sri Lanka	.99	.03	.57	.67	.99	.17	.70	.72
Lower-middle-income economies								
Colombia	.47	.23	.75	.36	.95	.71	.82	.75
Costa Rica	.88	.22	−.98	.26	.99	.88	.78	.89
Dominican RP	.98	.10	.08	.56	.99	.21	.68	.64
Ecuador	.99	.20	.72	.95	.99	.74	.65	.97
Egypt	.98	.20	.65	.77	.98	.07	.81	.78
El Salvador	.98	.26	.03	.73	.99	.49	.39	.82
Indonesia	.99	−.01	.67	.98	.99	.24	.56	.98
Ivory Coast	.90	.12	.03	.26	.99	.54	.47	.62
Morocco	.77	.24	.46	.70	.79	.16	.42	.70
Nicaragua	.95	.26	.14	.54	.99	.54	.61	.74
Peru	.41	.34	.85	.62	.31	.20	.81	.55
Philippines	.96	.26	.72	.85	.95	.18	.70	.83
Thailand	.96	−.01	.68	.64	.96	−.05	.50	.61
Turkey	.99	.14	.67	.93	.99	−.08	.37	.90
Cameroon	.99	.19	.68	.83	.99	.63	.82	.92
Upper-middle-income economies								
Argentina	.64	.22	.18	.36	.95	−.15	.20	.17
Brazil	.97	.48	.19	.91	.96	.39	.07	.90
Greece	.99	.08	.63	.90	.99	.14	.43	.88
Hong Kong	.88	−2.97	.59	.57	.97	−.72	.95	.93
Israel	.99	.13	.31	.80	.99	.12	.20	.78
Jordan	.93	−.94	.33	.76	.95	.37	.59	.86
Malaysia	.94	.12	.75	.65	.95	.15	.72	.67
Panama	.99	.18	.59	.89	.99	.51	.69	.92
Portugal	.99	.09	.83	.89	.99	−.00	.74	.87
Singapore	.99	−4.45	.38	.93	.99	.57	.91	.99
Trindad and Tobago	.98	−4.57	−.22	.88	.99	−1.74	.52	.95
Yugoslavia	.98	−.17	.55	.84	.97	−.02	.30	.78
High-income oil exporters								
Oman	.95	−2.81	.52	.58	.98	−.35	.74	.79
Saudi Arabia	.99	.64	.98	.99	.99	−5.53	.68	.99
United Arab Emirates	.78	−10.56	.65	.56	.94	−2.44	.63	.65
Industrial market economies								
Australia	.82	.43	.59	.67	.30	−.25	.65	.29
Austria	.96	.00	.37	.70	.90	.03	.22	.64
Belgium	.97	−.33	.36	.82	.95	−.15	.18	.77
Canada	.99	.98	.97	.98	.86	.02	−.02	.32
Denmark	.90	.19	.15	.58	.90	.04	.03	.52
Finland	.91	.55	.18	.65	.95	.00	.10	.38

Table 6.5   (continued)

	Unscaled Model				Scaled Model			
	R	A	M	O	R	A	M	O
France	.99	.88	.91	.99	.99	.10	.37	.94
Germany FR	.99	.99	.99	.99	.98	−3.62	.76	.80
Ireland	.94	.40	.07	.61	.97	−.17	.17	.50
Italy	.99	.94	.98	.99	.99	−.22	.19	.85
Japan	.99	.99	.99	.99	.97	−1.98	.65	.84
Netherlands	.99	.90	.90	.98	.99	.09	−.14	.86
New Zealand	.78	.27	.36	.42	.94	−.08	.51	.24
Norway	.97	−.61	.45	.92	.98	.57	.80	.96
Spain	.99	.26	.51	.96	.99	.06	.11	.93
Sweden	.96	.67	.66	.82	.98	.13	.49	.65
Switzerland	.93	−1.74	.58	.64	.98	−.09	.16	.39
U.S.A.	.99	1.00	.99	.99	.97	−.04	.17	.74
United Kingdom	.98	.77	.88	.94	.98	−.11	.09	.65
East European nonmarket economies								
Czechoslovakia	.10	.46	.64	.56				
Hungary	.68	−.01	.01	.24	.69	−.01	−.05	.23
Other								
Bermuda	.96	−1.12	.07	.50	.99	.61	.67	.86
Brunei	.98	−517.61	−8.04	.92	.99	.26	.98	.99
Cyprus	.98	.17	.62	.72	.99	.07	.64	.71
Faeroe Islands	.86	.08	−1.58	.17				
Fiji	.93	.01	−.89	.27	.99	.06	−.01	.34
French Polynesia	.96	−1.04	.17	.54	.99	.68	.78	.90
Greenland	.63	.08	−.57	.32				
Guadeloupe	.95	−.25	.40	.48	.99	.46	.85	.82
Iceland	.65	.11	−.18	.16	.99	.99	.96	.99
Martinique	.96	−.34	.37	.49	.98	.42	.83	.82
New Caledonia	.66	−2.48	.01	.21	.70	−.11	.17	.34
New Hebrides	.94	.22	−.12	.41				
Reunion	.94	−.16	.51	.38				
Seychelles	.95	−.60	.17	.38				
St. Pierre and Miquelon	.98	−.01	−1.73	.70				
Tonga	.96	−.14	−.09	.42	.99	.19	.59	.67

Notes: Nine factors for unscaled model, seven for the scaled model. R = resources; A = agriculture; M = manufacturing; O = overall.

its peculiar trade pattern. Other industrial countries in this group with unusual trade patterns are Australia and Switzerland. Outside of this group, Argentina, Hungary, and Bangladesh are the most peculiar countries.

The commodities that contribute most to the absolute residuals, and consequently to the measures of openness, are listed in table 6.6. The real outlier in this table is road vehicles for the scaled model. The list

Table 6.6   **Influential Commodities, Factor Analytic Model** $(\Sigma_j|E_{ij}|\Sigma_{ij}|E_{ij}|)$

Scaled Model		Unscaled Model	
Resources			
coal	.022	coal	.016
iron ore	.010	iron ore	.014
base metal	.009	gas	.012
petroleum products	.006	petroleum products	.009
aluminium	.005	base metal	.008
fertilizers	.005	aluminium	.007
copper	.004	copper	.006
tin	.004	tin	.005
gas	.003	electric energy	.004
other minerals	.003	other minerals	.004
Agriculture			
meat, fresh	.023	meat, fresh	.022
wheat 1	.021	coffee	.020
paper	.021	wheat, unmilled	.019
oil seeds	.014	paper	.017
maize	.013	sugar and honey	.012
wood, shaped	.012	animal food	.012
sugar and honey	.011	fruit, fresh	.012
coffee	.011	maize	.012
animal food	.011	wood, shaped	.011
alcoholic beverages	.010	wool	.011
Manufacturing			
road motor vehicles	.051	clothing	.020
machinery, nonelect.	.026	special transactions	.016
aircraft	.020	footwear	.013
special transactions	.020	ships	.013
special machines	.017	plastic materials	.013
office machines	.015	aircraft	.012
telecom equipment	.013	iron and steel shapes	.012
sound recorders	.013	universals, plates, etc.	.012
footwear	.012	organic chemicals	.011
electrical machinery	.011	power machinery	.011

of the influential commodities is about the same for the scaled and unscaled model for both the resource trade and the agricultural trade, but rather different for trade in manufactures. Some other influential commodities are coal, iron ore, meat, coffee, wheat, paper, special transactions, and footwear.

Finally, table 6.7 reports the commodities for each country with the largest estimated residuals based on the scaled model. This table seems to be ultimately destructive of the interpretation of the residuals as trade barriers. Most of the table is composed of export items that are unusual for reasons other than trade barriers. To select a few: Swiss

Table 6.7   **Extreme Commodities, Scaled Factor Analytic Model ($E_{ij} / \Sigma_j |E_{ij}|$)**

Resources		Agriculture		Manufacturing	
Argentina					
iron ore	−.009	wheat, unmilled	.082	machinery, nonelect.	−.030
coal	−.008	maize	.070	telecom equipment	−.023
Australia					
coal	.092	wheat, unmilled	.076	inorganic elements	.036
iron ore	.054	meat, fresh	.066	office machines	−.018
Austria					
coal	−.040	wood, shaped	.040	road vehicles	−.059
base metal	−.018	paper	.035	steel SITC 674	.043
Bangladesh					
aluminium	−.009	wheat, unmilled	−.092	textile products	.084
coal	−.006	jute	.051	woven textiles	.066
Belgium					
coal	−.040	oil seeds	−.019	steel SITC 674	.062
nonferrous metal	−.016	paper	−.016	special transactions	.059
Bermuda					
base metal	−.015	meat, fresh	−.031	pig iron	−.043
nickel	−.010	fruit, fresh	−.020	office machines	−.037
Brazil					
iron ore	.089	animal food	.087	power machinery	−.032
coal	−.016	fruit, fresh	.045	road vehicles	.032
Brunei					
aluminium	−.031	meat, fresh	−.043	pig iron	−.029
nickel	−.013	paper	.028	steel SITC 674	.025
Cameroon					
aluminium	.015	cocoa	.100	special transactions	.035
petroleum products	−.009	fruit, fresh	−.082	inorganic elements	−.028
Canada					
electric energy	.019	paper	.074	machinery, nonelect.	−.043
base metal	.015	wheat, unmilled	.071	road vehicles	.040
Sri Lanka					
tin	−.009	tea	.191	telecom equipment	−.040
fertilizers	−.008	rubber	.060	special transactions	−.033
Colombia					
fertilizers	−.005	coffee	.100	special transactions	.027
tin	−.004	fruit, fresh	−.097	organic chemicals	−.020
Costa Rica					
nickel	.007	fruit, fresh	.131	medicinal products	.031
base metal	.006	cocoa	−.113	pig iron	.028
Cyprus					
other minerals	.013	vegetables, fresh	.068	cement	.047
fertilizers	−.007	alcoholic beverages	.035	footwear	.037
Denmark					
coal	−.045	meat, fresh	.085	road vehicles	−.035
aluminium	−.012	meat, tinned	.042	furniture	.031

Table 6.7   (continued)

Resources		Agriculture		Manufacturing	
Dominican RP					
petroleum products	.010	sugar	.274	medicinal products	− .026
gas	− .007	fruit, fresh	− .066	pig iron	.019
Ecuador					
aluminium	− .015	fruit, fresh	.053	special transactions	.048
gas	− .008	wood, rough	− .034	machinery, nonelect.	− .023
Egypt					
aluminium	.018	wheat, unmilled	− .089	cement	− .032
coal	− .014	cotton	.057	iron SITC 673	− .022
El Salvador					
fertilizers	− .004	fruit, fresh	− .099	medicinal products	− .044
tin	− .002	cotton	.058	telecom equipment	− .031
Ethiopia					
fertilizers	− .005	fruit, fresh	− .111	machinery SITC 718	− .026
tin	− .002	coffee	.105	road vehicles	− .023
Fiji					
gas	− .010	sugar	.331	machinery, nonelect.	− .022
petroleum products	.006	coffee	− .030	woven textiles	− .022
Finland					
coal	− .030	paper	.192	ships	.064
petroleum products	.007	wood, shaped	.048	road vehicles	− .041
France					
coal	− .033	alcoholic beverages	.046	aircraft	.033
base metal	− .013	wheat, unmilled	.033	office machines	− .030
French Guiana					
base metal	− .030	alcoholic beverages	− .046	pig iron	− .078
fertilizers	− .022	wood, shaped	.035	structures	− .026
French Polynesia					
base metal	− .017	wood, shaped	− .038	electrical machinery	− .070
fertilizers	− .014	meat, fresh	− .034	war firearms	.047
Germany, FR					
iron ore	− .009	meat, fresh	− .031	road vehicles	.081
petroleum products	− .009	paper	− .024	aircraft	− .025
Greece					
aluminium	.020	meat, fresh	− .041	ships	− .056
fertilizers	− .011	fruit, fresh	.025	cement	.046
Guadeloupe					
base metal	− .012	fruit, fresh	.089	road vehicles	− .031
fertilizers	− .010	coffee	− .050	pig iron	− .029
Hong Kong					
base metal	.018	tea	− .039	pig iron	.061
nickel	.014	rubber	− .031	toys	.035
Hungary					
electric energy	− .109	animals	.203	medicinal products	.132
petroleum products	− .006	animal food	− .123	footwear	.076

Table 6.7   (continued)

Resources		Agriculture		Manufacturing	
Iceland					
tin	−.007	meat, fresh	−.115	machinery, nonelect.	.028
petroleum products	.006	cocoa	.068	steel SITC 674	.019
Indonesia					
tin	.022	rubber	.030	road vehicles	.041
base metal	.018	veneers	.027	machinery, nonelect.	−.039
Ireland					
coal	−.014	meat, fresh	.099	organic chemicals	.055
aluminium	−.011	food prep.	.035	office machines	.051
Israel					
petroleum products	.007	fruit, fresh	.032	pearl	.095
fertilizers	.005	coffee	−.027	metal manufactures	.087
Italy					
coal	−.021	meat, fresh	−.045	machinery, nonelect.	.057
petroleum products	.010	animals	−.024	footwear	.054
Ivory Coast					
petroleum products	−.007	cocoa	.192	machinery SITC 718	.017
gas	.006	fruit, fresh	−.095	road vehicles	.017
Japan					
coal	−.031	meat, fresh	−.030	road vehicles	.073
iron ore	−.020	wheat, unmilled	−.016	sound recorders	.038
Jordan					
fertilizers	.082	sugar	−.029	aircraft	−.081
tin	−.009	wheat, unmilled	−.019	special transactions	−.048
Malaysia					
tin	.055	wood, rough	.123	road vehicles	.031
petroleum products	−.012	veg. oil 2	.114	clothing	−.023
Martinique					
base metal	−.012	fruit, fresh	.079	pig iron	−.029
fertilizers	−.011	coffee	−.039	furniture	−.025
Morocco					
fertilizers	.138	wheat, unmilled	−.051	inorganic elements	.063
sulphur	−.033	fruit, fresh	.032	ships	−.031
Oman					
fertilizers	−.011	alcoholic beverages	.029	machinery SITC 718	−.058
base metal	−.009	fruit, fresh	−.023	special transactions	−.057
Netherlands					
coal	−.018	meat, fresh	.048	plastic materials	.052
petroleum products	.009	veg. materials n.e.s.	.035	road vehicles	−.049
New Caledonia					
base metal	.107	coffee	.026	pig iron	.304
nickel	.069	sugar	−.011	clothing	.050
New Zealand					
aluminium	.016	meat, fresh	.157	road vehicles	−.035
fertilizers	−.010	wool	.090	machinery, nonelect.	−.021

Table 6.7   (continued)

Resources		Agriculture		Manufacturing	
Nicaragua					
aluminium	−.005	cotton	.128	medicinal products	−.043
fertilizers	−.004	fruit, fresh	−.088	agricultural machinery	−.029
Norway					
aluminium	.079	paper	.046	aircraft	−.032
base metal	−.036	fish, tinned	.019	fertilizer, manufact.	.028
Pakistan					
aluminium	−.007	rice	.065	woven textiles	.064
fertilizers	−.006	cotton	.060	textile products	.045
Panama					
petroleum products	.015	coffee	−.047	special transactions	−.041
fertilizers	−.011	fruit, fresh	.032	road vehicles	−.039
Peru					
copper	.106	wheat, unmilled	−.033	telecom equipment	−.018
base metal	.091	animal food	.024	ships	.018
Philippines					
base metal	.062	sugar	.073	machinery, nonelect.	−.031
silver	.029	veg. oil, hard	.062	road vehicles	.026
Portugal					
fertilizers	−.011	maize	−.041	road vehicles	−.032
tin	−.007	alcoholic beverages	.033	textile products	.032
Saudi Arabia					
gas	−.014	wood, rough	−.056	special transactions	.073
coal	−.013	sugar	.036	coal	.049
Singapore					
fertilizers	−.031	sugar	.023	special transactions	.095
tin	.018	coffee	.022	coal	.066
Spain					
coal	−.024	oil seeds	−.039	iron SITC 673	.036
iron and steel	−.021	maize	−.035	machinery, nonelect.	−.033
Sweden					
iron ore	.012	paper	.098	road vehicles	.041
coal	−.009	wood, shaped	.053	telecom equipment	.029
Switzerland					
base metal	−.006	cheese	.011	watches	.076
aluminium	.005	paper	−.009	road vehicles	−.073
Thailand					
tin	.037	rice	.115	special transactions	−.035
aluminium	−.012	vegetables, fresh	.100	organic chemicals	−.021
Tonga					
other minerals	−.008	wood, shaped	−.086	structures	−.035
base metal	−.007	wheat 2	−.044	pig iron	−.021
Trinidad and Tobago					
petroleum products	.020	sugar	.038	special transactions	−.078
tin	−.018	cocoa	−.025	coal	−.047

Table 6.7   (continued)

Resources		Agriculture		Manufacturing	
United Arab Emirates					
fertilizers	− .010	meat, fresh	.021	machinery, nonelect.	− .087
silver SITC 681	− .008	alcoholic beverages	.017	steel tubes	− .060
Turkey					
other minerals	.014	animals	.044	textile yarn	.036
iron and steel	− .010	tobacco, unmanuf.	.043	organic chemicals	− .032
United Kingdom					
base metal	− .014	paper	− .045	road vehicles	− .046
copper	− .010	alcoholic beverages	.022	power machinery	.036
U.S.A.					
coal	.033	oil seeds	.037	road vehicles	− .077
petroleum products	.009	wheat, unmilled	.036	aircraft	.049
Yugoslavia					
coal	− .026	rubber	− .020	footwear	.060
aluminium	.017	cotton	− .019	organic chemicals	− .040

watches, wheat for Argentina, coal for Australia, road vehicles (−) for Austria, iron and steel for Belgium, paper for Canada, beverages for France.

For one such as myself who started this exercise with high hopes of detecting barriers in net export data, this table is sobering indeed. It now seems pretty clear that the unusual aspects of patterns of net exports occur mostly from the export side and are related to historical factors or to special resources, and not to trade barriers. It may well be that a separate study of the import side would be productive.

6.5   Measures of Peculiarity and Openness using a Regression Model

The alternative to factor analysis is a regression study in which the determinants of net exports are explicitly identified. A model of this form was used by Leamer (1984) to explain net exports in 1958 and 1975. The same model with two additions is estimated here using the 1982 three-digit SITC data. The following explanatory variables are more fully defined in Leamer (1984):

Capital: Accumulated and discounted gross domestic investment, assuming an average life of fifteen years.

Labor: Three labor variables distinguishing levels of skill. (The lowest skill category is an estimate of the illiterate work force.)

Land: Four land variables distinguishing climate types.

Oil production: Value of oil and gas production.

Coal: Value of production of coal.

Minerals: Value of production of minerals.

Distance: GNP-weighted average distance to markets. The distance between countries is the airline distance between capitals.

Trade balance: Net exports of the 183 three-digit SITC commodities.

Two new variables not used in Leamer (1984) are included in this list. The first is distance to markets, which serves as a proxy for natural barriers to trade. Distance ought to reduce net exports in absolute value, which is a feature that cannot be captured in a net export model that is easy to estimate. For ease of estimation, the distance variable is simply entered linearly in the equation. The second variable is the trade balance, which the theory in section 6.2 suggests can affect the level of trade intensity. The decision to exclude the trade balance in Leamer (1984) reflects concerns about the endogeneity of this variable, which would affect the estimation and interpretation of the other coefficients in the model. In this chapter, interest focuses on the residuals, not the coefficients, and the question of endogeneity is secondary.

A heteroskedastic model with residual standard error proportional to GNP (the scaled model) is superior to a homoskedastic model in terms of overall fit. Estimates based on both models are generally reported in the tables. Table 6.8 contains the adjusted trade intensity ratios for the set of countries for which it is possible to compile the data on the variables listed above.[4] Table 6.9 contains the corresponding

Table 6.8   **Openness Measures: Adjusted Trade Intensity Ratios; Regression Model**

	Unscaled Model				Scaled Model			
	R	A	M	O	R	A	M	O
Low-income economies								
Bangladesh	−.16	−.18	−.41	−.75	−.01	−.03	−.03	−.07
Ethiopia	−.24	−.50	−1.2	−1.9	−.02	−.02	.01	−.04
Pakistan	−.04	−.01	.02	−.03	−.02	−.03	.03	−.02
Sri Lanka	−.14	−.13	−.36	−.63	.00	−.00	.01	.01
Lower-middle-income economies								
Peru	−.24	−.19	−.30	−.73	−.08	−.08	−.05	−.21
Cameroon	−.15	−.21	−.44	−.80	−.02	−.08	−.09	−.19
Colombia	−.06	−.00	−.10	−.16	−.07	−.05	−.00	−.13
Egypt	−.09	−.03	−.21	−.33	−.00	−.02	−.06	−.08
Philippines	−.01	−.04	−.10	−.15	−.03	−.03	.00	−.05
El Salvador	−.20	−.30	−.52	−1	.02	−.01	−.06	−.05
Nicaragua	−.34	−.38	−.68	−1.4	−.00	−.02	−.03	−.05
Ecuador	−.04	−.02	−.07	−.14	−.05	.01	.00	−.04
Indonesia	.04	−.02	.01	.04	.03	−.02	−.02	−.02
Morocco	.04	−.09	−.24	−.29	.00	−.01	−.01	−.02

Table 6.8 (continued)

	Unscaled Model				Scaled Model			
	R	A	M	O	R	A	M	O
Dominican RP	−.08	−.12	−.26	−.46	.01	.02	−.03	−.01
Thailand	.01	−.01	−.14	−.14	.01	.03	−.01	.03
Costa Rica	−.30	−.36	−.70	−1.4	−.04	.08	.01	.05
Turkey	.03	−.00	−.01	.02	.01	.01	.02	.05
Ivory Coast	−.14	.05	−.23	−.32	.02	.11	.06	.19
Upper-middle-income economies								
Panama	−.27	−.26	−.46	−.99	−.12	−.04	−.05	−.21
Argentina	.04	−.03	−.07	−.14	−.01	−.07	−.05	−.13
Brazil	.00	−.00	−.00	.00	−.02	−.07	−.02	−.11
Portugal	−.06	.02	.10	−.15	−.12	.05	−.02	−.10
Greece	−.02	.03	−.03	−.02	−.06	.03	−.01	−.04
Yugoslavia	.01	−.01	.00	−.00	.00	−.01	.05	.04
Israel	.02	.01	.05	.09	−.01	.02	.11	.12
Trinidad and Tobago	.04	−.16	−.09	−.21	.14	−.01	.14	.27
Malaysia	−.01	.09	−.01	.07	.04	.14	.13	.31
Hong Kong	−.05	.05	.29	.29	−.02	.06	.37	.42
Singapore	.37	−.11	−.11	.15	.32	−.03	.22	.51
High-income oil exporters								
Saudi Arabia	−.00	−.01	.00	−.01	−.04	−.05	.01	−.08
Industrial market economies								
Australia	−.01	−.00	.01	−.01	.05	−.03	−.04	−.11
Canada	−.00	−.00	−.00	−.00	−.01	−.05	−.02	−.07
U.S.A.	.00	.00	−.00	.00	−.02	.01	.02	−.05
France	−.01	.01	.00	.00	−.01	−.01	.00	−.03
Austria	−.01	.01	.04	.03	−.02	−.01	.03	.00
U.K.	.02	.02	.02	.06	−.02	.01	.01	.00
Spain	.02	.01	.01	.04	−.00	.01	−.00	.00
Japan	.00	−.00	.00	.00	.00	−.05	.04	−.00
Sweden	.01	.00	−.05	−.03	−.01	−.01	.03	.01
Germany FR	.00	.00	.01	.01	.03	−.03	.07	.07
Switzerland	−.02	.01	.12	.12	−.03	−.02	.13	.08
Italy	.01	.03	.06	.10	.02	.01	.08	.10
Norway	.10	.00	.04	.14	.05	.01	.05	.11
Denmark	.03	.07	.04	.14	.01	.06	.06	.12
Finland	.03	.07	.03	.14	−.00	.06	.06	.12
Belgium	.05	.04	.14	.22	.05	.02	.13	.20
Netherlands	.10	.06	−.02	.14	.10	.05	.05	.20
New Zealand	−.09	.02	−.03	−.10	−.00	.10	.11	.21
Ireland	.02	.03	−.05	.00	.02	.12	.12	.26
Other								
Cyprus	−.37	−.59	−.93	−1.9	−.01	−.04	−.01	−.06
Fiji	−1.7	−2.1	−3.9	−7.7	.00	−.04	−.02	−.05
Iceland	−.76	−.73	−1.3	−2.8	.02	.04	.01	.07

Notes: R = resources; A = agriculture; M = manufacturing; O = overall. Sorted by overall measure.

Table 6.9   **Ranks of Openness Measures: Adjusted Trade Intensity Ratios; Regression Model**

	Unscaled Model				Scaled Model				
	R	A	M	O	R	A	M	O	TIR
Low-income economies									
Bangladesh	10	11	10	10	25	12	9	12	13
Ethiopia	7	4	3	3	14	18	26	20	23
Pakistan	22	22	43	26	19	13	34	24	16
Sri Lanka	13	13	11	12	32	31	29	31	44
Lower-middle-income economies									
Peru	8	10	12	11	3	2	5	2	22
Cameroon	11	9	9	9	18	1	1	3	29
Colombia	18	26	21	18	4	6	23	5	8
Egypt	15	18	16	14	31	21	2	9	28
Nicaragua	4	5	6	5	29	19	10	14	35
El Salvador	9	7	7	7	42	25	3	16	26
Philippines	29	17	20	20	10	15	25	17	21
Ecuador	20	20	23	22	6	33	24	19	27
Morocco	48	16	14	16	36	24	18	23	39
Indonesia	49	21	41	40	47	20	11	25	38
Dominican RP	16	14	13	13	38	39	8	26	15
Thailand	37	25	17	21	39	42	20	33	31
Turkey	45	28	30	38	40	35	32	35	17
Costa Rica	5	6	5	6	8	49	31	36	47
Ivory Coast	12	49	15	15	44	51	42	45	45
Upper-middle-income economies									
Panama	6	8	8	8	2	10	4	1	40
Argentina	21	19	24	23	22	4	6	4	6
Brazil	34	30	33	32	16	3	14	7	2
Portugal	17	41	19	19	1	44	12	8	42
Greece	24	44	27	27	5	41	19	21	25
Yugoslavia	36	23	35	31	33	27	39	34	14
Israel	42	40	49	44	24	38	45	43	32
Trinidad and Tobago	47	12	22	17	52	29	51	50	49
Malaysia	26	53	31	43	48	53	48	51	51
Hong Kong	19	48	53	53	15	48	53	52	50
Singapore	53	15	18	51	53	14	52	53	53
High-income oil exporters									
Saudi Arabia	30	24	38	29	9	5	28	10	52
Industrial market economies									
Australia	28	27	40	28	7	17	7	6	12
Canada	31	29	32	30	23	8	15	11	9
U.S.A.	32	32	34	34	13	26	16	18	1
France	27	38	37	35	21	23	22	22	4
Japan	33	31	36	36	35	7	36	27	10
Spain	40	39	42	41	27	32	21	28	5
U.K.	41	43	44	42	12	36	30	29	3
Austria	25	37	46	39	17	28	33	30	7
Sweden	38	34	26	25	20	30	35	32	18

Table 6.9   (continued)

	Unscaled Model				Scaled Model				
	R	A	M	O	R	A	M	O	
Germany FR	35	35	39	37	46	16	43	38	11
Switzerland	23	36	51	46	11	22	49	39	20
Italy	39	46	50	45	41	34	44	40	19
Norway	52	33	47	50	50	37	38	41	33
Finland	46	52	45	47	30	47	40	42	30
Denmark	44	51	48	49	37	46	41	44	24
Netherlands	51	50	29	48	51	45	37	46	34
Belgium	50	47	52	52	49	40	50	47	36
New Zealand	14	42	28	24	28	50	46	48	37
Ireland	43	45	25	33	43	52	47	49	43
Other									
Cyprus	3	3	4	4	26	9	17	13	46
Fiji	1	1	1	1	34	11	13	15	41
Iceland	2	2	2	2	45	43	27	37	48

Notes: R = resources; A = agriculture; M = manufacturing; O = overall; TIR = rank of trade intensity ratio.

ranks. The last column of table 6.9 reports the ranks of the unadjusted trade intensity ratios.

Controlling for the resources listed, and for distance and the trade balance, the regression analysis makes some dramatic changes in the measures of openness. For example, Panama, which has a very high overall trade intensity ratio, has the lowest adjusted ratio, using the scaled model. Thus, although Panama is very trade dependent, her resources suggest that she should be even more so. Peru and Cameroon are essentially the same.

According to the adjusted trade intensities in table 6.9 the countries with the highest barriers to trade are Panama, Peru, Cameroon, and Argentina. The most open countries are Singapore, Hong Kong, and Malaysia.

For many of the less-developed countries, the adjustment to the trade intensity ratio makes them appear less open. The measures for the industrial market economies tend to adjust in the opposite way, with relatively low trade intensity ratios but relatively high openness measures. For example, the United States has the lowest trade intensity, equal to 7 percent of GNP (table 6.1). If the scaled model is used, the United States ranks eighteenth in terms of overall openness, though it is only third among the industrial market economies. If the unscaled model is used, which emphasizes these bigger countries, the United States moves up to number thirty-four. A fairly big change among these countries is that Australia and Canada are estimated as not very open, even though they rank ahead of several other of these countries in terms of trade intensity. Note also that the anomaly of low Japanese trade in agricultural products remains unexplained; similarly for West Germany. Two other anomalies are the relatively low resource trade of Switzerland and New Zealand.

The choice between the ordering in table 6.2 and the adjusted ordering in table 6.9 depends completely on the quality of the model that underlies the adjustment. Now we must begin the criticism phase of the analysis to decide if the model seems to be doing the job as well as it can be done. We are attributing the residuals in the model completely to the trade barriers, which is obviously incorrect if there are omitted variables that could account for a significant portion of the unexplained variability of trade.

The first criticism of the model is that it does not explain the trade of many countries very well. Table 6.10 contains country R^2's indicating the proportion of the variability of trade that is explained by the model. These R^2's are much lower than the factor-analytic R^2's reported in table 6.5. Table 6.10 indicates that in terms of R^2's, the model does a relatively poor job of explaining the trade composition of about a third of the countries. Remember that the model is estimated separately for each commodity. Although the R^2's for each commodity must be positive, the R^2's for each country need not be. In fact, there are quite a few negative country R^2's. Unlike the factor-analysis results, there appears in table 6.10 to be no tendency for the model to work relatively well on one or more of the subsets of commodities.

Table 6.10   Country R^2, Regression Model

	Unscaled Model				Scaled Model			
	R	A	M	O	R	A	M	O
Low-income economies								
Pakistan	.67	.22	.27	.54	.15	− .90	.43	.12
Bangladesh	− 17	− 2.9	− 15	− 11	.85	.70	.91	.82
Sri Lanka	.62	− .34	− 2.2	.01	.97	.65	.88	.87
Ethiopia	− 4.2	− 2.7	− 100	− 13	.74	.98	.79	.90
Lower-middle-income economies								
Peru	− 27	− 19	− 7.7	− 16	− 3.2	− 4.2	.59	− 1.5
Colombia	− 31	.41	− 2.2	.92	− 38	.52	.79	− .44
Costa Rica	− 12	− .51	− 16	− 2.3	− 1.6	.64	.45	.43
Dominican RP	− 3.1	− 1.3	− 25	− 3	.95	.02	.10	.51
Philippines	.66	− .17	− 1.9	.24	.70	− .92	.57	.52
El Salvador	− 3.5	− 4.7	− 41	− 6.2	.77	.09	− .18	.53
Thailand	.52	.07	− 1.7	.21	.78	.14	.33	.56

Table 6.10   (continued)

	Unscaled Model				Scaled Model			
	R	A	M	O	R	A	M	O
Cameroon	−1.5	−2.1	−15	−2.7	.66	.23	.50	.60
Morocco	−.69	−2.5	−3.2	−1.1	.79	−1	.36	.61
Ivory Coast	−.51	.07	−4.7	−.13	.08	.74	−.11	.62
Egypt	−.16	−.38	−4.8	−1.2	.70	.24	.62	.62
Nicaragua	−11	−2.6	−31	−8.2	.96	.60	.64	.76
Turkey	.63	−.47	.08	.56	.96	−.44	.53	.87
Ecuador	.96	−.26	−.69	.85	.92	.55	.69	.90
Indonesia	.97	.30	.81	.96	.90	−.37	.81	.90
Upper-middle-income economies								
Argentina	−7.3	.62	−2.7	.82	−3	−1.3	−.93	−1.2
Portugal	.65	.12	−.31	.41	−.46	−.03	.40	−.19
Hong Kong	−2.9	−.75	.18	−.18	−1.8	−.39	.14	−.08
Panama	−1	−7.8	−10	−2.6	.08	.12	.28	.14
Brazil	1.00	.99	.97	1.00	.83	−6.6	−1.1	.19
Trinidad and Tobago	.13	−13	−.10	11	.39	−1.1	.60	.43
Greece	.97	−.25	−.33	.75	.63	−.40	.25	.54
Yugoslavia	.88	−1.1	−.75	.45	.70	−1.1	.38	.58
Malaysia	.89	.41	.26	.69	.92	.29	.60	.69
Israel	.85	−.48	.24	.66	.99	.34	.25	.79
Singapore	.74	−2.4	−.43	.65	.84	−.49	.80	.83
High-income oil exporters								
Saudi Arabia	1.00	.91	.99	1.00	.99	−3.9	.94	.99
Industrial market economies								
U.S.A.	1.00	1.00	1.00	1.00	−5.1	−1.8	−1.5	−3.9
Australia	.72	.95	.88	.84	−4.4	.38	.06	−1.5
Austria	−.59	−.26	.28	−.20	−.94	−.97	−.36	−.63
U.K.	.30	.09	.67	.39	−.47	.09	1.1	−.54
Switzerland	−1.6	−.58	−.18	−.51	−.89	−5.5	−.09	−.36
Ireland	−.70	.26	−.95	−.45	−.85	.13	.10	−.32
Netherlands	.54	.30	−1	.42	−.04	.18	.14	−.01
Germany FR	.98	.89	.98	.98	.06	−9	.11	.06
New Zealand	−9.5	.18	−2.3	−1.4	−.25	.30	.13	.26
Denmark	.24	−.03	−.06	.18	.59	−.12	.05	.33
Finland	.70	.15	−.85	.27	.69	.25	.18	.43
Japan	1.00	.98	1.00	1.00	.66	−9.3	.14	.44
Sweden	.77	.14	−.05	.44	.87	.01	.09	.48
Canada	.99	1.00	.99	1.00	.89	.26	.78	.60
France	.92	.49	.35	.89	.88	−2.9	−1.7	.67
Belgium	.92	−.09	.02	.71	.92	−.61	−.08	.68
Norway	.66	.11	.24	.66	.70	.24	.66	.72
Italy	.89	.47	.25	.80	.88	−1.3	.12	.73
Spain	.96	.09	−.99	.87	.98	−.22	−1.5	.85
Other								
Cyprus	−16	−18	−15	−15	.46	−2.1	.66	.15
Iceland	−43	−.71	−54	−6.3	.81	.69	.63	.71
Fiji	−235	−15	−1E3	−102	.87	.96	.82	.93

Notes: R = resources; A = agriculture; M = manufacturing; O = overall.

The lack of fit is meant to suggest inadequacies in the model: non-linearities, unmeasured resources, or trade barriers. Why does the scaled model do so poorly in explaining the trade of Peru, Argentina, the United States, and Australia? Note also the dramatic differences in the R^2's for the scaled and unscaled model. Many of these differences are due to the relatively heavy weight put on the larger countries in the unscaled version. An example is the United States, which is such an extreme country in the unscaled model that the fit is essentially perfect, but it is very poor in the scaled model in which the U.S. data are the very small numbers implied by very low trade intensity ratios. Because of the quality of the fits, it is best to think of the unscaled model as describing the larger countries, primarily the industrial market economies, and to think of the scaled model as describing the smaller countries.

Tables 6.11 and 6.12 contain "intervention" rates, which, like the R^2's, measure the size of the estimated residuals. The principal difference is that the intervention rates use the absolute residuals, not the squares thereof, which reduces the influence of the largest residuals. The residuals are compared with GNP in table 6.11 and with predicted net trade in table 6.12.

Countries are sorted in table 6.11 from largest to smallest values of the intervention rates to produce an ordering comparable with the adjusted trade intensity ratio (a country that intervenes little is an open country). Discrepancies between these intervention rates and the ad-

Table 6.11   **Intervention Rates, Regression Model ($\Sigma_j \mid E_{ij} \mid / GNP_i$)**

	Unscaled Model				Scaled Model			
	R	A	M	O	R	A	M	O
Low-income economies								
Bangladesh	.16	.26	.47	.89	.02	.05	.04	.11
Ethiopia	.24	.55	1.25	2.04	.03	.04	.05	.13
Pakistan	.04	.07	.11	.22	.05	.10	.08	.23
Sri Lanka	.14	.34	.48	.95	.04	.15	.09	.29
Lower-middle-income economies								
Turkey	.06	.08	.10	.24	.03	.08	.07	.17
Dominican RP	.19	.26	.32	.77	.02	.11	.06	.19
Ecuador	.05	.12	.17	.33	.05	.07	.07	.19
Indonesia	.05	.05	.06	.17	.09	.06	.06	.21
Philippines	.07	.10	.19	.36	.05	.09	.06	.21
Nicaragua	.36	.52	.79	1.68	.02	.12	.10	.24
Colombia	.08	.10	.19	.37	.09	.11	.06	.25
Egypt	.11	.15	.31	.57	.05	.11	.10	.25
Cameroon	.24	.29	.50	1.03	.07	.10	.10	.27

Table 6.11   (continued)

	Unscaled Model				Scaled Model			
	R	A	M	O	R	A	M	O
Thailand	.09	.18	.22	.49	.04	.14	.09	.27
El Salvador	.27	.42	.65	1.35	.04	.13	.11	.28
Peru	.31	.26	.38	.95	.13	.10	.08	.31
Morocco	.22	.23	.34	.79	.09	.15	.11	.34
Ivory Coast	.15	.46	.38	.99	.09	.20	.14	.43
Costa Rica	.39	.81	.94	2.13	.14	.26	.15	.55
Upper-middle-income economies								
Brazil	.00	.00	.01	.01	.04	.10	.05	.19
Yugoslavia	.04	.06	.15	.25	.05	.06	.09	.21
Israel	.05	.10	.17	.32	.02	.07	.15	.25
Greece	.03	.08	.13	.24	.07	.08	.11	.26
Argentina	.05	.07	.11	.23	.05	.14	.08	.27
Panama	.28	.35	.59	1.21	.12	.10	.16	.39
Malaysia	.10	.23	.18	.52	.09	.22	.14	.45
Portugal	.11	.13	.23	.47	.16	.13	.18	.47
Trinidad and Tobago	.35	.26	.34	.95	.24	.10	.15	.49
Hong Kong	.17	.13	.42	.72	.14	.12	.41	.67
Singapore	.50	.28	.85	1.63	.35	.15	.30	.80
High-income oil exporters								
Saudi Arabia	.01	.01	.02	.05	.06	.07	.06	.20
Industrial market economies								
Canada	.00	.01	.01	.01	.02	.06	.04	.11
France	.02	.02	.04	.08	.02	.06	.07	.15
Spain	.02	.04	.07	.13	.02	.05	.09	.16
U.K.	.02	.03	.04	.09	.04	.04	.08	.16
U.S.A.	.00	.00	.00	.00	.07	.03	.06	.16
Italy	.03	.04	.09	.15	.03	.07	.11	.21
Norway	.11	.06	.11	.28	.10	.05	.07	.22
Austria	.05	.05	.08	.19	.06	.07	.11	.23
Japan	.00	.00	.01	.01	.05	.08	.11	.23
Sweden	.04	.09	.14	.27	.03	.10	.11	.23
Australia	.02	.02	.03	.07	.10	.06	.08	.24
Germany FR	.01	.01	.02	.04	.05	.07	.12	.24
Denmark	.05	.11	.11	.27	.05	.13	.10	.28
Finland	.05	.13	.15	.34	.05	.13	.12	.30
Switzerland	.06	.04	.19	.29	.05	.07	.19	.31
Belgium	.05	.07	.19	.31	.05	.08	.19	.32
Netherlands	.11	.08	.13	.33	.14	.10	.11	.34
New Zealand	.17	.24	.23	.63	.06	.16	.14	.37
Ireland	.15	.18	.29	.62	.15	.18	.18	.51
Other								
Fiji	1.90	2.33	3.99	8.22	.05	.07	.05	.16
Iceland	.89	1.07	1.44	3.40	.06	.24	.12	.42
Cyprus	.58	.77	1.21	2.55	.09	.19	.18	.46

Notes: See table 6.10.

Table 6.12   **Intervention Rates, Regression Model ($\Sigma_j \mid E_{ij} \mid / \Sigma_j \mid N^*_{ij} \mid$)**

	Unscaled Model				Scaled Model			
	R	A	M	O	R	A	M	O
Low-income economies								
Bangladesh	.90	.99	.89	.92	.57	.43	.27	.36
Ethiopia	.85	.91	.98	.95	.50	.31	.53	.43
Sri Lanka	.54	1.13	.81	.83	.35	.88	.45	.57
Pakistan	.47	1.05	1.12	.87	.74	1.10	.97	.95
Lower-middle-income economies								
Cameroon	1.03	.98	.85	.92	.71	.56	.43	.53
Indonesia	.30	.82	.55	.47	.46	.97	.42	.53
Ecuador	.31	1.30	.89	.76	.32	1.04	.67	.57
Nicaragua	.89	.99	.94	.95	.33	.70	.53	.57
Egypt	.72	1.11	.88	.89	.77	.85	.47	.64
Peru	.95	1.11	.92	.98	.79	.79	.50	.69
Philippines	.82	.96	.94	.92	.53	1.01	.64	.72
Colombia	.99	1.29	.98	1.05	.99	.84	.59	.80
El Salvador	1.03	1.04	1.02	1.03	.89	1.03	.67	.83
Morocco	2.20	1.24	.87	1.17	.64	1.33	.67	.83
Dominican RP	1.42	1.24	.96	1.14	.41	1.54	.58	.84
Thailand	1.09	1.31	.86	1.02	.51	1.36	.71	.86
Turkey	1.31	1.47	.95	1.17	.40	1.70	.96	.94
Costa Rica	.99	1.18	1.06	1.09	1.09	1.07	.85	1.01
Ivory Coast	.68	1.70	1.00	1.14	1.35	.95	1.64	1.19
Upper-middle-income economies								
Panama	.74	1.01	.85	.86	.53	.81	.59	.61
Singapore	1.16	1.15	1.08	1.11	.72	.90	.66	.72
Greece	.29	1.85	.84	.78	.50	1.99	.80	.82
Brazil	.06	.12	.20	.11	.55	.95	1.07	.85
Argentina	.87	.59	.85	.75	1.41	.83	.74	.86
Portugal	.61	1.42	.73	.81	.66	1.92	.79	.87
Israel	.80	1.68	1.22	1.22	.24	1.38	1.88	1.08
Yugoslavia	.58	1.23	1.38	1.12	.74	1.24	1.54	1.16
Malaysia	.51	1.62	.72	.87	.60	2.28	1.26	1.27
Trinidad and Tobago	1.68	1.10	.90	1.16	2.23	1.20	1.02	1.44
Hong Kong	1.44	2.25	2.65	2.15	1.58	2.81	5.30	3.20
High-income oil exporters								
Saudi Arabia	.02	.27	.11	.06	.12	.76	.29	.23
Industrial market economies								
Canada	.05	.08	.08	.07	.29	.50	.41	.42
Australia	.27	.35	.35	.33	.91	.75	.59	.73
Norway	1.42	1.28	1.25	1.32	.79	1.54	.84	.91
Spain	.34	1.58	1.34	.96	.30	1.69	1.39	.96
France	.23	1.20	.94	.60	.33	1.37	1.54	.97
Sweden	.79	1.34	.95	1.01	.36	1.31	1.55	1.05
Japan	.04	.15	.06	.06	.68	1.04	1.60	1.11
Austria	.76	1.71	1.61	1.24	.74	1.37	1.81	1.25
U.S.A.	.03	.06	.02	.03	1.46	1.22	1.16	1.28
U.K.	2.36	2.33	1.06	1.59	.79	1.64	1.73	1.31

Table 6.12   (continued)

	Unscaled Model				Scaled Model			
	R	A	M	O	R	A	M	O
Finland	1.23	2.38	1.62	1.75	.67	1.94	1.83	1.43
Italy	.47	1.57	1.58	1.09	.57	1.61	2.97	1.52
Germany FR	.17	.34	.17	.19	1.87	1.18	2.15	1.70
Belgium	.62	2.33	3.46	1.89	.67	1.78	3.27	1.77
Denmark	1.26	2.70	1.94	1.98	.74	2.65	2.57	1.84
Switzerland	1.20	1.39	3.94	2.25	.80	1.32	4.42	1.92
New Zealand	1.12	1.51	1.24	1.29	1.06	2.30	3.19	2.09
Netherlands	1.88	2.23	1.07	1.49	2.53	1.80	2.02	2.12
Ireland	2.08	1.17	1.11	1.27	1.86	3.27	1.89	2.20
Other								
Fiji	1.04	1.03	.99	1.01	.57	.31	.28	.34
Cyprus	1.21	1.03	.96	1.03	.80	1.00	.55	.73
Iceland	1.04	1.08	.93	1.00	.87	1.07	.50	.79

Notes: See table 6.10.

justed trade intensity ratios occur when the large positive and large negative residuals offset each other in the computation of the adjusted trade intensity ratio, making a country appear to be only average on the openness scale, but nonetheless to intervene a great deal. For example, among the industrialized countries, Canada is the second least open economy, but also appears not to intervene very much. This suggests that many of the other industrialized countries have large positive residuals, which make them appear more open and more interventionist. Among low-income economies, Sri Lanka is estimated to intervene a lot, but is also estimated to be very "open." Generally speaking, there are major differences in the measures of intervention and the measures of openness.

The intervention rates in table 6.12 are comparable with R^2's and are ordered from smallest to largest. When these intervention rates exceed one, the model is not performing very well in the sense that the residuals are generally larger than predicted trade. There are a distressing number of large numbers in table 6.12. It seems highly unlikely that these large residuals should be attributed completely to trade barriers.

The commodities that contribute most to all of these measures are listed in tables 6.13 and 6.14. The biggest residuals are petroleum and petroleum products. In part, this is a consequence of the fact that these categories of trade are relatively large, but we hoped that the oil production variable together with capital and labor would offer a good

Table 6.13   **Influential Commodities, Scaled Model ($\Sigma_i \mid E_{ij} \mid /\Sigma_{ij} \mid E_{ij} \mid$)**

Resources		Agriculture		Manufacturing	
petroleum products	.093	fish, fresh	.035	clothing	.028
petroleum	.088	coffee	.028	road vehicles	.024
gas	.019	fruit, fresh	.027	special transactions	.021
fertilizers	.008	meat, fresh	.019	elect. machinery	.019
aluminium	.008	cocoa	.017	coal	.013
coal	.007	sugar	.014	ships	.011
tin	.007	paper	.013	telecom equipment	.010
base metal	.004	wood, rough	.013	organic chemicals	.009
copper	.004	tea	.012	steel plates	.009
iron ore	.004	veg oil, nonsoft	.011	woven textiles	.008

Table 6.14   **Extreme Commodities, by Country ($E_{ij}/\Sigma_j|E_{ij}|$)**

Resources		Agriculture		Manufacturing	
Argentina					
petroleum products	.08	fish, fresh	−.10	road vehicles	.03
petroleum	−.03	meat, fresh	−.05	mach., elec.	.02
gas	−.02	wool	−.04	special transactions	−.02
aluminium	−.02	coffee	.04	chemical n.e.s.	−.01
fertilizers	−.01	fruit, fresh	.04	clothing	−.01
iron ore	−.01	maize	.02	leather	−.01
Australia					
petroleum products	−.21	tea	.03	clothing	.04
gas	−.05	fruit, fresh	.03	ships	.03
coal	.04	wheat, unmilled	.03	machinery SITC 718	.02
iron ore	.02	wool	.02	mach., elec.	.02
petroleum	−.02	wood, shaped	.02	organic chemicals	.02
fertilizers	−.01	paper	.01	woven textiles	−.01
Austria					
petroleum	.14	coffee	−.03	clothing	−.05
petroleum products	−.03	fruit, fresh	−.03	road vehicles	−.05
gas	−.02	cocoa	−.02	steel SITC 674	.03
coal	−.01	paper	.02	mach., elec.	.02
electric energy	.01	wood, shaped	.02	special transaction	−.02
tin	−.01	fish, fresh	.01	iron SITC 673	.01
Bangladesh					
petroleum products	−.04	cocoa	−.10	mach., elec.	.04
gas	−.04	wood, rough	−.06	ships	.03
fertilizers	−.03	fruit, fresh	.03	road vehicles	.03
tin	−.01	rubber	−.03	steel SITC 674	.02
iron ore	.01	meat, fresh	.02	machinery SITC 718	.02
coal	.01	veg oil, hard	−.02	woven textiles	−.02

Table 6.14 (continued)

Resources		Agriculture		Manufacturing	
Belgium					
gas	−.04	coffee	−.02	steel SITC 674	.06
coal	−.02	fruit, fresh	−.02	special transactions	.05
petroleum	−.02	cocoa	−.02	clothing	−.05
nonferrous metals	−.01	wood, shaped	−.01	plastic material	.04
petroleum products	.01	oil seeds	−.01	road vehicles	.03
iron ore	−.01	alcoholic beverages	−.01	iron SITC 673	.03
Brazil					
petroleum	.06	cocoa	−.10	road vehicles	.03
petroleum products	.04	coffee	−.10	footwear	.01
iron ore	.03	fish, fresh	.06	steel SITC 674	.01
gas	.02	wood, rough	−.04	medicinal products	.01
copper	−.01	fruit, fresh	−.03	chemical n.e.s.	.01
aluminium	.01	animal food	.02	organic chemicals	.01
Cameroon					
petroleum products	−.14	coffee	−.09	mach., elec.	.03
petroleum	.07	cocoa	−.05	special transactions	−.03
gas	−.02	cotton	−.01	coal	−.02
aluminium	.01	rice	.01	road vehicles	.02
coal	−.01	paper	.01	ships	.02
iron ore	−.01	animal food	−.01	organic chemicals	.02
Canada					
gas	−.04	paper	−.14	ships	.04
petroleum products	−.02	fruit, fresh	.05	road vehicles	.02
petroleum	.01	coffee	.05	special transactions	−.02
coal	.01	wood, shaped	−.03	clothing	.02
aluminium	−.01	pulp	−.03	electrical machinery	.01
base metal	.01	fish, fresh	−.02	organic chemicals	.01
Colombia					
petroleum	.14	fish, fresh	.06	clothing	.02
petroleum products	−.14	coffee	.06	road vehicles	.02
fertilizers	.01	cocoa	−.05	cement	.02
gas	−.01	tea	−.03	medicinal products	.01
tin	.01	cotton	−.03	organic chemicals	−.01
iron ore	−.01	fruit, fresh	−.02	chemical n.e.s.	.01
Costa Rica					
petroleum	−.14	fruit, fresh	.13	mach., elec.	−.03
petroleum products	.08	coffee	.09	coal	.03
coal	.01	fish, fresh	−.05	chemical n.e.s.	−.02
aluminium	−.01	paper	−.03	plastic material	−.01
tin	.01	meat, fresh	.02	organic chemicals	−.01
fertilizers	.01	sugar	−.02	medicinal products	.01
Cyprus					
petroleum products	−.09	fish, fresh	−.13	clothing	.04
petroleum	.05	veg., fresh	.05	mach., elec.	.03
aluminium	−.02	coffee	−.03	footwear	.03
other minerals	.01	tobacco manuf.	.02	cement	.02
fertilizers	−.01	alcoholic beverages	.02	ships	.02
gas	−.01	sugar	−.01	special transactions	−.02

Table 6.14   (continued)

Resources		Agriculture		Manufacturing	
Denmark					
petroleum products	−.06	meat, fresh	.07	mach., elec.	.03
petroleum	.05	coffee	−.03	road vehicles	−.02
coal	−.02	fish, fresh	.03	clothing	−.02
gas	.01	meat	.03	furniture	.02
base metal	.00	meat, dried	.03	steel tubes	−.02
aluminium	−.00	fruit, fresh	−.03	steel SITC 674	−.02
Dominican Republic					
petroleum products	−.04	sugar	.19	clothing	−.04
petroleum	−.03	fish, fresh	−.07	mach., elec.	.02
tin	−.01	fruit, fresh	−.03	road vehicles	.02
coal	.01	cocoa	.03	medicinal products	−.02
fertilizers	−.01	veg oil soft	−.03	organic chemicals	.02
aluminium	−.00	rubber	−.02	woven textiles	.01
Ecuador					
petroleum	−.14	fish, fresh	.05	special transactions	.03
petroleum products	.07	fruit, fresh	.04	mach., elec.	−.02
gas	−.03	tea	−.02	structures	.01
fertilizers	.01	wheat, unmilled	.02	medicinal products	−.01
coal	.01	fish, tinned	.02	telecom equipment	.01
aluminium	−.01	rubber	−.02	power machinery	−.01
Egypt					
petroleum products	−.08	fish, fresh	.05	special transactions	−.04
petroleum	.07	wheat, unmilled	−.03	coal	−.03
aluminium	.02	sugar	.03	road vehicles	.03
coal	−.00	cocoa	.03	mach., elec.	.02
fertilizers	.00	fruit, fresh	−.03	woven textiles	.02
gas	−.00	coffee	−.03	cement	−.02
El Salvador					
petroleum	−.10	fruit, fresh	−.07	road vehicles	.05
petroleum products	.03	fish, fresh	−.07	woven textiles	.02
aluminium	−.00	coffee	.06	mach., elec.	.02
coal	.00	cotton	.04	medicinal products	−.02
fertilizers	.00	veg., fresh	−.03	textile yarn	.02
gas	−.00	tea	−.03	machinery SITC 718	.02
Ethiopia					
petroleum products	.15	cotton	−.02	road vehicles	−.04
gas	.03	coffee	.02	special transactions	.04
petroleum	−.02	meat, fresh	.02	mach., elec.	−.03
fertilizers	−.02	fish, fresh	.02	clothing	−.03
coal	−.01	sugar	−.02	coal	.02
tin	.01	rice	−.02	ships	−.01
Fiji					
petroleum products	−.13	fish, fresh	.11	clothing	−.02
petroleum	.11	coffee	−.05	coal	−.02
aluminium	.02	fruit, fresh	−.05	mach., elec.	.02
tin	−.01	sugar	.03	special transactions	−.02
coal	−.01	meat, fresh	−.03	woven textiles	.02
gas	−.00	wool	−.02	inorganic elements	−.01

Table 6.14 (continued)

Resources		Agriculture		Manufacturing	
Finland					
petroleum products	.08	paper	.15	road vehicles	−.05
petroleum	−.04	coffee	−.04	ships	.04
coal	−.01	fruit, fresh	−.03	clothing	.01
electric energy	−.01	pulp	.03	special transactions	.01
zinc	.01	wood, shaped	.03	aircraft	−.01
aluminium	−.01	veneers	.02	mach., elec.	−.01
France					
petroleum	.08	coffee	−.03	clothing	−.05
gas	−.02	fruit, fresh	−.03	road vehicles	.04
tin	−.01	wheat, unmilled	.03	aircraft	.03
coal	.01	cocoa	−.02	mach., elec.	.02
iron and steel	.00	meat, fresh	−.02	toys	−.02
fertilizers	−.00	alcoholic beverages	.02	telecom equipment	−.02
Germany					
petroleum	−.11	coffee	−.04	road vehicles	.13
gas	−.03	fruit, fresh	−.04	mach., elec.	.05
coal	.02	meat, fresh	−.02	clothing	−.03
petroleum products	.01	cocoa	−.02	special transactions	.02
fertilizers	.00	fish, fresh	.02	coal	.02
copper	.00	wood, rough	−.01	machinery SITC 718	.01
Greece					
petroleum	.12	meat, fresh	−.05	special transactions	−.05
petroleum products	−.10	fruit, fresh	.03	ships	−.03
aluminium	.01	tobac., unman.	.02	coal	.03
tin	−.01	coffee	.02	cement	.03
base metal	.01	veg., preserved	.02	textile yarn	.02
copper	.01	milk	−.01	mach., elec.	.02
Hong Kong					
petroleum	.10	animals	−.02	clothing	.18
petroleum products	−.09	paper	−.02	toys	.06
tin	−.00	fruit, fresh	−.01	woven textiles	−.03
base metal	.00	meat, fresh	−.01	watches	.02
copper	−.00	sugar	−.01	textile yarn	−.02
gas	.00	veg., fresh	−.01	telecom equipment	.02
Iceland					
petroleum products	−.05	fish, fresh	.23	special transactions	.02
aluminium	.04	fruit, fresh	−.06	clothing	−.02
petroleum	−.02	coffee	−.05	inorganic elements	−.02
fertilizers	−.01	meat, fresh	−.02	footwear	−.02
other minerals	−.01	veg., fresh	−.02	electrical machinery	−.02
coal	−.00	sugar	.02	cement	−.01
Indonesia					
petroleum products	−.20	tea	−.04	road vehicles	.03
petroleum	.09	sugar	−.02	plastic material	−.02
gas	.07	fish, fresh	.02	telecom equipment	.02
coal	−.01	veg., fresh	−.02	organic chemicals	−.01
base metal	.01	wood, shaped	.02	special transactions	.01
fertilizers	.01	veneers	.02	inorganic elements	−.01

Table 6.14   (continued)

Resources		Agriculture		Manufacturing	
Ireland					
petroleum products	−.14	meat, fresh	.07	organic chemicals	.05
petroleum	.12	butter	.03	office machinery	.04
coal	−.01	food preparations	.03	clothing	−.04
base metal	.01	milk	.02	instruments	.02
aluminium	−.01	alcoholic beverages	.02	road vehicles	−.02
fertilizers	−.00	fruit, fresh	−.02	special transactions	.01
Israel					
gas	.02	fruit	.02	pearl	.09
petroleum	.01	coffee	−.02	metal manufactures	.08
coal	.01	meat, fresh	−.02	road vehicles	−.05
fertilizers	.01	fruit, fresh	.02	special transactions	−.04
copper	−.01	oil seeds	−.02	chemical n.e.s.	.03
tin	−.00	cotton	.02	office machinery	−.03
Italy					
petroleum	−.08	meat, fresh	−.05	mach., elec.	.06
petroleum products	.04	coffee	−.03	footwear	.04
gas	−.02	animals	−.02	jewelry	.03
iron and steel	−.01	wood, shaped	−.02	clothing	.03
tin	−.00	cocoa	−.01	woven textiles	.03
base metal	.00	fish, fresh	.01	furniture	.02
Ivory Coast					
petroleum products	.11	cocoa	.12	road vehicles	−.03
petroleum	−.06	wood, rough	.05	mach., elec.	−.03
gas	.01	coffee	.05	ships	−.02
coal	.01	meat, fresh	−.02	special transactions	.02
tin	.01	rice	−.02	aircraft	−.01
aluminium	−.00	fish, fresh	−.02	steel SITC 674	−.01
Japan					
petroleum	−.07	coffee	−.04	road vehicles	.10
petroleum products	.07	wood, rough	−.03	clothing	−.03
gas	−.02	cocoa	−.03	sound recorders	.03
iron ore	−.01	fruit, fresh	−.03	steel tubes	.02
copper	.01	meat, fresh	−.02	electrical machinery	.02
tin	−.00	wood, shaped	−.02	ships	.02
Malaysia					
petroleum	.04	wood, rough	.11	mach., elec.	−.03
tin	.04	veg oil, hard	.09	machinery SITC 718	−.03
petroleum products	−.03	rubber	.08	road vehicles	−.03
base metal	−.02	wood, shaped	.04	steel SITC 674	−.02
copper	−.01	sugar	−.02	ships	−.01
fertilizers	−.01	cocoa	.02	power machinery	−.01
Morocco					
fertilizers	.09	fruit, fresh	.06	special transactions	−.04
petroleum	.06	fish, fresh	−.04	inorganic elements	.04
sulphur	−.02	wheat	−.04	coal	−.02
tin	−.02	coffee	.03	road vehicles	.02
gas	.01	veg oil, hard	−.02	ships	−.02
petroleum products	.01	wood, rough	−.02	electrical machinery	.01

Table 6.14   (continued)

Resources		Agriculture		Manufacturing	
Netherlands					
petroleum	− .24	meat, fresh	.02	plastic material	.03
gas	.07	veg material	.02	organic chemicals	.03
petroleum products	.05	veg,. fresh	.02	road vehicles	− .02
coal	− .01	coffee	− .02	ships	.02
fertilizers	.01	fruit, fresh	− .02	clothing	− .02
iron ore	− .00	fish, fresh	.01	special transactions	.02
New Zealand					
petroleum	.07	meat, fresh	.11	road vehicles	− .05
petroleum products	− .05	wool	.06	mach., elec.	− .02
aluminium	.02	butter	.05	steel SITC 674	− .02
fertilizers	− .01	milk	.04	plastic materials	− .02
gas	.00	sugar	− .02	machinery SITC 718	− .01
coal	.00	cheese	.01	woven textiles	− .01
Nicaragua					
petroleum products	− .04	cotton	.09	medicinal products	− .02
aluminium	− .01	cocoa	− .07	agricultural manufactures	− .02
coal	− .01	fruit, fresh	− .06	plastic materials	.02
base metal	− .01	fish, fresh	− .06	road vehicles	.02
iron ore	− .00	meat, fresh	.04	cement	− .02
tin	.00	paper	.02	mach., elec.	.02
Norway					
gas	.20	fish, fresh	.03	clothing	− .03
petroleum products	− .11	paper	.02	pig iron	.02
aluminium	.04	wheat	− .02	inorganic elements	− .02
petroleum	− .02	animal food	.02	road vehicles	− .02
base metal	− .01	meat, fresh	− .01	fertilizer manufactures	.01
nickel	.01	fish, tinned	.01	furniture	− .01
Pakistan					
petroleum products	− .15	rice	.06	clothing	.05
petroleum	.03	coffee	− .04	woven textiles	.03
tin	.01	fish, fresh	.03	agricultural manufactures	− .02
coal	− .01	sugar	.02	floor covering	.02
gas	− .01	cotton	.02	steel SITC 674	− .01
aluminium	− .01	fruit, fresh	− .02	fertilizer manufactures	− .01
Panama					
petroleum	.22	coffee	− .04	special transactions	− .05
petroleum products	− .09	cocoa	− .02	coal	− .04
tin	− .00	cotton	− .02	clothing	− .03
aluminium	− .00	fruit, fresh	.02	mach., elec.	.02
fertilizers	− .00	meat, fresh	.01	telecom equipment	− .02
base metal	− .00	wheat	.01	steel tubes	.02
Peru					
petroleum products	.16	wood, rough	− .05	special transactions	.02
petroleum	− .13	veg oil, hard	− .05	coal	.02
fertilizers	− .03	rubber	− .04	clothing	.01
copper	.02	fruit, fresh	− .03	inorganic elements	− .01
tin	− .02	wood, shaped	− .02	machinery SITC 718	.01
coal	− .01	fish, fresh	.02	telecom equipment	.01

Table 6.14   (continued)

Resources		Agriculture		Manufacturing	
Philippines					
petroleum	.11	tea	−.06	clothing	−.04
base metal	.03	sugar	.06	special transactions	.03
petroleum products	.02	fish, fresh	.05	mach., elec.	−.02
silver	.02	rubber	−.04	steel forms	−.01
tin	−.02	cocoa	.02	pearl	−.01
gas	.01	veg oil, hard	.02	power machinery	−.01
Portugal					
petroleum	.19	maize	−.03	special transactions	−.05
petroleum products	−.12	fish, fresh	−.02	coal	−.03
tin	−.01	oil seeds	−.02	road vehicles	−.03
fertilizers	−.01	cotton	−.02	textile products	.02
aluminium	−.01	pulp	.02	clothing	.02
coal	.00	alcoholic beverages	.01	woven textiles	.02
Saudi Arabia					
petroleum products	.18	wood, rough	−.04	road vehicles	−.02
gas	−.03	fish, fresh	−.04	special transactions	.02
petroleum	−.03	veg oil, hard	−.04	inorganic elements	.02
tin	−.02	rubber	−.03	mach., elec.	−.02
aluminium	−.02	coffee	.03	coal	.02
base metal	.01	meat, fresh	.02	power machinery	−.01
Singapore					
petroleum	−.23	coffee	.03	special transactions	.06
petroleum products	.17	fruit, fresh	.01	coal	.04
gas	.01	fish, fresh	.01	mach., elec.	−.03
tin	.01	rubber	.01	telecom equipment	.02
fertilizers	−.00	veg oil, hard	.01	clothing	−.02
coal	.00	sugar	−.01	steel tubes	−.01
Spain					
petroleum products	−.04	fruit, fresh	.03	road vehicles	.07
gas	−.02	maize	−.02	special transactions	−.04
iron and steel	−.01	oil seeds	−.02	iron SITC 673	.03
fertilizers	−.01	meat, fresh	−.02	clothing	−.03
tin	−.01	rubber	−.01	mach., elec.	.03
copper	.01	veg oil, hard	−.01	telecom equipment	−.02
Sri Lanka					
petroleum products	.06	tea	.10	clothing	.03
petroleum	−.02	sugar	−.05	woven textiles	−.02
fertilizers	.02	coffee	−.05	organic chemicals	.02
tin	−.01	rice	−.04	woven textiles	−.01
aluminium	.01	cocoa	.04	steel SITC 674	.01
base metal	−.01	rubber	.03	textile yarn	−.01
Sweden					
petroleum products	.05	paper	.07	road vehicles	.06
gas	.02	coffee	−.05	clothing	−.05
iron ore	.01	fruit, fresh	−.05	telecom equipment	.03
coal	.01	pulp	.03	special transactions	.02
petroleum	.00	wood, shaped	.03	electrical machinery	−.02
electric energy	−.00	fish, fresh	.02	sound recorders	−.01

Table 6.14   (continued)

Resources		Agriculture		Manufacturing	
Switzerland					
petroleum	.09	fruit, fresh	− .03	road vehicles	− .07
petroleum products	− .03	coffee	− .02	clothing	− .05
coal	.01	cocoa	− .02	watches	.04
gas	.01	meat, fresh	− .01	medicinal products	.03
aluminium	.01	fish, fresh	.01	mach., elec.	.03
base metal	.00	alcoholic beverages	− .01	textile machinery	.03
Thailand					
petroleum products	− .09	rice	.08	special transactions	− .04
gas	− .03	veg., fresh	.06	clothing	− .03
tin	.01	tea	− .06	woven textiles	.02
base metal	− .00	sugar	.05	mach., elec.	.02
iron and steel	− .00	fish, fresh	.04	woven textiles	.01
copper	− .00	maize	.02	coal	− .01
Trinidad and Tobago					
petroleum products	.32	fish, fresh	− .03	mach., elec.	− .04
petroleum	.09	meat, fresh	− .01	ships	− .03
gas	− .03	veg., fresh	− .01	machinery SITC 718	− .02
aluminium	− .01	wheat	− .01	aircraft	− .02
coal	− .01	paper	.01	inorganic elements	.02
iron ore	− .01	cocoa	.01	road vehicles	− .02
Turkey					
petroleum	− .07	cotton	.04	textile yarn	.03
petroleum products	− .02	fruit, fresh	.04	organic chemicals	− .02
other minerals	.01	tobac., unman.	.04	cement	.02
gas	− .01	animals	.04	special transactions	− .02
iron and steel	− .01	tea	− .03	floor covering	.02
tin	− .01	sugar	.02	power machinery	− .02
United Kingdom					
petroleum products	− .11	meat, fresh	− .02	mach., elec.	.06
gas	− .06	fruit, fresh	− .02	aircraft	.03
petroleum	− .03	paper	− .01	machinery SITC 718	.03
silver SITC 681	.01	alcoholic beverages	.01	power machinery	.03
fertilizers	.01	fish, fresh	.01	power machinery	.02
aluminium	− .01	veg., fresh	− .01	steel tubes	.02
United States					
petroleum products	− .17	oil seeds	.02	mach., elec.	.05
petroleum	− .15	maize	.02	aircraft	.03
gas	− .06	animal food	.01	machinery SITC 718	.03
coal	.01	fish, fresh	.01	ships	.02
fertilizers	.01	meat, fresh	− .01	office machines	.02
aluminium	− .00	wood, shaped	.01	electrical machinery	.02
Yugoslavia					
gas	− .06	fruit, fresh	− .03	footwear	.05
petroleum products	− .06	rubber	− .02	organic chemicals	− .03
petroleum	.05	fish, fresh	.02	furniture	.02
aluminium	.01	tea	− .02	road vehicles	.02
coal	− .01	pulp	− .01	clothing	.02
base metal	− .01	cotton	− .01	power machinery	.02

explanation of trade in petroleum products. Part of the problem may be the difficulty of predicting the location of petroleum refineries, which may indeed be greatly influenced by policy interventions. After petroleum, fish is a problem commodity. This is suggestive of an omitted resource variable: coastline or access to fisheries. Coffee and fruit are also problem commodities. The land variables include land suited to tropical agricultural production, and in principle this should help explain trade in coffee and fruit. Is it possible that trade in these items is influenced by policy interventions? The one clear positive note is that clothing is the manufactured commodity for which the interventions seem most significant. That seems to square well with the facts.

Table 6.14 contains the same information for each country. A negative number in table 6.14 means that actual net exports are less than predicted by the model. Either exports are too small or imports too great, at least as judged by the behavior of the other countries in the sample. A positive number means that net exports are large compared with the other countries; either exports are too large or imports too small. A positive number thus suggests either an export subsidy or an import barrier, higher than other countries'. A negative number, on the other hand, suggests either an unusually low export subsidy or an unusually low import barrier. In a word, positive means relatively protected, negative relatively unprotected.

Take a good look at this table and try to form a judgment as to whether it gives a sense of the products that are significantly affected by trade barriers. Keep in mind, however, that products with small valuation at the three-digit SITC level cannot appear in these tables since their residuals would be correspondingly small.

Consider the first country, Argentina, which has one of the lowest overall R^2's. Ten percent of its sum of absolute residuals is due to overpredicting fish net exports, 8 percent from underpredicting petroleum products net exports, and so forth. The data suggest that Argentina's fish sector is relatively unprotected and that the petroleum products sector is protected or subsidized, compared with other countries.

Look at a couple of other countries, say, the United States and Japan. The United States has unpredictably low levels of net exports of petroleum products and petroleum, but appears to protect or subsidize machinery and aircraft. Japan protects or subsidizes road vehicles. Japan's unusually high net exports of petroleum products are offset by unusually low net exports of petroleum. Incidentally, this feature recurs for many countries and suggests that the model is incapable of explaining the location of petroleum refining. The measures that depend on these residuals therefore need to be viewed with suspicion.

As I examine these results, I am left with a feeling of skepticism regarding the usefulness of the adjusted trade intensity ratios as indicators of trade barriers. I see tastes (Japan's coffee), omitted resources (Iceland's fish), and historical accidents (Switzerland's watches). I am not sure that I see trade barriers. What seems clear is that, in the absence of direct measures of barriers, it will be impossible to determine the degree of openness for most countries with much subjective confidence.

Notes

This research has been partially supported by NSF grant SES 84 19932 and by the World Bank. Able research assistance has been provided by Shu-heng Chen and Kishore Gawande. Comments by Robert Baldwin, Anne Krueger, Alan Deardorff, and other attendees at the NBER conference are gratefully acknowledged.

1. This model leaves unspecified certain details of the structure of world demand and supply that would determine international product prices. These prices may change in response to changes in technology, shifts in world trade barriers, or worldwide growth of factor supplies. Policy analysis and econometric estimation that take international product prices as exogenous will nonetheless be appropriate provided that countries are small enough that internal events such as the imposition of trade barriers have no noticeable effects on international prices.

2. Here I am assuming that the tariff proceeds are redistributed in a lump sum or that the government utility function conforms with the private sector.

3. In the Bayesian language, it would be better to say that the unobservables are treated as if they came from a distribution with an infinite variance.

4. These numbers have been truncated after two decimals, and the columns for R, A, and M therefore appear not to add to the column for O.

References

Balassa, Bela. 1965. Trade liberalization and 'revealed' comparative advantage. *Manchester School* (May): 99–123.

———. 1971. *The structure of protection in developing countries*. New York: Pergamon Press.

———. 1979. The changing pattern of comparative advantage in manufactured goods. *Review of Economics and Statistics* (May): 259–66.

Balassa, Bela, and Carol Balassa. 1984. Industrial protection in the developed countries. *World Economy* 7: 179–96.

Bergsten, C. Fred, and William R. Cline. 1983. Trade policy in the 1980s: An overview. In William R. Cline, ed., *Trade policy in the 1980s*, 59–98. Washington, D.C.: Institute for International Economics.

Cline, William R., Noboru Kawanabe, T. O. M. Kronsjo, and Thomas Williams. 1978. *Trade negotiations in the Tokyo Round: A quantitative assessment*. Washington, D.C.: The Brookings Institution.

Godek, Paul E. 1986. The politically optimal tariff: Levels of trade restrictions across developed countries. *Economic Inquiry* 24: 587–93.

Hughes, Helen, and Anne O. Krueger. 1984. Effects of protection in developed countries on developing countries' exports of manufactures. In Robert Baldwin and Anne Krueger, eds., *The structure and evolution of recent U.S. trade policy,* 389–418. Chicago: University of Chicago Press.

Leamer, Edward E. 1978. *Specification searches.* New York: John Wiley.

———. 1984. *Sources of international comparative advantage: Theory and evidence.* Cambridge: MIT Press.

———. 1987a. Cross section estimation of the effects of trade barriers. In Robert Feenstra, ed., *Empirical methods for international trade.* Cambridge: MIT Press.

———. 1987b. Paths of development in the three-factor N-good general equilibrium model. *Journal of Political Economy* 95: 961–99.

Morrison, Thomas K. 1976. Manufactured exports and protection in developing countries: A cross-country analysis. *Economic Development and Cultural Change* 25: 151–58.

Nogues, Julio J., Andrzej Olechowski, and L. Alan Winters. 1986. The extent of nontariff barriers to industrial countries' imports. *World Bank Economic Review* 1: 181–99.

Pryor, Frederic L. 1966. Trade barriers of capitalist and communist nations against foodstuffs exported by tropical underdeveloped nations. *Review of Economics and Statistics* 48: 406–11.

Ray, Edward J., and Howard P. Marvel. 1984. The pattern of protection in the industrialized world. *Review of Economics and Statistics* 66: 452–58.

Sampson, Gary P., and Alexander Yeats. 1977. An evaluation of the common agricultural policy as a barrier facing agricultural exports to the European economic community. *American Journal of Agricultural Economics* 59: 99–106.

Saxonhouse, Gary R. 1983. The micro and macro economics of foreign sales to Japan. In William R. Cline, ed., *Trade policy in the 1980s,* 259–85. Washington, D.C.: Institute for International Economics.

Schwarz, G. 1978. Estimating the dimension of a model. *Annals of Statistics* 6: 461–64.

U.S. Tariff Commission. 1974. *Trade barriers.* Report to the Committee on Finance of the U.S. Senate. Pt. 2. Washington, D.C.

Comment   Drusilla K. Brown

Measures of the degree to which countries interfere with international commerce have typically been based on a bottom-up approach: measuring tariff and nontariff barriers, product by product and country by country. Alternatively, one could estimate a theoretical model that could predict the pattern and volume of trade under free trade conditions. The degree to which countries are "open" can be evaluated by comparing actual trade with the pattern of free trade predicted by the

Drusilla K. Brown is assistant professor of economics at Tufts University.

model. Countries that deviate most from the trade pattern predicted by the model would be deemed relatively more protectionist.

This second approach is adopted by Leamer in chapter 6, "Measures of Openness." In this chapter, factor endowments of land, labor, capital, oil production, and minerals, along with distance and the trade balance, are used to predict net trade within a product category for each country. Net trade within a product category is regressed on factor endowments for a cross section of countries. A separate equation is estimated for each product category.

While this model does not predict the pattern of trade under free trade conditions, it would predict trade if each country were to adopt the world's average level of protection. Thus, a country that trades less than the model predicts must have a higher than average level of protection, and those that trade more have a lower than average level of protection.

This is an extremely ambitious project and will yield information of great interest to both academic economists and policymakers. This approach is also a great improvement over measuring openness by calculating imports and exports as a fraction of GNP. As the chapter points out, such an approach merely indicates the degree to which countries differ in their factor endowments, not in the level of protection.

The question I address first is, What does this approach tell us? Suppose for a moment we really have found the true model that predicts trade, and we have found a country and product for which the regression equation fits the pattern of trade poorly. This procedure will tell us how a country's trade pattern is deviating from the average trade pattern for countries similarly endowed. If that is what we mean by "openness," this is an appropriate procedure.

However, will this approach tell us which countries are most protectionist? In a two-country model, if one country is protectionist the trade for both partners will deviate from the free trade pattern, and thus both countries will appear "closed" by this measure. Nonetheless, in a world of more than two countries the problem is not very damaging. If in a multicountry system some countries are open and trade mutually, we would expect that their actual trade pattern would be closely correlated with the free trade pattern, although countries close to protectionist countries may trade less than expected.

A second problem along these lines was noted in the chapter. The model will give misleading results if similarly endowed countries adopt similar structures of protection. Countries following the protection standard will appear normal, while countries with peculiar structures of protection will be singled out.

According to the measures used in the chapter, a country that is peculiar in its choice of intervention may be "open" as measured by the adjusted trade intensity ratio, but will also have a high index of intervention. This discrepancy occurs because the measure of openness compares the total amount of actual trade to the total amount of predicted trade. The intervention index, on the other hand, focuses on the absolute value of the residuals, thus checking to see if a country is trading in the "right" product categories. Therefore, a country that has a level of protection equal to the world average but applying to unusual product categories will have an appropriate level of trade but in the "wrong" product categories. As a result, the intervention index will be high.

A third problem with the interpretation of results will arise if some factors have a variable supply. Trade barriers that raise the return to capital will increase a protectionist country's "endowment" of capital over time. Consequently, if protection in a country has occurred over several years, such a country may cease to appear protectionist.

Problems with interpretation, however, do not pose insurmountable obstacles. If we accept the approach, then the next step is the choice of a theoretical model. The model chosen must satisfy very stringent conditions, for it is insufficient that it be a model with some statistical power to explain the pattern of trade. Rather, it must be *the* model of international trade, for all residuals are attributed to protection.

The framework chosen in the chapter is the n-factor n-good version of the Heckscher-Ohlin model. It is hard to imagine that the $n \times n$ version of the Heckscher-Ohlin theorem adequately explains the actual pattern of trade for the purposes of this study. Factor endowments undoubtedly play a role in determining the pattern of trade in goods, but there are many other factors, such as differences in taste and the presence of scale economies.

Scale economies, in particular, pose problems for the factor proportions theory. A small country may be heavily endowed with an input used intensively in the production of a particular good but may not be large enough to accommodate a firm that fully exploits the available economies of scale. Consequently, the small country may specialize in the production of goods produced with constant-returns-to-scale technology, while a large country specializes in the increasing-returns-to-scale industry. In this event, the model will be biased toward the result that small countries are more open than large countries in goods produced with increasing returns to scale but less open in goods produced with constant returns to scale. For example, scale economies and country size may explain the unusually large exports of aircraft by the United States or the absence of Austria's exports of road vehicles.

A second problem associated with scale economies is that in industries dominated by monopolistically competitive firms, trade may occur even between countries with identical tastes and factor endowments. In cases where a single monopolistically competitive industry straddles two or more product categories, trade in goods will be driven by product differentiation. Factor endowments may have little explanatory power.

A second difficulty with applying the Heckscher-Ohlin model to this problem is that higher dimensional trade theory does not predict the commodity composition of trade when the number of goods exceeds the number of factors. Rather, only the direction of factor trade is predictable. As a result, it would be more appropriate to use net factor trade as the dependent variable rather than net commodity trade.

For example, watches from Switzerland and beverages from France are offered as cases in which the model performed poorly because of omitted factors of production or as the result of an "accident of history." Similarly, the model had difficulty predicting the location of petroleum refining. Given the indeterminacy of the pattern of trade in goods when the number of goods exceeds the number of factors, it is likely that accidents of history will indeed affect the pattern of trade in goods.

Comparing actual trade against predictions of the $n \times n$ Heckscher-Ohlin theorem thus may be largely a measure of the inadequacies of this model, rather than a measure of trade barriers. This is similar to the criticism applied to the simple technique of calculating trade as a fraction of GNP, which is primarily a measure of the disparity of factor endowments among countries.

However, adopting net factor trade as the dependent variable will sidestep the indeterminacy problem when the number of goods exceeds the number of factors and should help to resolve some of the difficulties associated with trade in products produced with increasing returns to scale by monopolistically competitive firms. No matter what the pattern of trade in goods in these two instances, it should still be the case that factors of production embodied in the net trade bundle will unambiguously reflect relative factor abundance in the absence of protection. In these instances, the model predicting trade in goods may perform poorly, while a model predicting trade in factors could capture the essence of trade fairly well.

Despite these problems, some of the results presented in the chapter are highly effective in challenging conventional wisdom. For example, according to this study Japan is not dramatically more protectionist than the United States, and for most calculations Japan appears to have less intrusive barriers to trade. This is a result that many trade economists and Japan specialists suspect to be the case, but is not widely accepted outside of the profession. However, some of the results are impossible to believe. For example, according to this study one of the least protected industries in the United States is meat. Similarly, the results suggest that meat is an unprotected sector in Japan, which is clearly not the case.

This method of detecting protectionism is nevertheless very promising. The fundamental problems can be addressed simply by adding a few more factors of production, such as coastline for fishing and tropical weather conditions, and adopting a more general model that can accommodate accidents of history, scale economies, and trade pattern indeterminacies of the Heckscher-Ohlin model.

7   The Effects of Protection on Domestic Output

Robert E. Baldwin and Richard K. Green

Raising the level of import protection has become the standard government policy to assist industries seriously injured by increased imports. The political reasons for preferring import restrictions over alternative means of assistance, such as subsidizing domestic production or providing adjustment assistance to workers and firms, are not hard to understand. The benefits of protection are concentrated on the injured industry, whereas the costs are usually thinly spread over a large number of users of the protected product. Furthermore, unlike subsidies, no unpopular budgetary costs are involved, nor does protection, in contrast to adjustment assistance, send the unpopular message to the affected industry that the government thinks a decline in the number of firms and employed workers is appropriate.

A well-established body of partial equilibrium analysis demonstrating the output-increasing effects of import protection reinforces the preference of governments and import-injured industries for this policy. In the standard competitive model of profit-maximizing behavior, a tariff increase in an industry producing a homogeneous product enables domestic firms to increase output and capture a larger share of the home market by raising the costs of delivering the product from foreign compared to domestic production sources. If the product is differentiated, the increased delivery price of the variety produced abroad acts to shift demand toward the domestic substitute. The same expansion of domestic output also occurs in oligopolistic models under such commonly assumed conjectural behavior as Cournot-Nash or Bertrand.

Robert E. Baldwin is Hilldale Professor of Economics at the University of Wisconsin–Madison and a research associate of the National Bureau of Economic Research. Richard K. Green is a Ph.D. candidate in the Department of Economics at the University of Wisconsin–Madison.

There is also a body of analysis, however, utilizing a more general equilibrium framework, that points out the ineffectiveness of import protection in stimulating domestic production under some conditions. Metzler (1949) demonstrates, for example, that, if the income effects associated with price changes are taken into account, protection may not accomplish its intended purpose. Specifically, if the sum of the elasticity (in absolute terms) of foreign demand for the exports of the tariff-imposing country and that country's own marginal propensity to spend on imports is less than unity, the domestic price of the protected good will decline and thus act to reduce rather than increase domestic production.[1]

Baldwin (1982) analyzes a number of situations in which certain protection effects that are usually ignored in the standard partial equilibrium analysis cause a smaller-than-expected increase in home production. Under conditions often satisfied, introducing quantitative restrictions induces a shift in the product mix of foreign suppliers toward higher-priced varieties of the protected product.[2] Thus, since the value of imports in the protecting country falls less than the quantity of imports, the value of domestic output and employment increases less than is expected and, in particular, less than if an ad valorem tariff had been used to reduce the total quantity of imports to the same level. Even when foreign firms shift production to the tariff-imposing country, the output-increasing benefits often accrue to firms and workers other than those that were injured by increased imports.

Another response that weakens the domestic output-increasing effects of protection is importing the protected product in either a less or more processed form than is covered by the protectionist action. Switching to substitute products is still another means by which consumer responses lessen the price-increasing and, thus, output-increasing effects of protection.

Protection will have no output-increasing effects at home when a quota on a homogeneous good is imposed selectively against suppliers in only a few foreign countries, and this quota, plus the quantity of the import good initially supplied in world markets by producers in nonaffected countries, is greater than the import demand of the restricting country. The latter producers merely shift to supplying the market of the restricting country, while producers in the country against which the selective quota is imposed shift their exports to other countries. Even when these required conditions are not satisfied, the selective quotas may have a very limited effect on domestic production due to transshipments through nonquota countries or the transfer of production facilities to these countries.

Recent theoretical work analyzing international behavior in imperfectly competitive markets suggests still other reasons why protection may not lead to the increased domestic production expected on the basis of the standard competitive model. Assume, for example, that foreign producers of differentiated products that compete with similar domestic products have incurred substantial sunk costs in setting up distribution and service systems abroad and in acquiring knowledge about the foreign government's relevant regulations. While some of these costs can be recouped if the foreign firms reduce foreign sales, others cannot be recovered. Consequently, when temporary protection increases their costs of selling abroad, these foreign firms may decide that the best policy in the long run is not to raise their prices and suffer a decline in market share abroad as domestic producers expand capacity, but instead to accept lower profits and maintain their market position. Yet these firms would not have initially expanded production and entered the domestic market so extensively had profits originally been at this lower level. Hysteresis in trade has occurred (Richard Baldwin 1986),[3] and the reduction in imports expected under the competitive paradigm does not occur.[4]

In some circumstances, the long-term profit prospects for the domestic industry may be so unfavorable that even if foreign supply does decrease and domestic profits rise, local firms do not utilize the increased profits to expand their output. Instead, managers of firms in the protected industry invest the profits in other industries.

Other writings that deal with the ineffectiveness of protection include Bhagwati and Hansen's (1973) analysis of how smuggling in response to protection can prevent the attainment of the desired level of domestic production, and Bhagwati and Srinivasan's (1980) analysis of the ways in which lobbying for protection or for obtaining the revenues resulting from protection may reduce domestic output in the protected sector.

The foregoing summary of the standard economic analysis of protection and also of the literature indicating why protection may be relatively ineffective in increasing domestic output suggests that empirical investigation of whether an increase in protection leads to increased domestic output in the protected industry is a worthwhile research topic. We use two approaches in carrying out such an investigation. The first involves examining reports by the International Trade Commission on the probable economic effect on a domestic industry if import relief is terminated. These reports invariably assess the effectiveness of the protection that had been granted and indicate if the commission finds any evidence in individual cases that supports the above analysis as to why protection may prove relatively ineffective in stimulating domestic output. We discuss the assessments of the commission on this matter in section 7.1.

Sections 7.2, 7.3, and 7.4 describe the more formal approach used to test for the effectiveness of import protection by utilizing cross-section and time-series data on output and protection levels within different industries. Specifically, section 7.2 outlines the vector autoregression model used to test the hypothesis that a change in the level of protection in an import-competing industry does not cause a change in the level of domestic output in the industry. Section 7.3 describes the estimation techniques, section 7.4 presents the estimation- and hypothesis-testing procedures, and section 7.5 discusses the data and testing results. The last section draws some conclusions from the two approaches used to study the effects of protection on domestic output.

We wish to stress that in using vector autoregression techniques we are not attempting to draw causal inferences without relying on a priori theory, a procedure that has recently been criticized by Leamer (1985). On the basis of a well-established economic model, one can hypothesize that increases in protection in an industry regularly precede increases in output in the industry. Failure to obtain statistical support for the null hypothesis is consistent with an economic model in which protection causes an increase in industry output. Such a finding, by itself, does not, as Leamer stresses, tell us anything about the direction of causality between protection and output.[5]

7.1   An Analysis of Section 203 Cases

Sections 201–3 of the Trade Act of 1974 specify the conditions under which an industry can obtain relief from injury caused by import competition. Representatives of the industry first file a petition with the International Trade Commission (ITC) seeking a finding of serious injury (or threat of serious injury) due to increased imports. If the ITC makes an affirmative determination, the president is directed to provide import relief for the industry unless he or she determines that such a step is not in the national economic interest of the United States. When the national interest condition is satisfied, the protection provided by the president must not exceed five years and must be sufficient to prevent or remedy serious injury or the threat thereof to the industry in question and to facilitate the industry's orderly adjustment to new competitive conditions.

Under the provisions of section 203, the president can extend protection for three years beyond the period for which import relief was initially granted, but first must take into account the advice of the ITC based on its study of the probable economic effect on the industry of the termination of the import relief.[6]

There have been thirteen section 203 reports under the Trade Act of 1974. In eight of these a majority of the commissioners concluded that termination of import relief would have an adverse effect on the industry and recommended continued protection. In four cases the commission determined that termination would not adversely affect the industry and recommended an end to import relief, while in one case the vote was evenly split. This section discusses the commission's views on whether the types of offsetting responses to protection described in the introductory section did occur in the cases investigated and, if they did, how important they were in rendering the initial protection ineffective. The views of other economists who have examined these protectionist experiences will also be considered.

7.1.1 Color Television Sets

Almost every report mentions responses that have tended to offset the output-increasing effects of increased protection, in some cases to a significant degree. As would be expected, protection was often the least effective when it involved selective quantitative restrictions, as in the example of the protection granted the domestic color television industry. In 1977 the U.S. government negotiated an orderly marketing agreement (OMA) quantitatively limiting Japanese exports of color television receivers and subassemblies thereof to the United States to about 70 percent of Japan's 1976 level. As a result, Japan's share of the U.S. market fell from 18.7 percent to 10.8 percent between 1976 and 1978.

But there was a fourfold increase in exports of color television sets from Taiwan and Korea, with their share rising from 1.5 percent to 7.2 percent in the same period, and the net result was that the import share from all sources only declined from 21.3 percent to 20.9 percent (Morici and Megna 1983, 19). Accordingly, the Carter administration negotiated OMAs with both Taiwan and Korea that became effective in 1979. That dropped the import share from all sources to 13.7 percent in 1979. But imports from Mexico and Singapore continued to rise during the period; their share of imports of complete and incomplete color television receivers increased from 16 percent in 1976 to 37 percent in 1979, while the share of the countries covered by the OMAs fell from 82 percent to 59 percent (ITC Report, 203-6, 1980, A-12).

Since unlimited imports of some subassemblies were allowed, another effect of the protection was to increase Japanese and Taiwanese investment in assembly facilities in the United States (ITC Report, 201-6, 1980, 6). Imports of subassemblies not covered by the OMAs doubled between 1976 and 1979. Production of the two largest U.S. producers fell, however (ITC Report, 203-6, 1980, A-18). Thus, as Hufbauer, Berliner, and Elliott (1986, 220) conclude, the overall impact of the OMAs on the injured firms was limited because of the shift in supply sources and the change in the composition of imports. The ITC recommended continued protection, however.

7.1.2   Nonrubber Footwear

The government negotiated OMAs with Taiwan and Korea in 1977 to protect the domestic nonrubber footwear industry. As in the color television case, a significant increase in imports from noncontrolled countries followed. While the volume of imported nonrubber footwear from Taiwan and Korea declined from 225 million pairs to 148 million pairs in the year after the OMA went into effect, imports from other sources increased from 142 million pairs to 225 million pairs (ITC Report, 203-7, 1981, A-8). To circumvent the quantitative restrictions in 1978, exporters from Taiwan allegedly tried transshipping through Hong Kong, but the practice was curtailed by requiring certificates of origin. With the increase in imports from noncontrolled sources, the total U.S. import share by volume increased from 47.0 percent in 1976, the last year before import restraints, to 51.0 percent in 1981, the last year of the restraint period, even though the import share of Taiwan and Korea fell from 25.4 percent to 22.0 percent between these years (Hufbauer, Berliner, and Elliott 1986, 210–11).

Significant quality upgrading by Taiwanese and Korean footwear exporters also occurred and served to reduce the impact of protection on domestic employment (Aw and Roberts 1986; Chang 1987). This is evident from the increase in the value share of imports from these countries in the U.S. market from 9.0 percent in 1976 to 13.1 percent in 1981, in contrast to a decline in their volume share from 25.4 percent to 22.0 percent between these years.

Still another response that weakened the positive effect of protection on the domestic industry was a manufacturers' change in the composition of athletic shoes that shifted their U.S. Customs classification from nonrubber footwear, on which quantitative restrictions were imposed, to noncontrolled rubber footwear. To be classified as nonrubber footwear, the upper part of footwear must be composed of more than 50 percent leather. Foreign producers simply changed the ornamental stripes on jogging shoes from leather to vinyl, thereby qualifying them for classification as rubber footwear. The domestic industry estimated that 55 million pairs of jogging shoes entered the United States through this loophole in 1978 (ITC Report, 203-7, 1981 A-10).

While the more rapid increase in the ratio of imports to consumption after decontrol in 1982 than during the control period suggests that the quantitative control had some restraining effect, the gradual rise in the import penetration ratio during the restraint period and the concomitant appreciable decline in domestic output and employment can hardly be regarded as a fulfillment of the president's presumed intention to "prevent or remedy serious injury" after the affirmative ITC finding.

7.1.3   Ceramic Tableware

Protection provided to the ceramic tableware industry is an example of import relief that became progressively less effective due to foreign suppliers shifting toward higher-priced import categories not covered by the escape clause action. For the first three years after the president granted import relief in 1972 by sharply increasing duties, this shift was modest but enough to prevent the import/consumption ratio for all earthen table and kitchen articles from falling. The ratio stood at 55 percent in 1971, 57 percent in 1972, and 58 percent in 1975 (ITC Report, 203-1, 1976, A-43). The recession of 1974–75 reduced the consumption of earthen tableware, but the import decrease between 1972 and 1975 in items covered by the escape clause action was 58 percent compared to only 17 percent for the products on which tariffs were not raised. Domestic shipments declined by 19 percent.

During 1976 and 1977, when total consumption of earthen table and kitchen articles increased appreciably, the shift toward noncovered items became so pronounced that the commission concluded that the probable effect on the industry of terminating the protection would be "minimal" (ITC Report, 203–4, news release). Imports of protected articles declined by 85 percent between 1975 and 1977 whereas imports of nonprotected varieties increased by 87 percent. The import penetration ratio for all earthen table and kitchen articles rose from 58 percent in 1975 to 69 percent in 1977, with protected items making up only 9 percent of total imports in 1977 in contrast to 28 percent in 1972 (ITC Report, 203-4, 1978, 40). Domestic shipments declined 2 percent between 1975 and 1977, while domestic consumption rose 35 percent. As a result of inflation in 1976 and 1977, an increasing percentage of imports originally subject to higher duties entered under noncovered higher value import categories (ITC Report, 203-4, news release).[7]

7.1.4   Bolts, Nuts, and Large Screws

Interestingly, the lack of substitution between imports and domestic production was the basis for the ITC's recommending termination of the 1979 tariff increase on bolts, nuts, and large screws. A majority of the commissioners, backed by an econometric study done by the ITC staff, concluded that "imposition of import relief in 1979 appears to have had at most a minor effect on import levels and domestic production" (ITC Report, 203-11, 1981, 9).

7.1.5   Stainless Steel and Alloy Tool Steel

The protection of domestic producers of stainless steel and alloy tool steel in the late 1970s by quantitative import restrictions illustrates another problem associated with protection, that in helping one industry, a restriction may injure another. Users of specialty steel were forced to hold larger inventories than prior to the quota system because of the surge of imports of specialty steel at the beginning of each quota period when foreign suppliers rushed to fill their country quota. These steel consumers complained that the higher financing and storage costs reduced the competitiveness of their end products with similar imported products (ITC Report, 203-5, 1979, A-14). The upgrading in product mix by foreign suppliers had a similar effect. Foreign steel producers reduced their exports of steel used to manufacture cutting blades, thereby forcing domestic manufacturers of cutting blades to purchase higher-priced domestic tool steels, putting them at a disadvantage vis-à-vis foreign competitors.

The U.S. stainless steel wire–producing industry was also severely affected by a shift in the product mix of imported steel. Wire is drawn from stainless steel rods, which were covered by the quota. The increase in the price of steel rods caused by the quota raised the production costs of domestic wire suppliers and led to an increase in imports of wire. Thus, as the commission report stated, "The result is that the U.S. stainless steel wire-producing industry is caught between tight supplies and rising prices of its raw material, which is under quota, and increased availability and more favorable prices from imports of its end product, wire, which is not under quota" (ITC Report, 203-3, 1977, A-36).

Even though there were these consumer problems with the quantitative restrictions, the commission staff concluded on the basis of its own econometric study that, while U.S. business expansion was the most important cause for the expansion of domestic output in the first year of the quota system (1977), the contribution of the import restraint program approached about half that of the business cycle.

7.1.6   Some Conclusions

A review of section 203 cases supports the view that market responses to protection sometimes significantly undermine its intended purpose of remedying the injury caused by increased imports. Such seems to have occurred in the television, footwear, and ceramic tableware cases. A more formal test of this proposition is undertaken in the next three sections, but some conclusions about situations in which protection is likely to be less effective can be drawn from the section 203 cases.

The television and footwear cases illustrate the problem of trying to increase domestic production by imposing selective quantitative import restrictions. Domestic producers are attracted to this approach because protection is likely to be granted more quickly. Also, it avoids their having to deal with the opposition of foreign suppliers whose exports to the country have not increased significantly and who would be injured themselves by a general cutback in imports, which government officials also appreciate. Even the country being discriminated against often does not object strongly because its producers receive the windfall gain associated with quantitative restrictions. The possibility of upgrading and shifting production to noncontrolled countries also helps to reduce its objections.

Yet, once there is acceptance of the principle of imposing import restrictions against only those countries from which imports have increased significantly, protection is likely to be ineffective during the often lengthy period of lobbying by the affected industry for protection from one country after another as production expands in noncontrolled countries. Both firms and workers are likely to believe that protection will work, and they tend to postpone the hard adjustment decisions that eventually must be made.

As the ceramic tableware case illustrates, a similar problem arises from changes in the import relief provisions of U.S. trade law that enable an industry to be defined narrowly. It is easier for a group of domestic firms competing with a selected set of products being imported in significantly greater quantities to show serious injury when the industry is less broadly defined. But the firms often discover that there is such a high degree of substitutability between the items covered by the protectionist action and other items covered by a broader definition of the industry that they are unable to increase their output and employment after receiving protection. The time elapsing before all the relevant products are covered by a protectionist action often seems longer than if the firms had waited until the entire industry was threatened with serious injury.

7.2   The Econometric Model

We now turn to a more formal approach for investigating the efficacy of protection: we use vector auto-regression techniques to test whether changes in protection from 1972 to 1982 in five major industries regularly preceded changes in output in these industries.

Consider the detrended variables x and y, which have many observations. The variable x is said not to "Granger-cause" the variable y if

(1) $\quad E\{y_t : y_{t-1}, y_{t-2}, \ldots, y_1, x_{t-1}, x_{t-2}, \ldots, x_1) =$
$$E(y_t : y_{t-1}, y_{t-2}, \ldots, y_1\},$$

where $E\{y : \Theta)$ is the linear least-squares projection of y on the information Θ. Thus, if given the history of the y process, the history of the x process cannot improve the prediction of y_t, x does not help predict, or to use Granger's (1969) terminology, "cause" y. This is tantamount to saying that knowledge of the future of x gives us no knowledge of the future of y.[8]

To test empirically whether x "causes" y, we first estimate the equation

$$
(2) \qquad y_t = \alpha_o + \sum_{l=1}^{m} \alpha_1 y_{t-1}
$$

$$
+ \sum_{k=1}^{n} \delta_k x_{t-k} + u_t ,
$$

where the α's and δ's are parameters and the lag lengths m and n are sufficient to assure that $\{u_t\}_{t-l}^s$ is a white noise process. We then use an F-test to test the hypothesis $\delta_1 = \delta_2 = \ldots = \delta_n = 0$. Should we reject this hypothesis, we cannot say that x does not "Granger-cause" y.

For these tests to have sufficient power to be meaningful, large numbers of observations of x and y are needed. We have eleven years of consistent annual data of output, and tariffs at the four-digit SIC industry level; this is not enough observations for individual industries to test for Granger causality using the method outlined above. To overcome this problem, we can create panels at the two-digit level, with observations x_{it}'s, where i represents an observation on an industry at the four-digit level of detail, and t represents an observation on one year.

Obviously, looking at a panel multiplies the number of observations available for an individual industry. The procedure for determining Granger causality using panel data is not, however, a straightforward application of the model described above. Specifically, we must consider the impact of the individual characteristics of the various four-digit industries on their response to protection, and we therefore may not stack all the time series–cross section observations to estimate equation (2). Moreover, the problem of testing for Granger causality renders inappropriate many standard models of handling panel data.

We therefore use the techniques developed by Chamberlain (1983) and Holtz-Eakin, Newey, and Rosen (1985), and follow the exposition of these authors to describe the model we use. Consider a panel with N cross-sectional units observed over T periods, and let i index the cross-sectional observations and t the time periods. Because each cross-sectional unit has individual characteristics, we change equation (2) to

$$
(2a) \qquad y_{it} = f_i + \alpha_o + \sum_{l=1}^{m} \alpha_l y_{it-l}
$$

$$
+ \sum_{k=1}^{n} \delta_k x_{it-k} + u_{it} ,
$$

where f_i represents the individual characteristic of cross-sectional unit i. The common practice for estimating equation (2a) is to difference the data to eliminate f_i and then use ordinary least-squares (OLS) or generalized least-squares (GLS) on the equation:

$$(3) \qquad y_{it} - y_{it-1} =$$
$$+ \sum_{l=1}^{m} \alpha_l(y_{it-l} - y_{it-l-1})$$
$$+ \sum_{k=1}^{n} \delta_k(x_{it-k} - x_{it-k-1})$$
$$+ u_{it} - u_{it-1} \,.$$

The flaw with this approach in our context is evident. Because y_{it} depends on u_{it}, the error term $(u_{it} - u_{it-1})$ is correlated with the regressor $(y_{it} - y_{it-1})$, so any estimate produced using OLS or GLS on this equation will be biased.

We shall use instrumental variables to eliminate this problem. But before discussing the procedure we use to instrument out the bias, we should consider another problem with equation (3)—heteroskedasticity.

Equation (3) specifies that the parameters are constant not only across different units but also across time. It also specifies that individual characteristics are time-invariant. Such a specification is needlessly limiting, thanks to Chamberlain's procedure for allowing the parameters and individual characteristics to vary over time.

For expository purposes, consider a panel extending over four periods and a model with a first-order lag structure. So we have

$$(4) \qquad y_{i1} = \alpha_{o1} + \alpha_{11}y_{i0} + \delta_{11}x_{i0} + \phi_1 f_i + u_{i1} \,,$$
$$y_{i2} = \alpha_{o2} + \alpha_{12}y_{i1} + \delta_{12}x_{i1} + \phi_2 f_i + u_{i2} \,,$$
$$y_{i3} = \alpha_{o3} + \alpha_{11}y_{i2} + \delta_{13}x_{i2} + \phi_3 f_i + u_{i3} \,, \text{ and}$$
$$y_{i4} = \alpha_{o4} + \alpha_{11}y_{i3} + \delta_{14}x_{i3} + \phi_4 f_i + u_{i4} \,,$$

where ϕ_t is the coefficient multiplying the individual effect in period t. The model in equation (2a) implicitly restricts the ϕ's to one in each period. Because y_{i0} and x_{i0} are not observed, the equation for y_{i1} cannot be estimated; it is included here because of the implication for later observations.

To test for Granger causality, we estimate the equation (4) jointly and determine if the restriction

$$(5) \qquad \delta_{11} = \delta_{12} = \delta_{13} = \delta_{14} = 0$$

can be accepted under the F-test. But the procedure for estimating equation (4) is not straightforward. Differencing will clearly not work, as the individual effects will not disappear. Rather, we must perform Chamberlain's transformation: we multiply each equation for time t by (ϕ_{t-1}/ϕ_t) and then subtract the result from the equation for time $t + 1$, yielding

(6)
$$y_{i2} = (\alpha_{o2} - r_2) + (\alpha_{12} + r_2)y_{i1}$$
$$- r_2\alpha_{11}y_{i0} + \delta_{12}x_{i1} - r_2\delta_{11}x_{i0}$$
$$+ u_{i2} - r_2u_{i1},$$

$$y_{i3} = (\alpha_{o3} - r_3) + (\alpha_{13} + r_3)y_{i2}$$
$$- r_3\alpha_{12}y_{i1} + \delta_{13}x_{i2} - r_3\delta_{12}x_{i1}$$
$$+ u_{i3} - r_2u_{i2}, \text{ and}$$

$$y_{i4} = (\alpha_{o4} - r_4) + (\alpha_{14} + r_4)y_{i3}$$
$$- r_4\alpha_{13}y_{i2} + \delta_{12}x_{i3} - r_2\delta_{11}x_{i2}$$
$$+ u_{i4} - r_2u_{i3},$$

where $r_t = (\phi_t/\phi_{t-1})$. We then jointly estimate equation (6) and test the hypothesis (5). Now it is apparent why we postponed the discussion of instrumental variables: equation (6), the model we wish to estimate and use for testing, has some right-hand variables correlated with the transformed error term, so we are interested in finding the instruments required to consistently estimate the model.

The natural candidates for instruments are appropriately lagged values of x and y. It is therefore clear that not all the equations in (6) may be identified; in fact, in this specific setup, only the equation at time 4 is identified. The last equation (6) has four right-hand-side variables, so four instruments are required. We have four available instruments: $x_{i1}, x_{i2}, Y_{i1},$ and Y_{i2}; none of these variables is correlated with the error term in the last equation of (6). But it is clear that the other three equations may not be identified. Moreover, were we to add any further lags, none of the four equations could be identified. In general, to identify an equation for one time period under an m-order lag structure, we must have greater than $m + 3$ periods of data available. To put it another way, given that we have eleven years of annual data available, the longest lag structure we may try is eight years.

We have now described the Chamberlain-Holtz-Eakin et al. econometric model. It is a model that will test for Granger causality in a panel setup, allowing individual effects to vary with time and employing appropriate lagged variables to instrument out any bias. Following Holtz-Eakin, Newey, and Rosen, we now discuss precisely how such a model is estimated.

7.3   Estimation

The general form of equation (6) is

$$(7) \qquad y_{it} = a_t + \sum_{l=1}^{n+1} c_{lt} y_{i,t-l}$$

$$+ \sum_{l=1}^{n+1} d_{lt} x_{i,t-l} + v_{it},$$

where $r_t = (\phi_t/\phi_{t-1})$,

$a_t = \alpha_{ot} - r_t \alpha_{0t-1}$,

$c_{1t} = r_t + \alpha_{1t}$,

$c_{lt} = \alpha_{lt} - r_t \alpha_{l-1,t-1}$,

$c_{m+1,t} = -r_t \alpha_{m,t-1}$,

$d_{1t} = \delta_{1t}$,

$d_{lt} = \delta_{lt} - r_t \delta_{l-1,t-1}$,

$d_{m+1,t} = -r_t \delta_{m,t-1}$, and

$v_{it} = u_{it} - r_t u_{i,t-1}$.

Note that the hypothesis $\delta_m = 0$ is the same in our case as $d_m = 0$ for all m.

Introducing additional notation, let

$Y_t = [y_{1t}, \ldots, y_{Nt}]$, where N is the number of four-digit industries, and analogously for X_t. In our context, Y is output or employment of the industries, and X is some measure of protection. Let

$$W_t = [l, Y_{t-1}, \ldots, Y_{t-m-1}, X_{t-1}, \ldots, X_{tim-1}],$$

where m is the number of lags assumed. W_t is the $N \times (2m + 3)$ vector of right-hand-side variables in our general model, and l is an $N \times 1$ vector of ones.

$$V_t = [v_{1t}, \ldots, v_{nt}]$$

is the $N \times 1$ vector of transformed disturbance terms, and

$$\beta_t = [a_t, c_{1t}, \ldots, c_{m+1,t}, d_{1t}, \ldots, d_{m+1,t}]$$

is the $(2m + 3) \times 1$ vector of coefficients for the equations. So we may write equation (7) as

$$(8) \qquad Y_t = W_t \beta_t + V_t.$$

To combine all the observations, we can stack equation (8). Let

$$Y = [Y'_{m+3}, \ldots, Y'_T],$$

$$\beta = [\beta'_{m+3}, \ldots, \beta'_T],$$

$$V = [V'_{m+3}, \ldots, V'_T], \text{ and}$$

$$W = \text{diag}[W'_{m+3}, \ldots, W'_T],$$

where diag[ ] denotes a block diagonal matrix with the given entries along the diagonal. The observations for equation (8) may therefore be written

$$(9) \qquad\qquad Y = W\beta + V.$$

This appears to be a classical simultaneous equation system where the equations are indexed by t and the observations by i. In the classical system, however, the same instrumental variables are used for each equation. In our approach, the matrix of variables that qualify for use as instruments in period t is

$$Z_t = [e, Y_{t-2}, \ldots, Y_1, X_{t-2}, \ldots, X_1],$$

which, of course, changes with t. To allow for different instruments for each equation, we chose the matrix of instruments for the system in equation (9) to be block diagonal. So we have the matrix

$$Z = \mathrm{diag}[Z_{m+3}, \ldots, Z_t].$$

The orthogonality conditions assure that

$$\mathrm{plim}_{N\to\infty}(Z'V)/N = 0,$$

so Z is the appropriate choice of instruments for equation (9).[9]

To estimate β, premultiply equation (9) by Z' to obtain

$$(10) \qquad\qquad Z'Y = Z'W\beta = Z'V.$$

The orthogonality condition assures that GLS estimates of β will be consistent. To get a GLS estimator, we must have knowledge of the covariance matrix of disturbances $Z'V$. This covariance matrix, Ω, is given by

$$\Omega = E\{Z'VV'Z\}.$$

Clearly, Ω must be estimated. To do so, we get a preliminary estimator of β by estimating the coefficients of the equations for the time periods t using two-stage least squares on the equation for each time period alone. Call this estimator B_t. Now we use this estimator to form a vector of residuals for period t: $V_t = Y_t - W_t B_t$.

At this point, we depart from the procedure of Holtz-Eakin, Newey, and Rosen. In attempting to use their method, we found that in our case the difference between the largest and smallest eigenvalues of the Ω matrix is so large as to render it computationally singular. The method we use incorporates a restriction on the relationships of the variables across time that allows us to estimate a computationally nonsingular matrix. Because we have N different industries within each time period, we have no reason to believe that their error terms are homoskedastic.

We therefore use White's (1980) procedure to correct for heteroskedasticity. For each time period t, we estimate a covariance matrix

$$(11) \qquad (\Omega)_t = \sum_{i=1}^{n} (v_{it} v_{it} Z'_{it} Z_{it}),$$

where v_{ir} is the ith element of V_r and Z_{ir} is the ith row of Z_r. Now we reestimate B_t for each time period t:

$$B_t = [W_t'Z_t(\Omega_t)^{-1}Z_t'W_t]^{-1}W_t'Z_t(\Omega_t)^{-1}Z_t'Y_t .$$

We now use the residuals generated from this B_t to generate a covariance matrix $\tilde{\Omega}$ to use for joint estimation in the classical three-stage manner (see Judge et al. 1982).[10] Finally, we may use $\tilde{\Omega}$ to form a GLS estimator of the entire parameter vector, B, by using all the available observations:

$$(12) \qquad B = [W'Z(\tilde{\Omega})^{-1}Z'W]^{-1}W'Z(\tilde{\Omega})^{-1}Z'Y.$$

7.4 Hypothesis-Testing Procedure

We wish to determine if tariff protection "Granger-causes" output in protected industries. In our model—as described in equation (7)—this means testing whether $d_{lt} = 0$ for all l and t, subject to the provision that we have not estimated a model with lag-truncation bias. We follow the procedure outlined in Holtz-Eakin, Newey, and Rosen (1985). Let

$$(13) \qquad Q = (Y - WB)'Z(\tilde{\Omega})^{-1}Z'(Y - WB)/N,$$

where the terms on the right-hand side are defined as before. As N grows, Q has a chi-squared distribution. Now let

$$(14) \qquad Q_R = (Y - w\tau)'Z(\tilde{\Omega})^{-1}Z'(Y - w\tau)/N,$$

where w is the matrix of explanatory variables as transformed by our restrictions, and τ is the corresponding vector of restricted coefficients. Q_R is also distributed chi-squared as N grows. By analogy with the F statistic in the standard linear model, an appropriate test statistic is

$$(15) \qquad L = Q_R - Q,$$

which has the form of the numerator of the test statistic. The covariance matrix of the transformed residuals is by construction an identity matrix. L therefore has a chi-squared distribution as N grows with degrees of freedom equal to the degrees of freedom of Q_R minus the degrees of freedom of Q. When all parameters are identified under both the null and alternative hypotheses, the degrees of freedom of Q and Q_R are equal to the number of instrumental variables minus the number of parameters being estimated. L therefore has degrees of freedom equal to the dimension of B minus the dimension of τ.

7.5   Data and Results

Data on shipments, imports, and tariff revenues were collected at the four-digit SIC level for nineteen two-digit SIC industries for the years 1972–82. Many observations, however, are either missing or inconsistent. At this stage, we have been able to construct five panels of consistent data: four are the two-digit industries steel, food and kindred products, textiles, and apparel; the fifth is footwear, which is part of the two-digit industries leather products and rubber products. Information from Hufbauer, Berliner, and Elliott (1986) on nontariff trade barrier (NTB) tariff equivalents in the steel and footwear industries is also used. These data were used to estimate models for steel, footwear, textiles, apparel, and food and kindred products using tariffs alone, and for steel and footwear using tariffs plus the ad valorem equivalents of NTBs. All data were detrended; the detrended output and tariff data are available from the authors on request.

We used the general model outlined in section 7.3 to estimate steel, food and kindred products, textiles, and apparel; because of the small number of observations on footwear, a restricted form of the model was estimated by restricting all coefficients to be consistent across time.

We chose a lag length of three to estimate the covariance matrices for the models. Using these matrices, we performed tests to obtain the most parsimonious specifications possible, in order to get the sharpest consistent estimates of coefficients. In the cases of steel (both with NTBs added and without), food and kindred products, textiles, and apparel, we were able to specify consistent models with one lag. For footwear without NTBs added, we required three lags; for shoes with NTBs added, we required two. Guilkey and Salemi (1982) performed simulations indicating that in small-sample estimation, short lag lengths are less likely to produce errors in hypothesis testing.

We estimated equations for whether protection "Granger-causes" output for the last four available years. As the discussion on the econometric model suggests, we could identify coefficients for the last six years, but we wished to "reserve" data in the event that longer lag lengths were required. As we shall see, this is not the case, and an obvious extension is to estimate the data for six years. We did, of course, use all available data for instruments.

For the four unrestricted cases, we estimated nine coefficients in each time period—four lagged values of output, four lagged values of tariff rates divided by imports, and a constant—yielding a total of

Table 7.1 **Steel without Nontariff Barriers Added**

	Q	L	DF	.1 CV
1. $m = 3$	2.24	—	28	37.9
2. $m = 2$ (given 1)	3.80	1.56	8	13.4
3. $m = 1$ (given 2)	5.76	1.96	8	13.4
4. Exclude protection (given 3)	7.20	1.44	8	13.4

Notes: $N = 25$; Q = the test statistic representing the "fit" of each equation and follows a chi-squared distribution (see equation 13); L is the test statistic on the restrictions and also follows a chi-squared distribution (see equation 15); DF = degrees of freedom; and .1 CV is the 10 percent critical value of the chi-squared distribution.

Table 7.2 **Steel with Nontariff Barriers Added**

	Q	L	DF	.1 CV
1. $m = 3$	2.32	—	28	37.9
2. $m = 2$ (given 1)	3.89	1.57	8	13.4
3. $m = 1$ (given 2)	5.68	1.79	8	13.4
4. Exclude protection (given 3)	6.88	1.20	8	13.4

Notes: See table 7.1.

Table 7.3 **Food and Kindred Products**

	Q	L	DF	.1 CV
1. $m = 3$	1.22	—	28	37.9
2. $m = 2$ (given 1)	2.96	1.74	8	13.4
3. $m = 1$ (given 2)	4.46	1.50	8	13.4
4. Exclude protection (given 3)	4.73	0.27	8	13.4

Notes: See table 7.1. $N = 37$.

Table 7.4 **Textiles**

	Q	L	DF	.1 CV
1. $m = 3$	1.86	—	28	37.9
2. $m = 2$ (given 1)	3.27	1.41	8	13.4
3. $m = 1$ (given 2)	4.79	1.52	8	13.4
4. Exclude protection (given 3)	6.41	1.62	8	13.4

Notes: See table 7.1. $N = 28$.

Table 7.5   **Apparel**

	Q	L	DF	$.1\ CV$
1. $m = 3$	1.77	—	28	37.9
2. $m = 2$ (given 1)	2.33	0.55	8	13.4
3. $m = 1$ (given 2)	3.00	0.67	8	13.4
4. Exclude protection (given 3)	3.51	0.51	8	13.4

Notes: See table 7.1. $N = 33$.

thirty-six estimated coefficients. The numbers of instruments for the four time periods are 13, 15, 17, and 19, yielding a total of 64. The degrees of freedom in these cases are therefore 28. In the restricted case of footwear, we estimated a total of seven coefficients, and had 13 instruments at our disposal, yielding 6 degrees of freedom. In testing for lag length and Granger causality, degrees of freedom are equal to the number of coefficients we restrict to equal zero.

After jointly estimating the equations using the three-stage technique described above, we obtained the minimized chi-squared test statistics (i.e., Q) presented in tables 7.1–7.7. Because inferences about causality will be incorrect if the lag distribution is incorrectly truncated, we chose critical values at the 10 percent level to determine the correctness of lag lengths rather than the standard 5 percent or 1 percent levels. Tables 7.1–7.7 reveal that for all five industries, we may safely accept a lag length of three. Moreover, tables 7.1–7.5 reveal that for steel, food and kindred products, textiles, and apparel, we may truncate the lags to one without fear of lag-truncation bias. For footwear without NTBs added, we must use three lags (see table 7.6); for footwear with NTBs, we must use two (table 7.7).

A glance at the tables shows the striking results of our tests for Granger causality. In six of seven cases, our test statistics, L, for barriers having no effect are safely under the appropriate 10 percent critical value: in these cases, if we have prior reason to believe the hypothesis that tariff rates do not "Granger-cause" output to be true, we may reasonably accept that hypothesis. The significance of these

Table 7.6   **Shoes without Nontariff Barriers Added**

	Q	L	DF	$.1\ CV$
1. $m = 3$	1.81	—	6	10.6
2. $m = 2$ (given 1)	11.24	9.43	2	4.6
3. Exclude protection (given 1)	3.63	1.82	3	6.3

Notes: See table 7.1. $N = 5$.

Table 7.7 **Shoes with Nontariff Barriers Added**

	Q	L	DF	$.1\ CV$
1. $m = 3$	0.58	—	6	10.7
2. $m = 2$ (given 1)	4.16	3.58	2	4.60
3. $m = 1$ (given 2)	10.35	6.19	2	4.60
4. Exclude protection (given 2)	9.04	4.88	2	4.60

Notes: See table 7.1. $N = 5$.

results is even more clear when one considers that the one case in which the test statistic is significant at the 10 percent level (footwear with NTBs) is a close call, and that we are using the most parsimonious justifiable specifications, which, if anything, would cause us to err on the side of rejecting the hypothesis of no effect.

At the same time, we recognize that the arguments set forth in the model rely heavily on asymptotics. These arguments could be legitimately questioned in light of our small sample sizes. Moreover, the small sizes of our data sets invite speculation as to how powerful our tests are. At the same time, because we use panel data techniques, we are able to exploit several years of data in order to increase our effective sample size. And even keeping these caveats in mind, we believe that our results are sufficiently strong to suggest that the inefficacy of protection is a proposition with considerable empirical backing.[11]

7.6 Conclusions

Evidence from section 203 investigations by the ITC and our econometric analysis of the relationship between trade barriers and domestic output in five industries lend support to the proposition that protection is not an effective means of stimulating domestic output. Various reactions by users and producers of the protected product tend to offset its output-expanding effects. Not only has the imposition of higher tariffs and more restrictive nontariff trade barriers often produced a disappointingly small output expansion, but in some cases the barriers appear to have had no success in accomplishing their intended purpose of increasing domestic output or even preventing a further output decline.

Ironically, recent trade policy changes that enable industries to secure import protection sooner and more easily than before tend to make it easier for foreign suppliers to avoid reducing exports to the protected market. For example, it is politically easier for a government to quantitatively restrict imports of a product from a few foreign suppliers than from all foreign suppliers of the product. Yet, the quality upgrading by suppliers subject to quantitative restrictions, these suppliers shifting production to noncontrolled countries, and the increase in exports by noncontrolled suppliers that is caused by this protection method tend to offset the domestic output-expanding purpose of the protection. The use of ad valorem tariffs, imposed on an across-the-board basis, would not produce these offsetting effects.

Similarly, defining an industry narrowly in product terms enables domestic firms producing these items to show serious injury from imports more easily than if the industry is defined as also including other substitute products. But when protection is increased only on the narrow list of products, the shift by users and foreign suppliers to the substitute items undermines the output-increasing benefits of the protection.

The conclusion that protection is not an effective means of remedying or preventing injury to an industry from increased imports, of course, leaves the question of what means would be effective. There is clearly a need for more experimentation with alternative measures, but we are inclined to believe that some of the new adjustment-assistance proposals, for example, those of Lawrence and Litan (1986) and Hufbauer and Rosen (1986), are likely to prove more efficacious in dealing with the import-injury problem than with protection—especially the proposed selective quantitative restrictions.

Notes

1. An elasticity of foreign demand for imports of less than unity in absolute terms, for example, implies a backward-bending foreign export supply curve due to the effect of a high income elasticity of demand in the foreign country for its own exports that more than offsets the substitution and production effects associated with a price increase for these exports. Under these circumstances, a tariff can lower the domestic price of imports in the tariff-imposing country even if the income elasticity of demand for imports in the tariff-imposing country is positive.

2. See Baldwin 1982, 11 for these conditions. See also Falvey 1979.

3. Baldwin illustrates hysteresis in trade under imperfectly competitive market conditions by assuming a temporary shock to the value of a country's currency, but his model can be used to derive the same outcome as a consequence of a temporary increase in protection.

4. If the protection takes the form of quantitative restrictions, the capacity of domestic firms is more likely to expand and increase their share of the domestic market after the protection is withdrawn.

5. Political economy theory (Baldwin 1985) suggests that declining output in an industry leads to increased protection by stimulating increased lobbying for protection. In this chapter we are not concerned with this hypothesis.

6. The injured industry can request continuation of the import relief, or the president or the commission can initiate a commission study to determine

whether the protection should be removed prior to the end of the initial period of protection.

7. Not only were duty categories defined in unit-value terms, but the tariffs on imports were compound duties, that is, they included both an ad valorem and a specific component, so that the rate of protection in percentage terms declined as prices rose.

8. For a proof of this statement, see Sargent 1979.

9. Holding T fixed, as N goes to infinity.

10. Our procedure is slightly different from that presented in Judge et al. 1982 (379–86), which has instruments that remain constant across time. As already noted, our instruments change across time.

11. We also tested for whether protection "Granger-causes" domestic output changes using regressions that included lagged values of import prices as explanatory variables. We collected completely different data series for this test: import prices were taken from BLS import price indexes, and import and tariff data were taken from Census Bureau 990 Trade Reports. The data were at the three-digit SIC level and were quarterly. In contrast to the tests reported in the text of the chapter, we were unable to pick up any lag structure in the quarterly output data. Because we would expect to find a seasonal component in the quarterly output data, we are suspicious of the validity of our result—that protection did not "Granger-cause" changes in domestic output—based on these data. We will continue to work with these data to attempt to increase their power, and therefore get more reliable econometric results (see Green 1988).

References

Aw, Bee-Yan, and Mark J. Roberts. 1986. Measuring quality change in quota-constrained import markets: The case of U.S. footwear. *Journal of International Economics* 21 (1/2):45–60.

Baldwin, Richard E. 1986. Hysteresis in trade. Department of Economics, Columbia Graduate School of Business.

Baldwin, Robert E. 1970. *Nontariff distortions of international trade.* Washington, D.C.: Brookings Institution.

———. 1982. The inefficacy of trade policy. *Essays in International Finance,* no. 150. International Finance Section, Department of Economics, Princeton University.

———. 1985. *The political economy of U.S. import policy.* Cambridge, Mass.: MIT Press.

Bhagwati, Jagdish, and Bert Hansen. 1973. A theoretical analysis of smuggling. *Quarterly Journal of Economics* 87:172–87.

Chamberlain, Gary. 1983. Panel data. In Z. Griliches and M. Intriligator, eds., *Handbook of econometrics,* vol. 2. Amsterdam: North-Holland.

Chang, Eui Tae. 1987. Protective effects of discriminatory quantitative restrictions. *Korean Economic Journal* 1(1):15–28.

Falvey, Rodney E. 1979. The composition of trade with import-restricted product categories. *Journal of Political Economy* 87:1105–14.

Green, Richard. 1988. The inefficacy of protection. Ph.D. dissertation, University of Wisconsin–Madison.

Granger, C. 1969. Investigating causal relations by econometric models and cross-spectral methods. *Econometrica* 37:424–38.

Guilkey, D. K., and M. K. Salemi. 1982. Small sample properties for three tests for Granger causal ordering in a bivariate stochastic system. *Review of Economics and Statistics* 64(4):668–80.

Holtz-Eakin, D., Whitney Newey, and Howard Rosen. 1985. Implementing causality tests with panel data. NBER Technical Paper No. 48.

Hufbauer, Gary C., Diane T. Berliner, and Kimberly A. Elliott. 1986. *Trade protection in the United States: 31 Cases*. Washington, D.C.: Institute for International Economics.

Hufbauer, Gary C., and Howard F. Rosen. 1986. *Trade policy for troubled industries*. Policy Analyses in International Economics, no. 15. Washington, D.C.: Institute for International Economics.

Judge, G., R. Hill, W. Griffiths, H. Lutkepohl, and T. C. Lee. 1982. *Introduction to the theory and practice of econometrics*. New York: John Wiley.

Lawrence, Robert Z., and Robert E. Litan. 1986. *Pragmatic approaches for preserving free trade*. Washington, D.C.: Brookings Institution.

Leamer, Edward E. 1985. Vector autoregression for causal inference? In Karl Brunner and Allan H. Meltzer, eds., *Understanding monetary regimes*. Carnegie-Rochester Conference Series on Public Policy 22:225–304. Amsterdam: North-Holland.

Metzler, L. A. 1949. Tariffs, the terms of trade, and the distribution of national income. *Journal of Political Economy* 57 (February).

Morici, Peter, and Laura L. Megna. 1983. *U.S. economic policies affecting industrial trade: A quantitative assessment*. Washington, D.C.: National Planning Association Committee on Changing Economic Realities.

Sargent, T. 1979. *Macroeconomic theory*. New York: Academic Press.

U.S. International Trade Commission. Various years. Reports to the president on investigation no. 203-1-13 under section 203 of the Trade Act of 1974. Washington, D.C.

White, H. 1980. A heteroskedasticity-consistent covariance matrix estimator and a direct test for heteroskedasticity. *Econometrica* 5(48):817–38.

Comment   Robert C. Feenstra

This chapter follows the theme set in Baldwin's (1982) essay, "The Inefficacy of Trade Policy."[1] The author's efforts to bring a set of data to bear on this theme should be commended. This chapter is divided into two parts: the first looking at ITC reports and the second estimating the vector auto regressions (VARs). I found the ITC section helpful, but would have also liked to see summary statistics of the data set. Let me suggest that the authors construct unit values and price indexes at the two-digit level for each of their industries. A comparison of the unit values and price indexes should show *upgrading* for imports, fol-

Robert C. Feenstra is associate professor at the University of California, Davis, and a research fellow of the National Bureau of Economic Research.

lowing the method of Aw and Roberts (1986). I speculate below as to what the comparison of unit values and price indexes for domestic output might show.

Turning to the VARs, the basic estimating equation is (7). It is a regression of output on lagged output (in the same four-digit industry) and lagged protection. If the tariff coefficients are significantly different from zero, then we say that tariffs "Granger-cause" output. Looking at this equation, we could immediately think of also regressing tariffs on their lagged values and lagged output. This would be a test of a political economy model in which industry conditions lead to protection. However, this alternative regression would certainly be subject to the Lucas critique, that is, any change in trade policy would affect the coefficients of that regression.

Returning to equation (7), I discuss the economic model that could lie behind this equation and use this model to check the specification. Consider a multi-input, multi-output production function of the form

$$\text{(C1)} \qquad F(y_t, y_{t-1}, L_t, K_t) = 0,$$

where y_t is a vector of current outputs (e.g., various types of steel), y_{t-1} is lagged output, L_t is a vector of variable inputs, and K_t is fixed inputs. The firm chooses (y_t, L_t) to maximize profits $p'_y y_t - w'_t L_t$ subject to equation (C1), which gives

$$\text{(C2)} \qquad y_t = Y(p_t, y_{t-1}, w_t, K_t).$$

Equation (C2) is simply the solution for optimal domestic supply, depending on prices, lagged output, and input prices and quantities.

Comparing equation (C2) with equation (7), our first observation is that the authors have omitted the input prices and quantities from their output equation. This omission may not be too serious, since the input variables may be rather slow moving. It could be corrected by gathering more data.

A more serious omission is that equation (C2) includes the entire vector of domestic prices p_t needed to predict the output of any single four-digit industry. However, the authors include in equation (7) only the level of protection in that industry. Thus, an obvious omission from equation (7) is the level of international prices in each industry. If the application of protection is concurrent with falling international prices (which seems likely on political economy grounds), then this strengthened import competition could itself explain why domestic output does not rise following the protection.

A further problem is that the entire vector p_t entering equation (C2) has been reduced to scalars $x_t, x_{t-1}, \ldots$ in equation (7). To understand the importance of this, we need to consider the type of protection used in these industries.

First, suppose the protection takes the form of an ad valorem tariff, so that $p_t = p_0(1 + \tau)$ where p_0 is the vector of international prices. Under fairly weak assumptions (F homogeneous in y_t), a change in τ will have an *equiproportional* effect on each industry output y_{it}. In this case equation (7) is correct, with industry outputs measured in natural logs. A change in the level of protection would have the *same* effect on each four-digit industry, measured by the coefficients d_{mt}.

However, the more realistic case is where imports are constrained by some system of quotas. Then $p_t = p_0 + s$, where p_0 is international prices and s is the vector of quota rents on each product. Under a quota on physical units (e.g., tons of steel), s would be equal across product types (e.g., $10 of quota rents per ton of any kind of steel). More generally, selective quotas would lead to variations in the quota rents, reflected in the vector s.

A tightening of the quota will increase the quota rents. However, this will *not* generally lead to equiproportional changes in outputs across the four-digit industries. On the contrary, we would expect domestic firms to shift supply toward those products whose relative price has gone up. When s rises equally across product types, this means shifting supply toward the *lower*-priced products, or downgrading domestic output. This downgrading would occur for exactly the same reasons that imports are upgraded (see Falvey 1979): a dollar increase in all prices means that the relative price of the more (less) expensive goods goes down (up). It implies a *differential* effect of the quota on the domestic supplies of each product.

Looking again at equation (7), we see that the authors are forcing protection to have the same effect on each four-digit industry (measured by d_{mt}). This specification cannot capture the differential effects of a quota. I fear this misspecification is an important reason why d_{mt} is estimated as insignificantly different from zero. Thus, I would encourage the authors to move toward another specification for equation (7), which allows a differential response of domestic outputs. They could then test the weaker hypothesis that protection does not have an effect on "aggregate" industry output, while allowing some pattern of response at the four-digit level.

References

Aw, Bee-Yan, and Mark J. Roberts. 1986. Estimating quality change in quota-constrained import markets: The case of U.S. footwear. *Journal of International Economics* 21:45–60.

Baldwin, Robert E. 1982. The inefficacy of trade policy. *Essays in International Finance,* no. 150. International Finance Section, Department of Economics, Princeton University.

Falvey, Rodney E. 1979. The comparison of trade within import-restricted product categories. *Journal of Political Economy* 87:1105–14.

Comment   Robert M. Stern

My comments on the chapter by Baldwin and Green deal with four issues: (1) appropriateness of focusing on the domestic output effects of protection; (2) need for more discussion of the different types and consequences of protection; (3) use of the VAR model; and (4) selection of industries.

Policy Objectives

The focus on the domestic output effects of protection needs to be clarified and perhaps defended more explicitly in the chapter. Baldwin and Green assume that influencing domestic output is the objective of the policymakers, which it may well be, but they could have other objectives as well, for example, maintenance of employment, increased profitability, and providing more time for firms and workers to adjust (including a possible orderly decline in the industry and reallocation of resources to other sectors of comparative advantage).

The assumptions about firm behavior need to be clarified as well. That is, does it necessarily follow that protection will lead to increases in output in all cases? For example, if protection is viewed by firms as temporary, they might choose to diversify into other sectors, change the composition of their output to higher-value-added products, and maybe rationalize their production methods to become more cost-efficient. In these circumstances, output might well not increase.

This issue of firm behavior raises the more general point that firms in an industry may respond to protection in different ways and that perhaps the effects on profitability could be most important. Thus, for example, in the study by Hartigan et al. in the November 1986 *Review of Economics and Statistics,* the authors conclude (using events analysis) that there are perceptible effects of protection on firms as reflected in changes in stock prices. (These effects dissipate through time, however.) The issue, therefore, is that protection may have distinct effects on firms in the protected industry, but these effects may not necessarily show up in increases in output.

Different Types and Consequences of Protection

I would also like to have seen in the chapter more discussion of the different kinds of protection. From previous work by Baldwin and others we are familiar with the idea that trade policy may not be effective for a variety of reasons. The issue then is that some policies (for example, global quotas) may be more effective than others (such

Robert M. Stern is professor of economics and public policy at the University of Michigan, Ann Arbor.

as selective quotas), and it will not be surprising when we note the failures involved.

In their analysis of section 203 cases, Baldwin and Green focus on the escape-clause actions that were terminated for one reason or another. It would also have been interesting to examine those (eight) cases in which the ITC recommended that protection be continued. It would seem in these cases that protection must have mattered to the firms and industries in question and that the removal of protection would jeopardize the benefits they had realized. Thus, it is useful to point out the various reasons why protection does not work in particular cases. But does this mean that it does not work in all cases? And does it matter what kinds of policy (tariffs or quotas) have been used?

Use of the VAR Model

If it is granted that the output effects of protection are an appropriate criterion to use for purposes of analysis, the question then is whether the use of the VAR model is the best way to proceed. The model as set forth seems oversimplified since it posits a relation between changes in protection and output. Are there no other variables that enter? For example, changes in imports may affect both the amount of protection and output. How then do omitted variables enter into the estimation model?

If one wishes to study the output effects of protection, is there some way to select a reference point and ask what the situation would be without protection and, alternatively, with protection? The question here is whether protection makes a difference and, if so, how much of a difference and for how long. The VAR model unfortunately does not provide this kind of information.

Selection of Industries

Finally, I have some questions about the industries that were selected for the econometric analysis. It would have been helpful if more information had been given about the protection experiences of the five industries chosen. Presumably, such information is in the data appendix, but this was not made available.

The food and kindred products industry was one of those chosen, and I would be curious to know if this industry was subjected to increased tariff protection in the 1972–82 period. Here one can think of the U.S. sugar restrictions and periodic quotas on imports of beef (although these may not have been binding at all times). But these types of restrictions are not reflected in the tariffs used in the computations. Further, with respect to textiles and wearing apparel, the Multifibre Arrangement (MFA) is obviously an important factor affecting U.S. imports and domestic output. Yet, only tariffs were taken into account in the estimation.

NTBs were taken into consideration in the remaining two industries—steel and footwear. It would be interesting to determine whether protection of steel was essentially selective or global during the period. The "trigger price" system was operative in the late 1970s and early 1980s, but it may not have been effective in restraining imports. More generally, the U.S. steel industry was in chronic difficulty during much of this period, and protection may have affected only the rate of decline of output. Also, some segments of the steel industry, in particular the minimills, have been highly profitable, whereas the larger and more integrated firms have experienced considerable difficulties.

When NTBs were taken into account in the case of footwear, this was the only instance in which the null hypothesis was almost rejected. While footwear had some special problems because it was only part of the relevant two-digit industry and required more lags for estimation purposes, it nevertheless raises the question of how important NTBs may be with respect to the impact on domestic output in the textile and apparel industries. If these obviously important protectionist barriers were taken into account in these two industries, the conclusions reached in the chapter might be changed. But I am not entirely certain about this point since the textile and apparel industries may have responded to the nontariff protection by altering their product mix and rationalizing their methods of production to become more cost-efficient.

8 Trade Restraints, Intermediate Goods, and World Market Conditions

Val Eugene Lambson

Much of what is produced is not for final consumption. Products that are outputs from one process are often inputs in another, and a large portion of world trade is conducted in markets for such intermediate goods. Protectionist measures for industries producing these commodities can take different forms. In addition to the usual array of tariffs and quotas, domestic content requirements can be imposed.

When analyzing protection, most authors focus on the domestic price, factor use, and output effects of introducing a particular protective measure. Work on models with intermediate goods has followed this tradition. Sanyal and Jones (1982), for example, study the effects of imposing a tariff on an intermediate good in a general equilibrium context. In a partial equilibrium framework, Grossman (1981) analyzes the effects of domestic content legislation when domestic and foreign inputs are perfect substitutes in production. Mussa (1984) considers the possibility that domestic and foreign inputs might not be perfect substitutes in production. In addition to the case of perfect competition, he analyzes the effects of domestic content requirements when monopoly is present. Krishna and Itoh (1988) look at domestic content legislation in oligopolistic industries.

Another possible approach to analyzing protection, which is followed in this chapter, is to explore the effects of changes in economic conditions once protective policies are in place. Using a general equilibrium

Val Eugene Lambson is assistant professor of economics at the University of Wisconsin-Madison.

The author is indebted to Robert Baldwin, Christopher Flinn, Ronald Jones, Mark Kennet, Anne Polivka, and J. David Richardson. Remaining shortcomings are the author's responsibility.

233

framework, this chapter posits a change in a country's terms of trade and contrasts its effects on domestic prices, factor use, and consumption under four methods of protecting an import-competing sector that produces intermediate goods. The four methods of protection are (1) a tariff, (2) a quota, (3) a domestic content requirement defined in physical units, and (4) a domestic content requirement defined in value-added terms. Although any of these methods can be implemented with the goal of protecting a domestic industry, the behavior of the economy in the face of changing trading terms depends significantly on which protective policy is selected.

Section 8.1 exposits the general equilibrium model employed. A small country is assumed to have two production tiers. The input tier uses an industry-specific factor and labor to produce intermediate goods (inputs), while the output tier uses a different industry-specific factor, labor, and intermediate goods to produce final goods (outputs). Both inputs and outputs are traded on world markets. The small country imports inputs and exports outputs. Foreign and domestically produced inputs are perfect substitutes. Perfect competition is assumed throughout.

Section 8.2 reports the effects of terms-of-trade changes when protectionist measures are imposed. Perhaps the most interesting result is how the world and domestic prices of inputs are correlated. When a tariff is imposed the two prices, constrained to differ by the constant tariff rate, move together. Under a quota, by contrast, a change in the world price has no effect on the domestic price (although it does affect domestic welfare). When a domestic content requirement in physical units is imposed, the two prices are negatively correlated. Finally, if a domestic content requirement is implemented in value-added terms, the sign of the correlation seems to be ambiguous.

The results in section 8.2 report only the signs of the various effects. It is also interesting to have some feel for what their magnitudes might be. Section 8.3 explores a numerical example where the parameter values for the assumed Cobb-Douglas production technologies are derived from the 1977 input-output tables published by the *Survey of Current Business*. (Of course, the economy examined in section 8.3 should not be construed to be a good representation of the economy of the United States.) In addition to reporting the effects of terms-of-trade changes on employment and price in the input tier, the tables list the welfare effects of those changes in the presence of protection. It is shown that the magnitude of the welfare effects of changing trading terms depends on which protective measure is in place.

8.1 A Simple General Equilibrium Model

Assume that all production takes place in two stages. In the first stage, labor is combined with a specific factor to manufacture intermediate goods called *inputs*. In the second stage, labor and another specific factor are combined with inputs to produce final products called *outputs*. Industries that manufacture inputs comprise the *input tier* while industries that manufacture outputs comprise the *output tier*. Both inputs and outputs are traded competitively on the world market, and the country is sufficiently small that it cannot affect world prices. The country imports inputs and exports outputs. In the interest of tractability, differing factor intensities across industries in a given tier are ignored. This allows aggregation of the industries within the input tier and output tier, respectively, and simplifies the analysis considerably.

Let the level of input production be denoted by X_I. Inputs are produced using a specific factor, the supply of which is denoted by V_I, and labor. Labor is mobile between tiers. The amount of labor employed in the input tier is L_I.

Let the level of output production be denoted by X_O. Outputs are manufactured using a specific factor, the supply of which is denoted by V_O, inputs, the use of which is denoted by X_I^c, and labor. The amount of labor employed in the output tier is L_O.

The production functions in the input and output tiers are, respectively,

$$(1) \qquad\qquad X_I = f(V_I, L_I), \text{ and}$$

$$(2) \qquad\qquad X_O = g(V_O, L_O, X_I^c).$$

It is assumed that f and g are strictly concave functions exhibiting constant returns to scale. Derivatives of the production functions will be denoted by subscripts, for example, $g_{23} \equiv \partial^2 g / \partial L_O \, \partial X_I^c$. It is assumed throughout that $g_{23} \geq 0$, but most of the results are valid for general concave, linear homogenous production functions, and they are all valid as long as g_{23} is not too negative.

Let outputs be numeraire, so P is the relative price of inputs domestically, and P^* is the relative price of inputs on world markets. Four protectionist policies will be considered: a tariff, a quota, a domestic content requirement denominated in physical units (DCP), and a domestic content requirement denominated in value-added terms (DCV). If a tariff is imposed then the domestic price is given by

$$(3.\text{T}) \qquad\qquad P = (1 + t)P^*,$$

where t is the tariff rate. If a quota is imposed then imports are constrained as follows:

$$(3.\text{Q}) \qquad\qquad X_I^c - X_I \leq q,$$

where q is the quota level. If a domestic content requirement denominated in physical units is implemented then the economy must satisfy

$$(3.\text{DCP}) \qquad\qquad X_I / X_I^c \geq k.$$

This says that a fraction, k, of the produced inputs used domestically must be manufactured domestically. Finally, if domestic content legislation is written in value-added terms then

(3.DCV) $P^*(X_I^c - X_I) \leq (1-j)X_O$,

that is, domestic factors and inputs must make up at least a fraction, j, of value added.

It is assumed throughout that firms choose to exactly fulfill any requirements, so equations (3.Q), (3.DCP), and (3.DCV) hold with equality. Firms take all prices as given, and profits are maximized in each industry subject to any policy constraints. Hence, in the input tier V_I and L_I must solve

$$\max Pf(V_I,L_I) - r_I V_I - wL_I ,$$

where r_I is the return to the specific factor and w is the return to labor. The first-order conditions require, of course, that

(4) $r_I = Pf_1(V_I,L_I)$, and

(5) $w = Pf_2(V_I,L_I)$.

In the output tier the pertinent maximization problem depends on the policy restrictions imposed. Let X_I^* be the quantity of inputs imported, that is, $X_I^c = X_I + X_I^*$, and let r_O be the return to the specific factor used in the output tier. Then V_O, L_O, X_I, and X_I^* must solve

$$\max g(V_O L_O, X_I^c) - r_O V_O - wL_O - PX_I - P^*X_I^* ,$$

subject to equation (3.T) under a tariff, subject to equation (3.Q) under a quota, subject to equation (3.DCP) if a domestic content requirement is imposed in physical units, and subject to equation (3.DCV) if a domestic content requirement is imposed in value-added terms. The first-order conditions arising from the above maximization problem are presented below. (First-order conditions corresponding to the same factor are given the same equation number along with letters that denote the policy being imposed. For example, equation (6.T,Q) is the first-order condition for the specific factor in the output tier when either a tariff or a quota is imposed while equation (6.DCP) is the first-order condition for the same factor when a domestic content requirement in physical units is implemented.)

Under a tariff or a quota the first-order conditions imply

(6.T,Q) $r_O = g_1(V_O,L_O,X_I^c)$,

(7.T,Q) $w = g_2(V_O,L_O,X_I^c)$, and

(8.T,Q) $P = g_3(V_O,L_O,X_I^c)$.

Note that in (8.T,Q) the marginal revenue product of inputs is set equal to the domestic price of inputs. In the case of a tariff, $P = (1 + t)P^*$ and the same price is paid for domestic inputs as for foreign inputs. In the case of a quota $P > P^*$, but the *marginal* unit of inputs is purchased domestically.

If a domestic content requirement is legislated in physical units then the pertinent first-order conditions imply

$$(6.\text{DCP}) \qquad\qquad r_O = g_1(V_O, L_O, X_I^c),$$

$$(7.\text{DCP}) \qquad\qquad w = g_2(V_O, L_O, X_I^c), \text{ and}$$

$$(8.\text{DCP}) \qquad kP + (1 - k)P^* = g_3(V_O, L_O, X_I^c).$$

Note that equations (6) and (7) are the same, respectively, under tariffs, quotas, and domestic content requirements in physical units. The same is *not* true for equation (8). This is because under a domestic content requirement denoted in physical units, the marginal unit of inputs is partially foreign and partially domestically produced. The fraction of the marginal unit that is domestically produced is k. (For a fuller discussion of these relations see Grossman 1981.)

Finally, if a domestic content requirement is denoted in value-added terms then the first-order conditions of the appropriate maximization problem imply

$$(6.\text{DCV}) \quad r_O = \{1 + (1 - j)[(P - P^*)/P]\}g_1(V_O, L_O, X_I^c),$$

$$(7.\text{DCV}) \quad w = \{1 + (1 - j)[(P - P^*)/P]\}g_2(V_O, L_O, X_I^c), \text{ and}$$

$$(8.\text{DCV}) \quad P = \{1 + (1 - j)[(P - P^*)/P]\}g_3(V_O, L_O, X_I^c),$$

where j is the fraction of value added that must be domestically produced. Note that all three equations differ from their counterparts for the other cases. (For a fuller discussion see Grossman 1981.)

To close the model, balanced trade is assumed, that is,

$$(9) \qquad\qquad X_O + P^* X_I = X_O^c + P^* X_I^c,$$

where X_O^c is the amount of the output consumed in the country. Let $L \equiv L_I + L_O$ be total labor in the economy. If $L - L_I$ is substituted for L_O in the above systems of equations, there result four systems of nine equations in the nine unknowns X_I, X_O, X_I^c, X_O^c, r_I, r_O, w, L_I, and P. (Which nine equations are appropriate depends, of course, on the policy that is implemented.) In the next section these systems of equations are employed to derive the effects of a change in P^* on P, L_I, and X_I^c when the various protectionist policies are implemented.

8.2   Terms-of-Trade Effects in the Presence of Protection

The analysis of tariffs contains no surprises, but a few results are presented so they can be contrasted with those that are obtained for alternative protectionist measures. With a tariff imposed, the domestic and world prices of inputs are related by equation (3.T). Obviously, then, $\partial P/\partial P^* > 0$. The relationships between the world price and other domestic variables are also easy to ascertain. Combining equations (3.T), (5), and (7.T,Q) yields

$$(10) \qquad (1 + t)P^*f_2(V_I,L_I) = g_2(V_O,L - L_I,X_I^c).$$

Substitute equation (3.T) into equation (8.T,Q) to write

$$(11) \qquad (1 + t)P^* = g_3(V_O,L - L_I,X_I^c).$$

Finally, equations (1), (2), and (9) imply

$$(12) \qquad g(V_O,L - L_I,X_I^c) + P^*f(V_I,L_I) = X_O^c + X_I^c.$$

Now equations (10)–(12) constitute a system of three equations in the three unknowns L_I, X_I^c, and X_O^c. Totally differentiate all three with respect to P^* and solve for $\partial L_I/\partial P^*$, $\partial X_I^c/\partial P^*$, and $\partial X_O^c/\partial P^*$. Then the posited properties of the production functions imply that an increase in the world price of inputs when a tariff is in place (or when there is no protection at all, that is, when $t = 1$) has the following effects: employment of labor in the input tier rises (and hence, so does production in the input tier), employment of produced inputs declines, and domestic consumption of outputs (i.e., welfare) declines.

Now consider a quota that restricts the importation of inputs from abroad. Although for any tariff there is a quota that will yield equivalent protection to the input tier, an increase in the world price of inputs has none of the effects when a quota is in place that it has when a tariff is in place except that domestic consumption falls. The reason is that as long as the pattern of trade is not reversed, all the margins remain unaffected by a world price change because the marginal unit of inputs used in the output tier is domestically produced. Under a quota, the link between the world price and the domestic price of inputs is broken. Specifically, use equations (5) and (7.T,Q) to write

$$(13) \qquad Pf_2(V_I,L_I) = g_2(V_O,L - L_I,X_I^c).$$

In addition, substitute equation (1) into equation (3.Q) to write

$$(14) \qquad X_I^c - f(V_I,L_I) = q.$$

Finally, equation (8.T,Q) is reproduced here as equation (15) for the reader's convenience:

(15) $$P = g_3(V_O, L - L_I, X_I^c).$$

Now equations (13)–(15) constitute three equations in the three unknowns P, X_I^c, and L_I. Note, however, that these equations are entirely independent of P^*. Changes in the world price of inputs when there is a quota in effect have no effect on domestic production decisions. They do, however, affect domestic consumption. Differentiation of the budget constraint (9) establishes that

(16) $$\partial X_O^c / \partial P^* = X_I - X_I^c < 0.$$

Although no production decisions are affected, the price paid for the (constant) level of imports increases, resulting in a decrease in domestic consumption of outputs.

Economies with domestic content requirements in place behave differently, when faced with a terms-of-trade change, than do economies where tariffs or quotas are implemented. Furthermore, the difference depends on whether the requirements are imposed in terms of physical units or value added. First consider the case of a domestic content requirement denominated in physical units. Substitute equation (1) into equation (3.DCP) to write

(17) $$kX_I^c = f(V_I, L_I).$$

Now require that the marginal revenue product of labor be equated across tiers, that is, combine equations (5) and (7.DCP) to write

(18) $$Pf_2(V_I, L_I) = g_2(V_O, L - L_I, X_I^c).$$

Finally, equation (8.DCP) is reproduced here as equation (19) for the reader's convenience:

(19) $$kP + (1 - k)P^* = g_3(V_O, L - L_I, X_I^c).$$

Now equations (17)–(19) constitute a system of three equations in the unknowns P, L_I, and X_I^c. The usual methods verify that the derivative of each of these variables with respect to P^* is negative. The negative correlation between the domestic input price and the world input price contrasts with the positive correlation between them under a tariff and the absence of correlation between them under a quota. The same pattern holds for the correlation between the amount of labor employed in the input tier (and hence, the level of input production) and the world input price. By contrast, the correlation between input use and the world input price is the same as under a tariff. These results are summarized in table 8.1.

To gain some intuition consider figure 8.1, which illustrates two production possibility frontiers. The outer production possibility frontier

Table 8.1   Some Effects of Terms-of-Trade Changes

	$\delta P/\delta P^*$	$\delta L_I/\delta P^*$	$\delta X_f^C/\delta P^*$
Tariff	+	+	−
Quota	0	0	0
Domestic content (physical units)	−	−	−
Domestic content (value added)	?	+	−

describes the production set given the level of inputs (foreign and domestic) employed in the output tier before a price change. Suppose the economy produces at point A on that frontier. When P^* rises, the level of inputs used in the economy declines. The inner production possibility frontier describes the production set of the economy given the lower level of inputs. If the same level of inputs were produced as before, then production would occur at point B and the domestic price of inputs, as reflected in the slope of the inner frontier, would be lower. However, if the level of inputs used falls, and if equation (3.DCP) holds with equality as assumed, use of domestically produced inputs must fall proportionally. So production actually occurs at a point like C, yielding a domestic price of inputs that is lower still. Hence there are

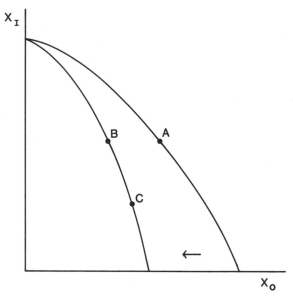

Fig. 8.1   Domestic content, physical units

two effects. First, since fewer produced inputs are used, the economy is comparatively less able to produce outputs. Second, since the ratio of domestically produced inputs to total inputs is constant, fewer inputs are produced at home. Both of these effects work in the same direction, resulting in a fall in P.

When the domestic content requirement is defined in terms of value added, the economy behaves differently once again. For that case, combine equations (5) and (7.DCV) to write

(20) $Pf_2(V_I,L_I) = \{1 + (1 - j)[(P - P^*)/P]\}g_2(V_O,L - L_I,X_I^c).$

Substitute equation (1) into equation (3.DCV) to write

(21) $P^*[X_I^c - f(V_I,L_I)] = (1 - j)X_O .$

Finally, equation (8.DCV) is reproduced here as equation (22) for the reader's convenience:

(22) $P = \{1 + (1 - j)[(P - P^*)/P]\}g_3(V_O,L - L_I,X_I^c).$

Now equations (20)–(22) are a system of three equations in the variables P, X_I^c, and L_I. Dividing (20) by (22) eliminates P:

(23) $f_2(V_I,L_I) = g_2(V_O,L - L_I,X_I^c)/g_3(V_O,L - L_I,X_I^c).$

Now equations (21) and (23) are a rather tractable two-equation system in L_I and X_I^c that can be used to show that $\partial L_I/\partial P^* > 0$ and $\partial X_I^c/\partial P^* < 0$. So, although an increase in the world price causes a decrease in the use of inputs just as it does when domestic content is counted in physical units, it causes an *increase* in the domestic *production* of inputs. The intuition is as follows. When P^* rises, the same level of foreign input use would violate the constraint (3.DCV). Hence there is a tendency for substitution away from imported inputs and into domestically produced inputs. Of course, the higher world price causes a decrease in the total derived demand for inputs. Nevertheless, the net effect is for the production of domestically produced inputs to rise.

To derive the sign of $\partial P/\partial P^*$ when domestic content requirements are denominated in value-added terms, the three-equation system (20)–(22) can be differentiated and the resulting system solved for $\partial P/\partial P^*$. That exercise yields a sign for $\partial P/\partial P^*$ which appears to be ambiguous. Some insight can be gained from figure 8.2 where, as before, the outer and inner production possibility frontiers describe the economy's production set given the level of inputs employed in the economy before and after an increase in the world price, respectively. As before, the decrease in the level of inputs used causes the production possibility frontier to rotate in. However, now labor flows *into* the input tier. Hence the two effects work in opposite directions. (In the Cobb-Douglas case considered in section 8.3, $\partial P/\partial P^*$ is positive.) A note of caution is in

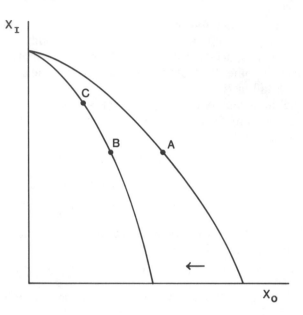

Fig. 8.2   Domestic content, value added

order as to the use of figure 8.2. While in figure 8.1 the slope of the production possibility frontier reflects the domestic price ratio, the same does not hold for figure 8.2. (These two facts can be seen from equations (5) and (7.DCP) and from equations (5) and (7.DCV), respectively.)

8.3   A Simulation

To get some idea of the magnitude of the effects described in section 8.2, consider a simple economy possessing a Cobb-Douglas technology in each tier, so that the production functions are given by

(24) $X_I = FL_I^\alpha V_I^{1-\alpha}$, and

(25) $X_O = GL_O^{\beta_1}(X_I^c)^{\beta_2}V_O^{1-\beta_1-\beta_2}$

For the purposes of the numerical example that follows, values for the parameters of equations (24) and (25) were derived from the 1977 input-output tables published by the *Survey of Current Business*. Attention was focused on the industries comprising the first seventy-nine columns of those tables. It is unfortunate for the purposes of this chapter that the disaggregation in the tables is not on the basis of intermediate and final products; in each industry some of the production is of intermediate goods and some of the production is of final goods. However, for each industry, i, total intermediate demand and total final demand are given. For the purposes of this example, assume that all imports reported in the input-output tables are of intermediate goods. Let ϕ_i be the fraction of output in each industry that is attributed to intermediate demand. Though imperfect, ϕ_i will be used as a measure of the fraction of value added in industry i that resulted from intermediate goods production. Multiplication of value added in each industry, i, by ϕ_i and summation over all industries yield a measure of the total production of intermediate goods, X_I. Similarly, multiplication of value added in each industry, i, by $(1 - \phi_i)$ and summation over all industries yield a measure of the total production of final goods, X_O. The input-output tables also give wages and other factor payments in each industry but, once again, do not divide them between intermediate and final good production. Multiplication of these figures by ϕ_i and $(1 - \phi_i)$ and summation over industries yield estimates, in dollar units, of how much labor and "other factors" (to be interpreted as immobile specific factors) are used in the input tier and in the output tier, respectively. That is, these calculations yield estimates of V_I, V_O, L_I, and L_O. Consistent with the earlier assumption that all imports are of intermediate goods, assume that input use in the economy is $X_I^c = X_I + \Sigma_i m_i$. These estimates can then be used to derive the factor shares, α, β_1, and β_2. Plugging all of these results into equations (24) and (25) determines values for F and G. The resulting values of α, β_1, β_2, L, V_I, V_O, F, and G are to be found near the bottom of table 8.2.

Consider a small, undistorted economy with production functions and factor endowments as derived above and listed near the bottom of table 8.2. Table 8.2 also reports the values of input production, X_I, input consumption, X_I^c, output production, X_O, output consumption,

Table 8.2   The Undistorted Economy

P^*	X_I	X_I^c	X_O	X_O^c	k	J
.1	.04	9.45	3.94	3.00	.005	.76
.2	.12	3.78	3.15	2.42	.03	.77
.3	.22	2.19	2.74	2.15	.10	.78
.4	.33	1.47	2.45	2.00	.22	.81
.5	.44	1.07	2.23	1.91	.41	.86
.6	.54	.81	2.03	1.87	.66	.92
.7	.63	.64	1.86	1.85	.99	.99

$\alpha = .53$			$\beta_1 = .29$		$\beta_2 = .24$	
$L = .96$			$V_I = .35$		$V_O = .46$	
		$F = 2.00$		$G = 3.36$		

Notes: Value of X_I, X_I^c, X_O, X_O^c, L, V_I, and V_O are in trillions of dollars. Rounding is to two decimal places.

X_O^C, domestic content in physical units, k, and domestic content in value-added terms, j, for such an economy facing world prices ranging from .1 to .7. Note that if world input prices exceed .7 by very much, the country will export inputs instead of importing them.

Table 8.3 reports the results of imposing an ad valorem tariff on the input tier for three different world prices. For the different world prices and different tariff rates the first five columns report the equilibrium levels of input production, input consumption, output production, output consumption (i.e., welfare), and domestic price, respectively. The final column reports the elasticity of labor employment in the input tier with respect to a change in the world price of the input. The elasticity of the domestic input price with respect to the world input price is, of course, always one by equation (3.T). The welfare costs of imposing an ad valorem tariff are easily determined from the table. For example, when the world price is .4, domestic welfare without a tariff (i.e., X_O^C when $(1 + t) = 1$) is $2.0 trillion. If a 25 percent tariff is imposed, this figure falls to $1.98 trillion.

It is well known that given perfectly competitive markets without distortions there is an equivalent quota for every tariff. As argued in section 8.2, however, economies with different policies in place will behave differently when faced with terms-of-trade changes. Table 8.4 reports the elasticities of equilibrium output consumption for different

Table 8.3   **Ad Valorem Tariffs**

	X_I	X_I^C	X_O	X_O^C	P	η_{L_I}
$P^* = .2$						
$(1+t) = 1.0$	.12	3.78	3.15	2.42	.2	3.60
$(1+t) = 1.5$	.22	2.19	2.74	2.35	.3	3.61
$(1+t) = 2.0$	.33	1.47	2.46	2.23	.4	3.64
$(1+t) = 2.5$	.44	1.07	2.23	2.10	.5	3.69
$(1+t) = 3.0$	.54	.81	2.03	1.98	.6	3.75
$(1+t) = 3.5$	.63	.64	1.86	1.86	.7	3.83
$P^* = .4$						
$(1+t) = 1.00$	.33	1.47	2.45	2.00	.4	3.64
$(1+t) = 1.25$	.44	1.07	2.23	1.98	.5	3.69
$(1+t) = 1.50$	.54	.81	2.03	1.92	.6	3.75
$(1+t) = 1.75$	.63	.64	1.86	1.86	.7	3.83
$P^* = .6$						
$(1+t) = 1.00$	.54	.81	2.03	1.87	.6	3.75
$(1+t) = 1.05$	.57	.75	1.98	1.87	.63	3.77
$(1+t) = 1.10$	.59	.70	1.93	1.86	.66	3.80
$(1+t) = 1.15$	.62	.65	1.88	1.86	.69	3.82

Notes: Values of X_I, X_I^C, X_O, X_O^C are in trillions of dollars. Rounding is to two decimal places.

Table 8.4   **Welfare Effects of Terms-of-Trade Changes**

	$\eta_{x_0^C}$ (Ad Valorem Tariff)	$\eta_{x_0^C}$ (Specific Tariff)	$\eta_{x_0^C}$ (Quota)
$P^* = .2$			
$P = .2$	$-.30$	$-.30$	$-.30$
$P = .3$	$-.32$	$-.27$	$-.17$
$P = .4$	$-.37$	$-.24$	$-.10$
$P = .5$	$-.47$	$-.22$	$-.06$
$P = .6$	$-.61$	$-.22$	$-.03$
$P = .7$	$-.81$	$-.23$	$-.001$
$P^* = .4$			
$P = .4$	$-.23$	$-.23$	$-.23$
$P = .5$	$-.27$	$-.24$	$-.13$
$P = .6$	$-.36$	$-.26$	$-.06$
$P = .7$	$-.49$	$-.28$	$-.002$
$P^* = .6$			
$P = .6$	$-.09$	$-.09$	$-.09$
$P = .63$	$-.11$	$-.10$	$-.06$
$P = .66$	$-.13$	$-.12$	$-.03$
$P = .69$	$-.15$	$-.13$	$-.01$

world prices and different levels of protection when protection takes the form of an ad valorem tariff, a specific tariff, or a quota. The domestic prices in the first column refer to the domestic prices that result from the protection, whatever its form. For example, the first row in the section headed $P^* = .2$ reports that when no protection is imposed, that is, when $P = .2$, the elasticity of equilibrium output consumption is $-.30$. The second row of the same section reports that when the domestic price is increased to .3 then the elasticity is $-.32$ if protection is by an ad valorem tariff, $-.27$ if protection is by a specific tariff, and $-.17$ if protection is by a quota.

Table 8.4 indicates that the welfare effects of terms-of-trade changes are of greatest magnitude under ad valorem tariffs and of smallest magnitude under quotas. The intuition follows from the analysis in section 8.2. When a quota is in place, changes in the world price of the input do not cause any reallocation of productive resources in the economy. An increase in that price reduces welfare only by increasing the price that the country must pay for its fixed level of imports. Given a tariff, however, an increase in the world price induces labor to flow into the input tier, where the country is at a comparative disadvantage. This intensifies the welfare loss relative to the quota case. Finally, note that the magnitudes of welfare changes are greater under an ad valorem tariff than under a specific tariff. This is because the specific tariff, being a per unit tax, becomes proportionally less important when prices rise than does an ad valorem tariff.

Table 8.5 reports the effects of terms-of-trade changes when domestic content requirements are imposed in physical units. The first five columns are as in table 8.3; the last three columns report the elasticities of the domestic price, labor employment in the input tier, and output consumption, respectively, with respect to changes in the world price of inputs. Note that the elasticity of the domestic price of inputs with respect to the world price of inputs can be significant; when $P^* = .2$ and $k = .1$, for example, $\eta_P = -1$. Table 8.6 reports similar results for domestic content requirements denominated in value-added terms. Since domestic content requirements are not, by themselves, equivalent to tariffs, direct comparisons of welfare elasticities are not as meaningful as they are in table 8.4. Nevertheless, if one makes the comparison in terms of domestic prices it appears that the welfare effects of terms-of-trade changes are smaller under quotas than under domestic content legislation. For example, in table 8.5 with $P^* = .2$, elasticities range from $-.24$ to $-.01$ for protection that yields domestic prices from .46 to .71,

Table 8.5   **Domestic Content in Physical Units**

	X_I	X_I^C	X_O	X_O^C	P	η_P	η_{L_I}	$\eta_{X_O^C}$
$P^* = .2$								
$k = .1$	.31	3.14	2.95	2.39	.46	-1.00	-1.30	$-.24$
$k = .2$	.45	2.25	2.66	2.30	.62	$-.52$	$-.64$	$-.16$
$k = .3$	.51	1.71	2.45	2.21	.68	$-.32$	$-.38$	$-.11$
$k = .4$	.55	1.38	2.30	2.13	.70	$-.21$	$-.25$	$-.08$
$k = .5$	.58	1.15	2.18	2.07	.71	$-.14$	$-.16$	$-.06$
$k = .6$	.59	.99	2.09	2.01	.71	$-.10$	$-.11$	$-.04$
$k = .7$	.61	.87	2.02	1.97	.71	$-.07$	$-.07$	$-.03$
$k = .8$	.62	.77	1.96	1.93	.71	$-.04$	$-.04$	$-.02$
$k = .9$	.63	.69	1.90	1.89	.71	$-.02$	$-.02$	$-.01$
$P^* = .4$								
$k = .3$	.40	1.34	2.37	2.00	.48	$-.69$	$-.85$	$-.19$
$k = .4$	.47	1.17	2.26	1.98	.56	$-.46$	$-.56$	$-.14$
$k = .5$	.52	1.04	2.17	1.96	.61	$-.31$	$-.37$	$-.11$
$k = .6$	.55	.92	2.09	1.94	.64	$-.21$	$-.24$	$-.08$
$k = .7$	.58	.83	2.02	1.92	.66	$-.14$	$-.16$	$-.05$
$k = .8$	.60	.75	1.96	1.90	.68	$-.08$	$-.09$	$-.03$
$k = .9$	.62	.69	1.90	1.87	.69	$-.04$	$-.04$	$-.01$
$P^* = .6$								
$k = .7$	.55	.79	2.01	1.89	.62	$-.21$	$-.24$	$-.07$
$k = .8$	.58	.73	1.95	1.87	.65	$-.12$	$-.14$	$-.05$
$k = .9$	.61	.68	1.90	1.86	.68	$-.05$	$-.06$	$-.02$

Notes: Values of X_I, X_I^C, X_O, and X_O^C are in trillions of dollars. Rounding is to two decimal places.

Table 8.6   **Domestic Content in Value-Added Terms**

	X_I	X_I^C	X_O	X_O^C	P	η_P	η_{L_I}	$\eta_{X_O^C}$
$P^* = .2$								
$j = .8$	.15	3.17	3.02	2.41	.23	.81	3.03	−.30
$j = .825$	.18	2.72	2.90	2.39	.27	.77	2.88	−.29
$j = .850$	.21	2.30	2.78	2.36	.31	.71	2.65	−.28
$j = .875$	.26	1.91	2.64	2.31	.35	.62	2.32	−.26
$j = .90$	.31	1.56	2.50	2.25	.40	.50	1.89	−.24
$j = .925$	.38	1.26	2.35	2.17	.47	.35	1.37	−.20
$j = .950$	.46	1.01	2.19	2.08	.54	.21	.84	−.15
$j = .975$	.55	.80	2.02	1.97	.62	.09	.36	−.08
$P^* = .4$								
$j = .825$	.35	1.41	2.42	2.00	.42	.32	1.59	−.22
$j = .850$	.38	1.26	2.37	1.99	.45	.27	1.33	−.20
$j = .875$	.42	1.13	2.27	1.98	.49	.21	1.07	−.18
$j = .9$	.46	1.01	2.19	1.97	.53	.16	.82	−.15
$j = .925$	.50	.90	2.10	1.95	.58	.11	.58	−.12
$j = .950$	.55	.80	2.02	1.92	.62	.07	.35	.08
$j = .975$	.59	.71	1.94	1.89	.66	.03	.16	−.04
$P^* = .6$								
$j = .925$	.55	.80	2.02	1.87	.61	.02	.35	−.08
$j − .950$	.57	.74	1.96	1.87	.64	.01	.22	−.06
$j = .975$	.60	.68	1.91	1.86	.67	.01	.01	−.03

Notes: Values of X_I, X_I^C, X_O, and X_O^C are in trillions of dollars. Rounding is to two decimal places.

while in table 8.4 with $P^* = .2$, elasticities range from $-.10$ to $-.001$ for quotas resulting in domestic prices from .4 to.7.

8.4 Concluding Remarks

The simulation in section 8.3 reports the comparative statics effects of world price changes on a small open economy when producers of all intermediate goods are protected. Obviously, as both Dixit and Grossman assert in their comments on this chapter, in the more likely event that less sweeping measures are considered, one would want to focus on the particular industries in question. Of course, a careful empirical application of this theory to, for example, the United States economy would require a more complex model and more detailed data than were used here. The results reported in section 8.3 are best interpreted as being illustrative in nature.

The results derived above demonstrate that, although two policies may be equivalent in a static sense, they may behave very differently in the face of changes in market conditions. Hence, if it is difficult to change policies once they are in place, the criteria for choosing a policy should include how it will cause the economy to behave in the future, given what is likely to occur.

References

Grossman, Gene. 1981. The theory of domestic content protection and content preference. *Quarterly Journal of Economics* 96:585–603.
Jones, Ronald. 1965. The structure of simple general equilibrium models. *Journal of Political Economy* 73:557–72.
Krishna, Kala, and Motoshige, Itoh. 1988. Content protection and oligopolistic interactions. *Review of Economic Studies* 56:107–26.
Mussa, Michael. 1984. The economics of content protection. National Bureau of Economic Research Working Paper No. 1457.
Sanyal, Kalyan, and Ronald Jones. 1982. The theory of trade in middle products. *American Economic Review* 72:16–32.

Comment   Avinash K. Dixit

This chapter compares the performance of alternative methods of content protection when the world price can change after the policy has been fixed. This is very useful in drawing our attention to a dimension of "robustness" of policy that is seldom analyzed. Major policy changes are infrequent, therefore, the design of policy should bear in mind its suitability to a variety of future circumstances where it will be in force. The idea should have much wider applicability, but the analysis needs to be taken further before it can be used in this way.

In quite general notation, the equilibrium of an economy is determined given the world prices p^* and policy instruments z. Let x denote some variable of economic interest, such as the consumption of the output good, or the rental rate for the specific factor in the input tier. Now x is a function $x(z,p^*)$. What Lambson does is to compare the partial derivatives $x_2 (z,p^*)$ for different instruments z. What can we learn from this? Presumably the variable x is a maximand or a target of policy. If we choose z having in mind one value of p^* and then a higher value emerges, then x might overshoot, or move the wrong way, depending on the sign of $x_2 (z,p^*)$.

This is not as systematic as one would like. We should view the problem as one of decision making under uncertainty. We must fix z before p^* is realized, but we have a subjective or objective distribution

Avinash K. Dixit is professor of economics at Princeton University.

over it, and some attitude to risk about x. The simplest such problem would be to maximize $E[U(x(z,p^*))]$. Another might be to maximize Prob $\{x(z,p^*) > \underline{x}\}$ where $\underline{x}$ is a target level.

If the uncertainty in p^* is small, Lambson's comparative statics will be a useful component of this more general analysis. Thus we have, approximately,

$$x(z,p^*) = x(z,Ep^*) + (p^* - Ep^*) x_2 (z,Ep^*).$$

Therefore

$$\text{Var}[x(z,p^*)] = \text{Var}[p^*] \cdot [x_2 (z,Ep^*)]^2.$$

The policymaker can then choose z to maximize a quadratic utility function over x. Alternatively,

$$\text{Prob } \{x(z,p^*) > \underline{x}\} =$$
$$\text{Prob } \{p^* > Ep^* + [\underline{x} - x(z,Ep^*)]/x_2(z,Ep^*)\},$$

which enables us to calculate the approximate policy to ensure fulfillment of the target with maximum probability.

Once uncertainty is made explicit, it becomes important to introduce markets to deal with it. Even with the aggregate or systematic uncertainty that is inherent in p^*, the real incomes of different factors are affected differently. They therefore have the desire to trade Arrow-type securities whose payoff is conditional on p^*. Such markets are feasible since p^* is easily observable. The equilibrium, and therefore the policy analysis, should be conducted relative to such a market structure.

Turning to the specific problem of content protection, I think this whole literature needs to distinguish two concepts: protection of the input tier and protection to value added in the output tier. When we think of content protection for the automobile industry, we mean a requirement that a greater proportion of transmissions, chassis, engines, and so forth be of domestic manufacture, not that the industry use a certain proportion, whether in physical or value terms, of domestic steel. In fact, an import tariff or quota on steel will reduce the effective rate of protection to the domestic auto industry.

Of course, this is in part a matter of definition: if auto parts are classified in the input tier and only the final assembly stage in the output tier, content protection may properly be modeled as protection of the input tier. Therefore, theoretical work may legitimately blur the distinction. However, in empirical work, an appropriate choice of definitions becomes crucial. Here Lambson's formulation seems unfortunate. He assumes that all imports are of intermediate goods and chooses his parameter values accordingly. Now in 1984, out of a total of $341 billion of U.S. merchandise imports, $39 billion were road vehicles (excluding parts), $14 billion were clothing and accessories, $5 billion were footwear, and $3.6 billion were toys and sporting goods. If all these goods, comprising almost 20 percent of all imports, are to be intermediate, the output tier must be essentially only retailing. This makes content protection, or protection of the input tier, virtually tantamount to general protection for manufacturing. I doubt if that is what most people would understand by the term.

In reality, what we understand by the scope of the input and output tiers differs very widely across industries, depending on the extent of vertical integration, organization of labor, or even pure historical custom. This leads me to think that aggregate economywide equilibrium models are not really the best way to do empirical work on content protection. An industry-by-industry approach would allow more precision in capturing the kind of protection that is relevant in each context. It would also allow a more accurate specification of demand and cost conditions, and so improve the calculation of the efficiency and distributive effects of the policies.

Comment   Gene M. Grossman

This chapter is a fine example of the Rochester school of trade theory. Lambson constructs a simple, tractable general equilibrium model to study various trade policies that might be used to protect producers of intermediate inputs. Unlike much of the literature that focuses on the implications for resource allocation of different policies set to achieve some common objective, Lambson is concerned with what happens when policies are already in place and some external conditions change. In particular, he studies how changes in the terms of trade affect equilibrium in the domestic market when tariffs, quotas, or two types of content protection schemes are used to protect intermediate-goods producers. A main finding is that a fall in the international price of intermediates causes the local price of intermediates to fall when a tariff is in effect, has no impact on domestic prices under a quota regime, and actually causes the local price of intermediates to rise when a physical content protection scheme is in place.

My remarks are in three parts. First, I provide an interpretation of Lambson's results that makes use of some simple, partial equilibrium, supply and demand diagrams. These diagrams helped me to understand

Gene M. Grossman is associate professor of economics and international affairs at the Woodrow Wilson School, Princeton University, and a research associate of the National Bureau of Economic Research.

the findings and also convinced me that they would survive in alternative but equally reasonable specifications of the general equilibrium structure. Second, I argue that the general equilibrium approach perhaps is not the most appropriate for the question at hand, especially when it comes time for the empirical application presented in the last section of Lambson's chapter. Finally, I offer some suggestions for possible extensions of the research reported here.

Interpretation of Results

The theoretical portion of Lambson's chapter stresses that foreign price changes will have qualitatively different effects on the domestic intermediate goods market when different policies are used to protect that industry. This point is seen most clearly, I believe, when we consider how the *net* derived demand curve for domestic intermediates shifts in response to the terms-of-trade change under the alternative policies. In figure C8.1, I have shown the equilibrium in the domestic market for locally produced intermediate goods under a tariff regime. The curve labeled DD′ is the total derived demand for intermediates by domestic final-goods manufacturers, and SS′ is the supply of intermediates by local producers. Under a tariff, imports are available in perfectly elastic supply at the tariff-augmented international price, so initially the net (or residual) derived demand for the domestic input is given by ACD′. When the world price of imported intermediates falls to p_i^*, the net derived demand shifts to A′C′D′, causing the domestic price to fall to $p_i^*(1 + t)$. As is well known, incipient *substitution* toward imports causes demand for the domestic product to fall, thereby exerting downward pressure on the local price.

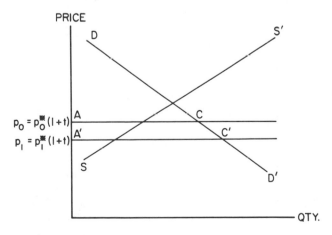

Fig. C8.1   Tariff protection

Contrast this result with that for a quota, illustrated in figure C8.2. Here the net demand curve at the initial world price of foreign intermediates is given by ABCD'. This curve is found by subtracting from total demand DD' the fixed amount of the quota, BC, for all domestic prices exceeding the world price of intermediates. Now when the world price falls to p_1^*, the net demand for domestic intermediates becomes AB'C'D'. As is clear from this figure, this shift has no effect on the equilibrium price of the domestic product. The reason, of course, is that substitution toward the now cheaper import is not possible when the quota is binding, so the fall in p^* induces no change in demand.

Next consider the case of a physical content protection scheme (PCP). In Grossman (1981) I described the construction of the net derived demand curve associated with this policy instrument, as depicted in figure C8.3. To review briefly, a PCP requires domestic manufacturers to use at least a specified proportion $1 - k$ of domestic intermediates (relative to imported intermediates) in their production processes. Again let DD' be the total demand for intermediates by domestic manufacturers, and note that this curve is drawn as a function of the *effective* price of an intermediate good faced by the final-goods sector. As an intermediate step, we construct the curve labeled DE by finding all quantities that are a fraction $1 - k$ of total demand along DD'. Then, the relevant portion of the net derived demand curve is found by vertically displacing DE, so that a weighted average of the domestic price on the net derived demand curve and the (given) international price p^* (with $1 - k$ and k as the weights) gives the corresponding price on the curve DE. Take the point X, for example. When the domestic price is given by the ordinate of this point, the weighted average of the domestic

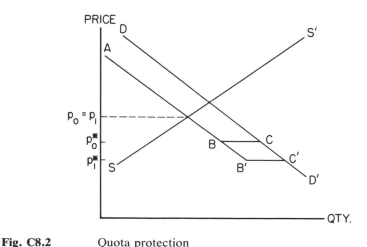

Fig. C8.2   Quota protection

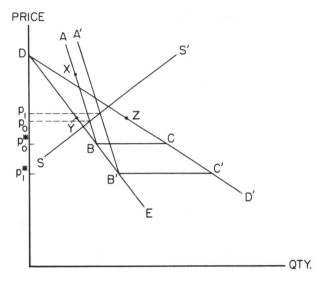

Fig. C8.3   Content protection

and foreign price is given by the ordinate of Y, on DE. This is the effective price of intermediates faced by domestic manufacturers, so total demand is given by the abscissa of Z on DD'. But then the PCP requires that at least a fraction $1 - k$ of this amount be purchased domestically. By construction, this quantity is given by the abscissa of Y and hence X. (Note that the complete net derived demand curve is given by ABCD', where the policy is not binding along BCD'.)

When the international price falls to p_1^*, the net demand curve shifts to A'B'C'D'. This increase in demand in the relevant region causes the domestic price to rise, thus confirming Lambson's result. How do we account for this finding? Because the PCP requires that imported and domestic inputs be used in fixed proportions, the two intermediate goods become complements, rather than substitutes, when the policy is in effect. The fall in p^* induces domestic manufacturers of final goods to expand their production. Substitution between the intermediates does not take place, but the "output effect" implies an increase in demand for the domestic product.

Finally, consider the value-added content scheme (VACP). Here there are two effects working in opposite directions. The fall in p^* means that more foreign intermediates can be imported without the content constraint being violated. Hence, substitution of imported for domestic intermediates takes place. At the same time, because the fall in p^* eases the constraint, local final-goods producers have an incentive to expand their outputs by purchasing more inputs of all kinds. Evidently, the net impact of the output and substitution effects is ambiguous, as Lambson has shown.

General versus Partial Equilibrium Modeling

As should be clear from the logic of the discussion, Lambson's theoretical results would survive in many alternative general equilibrium models to the one he chooses. But where the theory is robust to model specification, the empirical calibration is not likely to be so. In practice, content protection always is applied at the level of a specific industry and enforced on a firm-by-firm basis. Indeed, it is hard to imagine what would be meant by an economywide content protection scheme. Are we to imagine that the economy as a whole is to achieve a certain average domestic content? If so, how would such a scheme be implemented? If the content requirement is to apply to each and every firm, surely the constraint would have differential impacts across sectors.

The general equilibrium structure forces Lambson to treat all imports as intermediates. While he justifies this approach with appeal to the notion of "middle products" as developed by Sanyal and Jones (1982), it is hard to imagine how French wine could be made to conform to a 60 percent domestic content requirement, even after allowance is made for domestic value added in packaging and retailing.

An alternative approach would have been to follow the partial equilibrium modeling outlined above. Then, detailed consideration could have been given to each of two or three industries for which content protection has been proposed. While some points of detail would be different (there would be no need to have balanced trade between intermediates and final goods at the industry level), the general message would have been preserved and the numbers would have been more informative.

Extensions of the Research

Given the evident inertia in the policy-setting apparatus, the question raised by Lambson of the "robustness" of trade policy to a changing economic environment is an important one. Lambson's work might be fruitfully extended using the following general approach. First, one could state explicitly the assumed objective of trade policy. Next, the various instruments that might be used to achieve that objective would be identified. The policy control variables then would be set at the levels needed to achieve the objective. Finally, shocks to the environment are introduced, and implications for domestic *welfare* are compared. The approach could apply not only to changes in the terms of trade, but also to shifts in domestic supply and demand conditions. This would provide an additional basis for ranking policies beyond the usual, static, deadweight-loss measures: which policy will cause least harm if conditions change before the policymakers have a chance to act again?

References

Grossman, Gene M. 1981. The theory of domestic content protection and content preference. *Quarterly Journal of Economics* 96(4): 585–603.

Sanyal, Kalyan, and Ronald W. Jones. 1982. The theory of trade in middle products. *American Economic Review* 72(1): 16–32.

III Determining the Relationship between Foreign Direct Investment and Exports

9   U.S. and Swedish Direct Investment and Exports

Magnus Blomström, Robert E. Lipsey, and Ksenia Kulchycky

The effect of foreign production by a country's firms on the home country's exports continues to be a puzzle after many years of controversy and a considerable amount of empirical research. Theoretical models of direct foreign investment typically treat the size of a market as exogenous and a company's share of a market as a function of its firm-specific capital. The decision as to whether to produce abroad is then a matter of choosing among possible methods of serving the foreign market, including exporting from the home country, producing abroad, and licensing others to produce the firm's product. That decision will depend on the nature of the firm's intangible assets, on transport costs, economies or diseconomies of scale, barriers to trade and other government regulations, on factor prices at home and in other countries,

Magnus Blomström is associate professor of economics at the Stockholm School of Economics and a research economist at the National Bureau of Economic Research. Robert E. Lipsey is professor of economics at Queens College and the Graduate Center of the City University of New York and a research associate of the National Bureau of Economic Research. Ksenia Kulchycky is a Ph.D. candidate in the Department of Economics of the University of Pennsylvania.

   This research is part of the NBER program in International Studies. Magnus Blomström's part of the research took place while he was a member of the staff of the Industriens Utredningsinstitut of Stockholm. Robert Lipsey's research was supported first by an SSRC-Fulbright Fellowship and later by a PSC-CUNY grant and a grant of computer time from the City University of New York. The authors are grateful to the Industriens Utredningsinstitut and the Bureau of Economic Analysis of the U.S. Department of Commerce for use of their data and to Robert Baldwin, Jeffrey Zax, and participants in the NBER Conference on Trade Policy Issues and Empirical Analysis, particularly the discussants, Steven J. Matusz and John Mutti, for useful comments and suggestions. Linda Molinari assisted with statistical work and computer programming and James Hayes and Rosa Schupbach with the preparation of the manuscript.

as well as on the need to adapt the product to differences among markets in the characteristics demanded. This more or less standard view of the multinational firm implies that production in a market is a substitute for production at home for export to that market.

A more neutral viewpoint would be to regard a firm's share of a market as being at least partly dependent on whether it produces there, even though local production does not affect the demand for the firm's products. That would be the case, for example, if a product were totally nontradable: that may be true for some services, such as tourism or medical care. If all the firm's products were nontradable, there could, of course, be no effect of overseas production on exports. A more interesting example would be a firm that can increase its market share in a country by producing there, because local production reduces the cost of supplying the market. If that local production requires some input from the parent, such as components, it might raise or lower parent exports, depending on the size of the gain in market share and the importance of parent input in the affiliate's output.

A third possibility is that a firm's production in a host country increases that country's demand for the firm's products. In that case, higher production abroad by a country's firms would be more likely to lead to larger home country exports. That is most obvious if the production abroad is in activities ancillary to exporting, such as sales and service operations. A positive effect of production abroad on home country exports could also result if production of one part of a parent company's range of products familiarizes a market with the parent company's name and reputation. Production in a country by a multinational might also raise that country's demand for the product in general, rather than for only the output of the multinational firm. That might be the case, for example, if a company like Coca Cola entered a country and advertised heavily. The demand for cola drinks might increase enough to open the market to local or other foreign producers.

With all these possibilities, the assumption of fixed market shares for a parent firm, convenient though it is, seems inappropriate to us. Furthermore, even if a firm's overseas production added to exports by the parent, for one of the reasons mentioned above, that addition might be at the expense of exports by rival companies in the home country. For this reason we examine the effects of production abroad by a country's firms on the home country's exports rather than on the exports of the parents themselves.

We analyze the effects of foreign production on home country exports, using cross-section data from Sweden and the United States. In addition, for Swedish exports, we also study the determinants of changes over time in exports to each destination.

9.1   Earlier Empirical Findings

Despite the implications of theoretical models of direct investment, empirical studies have rarely observed substitution between overseas production and exports. A cross-sectional study for 1970 covering fourteen industries, based on foreign production data for about two hundred of the larger U.S. investors, found only positive coefficients among those that were significant in equations in which U.S. exports to a country in an industry were related to U.S. companies' production in that country and industry as well as to other variables (Lipsey and Weiss 1981). At the same time, coefficients for U.S. companies' production were mostly negative in equations explaining exports to each country by other industrial countries. There was weaker evidence, from data on numbers of affiliates, that investment by countries other than the United States was negatively related to U.S. exports, and positively related to exports by other countries. The positive (complementary) relationship between U.S.-owned production and U.S. exports was also evident in equations for individual U.S. firms' exports, based on the same data (Lipsey and Weiss 1984).

Bergsten, Horst, and Moran (1978), using published IRS and U.S. Department of Commerce data, concluded that "the relation between foreign investment and exports or imports is largely haphazard" (p. 97), although they suggested that there is a noticeable complementarity for investment up to a certain level, because most of the initial investment goes into marketing and assembly.

The most elaborate examination of trade investment relationships for individual firms has been performed by Swedenborg (1979, 1982) for Swedish multinationals. OLS (ordinary least squares) equations relating the ratio of exports to home production to the ratio of foreign to home production across all industries showed a positive and significant influence of foreign production on firm exports, and of foreign production in a country on firm exports to the country. A 2SLS (two-stage least squares) estimate of the relationship found it statistically insignificant, although the coefficients across all firms, and across all firms and countries, did not change greatly. As compared with those in the OLS equations, they fell by 25 percent to 30 percent. Equations confined to firms with more than five affiliates produced lower coefficients in OLS equations, and more of a decline in 2SLS.

Swedenborg (1982) also combined data from four Swedish surveys, again using 2SLS, and found that each increase by $10 of foreign production in a country produced an increase of exports to that country by the parent company of $1. That $1 increase was the net outcome of $1.20 added to exports to the affiliate and $.20 subtracted from exports to nonaffiliates in the country.

9.2 Estimating the Effects of Foreign Production

The fear that foreign production by a country's firms means the export of jobs to other countries is an old one. Bergsten, Horst, and Moran (1978) trace the discussion in the United States back to the 1920s; the discussion occurred despite the fact that much of the flow of U.S. investment at that time was in public utilities, not likely to be competitive with U.S. production.

While the idea of exporting jobs in the aggregate is a fuzzy one, and while economists have not generally considered the maximization of commodity exports to be a sensible objective for economic policy, these fears have led to recurrent efforts to measure the effect that U.S. firms' overseas production has on exports and to proposals for government action to hinder the growth of such production.

There are several possible ways of defining the proposition that production overseas by a country's firms substitutes for, or is complementary to, exports by the country or by the parent firms themselves. Each way is associated with a different implied model of the behavior of firms or a different policy question.

The simplest, if unrealistic, view might be that the factors determining the location and extent of affiliate production in a country are unrelated to the factors that determine parent exports to a country. This would be the case if affiliates were handed out to parents in a lottery. What might amount to much the same thing would be if the decision to establish an affiliate in a country were a very long-term one, and virtually permanent once made, while the export decision was a short-term one, easily adjusted to contemporary circumstances. Then, even if the existence and size of an affiliate reflected the same influences, such as exchange rates or price levels, which also played an important role in determining trade flows, the investment and the exports would reflect these influences from different periods. In that case, we could still interpret a coefficient for affiliate production, for example, in an equation explaining exports from the home country as representing the effect of affiliate production on exports.

The persistent problem in these analyses is the likelihood that the variables that determine investment in a country and affiliate production are the same as the ones determining trade flows. Some of the obvious ones, such as host country income and income per capita, can be included in the equation for trade flows to avoid attributing their effect to affiliate activity. But the risk that always remains is that there are unaccounted-for variables—such as host country regulation—that influence both investment and trade, and that we attribute their effects to investment.

There have been various attempts to escape this problem. The most obvious way is to include all relevant explanatory variables in the trade equation, but one can never be sure that there are not important additional variables omitted. In studies of exports by Swedish multinationals, Swedenborg (1979, 1982) used 2SLS, with the first-stage equation estimating affiliate production and the second-stage equation estimating parent exports as a whole and parent exports to individual countries. One difficulty was that the first-stage equation explained little of the variation in affiliate production. Consequently, a good deal of what may have been relevant variation in affiliate production was omitted in the second stage.

Lipsey and Weiss (1981, 1984) attempted to escape the problem by including a larger number of variables in the OLS equations, by working within fairly detailed industries, and by examining the relationships of affiliate production, not only to home-country exports but also to exports by others. The idea behind the last procedure was that it was likely to reveal some spurious relationships based on omitted characteristics of countries, provided that the omitted variables did not produce opposite effects on U.S. exports and exports by others.

Another method of dealing with the simultaneity issue, which we have tried in this chapter, is to study not only the levels of exports at one time, but also changes over time in home country exports to each destination. The assumption involved is that the effects of the most troublesome unaccounted-for factors that simultaneously influence investment and exports do not determine changes in these, or that their influence is incorporated in the initial levels of affiliate production and exports. We do not believe that such a cross section of changes over time has been tried before.

9.3 Trade Equations

The equations explaining U.S. and Swedish exports for each industry group are related to the trade equations of the type discussed in Leamer and Stern (1970) and used in studies by Chenery (1960), Linneman (1966), and others. They do differ, however, in a couple of respects. One is that they all relate to exports from one country and therefore do not involve any exporting-country variables. A second is that we use GDP and GDP per capita rather than GDP and population (only two of the three—income, population, and income per capita—can be used, because any two determine the third). A third difference is that we have dropped the distance variable, typically used as a measure of trade resistance, since it made little difference to the results and we needed to economize on independent variables. The implied trade equation for each industry is then

$$EXP_{ij} = f(GDP_j, GDPC_j),$$

where EXP_{ij} equals exports from the U.S. in 1982 or Sweden in 1978 to country j in products of industry i; GDP_j equals real GDP of country j in 1978 or 1982 in international prices (see appendix); and $GDPC_j$ equals real GDP per capita of country j in 1978 or 1982 in international prices.

We expect the coefficients for GDP to be positive, although one can imagine cases in which the expected influence of aggregate income on the aggregate demand for the product is more than offset by its influence on supply. For example, that may be the case in an industry in which economies of scale are of great importance and large markets are the preferred locations for production, so that while overall demand in a country is high, import demand is low. Coefficients for GDPC may be either positive or negative. Among the demand-side influences, a high income elasticity of demand should mean high demand in countries with high per capita income, given the aggregate GDP, and therefore a positive coefficient for GDPC. A low income elasticity should produce a negative coefficient. Obvious missing variables are tariff levels, for which we do not have information for a sufficient number of countries, and restrictions on imports or inducements to exports by affiliates, which are possibilities for further research. There are no industry characteristics, such as appear in some other studies of this issue, because each equation includes data for only one industry group.

To these trade equations we add several variables representing affiliate activity or production. These are NS_{ij}, which equals net sales of affiliates in industry i located in country j (sales minus imports from the home country); NLS_{ij}, which equals net local sales—sales of affiliates in industry i located in country j to buyers in country j, minus the portion of these sales accounted for by imports (that amount is estimated assuming that the ratio of imports to sales is the same for sales in the host country as for sales to other countries); and NES_{ij}, which equals net export sales—sales of affiliates in industry i located in country j to buyers outside country j, minus the portion of these sales accounted for by imports, estimated as for NLS.

We have no prior expectations for either net sales or net local sales. They include a mixture of influences in opposite directions. To the extent that affiliate production substitutes for exports from the United States or Sweden by either the parents or other firms, the effect on exports should be negative. That would be true if affiliate production of finished products substituted for exports of finished products, but also even if affiliate assembly of products substituted for only the final stages of output, provided that the U.S. or Swedish companies' share in the country's consumption was a fixed amount determined by country size and other country variables. Even if production in a host country increased exports of components or of other finished products by the parent, the effect on home country exports as a whole could be negative if some production replaced export sales by other U.S. or Swedish companies.

On the other side, if production in a host country by a U.S or Swedish company increased the size of that country's market for the products of that company's industry, or if it raised the company's share of the market even without increasing the size of the market, the effect on home country exports would be positive, provided that the increase in share came at the expense of local or other foreign companies rather than at the expense of other U.S. or Swedish companies. The positive effects could be on home country exports of raw materials or components or on home country exports of other finished products. The effect on finished products might occur if local production familiarized the host country with the parent's brand name or with U.S or Swedish goods more generally. The positive effect on home country exports may be enhanced by the fact that some of the affiliate production, even in affiliates classified as manufacturing, consists of distribution and service activities.

As between net sales and net local sales, we would expect negative coefficients to be more likely in the latter case. To the extent that affiliate production is for export rather than for local sale, it should not substitute for home country exports to the host country, even if it competes with home country exports to other countries. Thus, when we treat production for export separately, we expect the coefficient on net export sales to be positive.

9.3.1   Effects of Swedish Affiliate Production

Our examination of the consequences of Swedish firms' overseas production is based on the same set of data on multinational firms as was used by Swedenborg (1982), but in more aggregated form. Furthermore, it focuses on aggregate Swedish exports in each industry, including exports by nonmultinational firms, rather than on exports by the parent firms themselves. The data cover ten individual industries (see appendix for a description of the data). We have used equations for only the seven industries in which there are at least ten countries with Swedish-owned production.

The impact on Swedish exports of overseas production by Swedish firms is described by the set of coefficients for affiliate production in equations explaining Swedish exports to a country by GDP and GDP per capita, as in the trade equations described above, but adding a variable for being a Nordic country (Denmark, Finland, and Norway). We also performed a 2SLS regression on the Swedish data where the first-stage equations included a dummy variable for EEC membership. We expected the coefficients for GDP and GDP per capita, as well as that for being a Nordic country, to be positive (see table 9.1).

In the OLS regressions, all the coefficients are positive, implying that, other things equal, greater production by Swedish affiliates in a country is associated with larger exports from Sweden. The range of coefficients is wide, from 230 kronor of exports per thousand kronor of production in the host country, to exports greater than the host country production. There is no evidence here that host country production substitutes for exports from Sweden.

In the results there is some suggestion of unaccounted-for curvilinearity in the relationship, in the fact that the intercepts, supposedly showing the exports that would take place without any Swedish-owned production in the country, are mostly negative and fairly large, although they are not statistically significant (see appendix, table 9.A.1).

The coefficients in the 2SLS regressions are in general much larger than those in the OLS equations, although the story they tell is similar. All the coefficients in the 2SLS analysis are positive, and two of them indicate that a krona of Swedish-owned production in a foreign country draws in more than a krona of Swedish exports.

Table 9.1   **Coefficients for Affiliate Net Sales in Swedish Export Equations, 1978**

Industry Group	OLS	2SLS
Paper products	.229	.435
	(4.98)	(4.09)
Chemicals	.836	3.511
	(4.05)	(3.09)
Metal manufacturing	.379	.500
	(4.43)	(4.34)
Nonelectrical machinery	.359	.368
	(12.9)	(9.05)
Electrical machinery	.086	.516
	(1.40)	(1.15)
Transport equipment	.312	.921
	(3.49)	(2.85)
Other manufacturing	1.137	2.490
	(6.64)	(4.58)

Sources: Tables 9.A.1 and 9.A.2.

Notes: t-Statistics are in parentheses. Equations include, as independent variables, GDP, GDPC, a dummy variable for being a Nordic country, and Swedish manufacturing affiliate net sales. The instrument variable in the 2SLS is a variable for EEC membership.

We were able to distinguish affiliate production for local sale in the host country (net local sales) for only five industries. The result of substituting net local sales for net sales in these five industries is shown in table 9.2. The substitution produces larger coefficients for affiliate sales in most cases, but only two of the differences are substantial.

On the whole, then, while we would hesitate to place great weight on the estimated size of the coefficients, we think the evidence for a positive relationship is reasonably strong. There is certainly no sign of any negative relationship in this cross section.

Another way of looking at the relation between foreign production and exports is to relate changes in exports to a country, in each industry group over a period, to the initial levels of exports to and affiliate activity in that country, and to changes in real income and affiliate activity. We estimated the following equations:

$$\Delta EXP_{ij} = f(\Delta GDP_j, EXP70_{ij}, NS70_{ij}), \text{ and}$$

$$\Delta EXP_{ij} = f(\Delta GDP_j, EXP70_{ij}, \Delta NS_{ij}),$$

where ΔEXP_{ij} equals changes in exports from Sweden to country j in products of industry i, 1970–78 (thousand kronor); ΔGDP_j equals changes in real GDP of country j, 1970–78 (millions of dollars); $EXP70_{ij}$ equals exports from Sweden to country j in products of industry i in 1970 (thousand kronor); ΔNS_{ij} equals changes in affiliates' net sales, 1970–78 (thousand kronor); and $NS70_{ij}$ equals affiliates' net sales in 1970 (thousand kronor).

The variable for exports in the beginning of the period should incorporate the effects of not only the factors that we controlled for in

Table 9.2   **Coefficients for Affiliate Net Sales and Net Local Sales in Swedish Export Equations, 1978**

Industry Group	Net Sales	Net Local Sales
Paper products	.217	.351
	(2.11)	(2.79)
Chemicals	.809	.870
	(2.29)	(2.32)
Metal manufacturing	.330	.268
	(1.59)	(.80)
Nonelectrical machinery	.336	.508
	(5.87)	(6.32)
Electrical machinery	.083	.085
	(1.11)	(1.12)

Source: Table 9.A.3.

Note: Numbers in parentheses are t-statistics.

cross-section equations above, but also most of the unaccounted-for variables that we mentioned.

Initial foreign production and changes in it are included in separate regressions. The variable for the initial production position should tell us whether, as time goes by, affiliates substitute their own production for imports from the home country. In other words, do Swedish exports, given their initial level, increase less to countries with higher initial levels of Swedish-owned production? We should note that this is a different question from the one studied by Swedenborg (1979, 1982), which is whether the proportion of local sales that a company makes from local production changes with the age of the affiliate. The short- or medium-run effects of foreign production on exports should be reflected in the coefficients for changes in affiliate production. In other words, do Swedish exports increase less, given their initial level, to countries where Swedish-owned production increases more?

The results from these regressions are shown in table 9.3 These results strengthen our earlier impressions of a predominantly positive influence of affiliate production on home country exports. The variable for the initial level of affiliate production generally carries a positive and strongly significant coefficient. Metal manufacturing is the main exception. There is thus not much evidence here that Swedish firms'

Table 9.3   **Coefficients for Affiliate Net Sales in 1970 and Changes in Net Sales in Swedish Export Change Equations, 1970–78**

Industry Group	NS70	ΔNS
Paper products	.201	.058
	(1.36)	(1.62)
Chemicals	.448	.179
	(2.34)	(1.60)
Metal manufacturing	−.271	−.158
	(2.60)	(3.19)
Nonelectrical machinery	.122	.062
	(2.27)	(1.81)
Electrical machinery	.282	−.132
	(1.04)	(1.46)
Transport equipment	1.899	.276
	(2.71)	(3.64)
Other manufacturing	.836	.444
	(2.44)	(4.65)

Source: Table 9.A.4.

Notes: Numbers in parentheses are t-statistics. Both equations based on net sales in 1970 (NS 70), and equations based on changes in net sales, 1970-78 (Δ NS) include, as independent variables, Swedish exports to a country in 1970, in thousands of Swedish kronor, and the percentage change in real GDP between 1970 and 1978.

production in a country tends to reduce the country's subsequent imports from Sweden. The higher the level of Swedish-owned production in 1970, the larger the increase in Swedish exports between 1970 and 1978. The coefficient for changes in affiliate production is positive in five of the seven industries, and significantly different from zero at the 5 percent level in three of these. Only in metal manufacturing do we again find a negative and significant coefficient. On the whole, the larger the growth in Swedish-owned production in the host country, the greater the growth in exports from Sweden. This suggests a dominance of complementarity rather than of substitution between overseas production and exports.

9.3.2   Effects of U.S. Affiliate Production

For the United States we show two sets of equations and results. The U.S. data for majority-owned affiliates were available at a much more detailed industry level than the Swedish data: thirty-four industries, of which we show results for the thirty industries in which we had at least fifteen countries with some affiliate net sales. The second set of equations, in which we add data for minority-owned affiliates, was run for only seven broad industry groups.

The coefficients for various measures of production by majority-owned U.S. affiliates in U.S. export equations are summarized in table 9.4. The equations with only one affiliate production variable indicate that in about 80 percent of the industries, production in a country by majority-owned U.S affiliates was either unrelated to or positively related to exports by U.S firms in the same industry. In industries for which there was a statistically significant relationship and, more broadly,

Table 9.4   **Summary of t-Statistics for Coefficients of Affiliate Production in U.S. Export Equations, 1982 (30 industries)**

	Equations with One Production Variable		Equations with Two Production Variables	
	Net Sales	Net Local Sales	Net Local Sales	Net Export Sales
Coefficients with $t \geq 1$				
Positive				
$t \geq 2$	7	7	3	6
$1 \leq t < 2$	6	8	11	3
Negative				
$t \geq 2$	4	5	5	1
$1 \leq t < 2$	1	1	1	1
Coefficients with $t < 1$	12	9	10	19

Sources: Tables 9.A.5 – 9.A.7.

in all industries in which the coefficient for production was at least as large as its standard error, most of the coefficients were positive, suggesting complementarity between U.S. exports and U.S.-owned production in a country, rather than substitution of one for the other. The five industries in which there were negative coefficients twice their standard errors, suggesting some substitution of host country production for U.S. exports, were (1) other foods, (2) drugs, (3) industrial chemicals, (4) primary nonferrous metals, and (5) lumber, wood, furniture, and fixtures. The negative coefficient for drugs is particularly surprising because it contradicts the strong finding of complementarity for this industry in Lipsey and Weiss (1981).

When we separate production in each country into production for local sale and production for export, we find, as we expect, that indications of substitution are almost entirely confined to production for local sale (net local sales). For most industries, we find that production for export from the host country has no visible influence on U.S. exports to the host country, and where we do find a relationship, it is a positive one in the great majority of cases. The effects of production for local sale are not as clear. There are more instances of negative coefficients than of positive ones twice their standard errors, but the whole group of coefficients at least equal to their standard errors shows a large majority of positive (complementary) relationships. Evidence of substitution still is confined to a small minority of the thirty industries.

9.4 Production by Minority-Owned Affiliates

Most analyses of trade investment relationships have concentrated on majority-owned affiliates. The main reason is probably the paucity of data on affiliates that are 50 percent or less owned by the parent. The Swedish data used above include virtually no information on these affiliates, and the U.S. surveys have exempted them from large parts of the questionnaire, and particularly from the trade questions. One justification for that exemption is that the parent firms often would not know the answers and would not have the same ability to compel cooperation from minority-owned affiliates as from majority-owned affiliates.

The omission of affiliates 50 percent or less owned would be relatively harmless if they were randomly scattered over the world and over industries. We know, however, that they are not. They are virtually the only U.S. affiliates in Japan, for example, and are of considerable importance in that country. Their importance is also associated with industry and country characteristics, such as the technological level of the industry and the income level of the country, both characteristics often used in the examination of trade investment relationships.

Aside from its interaction with some of the explanatory variables, production by minority-owned affiliates (for convenience, we will refer to minority ownership, even though it includes a substantial number of cases of 50 percent ownership) might have different effects on trade from those of production by majority-owned affiliates. One possibility is that the effects would be simply a diluted version of those associated with majority ownership, because they are shared among several owners, some of which are often not U.S. firms. On the other hand, production by minority-owned affiliates might have a stronger effect on parent trade, because minority ownership is resorted to in cases in which the parent would otherwise be barred from a market, either because the host country has particularly stringent barriers to imports or because the parent company does not have a very large technological advantage over other firms. Minority ownership might represent a price for entry into a market more often than does majority ownership.

Because minority-owned affiliates did not receive the questionnaire on the disposition of their sales, we cannot calculate net local sales or net export sales for them. The activity measure for them in all the equations is net sales, whatever the measure used for majority-owned affiliates. Because these equations are based on published data, we are also limited here to equations for six industry groups (using net sales for majority-owned affiliates) or for four industry groups (using net local sales for majority-owned affiliates) instead of the thirty industries used earlier.

The coefficients for production by minority-owned affiliates in equations including various versions of production by majority-owned affiliates are summarized in table 9.5. Whatever the measure of production we use for majority-owned affiliates, the coefficients for production by minority-owned affiliates are all positive (table 9.A.9). Only a few are statistically significant at the 5 percent level, but almost all are larger than their standard errors. Thus, minority-owned affiliates' activity seems to be more clearly complementary to exports from the United States than that of majority-owned affiliates.

Adding the variable for production by minority-owned affiliates to the equations has another effect: it strengthens the case for complementarity between production by majority-owned affiliates and exports from the United States, as seen in table 9.5. In the equations for these broad industry groups that did not include any variable for minority-owned production, the results showed substitution between production in majority-owned affiliates and exports from the United States as often as, or more often than, complementarity. When the variable for production by minority-owned affiliates was included, the coefficients for production by majority-owned affiliates shifted toward showing greater evidence for complementarity. Thus, the addition of data for minority-

Table 9.5   Summary of t-Statistics for Coefficients of Production by Majority-
                   Owned Affiliates in U.S. Export Equations, With and Without
                   Production by Minority-Owned Affiliates, 1982 (6 industry groups)

	Production by Minority-Owned Affiliates	
	Excluded	Included
Coefficients with $t \geq 1$		
Positive		
$t \geq 2$	1	7
$1 \leq t < 2$	5	2
Negative		
$t \geq 2$	3	3
$1 \leq t < 2$	2	1
Coefficients with $t < 1$	7	5

Sources: Tables 9.A.8 and 9.A.9.

owned affiliates strengthens the case for a positive effect of affiliates' production on home country exports.

In view of the always present possibility that some missing variable could explain both the level of U.S. affiliate production in and the level of U.S. exports to a country, we would like to have information on production in each host country by affiliates from countries other than the United States. We could then test whether exports by each home country were reduced by the production of other countries' affiliates, while they were increased by the production of their own affiliates. Such a relationship was found in somewhat crude data for 1970 by Lipsey and Weiss (1981).

Unfortunately, we do not have recent data on the presence of, or production by, non-U.S. affiliates in each country. As the closest approach we could make to such a test, we have related exports to a host country by countries other than the United States to production in the host country by U.S. affiliates. If U.S.-owned production serves to increase the U.S. share in a country's imports without expanding the level of imports, U.S.-owned production should be negatively related to exports by other countries to the host countries. If U.S.-owned production increases U.S. sales by expanding markets in host countries, we might find no relation to exports by other countries or even a positive one. A positive relationship could also reflect an expansion of a U.S. company's exports to the host country from its operations in countries outside the United States. A more troublesome implication of a positive coefficient could be that it shows we have not successfully accounted for important determinants of a host country's imports, such as the activity of non-U.S. affiliates or, more generally, an open trade and investment regime.

The results, summarized in table 9.6, are not reassuring. The coefficients in equations for thirty industries, using net sales as the affiliate production measure, are all positive and all but a few are more than twice their standard errors. One might expect local sales by U.S. affiliates, rather than total sales, to be most closely associated with exports to that market by other countries. The use of net local sales leaves the predominance of positive relationships intact, although it reduces the frequency of strong positive relationships between U.S. affiliate production in a country and that country's imports from others.

A possible explanation for the apparently persistent positive coefficient is suggested by the equations using both net local sales and net export sales by U.S. affiliates as explanatory variables. Almost half of the coefficients for net local sales are close to zero, while most of the rest are positive. The coefficients for net export sales are overwhelmingly positive and statistically significant. The most likely explanation, we suspect, is that high export sales by affiliates, in particular, reflect policies that attract direct investment in production by firms from both the United States and other countries, and the imports associated with this production. The U.S. affiliate production, and particularly U.S. affiliate production for export, is therefore acting, to some extent, as a proxy for the openness of a country's trade and investment regime and for the presence of non-U.S. affiliates.

Table 9.6   **Summary of t-Statistics for Coefficients of U.S. Affiliate Production in Non-U.S. Export Equations, 1982 (30 industries)**

	Measure of Affiliate Production			
	Equations with One Production Variable		Equations with Two Production Variables	
	Net Sales	Net Local Sales	Net Local Sales	Net Export Sales
Coefficients with $t \geq 1$				
Positive				
$t \geq 2$	27	22	10	18
$1 \leq t < 2$	1	6	6	5
Negative				
$t \geq 2$				
$1 \leq t < 2$			1	2
Coefficients with $t < 1$	2	2	13	5

Sources: Tables 9.A.10 – 9.A.12.

Somewhat the same set of relationships can be observed in equations for the major industry groups, where we can include information on production by U.S. minority-owned affiliates (table 9.7). In the equations in which net sales are used as a production measure, the coefficients for majority-owned affiliates are all positive and mostly significant at the 5 percent level. Those for minority-owned affiliates are almost all negative, however. Two are statistically significant, and two others are larger than their standard errors. Thus, there is evidence that production by minority-owned U.S. affiliates does substitute for a country's imports from countries other than the United States.

Some further hint of what we may be missing by omitting minority affiliates from our earlier calculations can be gleaned from the equations in table 9.8. These separate production by majority-owned affiliates into production for local sale and production for export and include minority affiliate net sales. The large positive coefficients in the equations for exports by other countries are associated mainly with U.S. affiliates' production for export. We would not expect these to compete with foreign countries' exports to the production location, and we suspect they act as a proxy for production by foreign countries' affiliates, as mentioned earlier. Production by U.S. minority-owned affiliates in two industries and production for local sale by majority-owned affiliates in one industry do appear to substitute for imports from countries other than the United States.

Table 9.7   **Coefficients for Production by Majority-Owned and Minority-Owned U.S. Affiliates in Non-U.S. Export Equations, 1982**

Industry Group	Production of Majority-Owned Affiliates	Production of Minority-Owned Affiliates
Foods	585	−2,194
	(1.7)	(1.8)
Chemicals	255	−2,446
	(3.5)	(4.6)
Metals	2,279	−2,252
	(4.1)	(1.6)
Nonelectrical machinery	593	1,152
	(2.0)	(0.9)
Electrical machinery	2,043	−158
	(6.7)	(.2)
Transport equipment	512	−641
	(2.9)	(2.7)

Source: Table 9.A.13.

Notes: t-Statistics are in parentheses. Canada is excluded from export destinations. Equations include, as independent variables, GDP, GDPC, and net sales as the measure of affiliate production.

Table 9.8   Coefficients for U.S. Majority-Owned Affiliates' Local and Export Sales and Minority-Owned Affiliates' Sales in Non-U.S. Export Equations, 1982

Industry Group	Majority-Owned Affiliates		Minority-Owned Affiliates
	Net Local Sales	Net Export Sales	Net Sales
Chemicals	−270	1,141	−2,616
	(.8)	(3.0)	(5.0)
Nonelectrical machinery	−1,665	2,355	1,304
	(2.7)	(4.8)	(1.3)
Electrical machinery	1,212	3,408	−1
	(1.4)	(2.7)	(.0)
Transport equipment	586	15	−1,025
	(7.0)	(.2)	(15.0)

Source: Table 9.A.13
Notes: t-Statistics are in parentheses. Canada is excluded from export destinations. Equations include, as independent variables, GDP, GDPC, and measures of affiliate production.

There is a preponderance of positive coefficients for minority-owned U.S. affiliate production in U.S. export equations and of negative coefficients in equations for exports by others to a market. This suggests that minority-owned production, even more than production by majority-owned affiliates, is a way in which U.S firms buy entry into a market or market share for themselves and hinder it for their foreign rivals.

9.5   Conclusions

The predominant relationship between production in a country by affiliates of Swedish and U.S. firms and exports to that country from Sweden and the United States is something between neutrality and complementarity. By the former we mean no effect on home country exports at all, and by the latter we mean inducing a higher level of home country exports.

The higher the level of Swedish affiliate production in a country, the higher the level of Swedish exports to that country in that industry. This relationship in OLS equations is confirmed in a 2SLS analysis that attempts to remove the effects of simultaneous determination of Swedish exports and host country affiliate production by Swedish firms and is observed whether production is measured by affiliate net sales or by net local sales. The same conclusions are produced by an analysis of changes over time in Swedish exports. Both high initial levels of Swedish affiliate production in a country and increases in production are positively associated with increases in Swedish exports to the country.

The results for the United States are more mixed. At the most disaggregated industry level, there is a predominance of positive relationships between affiliate net sales and U.S. exports, but there are a few negative coefficients, implying substitution of U.S. affiliate production for exports from the United States. Part of the positive influence of affiliate production on exports from the United States is the effect of affiliate production for exports from the host country, the effects of which are overwhelmingly positive. That is what we expect, because any substitution would take place outside the host country. Production by minority-owned affiliates of U.S. firms was somewhat more likely to be a means of buying market shares for the United States and denying them to others than was production by majority-owned affiliates. Furthermore, inclusion of production by minority-owned affiliates in the U.S. export equations increased the evidence for complementarity between U.S. exports and production by majority-owned U.S. affiliates.

Appendix

Data

The U.S. affiliate production data are from the individual firm reports underlying U.S. Department of Commerce (1985), a presumably quite complete census of U.S. direct investment abroad in 1982. Since these reports are confidential, the calculations described here were carried out for us within the Bureau of Economic Analysis of the U.S. Department of Commerce. We have omitted Canada from the U.S. equations for fear that it would be an outlier and unduly influence the results, and we omitted Malaysia, Mexico, the Philippines, Taiwan, and Thailand from the detailed industry equations, because some of the observations for net sales were negative. The reason apparently was that some respondents in these countries reported exports to the United States under items 806.30 and 807.00 of the U.S. Tariff Schedules at value added in the host country, rather than at the total value of the exports.

The Swedish data for production of individual foreign affiliates come from the Industriens Utredningsinstitut (IUI) of Stockholm. The IUI has completed four surveys of Swedish multinationals' foreign investment abroad covering 1965, 1970, 1974, and 1978. These surveys cover virtually all Swedish firms investing abroad and are in general comparable to the BEA surveys (see Swedenborg 1979, 1982).

Exports by the United States and all market economies to different countries, by the industry classifications used in the U.S. direct investment survey, were taken from United Nations trade tapes and converted from the SITC to this industry classification. Swedish exports by industry are from Statistiska Centralbyrån (Utdrag ur Makrobasen).

Table 9.A.1   **OLS Regression Results for Swedish Exports, 1978**
                     (7 industry groups)

		Coefficients of				
Industry (No. Obs.)	Intercept	GDP	GDP per Capita (GDPC)	Nordic Country (NORDIC)	Net Sales (NS)	R^2
Paper products (66)	997	−.02	1.72	225	.229	.81
	(.16)	(1.82)	(1.28)	(11.3)	(4.98)	
Chemicals (66)	−30,912	−.03	14.89	1,032	.836	.78
	(1.03)	(.41)	(2.30)	(10.7)	(4.05)	
Metal manufacturing (66)	−21,199	−.01	9.86	459	.379	.75
	(1.26)	(.27)	(2.62)	(8.5)	(4.43)	
Nonelectrical machinery (66)	−15,989	.23	17.62	849	.359	.92
	(.68)	(4.22)	(3.40)	(11.5)	(12.9)	
Electrical machinery (66)	−16,629	.00	20.54	500	.086	.72
	(.91)	(.11)	(5.29)	(8.6)	(1.40)	
Transport equipment (66)	−43,300	.69	20.08	1,010	.312	.73
	(.97)	(7.60)	(2.06)	(7.1)	(3.49)	
Other manufacturing (66)	−44,522	.04	24.77	764	1.137	.68
	(1.07)	(.43)	(2.79)	(5.9)	(6.64)	

Notes: Dependent variable is Swedish exports to a country by an industry (thousand kronor). GDP = real GDP in 1978 in millions of international dollars, derived from data for 1980 in United Nations and Commission of the European Communities 1986 and extrapolated to 1978 and to countries not covered in the survey by methods described in Kravis and Lipsey 1984; GDPC = real GDP per capita in 1978 international dollars; NORDIC = dummy variable for membership in Nordic group (million kronor); and NS = affiliate net sales, derived as total affiliate sales minus imports from Sweden (thousand kronor). Numbers in parentheses are t-statistics.

Table 9.A.2   **2SLS Regression Results for Swedish Exports, 1978**
                      (7 industry groups)

Industry (No. Obs.)	Intercept	GDP	GDP per Capita (GDPC)	Nordic Country (NORDIC)	EEC Member (EEC)	Net Sales (NS)	$\bar{R}^2$
First Stage (Dependent Variable = Net Sales)							
Paper products (66)	−16,422	.13	3.68	119	138	—	.56
	(1.11)	(4.55)	(1.10)	(2.57)	(4.50)		
Chemicals (66)	−4,767	.18	3.96	93	106	—	.49
	(.27)	(5.22)	(1.01)	(1.71)	(2.93)		
Metal manufacturing	−4,723	.22	2.80	140	309	—	.76
(66)	(.28)	(6.48)	(.74)	(2.68)	(8.93)		
Nonelectrical	−72,056	.97	12.01	−120	1,201	—	.68
machinery (66)	(.91)	(6.10)	(.67)	(.48)	(7.29)		
Electrical machinery	19,358	.19	6.26	32	115	—	.17
(66)	(.51)	(2.56)	(.73)	(.27)	(1.46)		
Transport equipment	−6,631	−.10	15.21	−254	384	—	.16
(66)	(.11)	(.84)	(1.12)	(1.35)	(3.08)		
Other manufacturing	−14,096	.08	2.97	−5	225	—	.26
(66)	(.51)	(1.36)	(.47)	(.06)	(3.91)		
Second Stage							
Paper products (66)	6,172	−.05	−.26	201	—	.435	.75
	(.82)	(2.61)	(.14)	(7.9)		(4.09)	
Chemicals (66)	−122	−.51	−7.98	783	—	3.511	.50
	(.00)	(2.17)	(.51)	(3.7)		(3.09)	
Metal manufacturing	−18,247	−.04	7.90	443	—	.500	.75
(66)	(1.06)	(.85)	(1.97)	(7.9)		(4.34)	
Nonelectrical	−14,603	.22	17.02	850	—	.368	.91
machinery (66)	(.61)	(3.60)	(3.08)	(11.5)		(9.05)	
Electrical machinery	−21,828	−.08	15.73	487	—	.516	.60
(66)	(.87)	(.78)	(2.19)	(6.2)		(1.15)	
Transport equipment	−24,446	.76	.75	1,165	—	.921	.60
(66)	(.41)	(6.06)	(.05)	(5.7)		(2.85)	
Other manufacturing	−6,108	−.06	7.60	772	—	2.490	.50
(66)	(.10)	(.47)	(.54)	(4.2)		(4.58)	

Notes: EEC member = dummy variable for membership in European Economic Community. See table 9.A.1.

Table 9.A.3   **Comparison of OLS Regression Results for Swedish Exports Based on Net Sales and Net Local Sales, 1978 (5 industry groups)**

			Coefficients of				
Industry (No. Obs.)	Intercept	GDP	GDP per Capita (GDPC)	Nordic Country (NORDIC)	Net Sales (NS)	Net Local Sales (NLS)	$\bar{R}^2$
Paper products (19)	−25,102	−.03	5.83	217	.217	—	.74
	(.56)	(1.16)[a]	(.87)	(5.20)	(2.11)		
Chemicals (30)	−92,998	−.07	27.62	984	.809	—	.74
	(1.10)	(.61)	(1.91)	(6.52)	(2.29)		
Metal manufacturing (19)	−112,624	−.03	25.15	424	.330	—	.60
	(1.01)	(.35)	(1.52)	(3.68)	(1.59)		
Nonelectrical machinery (21)	−64,951	.21	29.79	794	.336	—	.85
	(.57)	(2.00)	(1.82)	(5.49)	(5.87)		
Electrical machinery (24)	−14,801	.01	19.98	504	.083	—	.80
	(.27)	(.24)	(2.39)	(7.54)	(1.11)		
Paper products (19)	−20,370	−.05	5.15	209	—	.351	.76
	(.50)	(1.79)	(.85)	(5.43)		(2.79)	
Chemicals (30)	−98,567	−.09	29.42	995	—	.870	.73
	(1.16)	(.73)	(2.06)	(6.64)		(2.32)	
Metal manufacturing (19)	−109,646	.02	30.34	400	—	.268	.52
	(.93)	(.22)	(1.77)	(3.18)		(.80)	
Nonelectrical machinery (21)	−56,852	.09	33.00	787	—	.508	.86
	(.52)	(.83)	(2.15)	(5.74)		(6.32)	
Electrical machinery (24)	−15,333	.01	20.19	505	—	.085	.79
	(.28)	(.25)	(2.42)	(7.55)		(1.12)	

Notes: Net local sales in thousands of kronor. See table 9.A.1.

Table 9.A.4   **OLS Regression Results for Changes in Swedish Exports, 1970–78 (7 industry groups)**

Industry (No. Obs.)	Intercept	Change in GDP (ΔGDP)	Exports 1970 (EXP70)	Change in Net Sales (ΔNS)	Net Sales (NS70)	$\bar{R}^2$
Paper products (66)	−.53	−.04	2.44	.058	—	.83
	(.02)	(.98)	(14.1)	(1.62)		
Chemicals (66)	−1,280	−.10	2.68	.179	—	.93
	(.14)	(.88)	(25.1)	(1.60)		
Metal manufacturing (66)	469	.05	2.27	−.158	—	.94
	(.11)	(.85)	(25.3)	(3.19)		
Nonelectrical machinery (66)	−7,683	.36	1.54	.062	—	.93
	(.73)	(2.96)	(14.6)	(1.81)		
Electrical machinery (66)	24,239	−.02	2.03	−.132	—	.46
	(1.64)	(.12)	(7.5)	(1.46)		
Transport equipment (66)	15,199	1.14	.84	.276	—	.61
	(.60)	(4.0)	(6.2)	(3.64)		
Other manufacturing (66)	16,233	−.21	1.68	.444	—	.89
	(1.40)	(1.64)	(17.3)	(4.65)		
Paper products (66)	−849	−.01	2.49	—	.201	.83
	(.28)	(.33)	(15.2)		(1.36)	
Chemicals (66)	−3,334	−.08	2.67	—	.448	.93
	(.38)	(.83)	(26.7)		(2.34)	
Metal manufacturing (66)	214	−.01	2.27	—	−.271	.93
	(.05)	(.18)	(22.5)		(2.60)	
Nonelectrical machinery (66)	−6,759	.31	1.56	—	.122	.93
	(.65)	(2.45)	(17.5)		(2.27)	
Electrical machinery (66)	21,589	−.15	1.78	—	.282	.47
	(1.44)	(.94)	(6.2)		(1.04)	
Transport equipment (66)	18,450	1.08	.87	—	1.899	.57
	(.70)	(3.59)	(6.1)		(2.71)	
Other manufacturing (66)	11,328	−.12	1.71	—	.836	.86
	(.88)	(.88)	(14.3)		(2.44)	

Note: Dependent variable is change in Swedish exports to a country by an industry (thousand kronor). For definitions of variables, see text.

Table 9.A.5   **OLS Equations for U.S. Exports Based on Net Sales by Majority-Owned U.S. Affiliates, 1982 (30 industries)**

Industry No.	Intercept ($ millions)	GDP	GDP per Capita (GDPC)	Net Sales (NS)	$\bar{R}^2$	No. of Obs.
1	−4.0	.094	4.5	.01	.23	48
	(0.3)	(2.0)	(2.0)	(0.5)		
2	−.2	.015	.26	−.00	.51	47
	(0.3)	(4.0)	(1.8)	(0.0)		
3	.3	.027	1.86	−.04	.05	43
	(0.0)	(1.2)	(1.5)	(1.4)		
4	−3.7	1.40	3.01	−.23	.72	48
	(0.1)	(10.4)	(0.4)	(3.7)		
5	2.2	.142	4.29	.17	.58	48
	(0.2)	(4.4)	(2.5)	(2.4)		
6			NA			
7			NA			
8	3.1	.04	.83	−.01	.17	48
	(0.7)	(2.5)	(1.1)	(0.3)		
9	2.1	.028	.58	.30	.79	48
	(0.6)	(2.2)	(0.9)	(9.9)		
10	−11.7	.44	1.6	−.083	.86	48
	(1.6)	(13.9)	(1.3)	(4.7)		
11	−.6	.020	1.0	.010	.43	48
	(0.3)	(1.8)	(2.4)	(1.3)		
12	15.5	.071	−1.13	.27	.61	47
	(3.8)	(5.3)	(1.6)	(4.5)		
13	16.0	1.52	2.51	−.01	.81	48
	(0.5)	(12.1)	(0.4)	(0.2)		
14	4.4	.31	1.7	−.01	.77	48
	(0.5)	(10.5)	(1.1)	(0.4)		
15	2.0	.030	1.48	.029	.34	48
	(0.5)	(2.1)	(2.1)	(1.8)		
16	−2.0	.036	1.44	.038	.56	48
	(0.7)	(3.2)	(2.9)	(1.5)		
17	17.2	.04	3.30	−.04	−.01	48
	(1.0)	(0.6)	(1.1)	(0.1)		
18	−22.5	.538	3.4	−.33	.85	48
	(2.1)	(13.6)	(1.8)	(3.3)		
19	2.2	.177	8.15	.02	.20	48
	(0.1)	(1.9)	(1.8)	(0.4)		
20			NA			
21	35.1	.036	6.8	.077	.07	48
	(1.2)	(0.3)	(1.4)	(1.0)		
22	−18.5	.115	16.8	.283	.83	48
	(0.5)	(0.7)	(2.9)	(7.5)		

Table 9.A.5   (continued)

			Coefficients of			
			GDP per	Net		
Industry	Intercept		Capita	Sales		No. of
No.	($ millions)	GDP	(GDPC)	(NS)	$\bar{R}^2$	Obs.
23	26.4	.694	22.6	.171	.46	48
	(0.4)	(3.1)	(2.1)	(1.4)		
24	− 2.7	.01	2.50	.026	.10	48
	(0.4)	(0.3)	(2.3)	(0.4)		
25	5.6	.25	2.5	− .002	.52	48
	(0.4)	(5.7)	(1.1)	(0.1)		
26	9.8	.146	− .08	.49	.76	48
	(0.6)	(2.1)	(0.0)	(7.5)		
27	− 21.1	.579	14.7	.06	.59	48
	(0.7)	(5.2)	(2.7)	(0.4)		
28	− 3.9	.002	19.6	.012	.09	48
	(0.1)	(0.0)	(2.2)	(0.7)		
29			NA			
30	− 39.3	1.27	− 1.18	− 3.84	.75	48
	(1.3)	(11.4)	(0.2)	(5.8)		
31	− .2	.030	1.17	.043	.38	48
	(0.1)	(2.5)	(2.1)	(1.4)		
32	− 1.4	.033	1.46	− .007	.35	48
	(0.4)	(2.8)	(2.7)	(0.2)		
33	− 39.6	.83	12.4	.162	.92	48
	(2.2)	(13.4)	(4.0)	(7.1)		
34	− 15.8	.133	6.12	.34	.53	48
	(1.1)	(2.4)	(2.5)	(2.3)		

Notes: Dependent variable is U.S. exports to a country by an industry (thousand dollars). Canada, Malaysia, Mexico, Philippines, Taiwan, and Thailand are excluded from the equations. GDP = real GDP in 1982 in millions of international dollars, derived from data for 1980 in United Nations and Commission of the European Communities 1986, and extrapolated to 1982 and to countries not covered in the survey by methods described in Kravis and Lipsey 1984; GDPC = real GDP per capita in 1982; and Net Sales = affiliate net sales, derived as total affiliate sales minus imports from the United States (thousand dollars). Number in parentheses are t-statistics.

The 34 industries are the following: (1) grain mill and bakery products; (2) beverages; (3) tobacco; (4) other food products; (5) textiles and apparel; (6) leather and leatherware; (7) pulp and paper; (8) paper products; (9) printing and publishing; (10) drugs; (11) soap, cleansers, toilet goods; (12) agricultural chemicals; (13) industrial chemicals; (14) other chemicals; (15) rubber products; (16) plastic products; (17) primary metals, ferrous; (18) primary metals, nonferrous; (19) fabricated metals; (20) farm and garden machinery; (21) construction and related machinery; (22) office and computing machinery; (23) other non-electrical machinery; (24) household appliances; (25) radio, TV, and communication equipment; (26) electronic components; (27) other electrical machinery; (28) motor vehicles and equipment; (29) other transport equipment; (30) lumber, wood, furniture and fixtures; (31) glass products; (32) stone, clay, cement, and concrete; (33) instruments and related products; and (34) other industries.

Table 9.A.6   **OLS Equations for U.S. Exports Based on Net Local Sales by Majority-Owned U.S. Affiliates, 1982 (30 industries)**

Industry No.	Intercept ($ millions)	GDP	GDP per Capita (GDPC)	Net Local Sales (NLS)	$\bar{R}^2$	No. of Obs.
			Coefficients of			
1	−4.0	.098	4.52	.01	.23	48
	(0.3)	(2.1)	(2.0)	(0.3)		
2	−.2	.015	.26	−.00	.51	47
	(0.2)	(3.9)	(1.8)	(0.2)		
3	.8	.026	1.67	−.04	.03	43
	(0.1)	(1.1)	(1.3)	(1.1)		
4	−1.7	1.44	1.97	−.31	.74	48
	(0.0)	(11.0)	(0.3)	(4.3)		
5	1.1	.105	4.83	.48	.63	48
	(0.1)	(3.2)	(3.1)	(3.6)		
6			NA			
7			NA			
8	3.1	.040	.82	−.01	.17	48
	(0.7)	(2.5)	(1.1)	(0.3)		
9	2.5	.029	.43	.40	.79	48
	(0.7)	(2.3)	(0.6)	(9.8)		
10	11.1	.514	1.06	−.162	.89	48
	(1.7)	(14.7)	(1.0)	(6.2)		
11	−.8	.018	1.06	.013	.43	48
	(0.3)	(1.6)	(2.5)	(1.4)		
12	14.9	.073	−.77	.300	.57	47
	(3.4)	(5.1)	(1.0)	(3.7)		
13	15.2	1.67	3.74	−.142	.83	48
	(0.4)	(12.5)	(0.6)	(2.1)		
14	4.5	.31	1.69	−.020	.77	48
	(0.5)	(10.4)	(1.1)	(0.6)		
15	1.6	.031	1.57	.033	.34	48
	(0.4)	(2.2)	(2.2)	(1.8)		
16	−2.2	.032	1.56	.059	.56	48
	(0.8)	(2.6)	(3.2)	(1.6)		
17	17.1	.035	3.26	.013	−.01	48
	(1.0)	(0.5)	(1.1)	(0.0)		
18	−21.4	.554	3.12	−.542	.86	48
	(2.1)	(14.1)	(1.8)	(3.8)		
19	2.1	.170	8.13	.031	.20	48
	(0.1)	(1.8)	(1.8)	(0.5)		
20			NA			
21	32.2	.014	7.5	.180	.09	48
	(1.1)	(0.1)	(1.6)	(1.5)		

Table 9.A.6   (continued)

		Coefficients of				
Industry No.	Intercept ($ millions)	GDP	GDP per Capita (GDPC)	Net Local Sales (NLS)	$\bar{R}^2$	No. of Obs.
22	− 14.3	.018	18.4	.488	.80	48
	(.4)	(0.1)	(3.0)	(6.7)		
23	25.1	.644	23.2	.361	.46	48
	(0.4)	(2.8)	(2.2)	(1.6)		
24	− 2.9	.003	2.5	.095	.12	48
	(0.5)	(0.2)	(2.3)	(1.1)		
25	5.4	.256	2.6	− .009	.52	48
	(0.4)	(5.8)	(1.1)	(0.2)		
26	21.3	.063	2.0	.782	.56	48
	(0.9)	(0.5)	(0.5)	(3.4)		
27	− 21.4	.586	14.9	.060	.59	48
	(0.7)	(5.2)	(2.8)	(0.3)		
28	− 5.2	− .027	19.4	.030	.11	48
	(0.1)	(0.2)	(2.2)	(1.1)		
29			NA			
30	− 47.1	1.229	− .049	− 4.404	.73	48
	(1.5)	(10.8)	(0.0)	(5.3)		
31	.0	.027	1.24	.077	.40	48
	(0.0)	(2.2)	(2.2)	(1.8)		
32	1.3	.031	1.43	.002	.34	48
	(0.4)	(2.4)	(2.6)	(0.1)		
33	− 39.9	.803	13.1	.282	.91	48
	(2.0)	(11.1)	(3.9)	(5.7)		
34	− 16.9	.147	6.5	.399	.52	48
	(1.2)	(2.8)	(2.7)	(2.2)		

Notes: For definitions and industry list, see table 9.A.5. Numbers in parentheses are t-statistics.

Table 9.A.7   OLS Equations for U.S. Exports Based on Net Local Sales and Net Export Sales by Majority-Owned U.S. Affiliates, 1982 (30 industries)

Industry No.	Intercept ($ millions)	GDP	GDP per Capita (GDPC)	Net Local Sales (NLS)	Net Export Sales (NXS)	$\bar{R}^2$	No. of Obs.
				Coefficients of			
1	−3.9	.081	4.20	−.023	.383	.28	48
	(0.3)	(1.8)	(1.9)	(0.9)	(2.0)		
2	−.2	.016	.25	−.002	.004	.50	47
	(0.2)	(3.8)	(1.7)	(0.3)	(0.4)		
3	.2	.026	1.92	−.034	−.067	.02	43
	(0.0)	(1.1)	(1.5)	(0.8)	(0.9)		
4	−.4	1.44	1.00	−.327	.142	.74	48
	(0.0)	(11.0)	(0.1)	(4.3)	(0.7)		
5	1.2	.106	4.72	.476	.022	.63	48
	(0.1)	(3.1)	(2.8)	(3.4)	(0.2)		
6			NA				
7			NA				
8	2.8	.040	.91	−.004	−.046	.16	48
	(0.6)	(2.5)	(1.1)	(0.1)	(0.3)		
9	2.2	.028	.53	.339	.202	.79	48
	(0.6)	(2.2)	(0.8)	(4.6)	(1.0)		
10	−10.7	.527	.79	−.181	.037	.89	48
	(1.7)	(14.1)	(0.7)	(5.6)	(1.0)		
11	−.9	.018	1.09	.014	−.008	.42	48
	(.4)	(1.5)	(2.5)	(1.3)	(0.3)		
12	16.1	.073	−1.32	.230	.381	.61	47
	(3.8)	(5.3)	(1.8)	(2.8)	(2.3)		
13	27.8	1.72	−1.23	−.238	.131	.85	48
	(0.8)	(13.5)	(0.2)	(3.2)	(2.6)		
14	4.9	.32	1.54	−.035	.034	.77	48
	(0.5)	(10.3)	(1.0)	(0.7)	(0.4)		
15	1.7	.030	1.53	.032	.013	.32	48
	(0.4)	(2.0)	(2.1)	(1.6)	(0.2)		
16	−2.1	.032	1.50	.056	.017	.55	48
	(0.7)	(2.55)	(2.9)	(1.5)	(0.4)		
17	13.7	.037	4.22	.183	−1.111	−.02	48
	(0.7)	(0.6)	(1.3)	(0.5)	(0.88)		
18	−21.0	.554	2.98	−.583	.108	.85	48
	(2.0)	(14.0)	(1.6)	(3.4)	(0.4)		
19	−3.4	.167	9.09	.143	−.313	.20	48
	(0.1)	(1.7)	(2.0)	(1.1)	(0.9)		
20			NA				

Table 9.A.7   (continued)

Industry No.	Intercept ($ millions)	GDP	Coefficients of GDP per Capita (GDPC)	Coefficients of Net Local Sales (NLS)	Coefficients of Net Export Sales (NXS)	$\bar{R}^2$	No. of Obs.
21	30.3	.021	8.0	.208	−.062	.07	48
	(1.0)	(0.2)	(1.6)	(1.5)	(0.4)		
22	−23.6	.238	16.2	.146	.440	.83	48
	(0.7)	(1.1)	(2.8)	(1.0)	(2.6)		
23	16.9	.589	26.2	.778	−.529	.46	48
	(0.3)	(2.5)	(2.4)	(1.5)	(0.9)		
24	−3.4	.010	2.61	.113	−.114	.12	48
	(0.5)	(0.4)	(2.4)	(1.2)	(0.9)		
25	4.6	.257	2.6	−.164	.402	.54	48
	(0.4)	(5.9)	(1.2)	(1.7)	(1.7)		
26	−5.4	.368	−.56	−.004	.721	.79	48
	(0.3)	(3.5)	(0.2)	(0.0)	(6.9)		
27	−18.8	.584	13.9	−.007	.280	.58	48
	(0.6)	(5.2)	(2.4)	(0.0)	(0.5)		
28	−10.4	−.003	19.7	.048	−.035	.10	48
	(0.2)	(0.0)	(2.3)	(1.4)	(0.8)		
29			NA				
30	−32.2	1.280	−2.3	−3.025	−7.130	.75	48
	(1.0)	(11.5)	(0.4)	(3.0)	(2.3)		
31	−.2	.027	1.31	.087	−.037	.39	48
	(0.1)	(2.3)	(2.3)	(1.8)	(0.5)		
32	1.7	.027	1.61	.043	−.127	.35	48
	(.5)	(2.1)	(2.9)	(0.8)	(1.1)		
33	−41.8	.904	11.88	−.053	.378	.93	48
	(2.5)	(13.5)	(4.1)	(0.6)	(4.0)		
34	−16.0	.135	6.20	.363	.290	.52	48
	(1.1)	(2.4)	(2.5)	(1.9)	(0.6)		

Notes: For definitions and industry list, see table 9.A.5. Numbers in parentheses are t-statistics.

Table 9.A.8   **OLS Equations for U.S. Exports Based on Production by Majority-Owned U.S. Affiliates, 1982 (6 industry groups)**

Industry Group	Intercept	GDP	GDP per Capita (GDPC)	Net Sales (NS)	Net Local Sales (NLS)	Net Export Sales (NXS)	$\bar{R}^2$	No. of Obs.
A	−54.6	1.80	5.98	−135.4			.87	23
	(0.89)	(11.16)	(0.52)	(4.26)				
B	17.7	2.53	11.85	−60.90			.87	27
	(0.21)	(11.22)	(0.83)	(1.96)				
C	7.9	.80	2.03	−6.99			.78	20
	(0.15)	(7.10)	(0.26)	(0.17)				
D	66.8	.59	48.14	222.1			.64	26
	(0.36)	(0.46)	(1.88)	(1.80)				
E	156.2	1.14	−9.50	155.6			.59	24
	(1.31)	(3.80)	(0.48)	(1.56)				
F	−81.1	.88	51.24	5.92			.52	24
	(0.67)	(2.82)	(2.83)	(0.22)				
B	21.9	2.88	17.92		−202.2		.92	17
	(0.20)	(11.0)	(0.88)		(3.82)			
D	20.0	.92	55.52		334.3		.63	24
	(0.10)	(0.52)	(2.09)		(1.13)			
E	103.0	1.07	6.99		185.8		.61	18
	(0.76)	(3.09)	(0.30)		(1.10)			
F	−72.0	.92	48.35		19.15		.53	22
	(0.56)	(2.88)	(2.54)		(0.40)			
B	110.2	3.11	−10.84		−255.3	125.3	.92	17
	(0.94)	(10.80)	(0.41)		(4.26)	(1.56)		
D	48.1	1.22	45.46		50.1	312.7	.62	24
	(0.24)	(0.68)	(1.57)		(0.12)	(0.90)		
E	44.9	1.32	4.64		−303.3	914.6	.73	18
	(0.39)	(4.34)	(0.24)		(1.32)	(2.73)		
F	−75.0	.93	48.64		37.0	−27.6	.51	22
	(0.57)	(2.83)	(2.49)		(0.50)	(0.32)		

Notes: Industry groups defined in terms of the industries of Table 9.A.5 are: (A) foods and kindred products (nos. 1–4); (B) chemicals and allied products (nos. 10–14); (C) metals (nos. 17–19); (D) Nonelectrical machinery (nos. 20–23); (E) electrical machinery (nos. 24–27); and (F) transport equipment (nos. 28 and 29).

Table 9.A.9   OLS Equations for U.S. Exports Based on Production by Both Majority-Owned and Minority-Owned U.S. Affiliates, 1982 (6 industry groups)

				Coefficients of					
				Majority-Owned Affiliate			Minority-Owned Affiliate Net Sales (MONS)		
Industry Group	Intercept	GDP	GDP per Capita (GDPC)	Net Sales (NS)	Net Local Sales (NLS)	Net Export Sales (NXS)		$\bar{R}^2$	No. of Obs.
A	−58.6	1.75	8.05	−133.6			25.4	.86	22
	(0.91)	(6.85)	(0.64)	(3.54)			(0.20)		
B	100.0	1.02	3.04	15.5			417.0	.95	27
	(1.88)	(3.82)	(0.35)	(0.70)			(6.55)		
C	−34.8	.75	5.17	2.7			66.4	.81	18
	(0.63)	(5.37)	(0.65)	(0.07)			(0.66)		
D	277.3	−.44	2.28	289.2			546.9	.85	24
	(2.41)	(0.54)	(0.13)	(3.03)			(1.37)		
E	149.0	.85	−7.03	142.3			320.2	.61	24
	(1.28)	(2.38)	(0.36)	(1.45)			(1.40)		
F	34.9	.36	18.53	50.0			43.8	.86	19
	(0.61)	(1.26)	(2.31)	(3.00)			(1.92)		
B	18.7	1.42	26.20		−74.9		335.9	.96	17
	(0.26)	(3.79)	(1.94)		(1.66)		(4.40)		
D	224.0	−.33	13.06		424.7		769.5	.82	22
	(1.65)	(0.27)	(0.68)		(1.81)		(1.70)		
E	90.0	.85	9.65		142.0		289.6	.62	18
	(0.67)	(2.16)	(0.42)		(0.83)		(1.16)		
F	18.3	.73	16.17		65.0		18.1	.92	17
	(0.40)	(3.23)	(2.46)		(3.04)		(1.02)		
B	108.3	1.64	−2.93		−124.0	127.1	337.1	.98	17
	(1.68)	(5.32)	(0.20)		(3.11)	(2.90)	(5.54)		
D	268.3	.06	−3.40		85.2	440.7	586.7	.85	22
	(2.11)	(0.05)	(0.17)		(0.31)	(2.03)	(1.34)		
E	−6.3	.95	9.25		−595.4	1,289.0	606.3	.85	18
	(0.07)	(3.88)	(0.64)		(3.19)	(4.81)	(3.59)		
F	23.1	.67	16.03		59.2	15.5	22.6	.92	17
	(0.48)	(2.59)	(2.37)		(2.42)	(0.55)	(1.13)		

Notes: See Table 9.A.8.

Table 9.A.10   **OLS Equations for Non-U.S. Exports Based on Net Sales by Majority-Owned U.S. Affiliates, 1982 (30 industries)**

Industry No.	Intercept ($ millions)	GDP	GDP per Capita (GDPC)	Net Sales (NS)	$\bar{R}^2$	No. of Obs.
			Coefficients of			
1	−11	.07	14.6	.12	.49	48
	(.5)	(1.0)	(3.5)	(3.3)		
2	−68	.34	19.6	.58	.65	47
	(1.9)	(2.2)	(3.2)	(3.1)		
3	−19	.16	6.6	.05	.26	43
	(.9)	(2.4)	(1.8)	(.5)		
4	−541	6.94	131.1	1.52	.77	48
	(1.9)	(6.9)	(2.6)	(3.3)		
5	−596	4.15	183.6	8.05	.63	48
	(1.8)	(3.9)	(3.2)	(3.4)		
6			NA			
7			NA			
8	−41	.08	16.1	.24	.47	48
	(1.9)	(1.1)	(4.3)	(2.2)		
9	−36	.10	19.8	.77	.56	48
	(1.3)	(1.1)	(4.7)	(3.5)		
10	−35	.50	23.1	.15	.81	48
	(1.5)	(4.6)	(5.6)	(2.6)		
11	−33	−.03	15.3	.18	.69	48
	(2.2)	(0.4)	(5.9)	(4.1)		
12	−22	.32	12.0	.99	.37	47
	(0.6)	(2.7)	(2.0)	(1.9)		
13	−159	3.6	96.0	1.13	.74	48
	(0.7)	(4.4)	(2.3)	(5.2)		
14	−46	.56	27.3	.35	.73	48
	(1.3)	(4.7)	(4.4)	(3.7)		
15	−85	.31	31.2	.32	.55	48
	(2.2)	(2.2)	(4.7)	(2.1)		
16	−52	−.09	19.1	1.37	.74	48
	(2.2)	(0.9)	(4.7)	(6.7)		
17	−210	1.46	137.9	9.31	.62	48
	(1.2)	(2.2)	(4.4)	(3.4)		
18	−229	2.71	58.1	3.93	.85	48
	(2.5)	(7.9)	(3.6)	(4.6)		
19	−132	−.01	88.8	.69	.66	48
	(1.5)	(.03)	(5.9)	(4.5)		
20			NA			

Table 9.A.10   (continued)

Industry No.	Intercept ($ millions)	Coefficients of			$\bar{R}^2$	No. of Obs.
		GDP	GDP per Capita (GDPC)	Net Sales (NS)		
21	.5	.05	33.7	.45	.54	48
	(0.0)	(.3)	(4.2)	(3.7)		
22	− 12	− .79	31.8	.58	.89	48
	(0.3)	(4.2)	(4.7)	(13.2)		
23	− 424	1.18	125.0	1.67	.72	48
	(0.0)	(2.0)	(4.5)	(5.1)		
24	− 49	.08	24.5	1.90	.71	48
	(1.7)	(.7)	(4.8)	(6.2)		
25	− 53	.63	51.1	.75	.57	48
	(0.5)	(2.0)	(3.1)	(3.9)		
26	− 8	− .09	15.1	1.40	.85	48
	(0.3)	(.7)	(2.8)	(11.9)		
27	− 114	.76	78.4	1.50	.65	48
	(1.3)	(2.4)	(5.0)	(3.3)		
28	− 385	1.78	240.5	.39	.55	48
	(1.1)	(1.5)	(4.0)	(3.5)		
29			NA			
30	− 286	3.28	69.7	.61	.85	48
	(3.4)	(10.7)	(4.8)	(0.3)		
31	− 20.7	.07	13.9	1.19	.79	48
	(1.3)	(1.1)	(4.9)	(7.6)		
32	− 51	− .02	35.1	1.88	.54	48
	(1.0)	(0.1)	(3.8)	(3.8)		
33	− 106	.81	65.8	.75	.77	48
	(1.2)	(2.7)	(4.4)	(6.7)		
34	− 204	.12	90.0	4.58	.56	48
	(1.6)	(0.2)	(4.2)	(3.5)		

Notes: Dependent variable is exports to a country by an industry from countries other than the U.S. For definitions and industry list, see Table 9.A.5. Numbers in parentheses are t-statistics.

Table 9.A.11   **OLS Equations for Non-U.S. Exports Based on Net Local Sales by Majority-Owned U.S. Affiliates, 1982 (30 industries)**

| Industry No. | Intercept ($ millions) | Coefficients of | | | $\bar{R}^2$ | No. of Obs. |
		GDP	GDP per Capita (GDPC)	Net Local Sales (NLS)		
1	−11	.10	14.71	.12	.47	48
	(0.5)	(1.2)	(3.5)	(3.1)		
2	−68	.48	20.92	.36	.59	47
	(1.8)	(2.7)	(3.2)	(1.4)		
3	−21	.17	7.21	−.03	.26	43
	(1.0)	(2.6)	(2.0)	(0.2)		
4	−555	7.10	143.57	1.56	.75	48
	(1.9)	(6.7)	(2.8)	(2.7)		
5	−655	3.81	222.75	11.55	.59	48
	(1.9)	(3.0)	(3.7)	(2.3)		
6			NA			
7			NA			
8	−40	.12	16.50	.16	.44	48
	(1.8)	(1.4)	(4.3)	(1.3)		
9	−34	.10	19.39	1.02	.57	48
	(1.3)	(1.2)	(4.1)	(3.5)		
10	−37	.51	24.30	.16	.79	48
	(1.5)	(3.8)	(5.7)	(1.7)		
11	−36	.02	16.2	.16	.62	48
	(2.2)	(0.3)	(5.8)	(2.6)		
12	−21	.34	12.9	.80	.33	47
	(0.6)	(2.8)	(2.0)	(1.2)		
13	−274	3.51	142.3	1.64	.65	48
	(1.0)	(3.4)	(3.0)	(3.0)		
14	−51	.57	29.3	.43	.70	48
	(1.4)	(4.4)	(4.6)	(2.8)		
15	−81	.37	31.4	.21	.52	48
	(2.0)	(2.7)	(4.5)	(1.2)		
16	−60	.00	23.9	1.21	.56	48
	(2.0)	(0.0)	(4.7)	(3.1)		
17	−239	1.48	145.9	10.73	.62	48
	(1.3)	(2.3)	(4.7)	(3.3)		
18	−251	2.95	65.8	3.90	.81	48
	(2.4)	(7.4)	(3.7)	(2.7)		
19	−144	.01	91.2	.90	.65	48
	(1.6)	(0.0)	(6.0)	(4.2)		
20			NA			

Table 9.A.11   (continued)

			Coefficients of			
Industry No.	Intercept ($ millions)	GDP	GDP per Capita (GDPC)	Net Local Sales (NLS)	$\bar{R}^2$	No. of Obs.
21	− 12	.19	37.6	.41	.44	48
	(0.2)	(1.0)	(4.3)	(1.8)		
22	− 4	− 1.20	34.2	1.06	.90	48
	(0.0)	(5.8)	(5.2)	(13.6)		
23	− 32	1.13	135.4	2.77	.69	48
	(0.2)	(1.8)	(4.7)	(4.4)		
24	− 58	.17	26.9	2.29	.65	48
	(1.8)	(1.6)	(4.9)	(5.0)		
25	− 52	.64	51.3	1.02	.56	48
	(0.5)	(2.0)	(3.0)	(3.7)		
26	30	− .43	20.7	2.43	.59	48
	(0.5)	(1.4)	(2.3)	(4.8)		
27	− 122	.87	83.8	1.51	.62	48
	(1.3)	(2.6)	(5.2)	(2.4)		
28	− 441	1.93	243.1	.63	.55	48
	(1.3)	(1.6)	(4.1)	(3.5)		
29			NA			
30	− 284	3.23	69.1	1.62	.85	48
	(3.3)	(10.8)	(4.8)	(0.7)		
31	− 28	.09	16.1	1.45	.72	48
	(1.5)	(1.3)	(5.0)	(5.7)		
32	− 57	− .08	37.7	2.57	.54	48
	(1.1)	(0.4)	(4.2)	(3.8)		
33	− 95	.49	67.0	1.57	.81	48
	(1.2)	(1.7)	(4.9)	(7.9)		
34	− 217	.26	94.9	5.56	.56	48
	(1.8)	(0.6)	(4.5)	(3.5)		

Notes: For definitions and industry list, see Table 9.A.5. Numbers in parentheses are t-statistics.

Table 9.A.12   **OLS Equations for Non-U.S. Exports Based on Net Local Sales and Net Export Sales by Majority-Owned U.S. Affiliates, 1982 (30 industries)**

		Coefficients of					
Industry No.	Intercept ($ millions)	GDP	GDP per Capita (GDPC)	Net Local Sales (NLS)	Net Export Sales (NXS)	$\bar{R}^2$	No. of Obs.
1	−11	.07	14.2	.07	.64	.50	48
	(0.5)	(0.8)	(3.5)	(1.6)	(1.8)		
2	−64	.51	16.9	.15	1.69	.71	47
	(2.0)	(3.4)	(3.0)	(0.7)	(4.3)		
3	−18	.18	5.8	−.08	.38	.30	43
	(0.8)	(2.7)	(1.6)	(0.7)	(1.8)		
4	−528	7.08	123.5	1.15	2.92	.77	48
	(1.8)	(6.94)	(2.4)	(2.0)	(2.0)		
5	−599	4.03	185.1	9.10	7.53	.62	48
	(1.8)	(3.4)	(3.1)	(1.8)	(2.4)		
6				NA			
7				NA			
8	−21	.099	9.8	−.07	3.52	.74	48
	(1.4)	(1.8)	(3.6)	(0.8)	(7.3)		
9	−35	.102	19.5	.96	.21	.56	48
	(1.3)	(1.1)	(4.1)	(1.8)	(0.1)		
10	−34	.63	21.8	− 00	.34	.81	48
	(1.4)	(4.6)	(5.2)	(0.0)	(2.4)		
11	−18	.084	12.0	−.077	1.15	.87	48
	(1.8)	(1.8)	(7.0)	(1.8)	(9.2)		
12	−12	.34	8.5	.245	3.02	.39	47
	(0.3)	(2.9)	(1.3)	(0.3)	(2.1)		
13	−133	4.07	86.9	.569	1.46	.74	48
	(0.6)	(4.5)	(2.0)	(1.1)	(4.0)		
14	−39	.62	24.9	−.041	.99	.75	48
	(1.1)	(5.2)	(4.1)	(0.2)	(3.2)		
15	−54	.27	24.8	.018	2.20	.65	48
	(1.5)	(2.2)	(4.0)	(0.1)	(4.1)		
16	−50	.02	17.4	.84	1.99	.76	48
	(2.3)	(0.2)	(4.5)	(2.9)	(6.2)		
17	−210	1.46	137.8	9.29	9.42	.61	48
	(1.1)	(2.2)	(4.1)	(2.4)	(0.7)		
18	−204	2.96	51.4	−.36	11.13	.89	48
	(2.5)	(9.6)	(3.6)	(0.3)	(5.4)		
19	−111	.03	85.3	.210	1.95	.67	48
	(1.2)	(0.1)	(5.6)	(0.5)	(1.8)		
20				NA			

Table 9.A.12 (continued)

			Coefficients of				
Industry No.	Intercept ($ millions)	GDP	GDP per Capita (GDPC)	Net Local Sales (NLS)	Net Export Sales (NXS)	$\bar{R}^2$	No. of Obs.
21	17	.10	29.5	−.01	.93	.59	48
	(0.4)	(0.6)	(3.8)	(0.0)	(4.1)		
22	1	−1.07	33.1	.88	.22	.90	48
	(0.0)	(4.5)	(5.0)	(5.2)	(1.2)		
23	38	1.59	111.0	−.67	4.37	.73	48
	(0.2)	(2.6)	(3.92)	(0.5)	(2.8)		
24	−50	.08	24.6	2.02	1.72	.71	48
	(1.7)	(0.8)	(4.8)	(4.6)	(3.0)		
25	−56	.65	51.4	.25	1.98	.56	48
	(0.6)	(2.0)	(3.1)	(0.3)	(1.1)		
26	−39	.35	14.2	.42	1.85	.88	48
	(1.3)	(1.9)	(2.9)	(1.2)	(10.0)		
27	−81	.83	67.7	.45	4.45	.70	48
	(0.9)	(2.7)	(4.3)	(0.7)	(3.0)		
28	−408	1.77	241.0	.52	.23	.55	48
	(1.1)	(1.4)	(4.0)	(2.1)	(0.8)		
29			NA				
30	−251	3.34	64.1	4.66	−15.71	.86	48
	(3.0)	(11.2)	(4.5)	(1.7)	(1.9)		
31	−19.4	.07	13.5	1.05	1.43	.78	48
	(1.2)	(1.2)	(4.7)	(4.3)	(3.8)		
32	−54	−.05	36.1	2.23	1.06	.53	48
	(1.0)	(0.2)	(3.8)	(2.4)	(0.6)		
33	−92	.31	69.3	2.18	−.68	.81	48
	(1.2)	(1.0)	(5.1)	(5.0)	(1.6)		
34	−211	.18	92.7	5.30	1.90	.55	48
	(1.7)	(0.4)	(4.2)	(3.2)	(0.5)		

Notes: For definitions and industry list, see Table 9.A.5. Numbers in parentheses are t-statistics.

Table 9.A.13   OLS Equations for Non-U.S. Exports Based on Production by Both Majority-Owned and Minority-Owned U.S. Affiliates, 1982 (6 industry groups)

| | | | | Coefficients of | | | | | |
| | | Majority-Owned Affiliate | | | | | Minority-Owned Affiliate | | |
Industry Group	Intercept	GDP	GDP per Capita (GDPC)	Net Sales (NS)	Net Local Sales (NLS)	Net Export Sales (NXS)	Net Sales (MONS)	$\bar{R}^2$	No. of Obs.
A	−1,289	8.96	353.7	584.8			−2,194	.80	22
	(2.14)	(3.76)	(3.0)	(1.66)			(1.85)		
B	−1,055	11.75	511.5	254.6			−2,446	.87	27
	(2.41)	(5.33)	(2.80)	(3.54)			(4.65)		
C	−810.4	5.20	323.3	2,278.8			−2,252	.81	18
	(1.07)	(2.70)	(2.98)	(4.14)			(1.63)		
D	52.4	2.68	181.4	592.6			1,152	.88	24
	(0.14)	(1.06)	(3.33)	(1.97)			(0.92)		
E	−255.1	−.08	151.7	2,042.7			−158	.80	24
	(0.70)	(0.07)	(2.52)	(6.72)			(0.22)		
F	−547.7	7.59	215.7	511.8			−641	.85	19
	(0.92)	(2.51)	(2.57)	(2.94)			(2.69)		
B	−2,034	11.27	615.4		170.9		−2,627	.89	17
	(3.27)	(3.45)	(5.22)		(0.43)		(3.95)		

Table 9.A.13 (continued)

				Coefficients of					
					Majority-Owned Affiliate				
Industry Group	Intercept	GDP	GDP per Capita (GDPC)	Net Sales (NS)	Net Local Sales (NLS)	Net Export Sales (NXS)	Minority-Owned Affiliate Net Sales (MONS)	$\bar{R}^2$	No. of Obs.
D	−201.3	5.93	211.6		148.8		2,282	.86	22
	(0.48)	(1.58)	(3.50)		(0.20)		(1.61)		
E	−208.5	−.57	215.1		3,160.4		−843	.78	18
	(0.44)	(0.41)	(2.62)		(5.20)		(0.95)		
F	−398.0	13.13	139.2		591.4		−1,030	.99	17
	(2.59)	(17.1)	(6.26)		(8.16)		(17.19)		
B	−1,230.5	13.26	353.8		−270.2	1,140.9	−2,616	.93	17
	(2.22)	(5.02)	(2.81)		(0.79)	(3.04)	(5.03)		
D	35.0	7.97	123.6		−1,665.3	2,355.2	1,304	.94	22
	(0.12)	(3.11)	(2.77)		(2.67)	(4.76)	(1.34)		
E	−463.1	−.29	214.0		1,211.2	3,407.5	−.6	.89	18
	(1.14)	(0.25)	(3.13)		(1.37)	(2.69)	(0.01)		
F	−393.2	13.07	139.1		585.7	15.4	−1,025	.99	17
	(2.41)	(14.75)	(6.01)		(7.00)	(0.16)	(15.0)		

Notes: See Table 9.A.8.

References

Bergsten, C. Fred, Thomas Horst, and Theodore H. Moran. 1978. *American multinationals and American interests*. Washington, D.C.: Brookings Institution.

Chenery, Hollis B. 1960. Patterns of industrial 'growth. *American Economic Review* 50 (September): 624–54.

Kravis, Irving B., and Robert E. Lipsey. 1984. The diffusion of economic growth in the world economy. In John W. Kendrick, ed., *International comparisons of productivity and causes of the slowdown*. Cambridge, Mass.: Ballinger for the American Enterprise Institute.

Leamer, Edward E., and Robert M. Stern. 1970. *Quantitative international economics*. Boston: Allyn and Bacon.

Linneman, Hans. 1966. *An econometric study of trade flows*. Amsterdam: North-Holland.

Lipsey, Robert E., and Merle Yahr Weiss. 1981. Foreign production and exports in manufacturing industries. *Review of Economics and Statistics* 63:488–94.

———. 1984. Foreign production and exports of individual firms. *Review of Economics and Statistics* 66:304–8.

Swedenborg, Birgitta. 1979. *The multinational operations of Swedish firms*. Stockholm: Industriens Utredningsinstitut.

———. 1982. *Svensk industri i utlandet*. Stockholm: Industriens Utrednings-institut.

United Nations and Commission of the European Communities. 1986. *World comparisons of purchasing power and real product for 1980*. Phase IV of the International Comparison Project: Part One: Summary Results for 60 Countries. New York: United Nations and Eurostat.

U.S. Department of Commerce. 1985. *U.S. direct investment abroad: 1982 benchmark survey data*. Bureau of Economic Analysis.

Comment   Steven J. Matusz

Does foreign direct investment substitute for exports, or is such investment complementary to exports? This is the question addressed by the authors. Using U.S. and Swedish data, they find that the preponderance of the evidence suggests that the relationship between direct foreign investment and export sales is one of complementarity. While they find some limited evidence of substitutability in the U.S. data, they find no evidence of substitutability in the Swedish data.

The following discussion focuses on two distinctly different issues, although both issues lead to the same general result. In particular, I argue that we should not be surprised that the preponderance of the evidence points toward complementarity. The first issue deals with the

Steven J. Matusz is assistant professor of economics at Michigan State University.

relationships mandated by the balance of payments under a regime of flexible exchange rates. The second relates to the distinction between the decision to invest and the decision to produce a given amount of output.

Concerning the balance of payments, we know that in a world of flexible exchange rates, the current account balance must exactly offset capital flows. An increase in foreign direct investment, all other things equal, will reduce the surplus or increase the deficit on the capital account. In turn, the exchange rate will adjust to induce an opposite change in the current account. Ignoring changes in unilateral transfers and returns to past investments, such a change implies either an increase in exports or a reduction in imports. While particular investment projects may change the relative composition of a bundle of exports, increasing exports of some products and reducing exports of others, the overall result must be an increase in net exports. This accounting identity suggests that in an industry-by-industry study such as the one undertaken by the authors, we should find a preponderance of evidence suggesting a positive relationship between current direct foreign investment and net exports, although there may be a few industries where the relationship is negative.

In at least two respects, the relationships necessitated by the balance of payments are not precisely the relationships that were tested by the authors, and therefore the a priori arguments in favor of finding complementarity are weakened. First, the authors use net sales of foreign affiliates to proxy for foreign direct investment. To the extent that such sales reflect past investment decisions, one might argue that these past investments can influence today's current account in a negative direction. However, one would have to argue that a high capital outflow in all previous periods leads to a low capital outflow in the present period, since it is the present capital account that is linked to the present current account. Second, the dependent variable is gross exports. Clearly, gross exports may decline even as net exports increase.

Regardless of the aggregate impact of direct foreign investment, the differential impact across industries is ambiguous. As the authors argue, most of the theory relating to the motive for direct foreign investment takes the size of the foreign market as given. Typically, one asks why a firm would choose to invest abroad rather than licensing a foreign agent or exporting the product. The very phrasing of the question implies that production abroad substitutes for exports. On the other hand, the authors correctly assert that theoretical arguments can be made to show that direct foreign investment and exports are complementary. For example, if the foreign affiliate is mostly a final assembly plant that imports the components from the parent, it follows that an increase in the activity of the foreign affiliate will stimulate exports from the parent. Alternatively, one might argue in favor of a microeconomic version of Say's law, that the foreign demand for a particular product is parameterized on the level of production undertaken in the foreign country.

Once the foreign affiliate is in operation, an increase in foreign demand can be expected to lead to an increase in production by the foreign affiliate as well as an increase in exports. If foreign demand is parameterized on the level of sales of the affiliate, any increase in demand initiated by, say, an increase in income will be magnified because the increased local production will stimulate further increases in demand. After controlling for other factors that might influence demand and holding all other things equal, we would expect to find a nonnegative coefficient on net sales of the foreign affiliate when trying to explain exports.

On the other hand, if the initial increase in the sales of the affiliate was due to a reduction in production costs abroad relative to those of the parent, we would see a substitution of affiliate sales for exports unless the added affiliate sales stimulate foreign demand so much that the substitution effect is swamped. It would seem that this is what is being tested in the cross-sectional study. In the cross section, investment is put in place and controls have been incorporated to account for variations in demand. Unobserved variations in production costs across countries induce firms to alter their mix of parent and affiliate production. In most of the results presented, it appears that the effect of affiliate sales on foreign demand outweighs the substitution effect due to relative cost differences.

Both of the above situations take as given the existence of the foreign affiliate, but if we wish to examine the relationship between direct foreign investment and exports, we must ask how the very existence of the affiliate influences the level of exports. In particular, if that affiliate did not exist, would the parent have expanded U.S. plant capacity and therefore production? Perhaps one way to address this question might be to separately estimate the elasticity of exports with respect to domestic investment, and the direct effect of foreign production on the size of the market. With such estimates in hand, it might then be possible to simulate the effect of an extra billion dollars of investment if undertaken at home and then if undertaken abroad. The difference in simulated export levels might then be a nearer approximation of the effect of direct foreign investment on exports for a given industry.

Comment   John Mutti

This chapter revisits a topic debated extensively in the 1970s. Such a reexamination allows new data and different analytical tools to be applied in evaluating the way foreign affiliate production affects a country's export performance. However, the policy context motivating such a reexamination differs from that of the 1960s and 1970s, when much of the attention focused on macroeconomic concerns in a world of fixed exchange rates. Fears of lost output in the United States and the potential exportation of jobs led to several legislative proposals to restrict foreign investment by U.S. firms. While those concerns may have been misdirected then, they seem even less relevant now that the United States is a large net importer of capital in a world of flexible exchange rates. The relationship between foreign investment and export performance does have a continued policy relevance today, given the role of direct foreign investment in current multilateral trade talks. In particular, would reduced barriers to foreign investment result in greater demand for U.S. exports and a consequent improvement in the terms of trade?

Chapter 9, by Blomström, Lipsey, and Kulchycky, presents estimates of the relationship between direct investment in one country by residents of another and the level of exports from the latter country to the former, based on Swedish and U.S. data. Two approaches are utilized, one based on cross-sectional data to explain the level of exports for a single year (1978 for Sweden and 1982 for the United States) and the other designed to explain the change in exports between two years (1970 and 1978 for Sweden). The underlying analytical framework is the gravity model of trade, which is modified to explain one country's exports to another as a function of economic activity in the recipient country, cost-related factors (distance, trade barriers, factor endowments), and production in the recipient country of affiliates controlled by the home country. The authors omit any of the cost-related variables. Omitted variables result in biased estimates of the remaining coefficients, but the direction of bias need not necessarily result in misleading inferences being drawn from the authors' work. For example, omitting the tariff variable could result in a downward bias in the estimated coefficient for affiliate sales. A tariff would be expected to reduce exports received and also to give an incentive for greater foreign affiliate production behind the tariff wall; thus, when the tariff is omitted, the estimated coefficient for affiliate sales may be smaller because it

John Mutti is the Sidney Meyer Professor of International Economics at Grinnell College.

reflects some of the negative influence of the tariff. In the absence of simultaneity bias, where affiliate sales are correlated with the error term in the export equation, a finding of complementarity would not likely be reversed if tariff data were collected and included in the analysis.

Because affiliate sales are likely to be influenced by exports and therefore to be determined endogenously, the authors report 2SLS estimates for the Swedish data. Both the OLS and 2SLS estimates suggest a definite complementary relationship between exports and affiliate sales. The estimated coefficients from 2SLS are larger than those from OLS, a contrast to results cited from Swedenborg's work. The 2SLS representation is problematic, though, due to the difficulty of specifying a variable that determines affiliate sales but does not belong in the export equation too. The authors rely on a dummy variable for membership in the EC, a choice that seems less easily justified than a measure directed at the investment process, such as taxes.

The time-series estimates are based on a different functional form, where the change in exports is regressed on the level of affiliate sales as well as the change in affiliate sales. The estimated coefficients for the change in affiliate sales are smaller than those obtained in either the OLS or 2SLS cross-sectional estimates. A potential caution in interpreting the time-series results is that the estimated relationship between exports and affiliate sales may instead be due to a common third factor operating over the period, such as inflation or technical innovation.

The authors are to be commended for reporting the full set of estimated equations in the appendix, including the intercepts obtained, the number of observations available, and other details frequently omitted in empirical work. As noted by the authors, several negative intercepts suggest that the estimated equation may rest on a misspecified functional form or the omission of some other critical variable. Because the full set of results is reported, the reader can evaluate how pervasive this problem is.

The U.S. estimates are based on much finer industry breakdowns than has been possible in previous work, due to the availability of the 1982 benchmark survey of U.S. direct foreign investment abroad. This disaggregation offers the potential advantage of avoiding combining several disparate types of activity together into a single group. Only OLS cross-sectional results are reported in this section of the chapter; they do not suggest as strong a complementary relationship as found in the Swedish data, but neither do they yield many cases of significant substitutability. The mixed outcome is similar in some respects to what Horst found in earlier work. Because heteroskedasticity often can be a problem in cross-sectional studies, some indication of its significance here is warranted. However, given the imprecision of many of the industry estimates reported, any adjustment may not be a high priority.

This more diaggregated data set also was used to see if greater U.S. affiliate sales in a foreign country reduced exports to that country from countries other than the United States. The effect of affiliate sales was positive and often statistically significant. This unexpected result again suggests that potential problems of misspecification exist. It may even raise the unsettling possibility that the relationship differs across countries and that cross-sectional analysis is inappropriate. In an analysis based on more aggregate industry groups, the authors were able to consider additional variables, such as the role of minority affiliates, whose importance differs substantially across countries. Those results suggest that in some industries minority operations represent a way to gain market access at the expense of foreign competitors. They also indicate that many possibilities remain in developing a more complete picture of the link between exports and foreign affiliate production.

IV Assessing U.S. Bilateral Trade Policy Disputes

10 United States–Japan Economic Relations

Rachel McCulloch

The bilateral relationship with Japan now dominates American thinking on the benefits and costs of foreign trade. Japan has become the model of all things modern and efficient, the standard against which the United States measures its own economy and finds itself wanting. But Japan is also firmly established as the villain in the industrial adjustment woes that have plagued the United States in recent years; most Americans remain unaware that Japan has encountered many of the same difficulties in reducing excess capacity, often in the same industries.

Such paradoxes typify the intense and stormy relationship between the world's economic superpowers. Against a background of ever-increasing bilateral imbalances, ever-escalating protectionist rhetoric, and even some action at the official level, individual Americans continue to vote with their dollars for still more Japanese imports. Can U.S. producers hope to reverse the trend? Can American consumers be persuaded to give up their Toyotas and their Sonys in favor of domestic goods? These questions are themselves rapidly becoming obsolete. Thanks to the recent flood of Japanese direct investments into U.S. manufacturing industries, it is now often possible to "buy American" without sacrificing Japanese design and quality.

This chapter reevaluates the past and future course of United States–Japan economic relations. The first section asks whether there is indeed a "Japan problem" and, if so, exactly what that problem is. Section 10.2 examines the macroeconomic roots of the United States–Japan bilateral trade imbalance and weighs alternative macroeconomic remedies. Section 10.3 deals with trade issues at the sectoral level. Section

Rachel McCulloch is professor of international finance at Brandeis University and a research associate of the National Bureau of Economic Research.

10.4 reviews the technological rivalry between the United States and Japan. Section 10.5 draws some conclusions and looks to the future of the relationship.

10.1   Is There a Japan Problem?

Given the surfeit of recent writings, both scholarly and popular, on the unprecedented size and continuing growth of the United States–Japan trade imbalance, it may seem odd to ask what the problem is, let alone whether a problem exists. Yet in some important respects, Japan is perhaps better seen as part of the solution rather than the source of the problem. To see why, it is helpful to examine the various aspects of the United States–Japan economic relationship that may underlie the continuing friction. Here there are at least six possible candidates: (1) growing bilateral imbalance on merchandise trade, particularly on trade in manufactured goods; (2) growing net capital inflows from Japan to the United States; (3) the yen/dollar exchange rate and perhaps also the present system of exchange rate determination; (4) sectoral nontariff barriers (whether real or imagined) limiting Japanese imports of U.S. products, Japanese trade-distorting industrial policies, and export incentives depriving U.S. firms of sales at home and in third-country markets; (5) successful emulation by Japan of the technological supremacy of U.S. industry; and (6) social, economic, political, and cultural differences between the two nations.

These categories are not mutually exclusive. Automotive products loom so large in total bilateral trade that this "sectoral" issue necessarily has implications for aggregate imbalances. The narrowing technological gap is intimately linked to the sectoral composition of trade and is itself affected by Japanese policies to promote economic growth. And while cultural and social conditions in, say, Indonesia are equally exotic to an American observer, Americans are much more interested in—and worried about—contrasts between Japan and the United States precisely because of the growing economic rivalry. Still, it is helpful to sort out the relative importance of each type of irritant and to examine the main causes and potential remedies in each.

10.1.1   Aggregate Imbalance

Highly aggregated measures of bilateral interaction are regarded by most economists as the visible "symptoms" of underlying macroeconomic conditions—and, specifically, *not* caused either by defects of trade or industrial policies at home or by skillful application of the same abroad. While the symptoms are themselves problematic, the causes and thus the effective potential remedies are to be found at the macroeconomic level. Yet the justification of every new proposal for trade legislation prominently features the latest hitherto unimaginable data on the nation's global external imbalance and bilateral deficit with Japan—with the strong implication that tough new trade policies (or creative new competitiveness policies) are the measures required for the United States to redress the present imbalance.

10.1.2 Capital Inflows

Matching Japanese global surpluses on merchandise trade and current account are massive foreign investments. The recent rates have been rivaled only by the petrodollar flood of the 1970s. But the petrodollars were recycled primarily through the Eurodollar market and went ultimately to many borrowers. In contrast, Japanese funds (autodollars?) have in large measure moved directly into U.S. financial markets. Thus, while there is no conceptual reason why the nation's largest bilateral merchandise trade deficit and its largest bilateral capital account surplus should be with the same trading partner, it is certainly true in this instance. If the oil surpluses had materialized later, or if U.S. fiscal policy had changed sooner, it is likely that more liabilities of the U.S. Treasury would now be held by Saudi Arabia and fewer by Japan.

The rapidly growing U.S. official debt to foreigners (or, indeed, to anyone) raises important issues of intergenerational equity. However, the concerns of many Americans focus on one particular component of the capital inflows, direct foreign investments in U.S. industries. On the one hand, state and local officials vie to attract new investments— jobs and the future tax base are the main reasons. But domestic firms worry about new competition as well as the effects on their own labor costs and taxes.

Apparently oblivious to U.S. official insistence on national treatment by foreign governments for U.S. subsidiaries abroad, the president of Ford Motor Company called in early 1987 for further reductions in auto imports from Japan, to compensate for increased production by Japanese plants in the United States. In the troubled U.S. semiconductor industry, national security concerns were raised in objection to the proposed acquisition of Fairchild Semiconductor by Fujitsu, Japan's largest computer company.[1]

10.1.3 The Dollar/Yen Exchange Rate

The exchange rate, too, is viewed by economists as fundamentally a symptom rather than a cause. However, the relationships determining exchange rate movements are poorly understood. Professional opinion remains divided particularly on the appropriate role and effectiveness of official intervention in foreign exchange markets, either directly, via purchases or sales of foreign exchange, or indirectly, via manipulation of discount rates.

Through 1985, dollar strength offered a plausible explanation of the nation's growing deficit on merchandise trade. But the subsequent dramatic decline in the dollar failed to induce a corresponding turnaround in U.S. trade performance. Analysts then rushed in to explain the nonevent with traditional J-curves and newer "hysteresis" effects. While differing in their microeconomic underpinnings, both theories suggest that for foreign trade, what goes up does not necessarily come down, or at least not as quickly as policymakers would like. As a result of continuing growth in the U.S. trade deficit, a yen/dollar exchange rate of 160, seen in 1986 by U.S. officials as an appropriate policy target, had given way to target values of 140 or below by mid-1987.

10.1.4   Who Is the Problem?

While the domestic consequences of large bilateral imbalances and major exchange rate movements surely constitute unsolved problems for U.S. policymakers, it is difficult to make a convincing case that the basic fault lies with the Japanese rather than elsewhere. True, the imbalances reflect mismatch between the macroeconomic conditions and policies of Japan and the United States. But if the main problem is simply the large aggregate imbalance, the main cause is macroeconomic policy in the United States.

Indeed, only Japan's offsetting surpluses permitted the U.S. economy to enjoy moderate growth during the 1980s while continuing on an unchanged macroeconomic course. In retrospect, perhaps the United States should have altered its fiscal policies sooner. Does that mean Japan is at fault for leaving the United States "free to choose" instead of being forced to confront immediately the full implications of its actions?

10.1.5   Sectoral Distortions

Although customarily raised along with the issue of growing bilateral imbalance, sectoral trade distortions present a conceptually different type of problem for the United States. The primary effect of such policies is to reduce the mutual benefits from trade based on comparative advantage. While individual firms and even industries often stand to gain from distortive sectoral policies, national gains from export promotion or import restriction are likely to be the exception rather than the rule.[2]

The conclusion that trade policies, whether good or bad, affect mainly the composition of trade rather than the aggregate balance stems from a general equilibrium view of economic activity. Simply put, although a trade policy may change the balance of trade for a particular product or even an industry, offsets arise via induced movements in exchange rates and input costs, foreign retaliation, and other indirect channels.[3]

Likewise, any positive employment effects in a specific sector are offset by reduced employment opportunities in other areas. Moreover, to the extent that the jobs "saved" are in relatively inefficient firms or in activities where the United States has lost comparative advantage, the overall composition of employment opportunities may be adversely affected.[4] Still, this does not alter the important economic and political issues raised by the distribution of the gains from maintaining relatively open international markets.

A separate concern is the changing composition of U.S. production. If the level of domestic activity in particular manufacturing industries has important positive effects on other parts of the economy, loss of market share in such "strategic" activities could reduce future U.S. industrial competitiveness across the board. No clear evidence of such externalities is yet available, but some fear that further delay in reversing present trends may leave the United States at a permanent competitive disadvantage.

10.1.6 How Important Are Trade Distortions?

The existence of subtle trade-distorting policies and industrial practices on the part of Japan is acknowledged by almost all international economists. The more interesting question is how important such policies are in shaping the overall relationship between Japan and the rest of the world, and particularly with the United States. While there are differences of opinion concerning the importance of such distortions to the performance of individual sectors (see, for example, Borrus and Zysman 1985), there is broad agreement that the consequences for the size of the aggregate imbalance are minor.

Even when there are significant benefits to be achieved by negotiating reductions in sectoral trade distortions, it is crucial that this task be divorced from the more pressing macroeconomic issues.[5] The persistent linkage of aggregate and sectoral issues allows policymakers to delay needed macroeconomic remedies and promotes U.S. allegations of bad faith on the part of Japanese officials when inappropriate means fail to achieve their stated ends.

10.1.7 Technological Rivalry

Perhaps most significant to the long-range development of the United States–Japan relationship is the successful emulation by Japan of U.S. technology–based economic growth. While many nations have sought to close the technology gap with the United States, only Japan has come so far so fast. Once primarily an importer and adapter of technologies developed elsewhere, Japan now rivals the United States in many areas of industrial innovation.

Japan's challenge to U.S. technological supremacy has important implications for the composition of bilateral trade flows. Through much of the post–World War II period, access to superior technology allowed the United States to compete effectively on world markets while maintaining average wages well above those abroad. U.S. industrial exports were increasingly concentrated in the high-technology industries, while the remainder of U.S. manufacturing lost ground to foreign suppliers. But with the loss of its decisive technological lead, U.S. industry can no longer compete on the basis of unique products or advanced processes alone. As a consequence, earnings in U.S. manufacturing are becoming more closely linked to those in Japan and other nations with access to advanced technologies and to the capital required to implement them.

Another long-term issue is the influence of the "Japanese model" of industrial development on policy choices of developing nations, especially in Asia. Does the future hold "many Japans" competing with the United States in world markets? South Korea is often labeled the next Japan because of its successes in promoting the same export industries—successes fostered in part by North American and European trade discrimination directed at Japan's most competitive export industries. Nationalistic Koreans reject the implied linkage with its one-time oppressor but often privately admire Japan's economic strategy. Other newly industrializing nations are also studying Japan's industrial policy and in some cases adopting certain elements. The specter of a world economy dominated by many nations all saving, innovating, and exporting at Japanese rates raises obvious concerns in the West.

Beyond the important but narrow issue of increased competition in high-technology manufacturing industries, the challenge to the U.S. lead in scientific and technological areas may have implications for the nation's key role in global security systems. This latter issue is linked to the ambivalence of the United States and its allies regarding increases in Japan's military expenditures. Japan's military budget for 1987 broached the "one percent threshold" relative to gross national product for the first time since the end of World War II.

10.1.8 Being Different

The final but by no means minor problem area in United States–Japan relations arises from the myriad social, political, and economic structures of the Japanese nation that contrast so sharply with their U.S. counterparts. While the net contribution of these differences to relative economic performance and to the bilateral imbalances remains largely in the realm of conjecture, many serious suggestions for relieving tensions between the two nations are based on efforts to reduce these differences, whether by making the United States more like Japan (higher savings, quality circles, a cabinet-level Department of Trade and Industry) or by making Japan more like the United States (deductability of mortgage interest, shorter work week, bigger defense budget). Made forcefully, such suggestions in effect challenge the relevance of traditional notions of national sovereignty in an increasingly interdependent world economy.

The importance of the many departures of Japanese governmental and business practice from Western norms remains an area of controversy even among scholars. Overall, political scientists such as Johnson (1982) seem more willing than economists to attribute Japanese industrial and trade successes to unique structural features. But even economists are divided on the importance of Japanese industrial policy and government-firm relationships in comparison to a high savings rate as key factors underlying the "Japanese miracle."

Contrasting economic and political systems also complicate the narrower issue of what constitutes a level playing field in trade and investment matters. Allegations of sectoral trade distortions often arise from differences in administrative structure and industrial organization. So far, neither U.S. trade law nor the General Agreement on Tariffs and Trade (GATT) has been able to deal effectively with the resulting disputes. Bilateral negotiations and ad hoc agreements, often short-lived, remain the major approach for addressing United States–Japan sectoral trade conflicts.

A darker side of the contrasts between the two nations lies below the surface. The overt U.S. racism of the World War II era has receded, but subtle racism is a plausible explanation for the very different official and private attitudes of Americans toward Japan (and the newly industrializing "four little dragons" of Asia) and toward Canada or Europe. Government officials and the media pass up no opportunity to remind the public of the gargantuan U.S. deficit on trade with Japan, but how many Americans realize that the nation's second largest bilateral deficit is on trade with Canada?[6]

However, racial prejudice is a two-way street, as Prime Minister Nakasone's well-publicized gaffe in 1986 amply demonstrated. In a nation where careful checks of ancestry are part of the usual preparation for marriage, many Japanese privately view the eclipse of U.S. industrial might as the inevitable consequence of its ethnic and racial diversity.

On this last score there may be grounds for some modest optimism. The intensification of economic ties between the United States and Japan has promoted a great desire on the part of each nation for better understanding of the other. Even if the primary motivation on each side springs from the lure of a large and lucrative foreign market, the resulting familiarity with a previously alien and inscrutable society can help to smooth those frictions based on differences alone.

10.2   Macroeconomic Roots of U.S. International Imbalance

Like an economic Sputnik, the rapid growth of the U.S. trade imbalance galvanized the American public. To many observers, escalation of the U.S. trade deficit in the 1980s was simply tangible and dramatic evidence of the nation's declining industrial competitiveness, in turn reflecting erosion of the commanding lead in science and technology the United States once enjoyed. Others variously sought explanations in trade-distorting practices abroad, export disincentives at home, and poor management practices of U.S. companies. Likewise, Japan's ever-increasing surpluses were interpreted either as evidence of Japanese bad faith in complying with agreements to open its markets to foreign goods or as confirmation of the wisdom of Japanese private and public economic management.

Each explanation spawned a detailed agenda of private and public action designed to arrest the decline. As with any broad policy initiative, both wise and foolish proposals have been advanced in the name of increased competitiveness. But for reasons discussed below, most of these proposals would do nothing to reduce the aggregate imbalance.[7]

10.2.1   The U.S. Budget Deficit

While the competitiveness frenzy continued unabated, an alternative analysis offered a very different assessment of the forces underlying rapid escalation of the U.S. trade deficit. According to this view, promoted as early as 1982 by the Council of Economic Advisors, the growth of the trade deficit was the largely predictable result of a single important macroeconomic development in the United States: a major increase in the size of the federal budget deficit. The corresponding prescription for restoration of U.S. competitiveness: cut the budget deficit.

The Council's macroeconomic explanation, initially met by disbelief and even ridicule, gained broad acceptance as the continued tandem rise of the "twin deficits" offered further circumstantial evidence in support of a linkage. The basic insight was, at least after the fact, a rather simple one. The large increase in the federal deficit translated into a comparable drop in the nation's total saving, pushing up U.S. interest rates. Drawn in by higher rates, foreign funds filled the gap. But the foreign demand for U.S. assets also drove up the value of the dollar, pricing U.S. goods out of many markets at home and abroad. Thus, rather than crowding out domestic capital formation as some had initially feared, the larger federal deficit crowded out domestic production of tradable goods.

Like most simple explanations, this one was too simple. The analysis focused on the U.S. demand for foreign funds but slighted important factors that influenced the supply of those funds to the U.S. market. While the enlarged federal deficit alone would have put upward pressure on domestic interest rates and promoted U.S. capital inflows, the actual size of those inflows was also the result of important "supply" factors in international capital markets.

10.2.2 Capital Inflows and Exchange Rates

In addition to its neglect of factors influencing the supply of funds to U.S. borrowers, the conventional wisdom implied that the appreciation of the dollar was a necessary consequence of the inflow of foreign funds. In fact, the theoretical consequences of a financial transfer for the exchange rate are ambiguous, depending crucially on spending patterns at home and abroad. The more similar those spending patterns and the larger the proportion of total expenditure devoted to tradable goods, the less the exchange rate would have to move to "effect" the transfer of current purchasing power to the United States.

Thinking in these terms helps explain how the dollar could fall so much with capital inflows still rising. The prolonged period of a very strong dollar caused permanent changes in consumer information and in producer costs of serving the U.S. market. Specifically, at a *given* exchange rate, more U.S. consumers would choose foreign products over their domestic counterparts when priced comparably in dollars, while foreign producers would be able to set lower dollar prices for goods aimed at the U.S. market. Both types of changes are hysteresis effects. They rest on once-and-for-all changes in demand and supply conditions, rather than on the short-term sluggishness, especially of demand, that underlies the J-curve analysis.[8]

10.2.3 The Supply of Foreign Funds

If growth in the federal budget deficit explains the greatly increased U.S. appetite for foreign funds, it is only one of many reasons why foreign lenders stood ready to satisfy that appetite. Other factors influencing the supply of foreign funds to U.S. capital markets can be grouped into three categories. Of these, two apply to lenders generally (including U.S. lenders, who cut back their own foreign loans in favor of domestic alternatives), while the third is specific to the most important foreign lender, Japan: (1) increased attractiveness of U.S. investments, reflecting, among others, enhanced tax incentives for capital formation, financial and industrial deregulation, repeal of the withholding tax on earnings of U.S. assets held by foreigners, and successful anti-inflationary macroeconomic policies; (2) reduced attractiveness of lending abroad, due to economic stagnation in much of Europe and the debt problems and capital flight affecting many less-developed countries; and (3) increased capital outflows from Japan, resulting from liberalization of restrictions on capital outflows (accelerated at the request of the United States as part of the 1984 dollar/yen agreement[9]) and lower Japanese budget deficits. Even without the large increase in U.S. federal deficits, these factors would have tended to push the U.S. capital account toward surplus, putting upward pressure on the international value of the dollar and downward pressure on U.S. merchandise trade performance.

10.2.4   Stock Adjustments and Continuing Flows

A further complication in the link between the U.S. budget deficit and U.S. borrowing from abroad is that the rise in the deficit created an ongoing demand for foreign capital, while the inflows from abroad have reflected both one-time readjustments of asset holdings in response to new market conditions and ongoing supply effects. In the specific case of capital inflows from Japan, the liberalization of capital outflows resulted in a sizable shift of accumulated Japanese assets into U.S. securities with higher yields. But the chronic surplus of Japanese private savings over domestic absorption of those savings (by domestic capital formation or government deficit spending) translates into an ongoing supply influence that can be expected to push new capital into world markets year after year.

Over time, the resulting increases in foreign holdings of U.S. assets and in U.S. holdings of foreign assets have direct implications for the composition of the current account and for the relative value of the dollar. The rising net indebtedness of the United States should mean rising net outflows of interest and profits, pushing the U.S. services account toward deficit. For a *given* level of net capital inflow, rising debt service entails a shrinking deficit on merchandise trade and less upward pressure on the value of the dollar.[10] This compositional effect within the balance of payments would tend to reinforce the influence of hysteresis on equilibrium exchange rates.

10.2.5   Correcting the Aggregate Imbalance

Given the full set of contributing macroeconomic conditions, what can be said about the outcomes of alternative corrective policies? The U.S. external imbalance reflects an excess of total "absorption"— spending (public plus private) for both consumption and investment purposes—over production in the United States, and a corresponding shortfall of absorption relative to production abroad. Measures to reduce the imbalance can seek to reduce the U.S. spending excess or to reduce the foreign shortfall.

Reducing U.S. Absorption

The most obvious choices for direct U.S. action have become the bread and butter of national policy debate: raise taxes, cut government spending, or both. A third alternative for bringing total U.S. spending into line is to reduce domestic capital formation. This option, seldom explicitly considered, has obvious negative implications for the future growth of U.S. productive capacity. However, it may be chosen by default if policymakers are unable to cut total public and private spending for other purposes, or if new taxes enacted to reduce the deficit also reduce incentives for domestic investment.

Moreover, even a successful effort to reduce the budget deficit need not produce a comparable reduction in the nation's demand for capital imports. Although customarily described in terms of the increased federal deficit, the root of the nation's increased appetite for foreign funds (or, equivalently, of its increased deficit on current account) is actually increased *spending*—specifically, the increase in total domestic absorption of goods and services. Because changes in the federal government's plans for taxing and spending usually have important effects on decisions of state and local governments and of the private sector, merely reducing the federal deficit does not necessarily have a comparable effect on total absorption; major offsets are possible.[11]

Raising Foreign Absorption

As a practical matter, progress on deficit reduction has been slow in coming, and conflicts between President Reagan and the Democratic-controlled U.S. Congress are likely to make things even more difficult in 1987 and 1988. Meanwhile, Treasury Secretary James Baker III has pushed U.S. trading partners, especially West Germany and Japan, to assume more responsibility for effecting the desired adjustment. In the case of Japan, proposals have focused on means to reduce the Japanese savings surplus by increasing domestic consumption and investment spending. This could perhaps be accomplished by general economic stimulation, but the prospects are most favorable for narrowly targeted policies intended to raise specific components of Japanese spending.

The two areas mentioned most often in this connection are housing and public works. For housing, relatively modest changes in Japanese tax laws and financial regulation could make mortgage-financed owner-occupied housing far more attractive than it is today, thereby presumably increasing total expenditures in that category and probably overall.[12]

Increased government spending for highways, railroads, and especially sewers is a second potential area of expanded domestic absorption. By Western standards, Japanese spending in these areas is surprisingly low. Fewer than three Japanese households in five are connected to a central sewer system; incredibly, the ratio is only about four out of five even in the Tokyo-Yokohama area, one of the world's most densely populated urban centers (*Japan 1986*, 88). But second-guessing such domestic spending decisions seems of doubtful efficacy, and of even more doubtful appropriateness.

One last area for a major increase in Japan's domestic absorption is defense. Currently at a postwar high of just over one percent of gross national product, Japan's defense expenditures are, for example, only about half those of neutral Switzerland and a third those of West Germany (*Japan 1986*, 86). Other major U.S. allies spend still more. Should the United States urge Japan to share more of the collective burden of global security? Viewed strictly on its economic merits, this seems a more appropriate area than housing or sewers for pressure from other nations. However, proposals for a substantial increase in Japanese defense spending have so far encountered formidable political resistance both in Japan and in the United States.

While acknowledging that Japan's capital account surplus mirrors the nation's imbalance between saving and domestic investment, some analysts believe that the underlying macroeconomic imbalance is not appropriately viewed as exogenous. Rapp (1986) and Balassa (1986) link high Japanese savings to profits generated by sectoral protection. If this effect were quantitatively important, import liberalization would, in addition to its expected effects on sectoral composition of trade flows, raise Japanese domestic absorption and thus reduce the aggregate trade surplus.

Redirecting Foreign Funds

If the United States does not want Japan's capital surpluses, perhaps other borrowers do. An important alternative to increasing Japanese domestic absorption is redirecting Japan's foreign lending toward other nations, especially less-developed nations. Debt problems have led many developing nations to restrict imports of capital equipment supplied by the United States and other industrial nations. With more purchasing power at their disposal, these nations would be able to resume such imports; U.S. exporters would benefit accordingly.

In the past decade Japan has increased by nearly 50 percent its share of GNP devoted to official development assistance, while the U.S. share, initially the same (0.24 percent), remained unchanged. But compared to other prosperous nations, Japan's spending is still on the low side.

Although the Japanese have in fact continued to step up their spending for foreign aid, the increases have not always met with cheers from other donor nations. The problem arises from informal arrangements that link aid to expenditures for Japanese goods and services. While little aid is explicitly tied, aid is rarely committed without specific project plans; potential borrowers rely on Japanese expert advice in formulating the plans, which typically call for imports of Japanese capital equipment and other products. Mixed-credit financing is a related problem, although Japan has not been the major offender in this area.

Commercial lending and direct foreign investments in developing countries are other means by which Japanese surplus savings could be "recycled." Given the ongoing debt problems of many developing nations, this route currently looks hazardous to both potential lenders and potential borrowers. In the longer term, however, it is likely that "normal" capital-flow relations between rich and poor nations will be reestablished, with funds from Japan playing an important role.

Taxing Capital Imports

Only the net inflow of capital from abroad has kept the greatly increased federal deficit from pushing U.S. interest rates through the roof. Instead, the U.S. trade deficit has gone through the roof. Until U.S. domestic absorption can be cut, the nation will continue to face the same basic choice between high interest rates and foreign borrowing. Over time, the exact terms of the trade-off will depend on investors' preferences, but the United States can tilt that choice by taxing capital imports.[13]

Controlling U.S. capital imports would shift a greater part of the adjustment to higher deficits onto U.S. lenders and borrowers, rather than allowing much of the "crowding out" to be exported. From the U.S. perspective, the effect is similar to what would be obtained via expansion abroad. However, there are two potentially important differences. First, without specific expansionary policies in place abroad, imposition of capital controls by the United States could push the rest of the world into a deflationary spiral. Second, and perhaps key for some U.S. officials, capital controls would reverse recent U.S. gains in penetrating foreign (especially Japanese) markets for financial services.

10.3 Sectoral Issues

Allegations about Japan's relatively closed markets for industrial products reflect concerns of much longer standing than the aggregate imbalances of recent years. The encroachment of Japanese products into the U.S. market and their displacement of U.S. exports in markets elsewhere is likewise an old story, not a new one. However, emergence of a very large bilateral imbalance has exacerbated those longtime concerns, since the impact of competition with Japan is concentrated in a small number of U.S. manufacturing industries.[14]

Bilateral friction on agricultural trade is also an old story. However, with U.S. global surpluses on agricultural trade shrinking rapidly, one consequence has been renewed focus on the import barriers of Japan, already the largest market for U.S. agricultural exports. Changes in Japan's current policies in support of domestic agriculture, and especially of rice farming, could mean still larger imports of food from the United States. But, like other industrialized nations, Japan has so far found reductions in its expensive agricultural support policies politically unpalatable. Indeed, were the United States to reform its own costly and distortionary policies toward agriculture as it has urged the Japanese to do, any increase in Japanese imports of rice might well come from Thailand or China rather than from the United States.

10.3.1   Are Exports and Imports Separate Issues?

Are the issues raised by Japan's low imports and high exports two separate concerns, or are they linked aspects of a single developmental policy? Some argue that market closure, along with government assistance for generic research and development projects, was an essential element of the Japanese national policy responsible for subsequent export successes in motor vehicles and electronics.[15]

Moreover, as described in the previous section, Japan's overall trade balance is determined largely by macroeconomic influences. Any broad import-inhibiting factors, whether national policy or industrial practice, ought therefore also to inhibit exports. Conversely, any successful move to liberalize imports will likewise promote exports—although this is hardly a result U.S. trade negotiators are likely to stress.[16]

A third link between exports and imports arises from Japan's poor endowment of natural resources. For any given trade balance consistent with macroeconomic conditions, Japan's heavy dependence on imported oil and food means a correspondingly larger surplus on trade in manufactures (or in services—but Japan currently runs a deficit on services trade).[17] Still, the required surplus could be achieved through higher-than-average manufactured exports, as in the case of West Germany, rather than lower-than-average manufactured imports (Lawrence 1987).

Perhaps more important than the direct effect on the composition of Japan's trade flows, perennial dependence on imports of raw materials and food has shaped national attitudes, public and private, toward importing. To many Japanese, their economy's extreme vulnerability to changes in global market conditions, both for raw material imports such as oil and for manufactured exports, casts an omnipresent shadow over today's prosperity.

10.3.2   Japan's Low Import Share

In terms of conventional trade-distorting government practices, Japan was formerly a major offender among industrial nations but now must be counted as one of the most open.[18] Foreign products and services, from IBM to McDonald's, are to be found everywhere. Yet the Japanese ratio of imports to gross national product, and especially of manufactured imports to total imports, remains strikingly low in comparison to other industrial countries. Many of the "foreign" goods now so conspicuous in Japanese daily life are in fact produced domestically by local affiliates or licensees of foreign companies.

Are the low import ratios evidence of subtle trade barriers or simply a reflection of transport costs and an atypical factor endowment? Much of the evidence on Japan's "hidden" barriers to entry is anecdotal (e.g., Rapp 1986; Balassa 1986). While attesting to real frustrations experienced by U.S. producers in their attempts to serve a potentially lucrative market, such anecdotes provide little indication of whether public or private action in Japan differs significantly from that in, say, France. Christopher (1986) goes further, suggesting that while disappointed would-be exporters have clear motives for making their grievances known, successful U.S. exporters and direct investors wisely shun publicity. Kept from the public eye, their successes—and resulting profits—are less likely to promote further entry by competing U.S. producers. If so, anecdotal evidence may be a seriously biased measure of import barriers.

10.3.3 Econometric Evidence

Several researchers have used econometric methods to determine whether Japan's trade structure is basically a reflection of relative costs or has been shaped significantly by hidden but important barriers to imports. Starting from standard models linking trade patterns to national factor endowments and other determinants of relative cost, these researchers examine the deviations of actual trade flows from those predicted by the underlying model.

While based on different specifications, data, and time periods, studies by Saxonhouse (1983, 1985), Bergsten and Cline (1985), and Noland (1987) all found Japanese trade to be adequately explained by the same basic determinants as that of other areas, thus rejecting a major role for import barriers in Japan compared to its trading partners. In contrast, Balassa (1986) found significant shortfalls of Japanese imports relative to values predicted from a model very similar to Bergsten and Cline's. Noland conjectures that the conflicting results reflect differences in the samples and in the definitions of the independent variables but emphasizes that neither set of regressions is derived from a formal model. Deviations of actual from predicted values, ascribed by Balassa to trade policies applied, may simply indicate misspecification of the regression equation.

Noland's own regression equations are derived from an explicit two-sector model incorporating differentiated products and scale economies, an approach motivated by recent developments in the theory of international trade (e.g., Helpman and Krugman 1985). Despite the different theoretical underpinnings, Noland draws basically the same conclusion as Saxonhouse and Bergsten and Cline, that Japanese exports, imports, and total trade "do not appear to be out of the ordinary." But in interpreting his own results as well as those of earlier researchers, Noland emphasizes the need for caution in making any strong inference from the size of residuals, given uncertainty as to specification of the "true model."[19]

Although intended to cast light on the extent of Japan's sectoral barriers to imports, the studies by Bergsten and Cline, Balassa, and Noland all used aggregate trade data, while the one by Saxonhouse employed industry data but focused on net exports rather than imports. To focus directly on sectoral anomalies, Lawrence (1987) used import, export, and production data for twenty-two manufacturing industries. Like Noland, Lawrence adopted a theoretical framework incorporating differentiated products and scale economies. However, while Noland treated manufacturing as a single sector, in the Lawrence model each manufacturing industry produces a separate differentiated product.

The critical step in Lawrence's analysis is the assumption that tastes are similar across countries. With the additional assumption of no transport costs or trade barriers, a country's share in each market will then be proportional to its share in world production and independent of the size of the aggregate trade balance; larger countries will thus be more "closed" as measured by trade flows as a share of GNP. The implied relationship between a country's production and trade in each industry is used by Lawrence to infer the existence of "unusual barriers" to imports at the industry level.

Lawrence's data show that the industrialized countries are remarkably similar in patterns of domestic production and use (consumption plus investment) by industry. Contrary to the conventional wisdom, Japan is not unusual in its overall export performance, although Japan's manufactured exports are highly concentrated in a small number of industries. But Japan is atypical in its low manufactured imports and the very minor extent of intra-industry trade. From his regression analysis of industry trade and production data, Lawrence concludes that "unusual barriers reduce Japanese imports of manufactured goods substantially—by about forty percent." As Lawrence notes, his results are not inconsistent with Noland's finding of no significant anomaly in Japan's aggregate trade. Since manufactured goods were less than a quarter of Japan's total imports in 1980, substantial "underimporting" in some sectors could be masked by the use of aggregate data.

Despite his striking result, Lawrence casts doubt on sectoral trade liberalization as a cure-all for aggregate imbalances, suggesting that the increase in manufactured imports thereby produced would be largely offset by an associated rise in exports. Thus, the main effect would be an expansion of Japan's intra-industry trade, rather than a dramatic reduction in the nation's surplus on trade in manufactured goods. A more basic issue is, as with the earlier studies, the extent to which Japan's import shortfalls from Lawrence's predicted values reflect model misspecification or errors in variables (e.g., transport costs, for which Lawrence used mileage) rather than import barriers.

10.3.4   Lack of Intra-Industry Trade

A somewhat different argument made by Borrus and Zysman (1985) also takes as its starting point Japan's atypically low level of intra-industry trade. Borrus and Zysman point to the virtual absence of two-way trade in specific manufactured products: Japan tends not to import the manufactured goods that it exports.

According to Borrus and Zysman, past protection from imports has allowed Japanese producers to achieve a decisive competitive advantage. Indeed, the resulting advantage is so great that even when import barriers are no longer in place, foreign firms are unable to penetrate the domestic market, while Japanese firms can quickly displace other suppliers in the United States and third-country markets.[20] But Borrus and Zysman supply no evidence that Japan's intra-product and intra-industry trade are systematically depressed in sectors previously protected by import barriers. Although the cases of semiconductors and autos are suggestive, generalization to manufacturing as a whole requires further support.

A more fundamental issue is, as with any post hoc ergo propter hoc argument, the lack of evidence establishing that past protection of the Japanese domestic market from imports played a key role in developing present technological superiority. If a large and profitable market were the main necessary condition for developing a decisive competitive advantage, U.S. automakers, not Japanese, ought to dominate world markets today. That the Japanese experience with import substitution actually ended with internationally competitive production and termination of infant industry protection makes it an exception to the global norm. But if the Japanese experience is so different from what has been observed with import substitution elsewhere, perhaps other Japanese policies, not barriers to imports, were the essential ingredient.

10.4   The U.S. Technology Race with Japan

A persistent technology gap between the United States and other industrialized nations shaped the nation's trade in manufactured goods for several decades after World War II. Over this period, large public and private expenditures on research and development created a continuing flow of new products and processes. Early access to this superior technology allowed U.S. firms to remain internationally competitive despite labor costs far in excess of those abroad. As late as 1980, the U.S. trade position in high-technology manufacturing was still rising almost every year, while net trade in other manufacturing followed an opposite trend.

10.4.1 Closing the Technology Gap

The breakdown of trading relationships based on U.S. technological superiority reflected several major changes in the global economic environment. First, other industrial nations, impressed by U.S. economic gains from technology-driven growth, stepped up their own R&D expenditures. Some of the funds went for basic research, but much was used to speed the acquisition and adaptation of technology from abroad, especially from the United States. At the same time, dramatic improvements in communications and transportation helped to internationalize both research and production activities.

The growth of U.S. multinational corporations served as an important vehicle for the international transfer of new commercial technologies, providing not only access to proprietary technological information but also to the know-how and financial capital needed to implement the new technologies. The technology-disseminating activities of multinationals, while profit motivated, were in many cases actively encouraged by host countries' policies toward direct investments.

The closing of the technology gap between the United States and its commercial rivals meant increased competition on other dimensions of cost. Labor productivity and earnings rose rapidly abroad, while the growth of U.S. earnings slowed. Although the catch-up abroad probably benefited the nation as a whole by raising foreign demand for U.S. goods and services and by opening the possibility of importing as well as exporting new technologies, some U.S. workers clearly lost ground. In a number of U.S. manufacturing industries, real earnings actually fell for the first time in the postwar period as U.S. producers attempted to remain internationally competitive.

10.4.2 Japan's Technological Development

In contrast to most other industrial nations, Japan virtually excluded foreign investments in industries targeted for development during its period of technological catch-up. Instead, it relied primarily on licensing to acquire critical technologies from abroad. Imports of technology were controlled by the Ministry of International Trade and Industry (MITI), which prepared lists of desired technologies and reviewed most licensing proposals.[21] As a supplement to MITI's role as "doorkeeper" to technology imports, the Ministry of Finance ensured access of innovating firms to financial capital.[22]

Some developing countries have modeled their own policies toward imported technologies on those of Japan, particularly screening of licensing agreements and allocation of capital. However, none are in a position to duplicate the commitment of skilled workers that facilitated Japan's success in adapting imported technologies. In 1969, two decades into its catch-up phase, Japan employed about thirty scientists and engineers per ten thousand workers in the labor force, less than half the comparable figure for the United States but similar to the major European nations (*Science and Technology Data Book 1987*, 37–38). Fifteen years later the Japanese proportion of scientists and engineers in the work force had more than doubled, closely approaching the U.S. figure, while the European nations had more modest increases. Japanese spending for research and development (R&D) tells a similar story. Although Japan is only average among industrial nations in its overall proportion of gross national product devoted to R&D, it now enjoys the world's highest ratio of nondefense R&D to GNP.

As with trade in manufactured goods, Japan has in recent years greatly liberalized its policies toward technology imports while rapidly expanding its own technology exports. Japan's "technological balance of payments," recording payments and receipts of royalties and licensing fees for the use of trademarks, copyrights, and patents, still shows a large deficit. However, this is mainly a reflection of agreements made in earlier years during Japan's catch up phase. Japan's gross receipts from technology exports have grown steadily. By 1984 Japan was the third, after the United States and the United Kingdom, in earnings from foreign use of its technology (*Japan 1986*, 26).

Like other technologically advanced nations, Japan has also increased its direct investments abroad, pairing financial capital, superior technology, and managerial know-how with the lower labor costs of developing countries. Current or anticipated import barriers have provided the main motivation for recent Japanese direct investments in the other industrialized nations, but even these investments may entail substantial transfers of technology.[23] For Japanese investments in U.S. high-technology industries, there is likely to be a two-way flow, with the Japanese gaining speedier access to state-of-the-art technical information while themselves disseminating superior methods of management and organization.

10.4.3 Japanese Productivity and Trade

Bilateral comparisons of industry-level productivity and trade performance confirm Japan's catch-up to the technological level of the United States. In their comparison of productivity levels for twenty-eight industries, Jorgenson, Kuroda, and Nishimizu (1987) found that by 1979 nine Japanese industries had already closed the productivity gap with the United States; in the remaining nineteen industries the difference narrowed over the period studied. The analysis indicated that Japan's rising productivity levels were strongly influenced by major increases in the relative capital intensity of production as well as improved technology.

A recent study of U.S.-Japanese trade patterns in 1977 (Audretsch and Yamawaki 1986) found bilateral U.S.-Japanese trade structurally different from trade between the United States and other countries. In contrast to the consistent empirical result that U.S. export strength is greatest in the high-technology industries with relatively large employment of skilled workers, U.S. trade performance in its bilateral trade with Japan was negatively related to the skill level of the U.S. labor force. A possible interpretation of this finding is that at least in trade with Japan, the U.S. technological lead is no longer an important factor; an abundance of skilled workers and a lower wage premium for technical skills can give Japan a cost advantage over the United States in these industries.

However, the experience of Japanese-owned auto plants in the United States has shown that neither massive capital investments nor state-of-the-art technologies are essential ingredients of the Japanese cost advantage. In autos, Japanese producers operating in the United States have achieved lower costs than their indigenous counterparts while typically using less capital per worker and no highly advanced production technology. This raises the possibility that at least in the auto industry, a significant aspect of the Japanese competitive advantage is "technological" only in a very broad sense that includes organizational and managerial know-how.

But recent findings of Lipsey and Kravis (1986) suggest that Japan's advantage in auto production may not be typical. In terms of overall manufacturing exports, Lipsey and Kravis found that U.S. multinational corporations have maintained a virtually unchanged share of world totals since 1966; declining exports from U.S. production have been offset by rising exports from subsidiaries abroad. These results imply that loss of U.S. international competitiveness in manufacturing as a whole cannot be attributed to deficiencies in U.S. management skills or technology. However, in the case of transport equipment, the United States did lose substantial ground; by 1983, both the United States as a country and U.S. multinationals had lost about a quarter of their 1966 global market shares.[24]

10.5 Looking Ahead

Japan's rapid growth during much of the postwar period has been based on technological catch-up. The slowing of that growth in recent years reflects, among other things, the completion of the catch-up phase.

Can the Japanese policies and institutions that facilitated successful importation and adaptation of existing technologies work as well in producing new ones? Some claim that the Japanese educational system, in comparison to its U.S. counterpart, ensures a uniformly high standard of performance but systematically crushes individuality and creativity. However, it is too early to judge whether these differences have any implications for scientific innovation, and in any case both systems are in the throes of significant change. The increasing economic intimacy between the two nations has itself served as one major impetus for change.

I have argued that the rapidly growing bilateral imbalances between the United States and Japan were produced by macroeconomic conditions, not trade or industrial policies. In this sense, the imbalances can be viewed as "temporary" factors rather than long-term developments. But elimination of the imbalances without serious damage to the U.S. economy and those of its trading partners may be difficult to achieve. If Japanese investors turn away from U.S. financial markets before the United States is able to reduce domestic absorption, U.S. interest rates will be forced upward, with potentially disastrous consequences for the economy.

In terms of sectoral adjustments, the U.S.-Japanese relationship may well be entering a new phase. As the nations grow more similar in terms of technology base, abundance of capital and skilled labor, and per capita income, intra-industry trade is likely to grow. In particular, two-way trade in technology and in technology-based services should become increasingly important as Japan moves from adaptation into innovation. In the mature industries and even in some that are now considered "high-technology" sectors, both Japan and the United States will be faced with increasing competition from a new tier of competitors in Asia and elsewhere.

For both nations, problems of sectoral adjustment will continue to generate strong pressures for import protection and other forms of assistance to industries losing ground to newcomers. Sectoral trade conflict between the United States and Japan will be concentrated on the two ends of the industrial spectrum in terms of technological sophistication, with issues raised both by contrasting approaches to the phasing out of industries losing their comparative advantage and by contrasting approaches to the nurturing of new industries.

Could the United States return to its one-time position of unquestioned technological preeminence? Even with vastly increased resources allocated to research and development, this kind of advantage probably can no longer be sustained—by the United States or any country—in a world that has become highly interdependent. The commercial advantage of being first in innovation has been undermined by the greatly increased speed with which new technical knowledge becomes available to potential competitors all over the globe. This does not mean that research and development have become less important. On the contrary, technological improvements will continue to provide the basis for a rising standard of living both in the United States and abroad. However, the benefits of R&D efforts can no longer be counted mainly in terms of the advantages conferred to one nation's industries over competitors elsewhere.

Notes

1. In August 1987, National Semiconductor Corporation announced that it would buy Fairchild—at what industry analysts described as a bargain price, far less than that offered earlier by Fujitsu. National was one of several U.S. companies that opposed the sale to Fujitsu.

2. For a summary of the practical difficulties in using trade policy "strategically" to promote national advantage, see Richardson 1986.

3. See McCulloch and Richardson 1986, 61–64. Although protectionist measures are traditionally condemned as beggar-thy-neighbor policies, in reality they often turn out to be beggar-thy-brother policies, impairing performance of other industries in the same country. This is an important distinction for public servants, who seem relatively unconcerned about costs inflicted outside the nation's (or even the congressional district's) borders. For some examples of undercutting indirect effects of trade restrictions, see Baldwin 1982.

4. An opposite argument is sometimes made by analysts concerned about deindustrialization of the U.S. economy. They believe that foreign targeting of basic and high-technology manufacturing industries reduces U.S. employment opportunities in "high-value-added" activities. But high value added per worker may simply reflect firms' optimizing responses to strong unions, rather than a technological characteristic of the industry. It is far from obvious that national policy ought to bolster the resulting wage advantage by limiting imports. In the case of steel, probably the industry most frequently targeted worldwide, employment in the United States and other industrialized countries has dropped dramatically while wages remain well above the U.S. average for comparable skills and experience.

5. Moreover, even the existence of a real distortion does not assure that "corrective" policies will actually make things better rather than worse. Examples such as textiles and apparel, steel, autos, and semiconductors suggest that cartelization, not active competition based on comparative advantage, is the likely outcome of sectoral policy initiatives.

6. Relative to gross national product, the Canadian surplus on trade with the United States actually exceeds Japan's. But in early 1987, Canadian government statisticians showed that U.S. recording procedures have systematically missed certain U.S. exports, particularly those transported by truck into Canada. U.S. statistics have thus overstated the U.S. merchandise trade deficit and particularly the bilateral deficit with Canada.

7. McCulloch 1985 and McCulloch and Richardson 1986 examine in detail the types of policies usually recommended to restore U.S. competitiveness

and evaluate their likely effects (or lack of effects) on the nation's overall trade balance or current account.

8. On supply-side hysteresis effects arising from economies of scale and sunk costs, see Baldwin 1986.

9. See Frankel 1984 for a review of this agreement. The agreement was promoted as a means to raise the value of the yen by increasing its role as a reserve currency. However, the predictable short-run result, borne out by subsequent events, was just the opposite.

10. The assumption that net capital inflows are independent of current earnings on past investments is, however, suspect. Tax law in the United States and some other nations tends to favor reinvestment abroad of current earnings from foreign investments. Other governmental policies toward international capital transactions may also link the rate of new investment to current interest and profits.

11. An ongoing debate concerns the relative effects of tax-financed and bond-financed government expenditures. The issues are complex, hinging on such imponderables as the public's anticipation of future changes in tax rates. An extreme view is that, because of public anticipation of future tax liability, bond-financed spending has the same overall effect on today's absorption as tax-financed spending.

12. Saxonhouse 1985 characterizes the Japanese as "notorious target savers," with future housing a main target. This is a critical point, since increased spending in any one category does not necessarily translate into higher overall spending (lower saving). Saxonhouse also notes a possible bonus from increased housing expenditures for other spending: more living space may lift a major constraint on purchases of consumer durables.

13. This has been proposed in recent years by James Tobin and Rudiger Dornbusch, among others. See Dornbusch and Frankel 1987.

14. Conversely, a return to a more "normal" pattern of global capital flows should reduce sectoral frictions. Krugman 1986 and Petri 1987 use this logic to anticipate some reversal of recent competitive pressures on U.S. industry. Based on simulation analysis, Petri concludes that output structures in the United States and Japan could become quite similar by the 1990s.

15. For example, this argument is made by Borrus, Tyson, and Zysman (1987) for the case of the semiconductor industry.

16. If sectoral liberalization does reduce aggregate Japanese savings, as suggested by Rapp 1986 and Balassa 1986, the induced rise in Japanese exports would not fully offset the rise in imports.

17. Krugman 1986 links the "Japan problem" of rapid growth of manufactured exports to the United States to large increases in world oil prices from 1973 until 1984. His analysis suggests that lower oil prices will translate into a higher value of the yen and slower growth of Japanese manufactured exports.

18. Komiya and Itoh 1986 provides a detailed account of the gradual liberalization of Japanese imports. Saxonhouse 1983 and 1985 document the minor importance currently of conventional instruments of protection. Ahearn 1985 divides current Japanese import barriers into four categories: formal, regulatory, strategic, and business and cultural. He concludes that the most onerous remaining barriers to manufactured imports are in the last category, where Japanese public policy has relatively little direct impact.

19. Leamer 1984 gives a more comprehensive discussion of both specification issues and data problems associated with empirically relating resource endowments to trade patterns, also emphasizing the problem of sensitivity. While he

acknowledges the probable importance of scale economies, for practical reasons his own specification is based on a model with constant returns. Leamer does not focus on the existence of significant distortions but concludes from his analysis that resource endowments provide a "surprisingly good" explanation of the trade data.

20. Although Lawrence's data support the contention that Japanese intra-industry trade in manufactured goods is unusually low, he attributes this finding to remaining current barriers to imports, not technological advantages resulting from past protection.

21. Harris 1985 gives a comprehensive review of past and current Japanese policies toward international technology transfers.

22. Yamamura 1986 suggests that the role of the Ministry of Finance (MOF) was perhaps the most essential element of Japan's progrowth policy in this period. Given the underdeveloped state of Japanese domestic capital markets, their insulation from world financial markets, and regulated below-market-clearing interest rates on loans, MOF exercised enormous economic leverage over domestic firms as a consequence of its ability to allocate loans in a situation of chronic excess demand.

23. Bhagwati 1982 has pointed out that some direct foreign investments may be used in heading off new protection rather than in anticipation of producing inside the restricted market.

24. The atypical performance of the auto industry relative to U.S. manufacturing as a whole points up the danger in generalizing from the experience of a single sector, even a very important one, as Halberstam 1986 does in comparing Ford and Nissan.

References

Ahearn, Raymond J. 1985. Market access in Japan: The U.S. experience. In *Japan's economy and trade with the United States*. Washington, D.C.: Joint Economic Committee of the U.S. Congress.

Audretsch, David B., and Hideki Yamawaki. 1986. Industrial policy, R&D, and U.S.-Japanese trade. Wissenschaftszentrum Berlin für Sozialforschung. April.

Balassa, Bela. 1986. Japan's trade policies. *Weltwirtschaftliches Archiv* (December): 745–90.

Baldwin, Richard E. 1986. Hysteresis in trade. Massachusetts Institute of Technology. July.

Baldwin, Robert E. 1982. The inefficacy of trade policy. *Essays in International Finance*, no. 150. International Finance Section, Department of Economics, Princeton University.

Bergsten, C. Fred, and William R. Cline. 1985. *The United States–Japan economic problem*. Washington, D.C.: Institute for International Economics.

Bhagwati, Jagdish N. 1982. Shifting comparative advantage, protectionist demands, and policy response. In Jagdish N. Bhagwati, ed., *Import competition and response*. Chicago: University of Chicago Press.

Borrus, Michael, Laura D'Andrea Tyson, and John Zysman. 1987. Creating advantage: How government policies shape international trade in the semiconductor industry. In Paul R. Krugman, ed., *Strategic trade policy and the new international economics*. Cambridge: MIT Press.

Borrus, Michael, and John Zysman. 1985. Japan's industrial policy and its patterns of trade. In *Japan's economy and trade with the United States*. Washington, D.C.: Joint Economic Committee of the U.S. Congress.

Christopher, Robert C. 1986. *Second to none: American companies in Japan*. New York: Crown.

Dornbusch, Rudiger, and Jeffrey A. Frankel. 1987. Macroeconomics and protection. In Robert M. Stern, ed., *U.S. trade policies in a changing world economy*. Cambridge: MIT Press.

Frankel, Jeffrey A. 1984. *The yen/dollar agreement: Liberalizing Japanese capital markets*. Washington, D.C.: Institute for International Economics. December.

Halberstam, David. 1986. *The reckoning*. New York: William Morrow.

Harris, Martha Caldwell. 1985. Japan's international technology transfers. In *Japan's economy and trade with the United States*. Washington, D.C.: Joint Economic Committee of the U.S. Congress.

Helpman, Elhanan, and Paul R. Krugman. 1985. *Market structure and foreign trade*. Cambridge: MIT Press.

Japan 1986: An international comparison. 1986. Tokyo: Keizai Koho Center.

Johnson, Chalmers. 1982. *MITI and the Japanese miracle*. Stanford, Calif.: Stanford University Press.

Jorgenson, Dale W., Masahiro Kuroda, and Mieko Nishimizu. 1987. Japan-U.S. industry-level productivity comparisons, 1960–1979. *Journal of the Japanese and International Economies* 1:1–30.

Komiya, Ryutaro, and Motoshige Itoh. 1986. International trade and trade policy of Japan, 1955–1984. Discussion paper 85-F-16. Research Institute for the Japanese Economy, University of Tokyo.

Krause, Lawrence B. 1985. Statement before the Subcommittee on Asian and Pacific Affairs. Committee on Foreign Affairs, U.S. House of Representatives. May 9.

Krugman, Paul. 1986. Is the Japan problem over? National Bureau of Economic Research Working Paper No. 1962.

Lawrence, Robert Z. 1987. Does Japan import too little? Closed markets or minds? Paper prepared for the Brookings Panel on Economics Activity.

Leamer, Edward E. 1984. *Sources of international comparative advantage*. Cambridge: MIT Press.

Lipsey, Robert E., and Irving B. Kravis. 1986. The competitiveness and comparative advantage of U.S. multinationals, 1957–1983. National Bureau of Economic Research Working Paper No. 2051.

McCulloch, Rachel. 1985. Trade deficits, industrial competitiveness, and the Japanese. *California Management Review* (Winter): 140–56.

McCulloch, Rachel, and J. David Richardson. 1986. U.S. trade and the dollar: Evaluating current policy options. In Robert E. Baldwin and J. David Richardson, eds., *Current U.S. trade policy: Analysis, agenda, and administration*. Cambridge: National Bureau of Economic Research.

Noland, Marcus. 1987. An econometric model of the volume of international trade. Institute for International Economics.

Petri, Peter A. 1987. Looking beyond the current account: World capital and trade flows in the intermediate term. Paper prepared for the Ministry of Trade and Industry's International Conference on Economic Structure and Trade Problems, Tokyo. January 28–29.

Rapp, William V. 1986. Japan's invisible barriers to trade. In Thomas A. Pugel, ed., *Fragile interdependence: Economic issues in U.S.-Japanese trade and investment*. Lexington, Mass.: Lexington Books.

Richardson, J. David. 1986. The new political economy of trade policy. In Paul R. Krugman, ed., *Strategic trade policy and the new international economics*. Cambridge: MIT Press.

Saxonhouse, Gary R. 1983. The micro- and macroeconomics of foreign sales to Japan. In William R. Cline, ed., *Trade policy for the 1980s*. Cambridge: MIT Press.

————. 1985. What's wrong with Japanese trade structure. Seminar discussion paper no. 166. Research Seminar in International Economics, University of Michigan.

Science and technology data book 1987. 1986. National Science Foundation 86–311. Washington, D.C.

Yamamura, Kozo. 1986. Caveat emptor: The industrial policy of Japan. In Paul R. Krugman, ed., *Strategic trade policy and the new international economics*. Cambridge: MIT Press.

Comment   Robert W. Staiger

Rachel McCulloch's chapter on the state of United States–Japan economic relations provides an excellent synthesis of an important and complex relationship, a synthesis from which I learned a great deal and can add very little. While covering both aggregate and sectoral sources of friction between the two countries, McCulloch is careful to keep these two broad issues separate. This is important for two reasons. First, the current high degree of friction between Japan and the United States stems predominantly from an aggregate imbalance, and may therefore be expected to decline in large part as the aggregate imbalance declines. Second, from the perspective of policy design, it is important to address the aggregate imbalance with aggregate policies that affect national absorption and/or income, reserving the use of sectoral policies for the pursuit of sectoral goals. But I would like to suggest several reasons why it may be appropriate in the midst of large aggregate imbalances for there to be heightened U.S. interest in the sectoral aspects of the United States–Japan relationship, though this attention should not be viewed as a way to address the aggregate issues, and why now may be a good time to take a hard look at both the sectoral policies of these countries and the importance for each country of the sectoral composition of its productive activity.

The first reason concerns the effect of the large U.S. trade deficit on the bargaining position of the United States with regard to tariff and nontariff barriers in Japan. The political pressure in the United States for protection has grown with the size of the U.S. trade deficit, making

Robert W. Staiger is assistant professor of economics at Stanford University.

credible the promise of protectionist measures if the United States cannot come to an agreement with its trading partners on the rules for a free and fair trading environment. This increased credibility augments the ability of the United States to gain trade concessions in the form of more open international markets, and ought to heighten the interest in identifying and determining the importance of existing trade barriers. Of course, there is no guarantee that this change in bargaining power will lead to more open trade: it is perhaps more likely that VERs and other forms of managed trade will be the result. Nonetheless, the link between aggregate and sectoral issues is likely to be strong, and for this reason renewed focus on just what sectoral barriers to trade remain seems appropriate.

The second reason concerns the permanence of the changes in the sectoral composition of production in Japan and the United States that have come about as a result of the temporary aggregate imbalance. It is quite possible that the sectoral makeup of U.S. production will be substantially altered long after the close of the "introductory sale" of many foreign products in U.S. markets brought on by the great real appreciation of the dollar in the first half of the 1980s. If these sectoral changes do prove to be permanent, then whether the United States (or any other country) should be concerned with the sectoral composition of its productive activity takes on an added importance whenever an aggregate imbalance arises.

In short, whether and to what extent Japan distorts its trade patterns seems especially relevant now, not because the elimination of those distortions will have a predictable effect on Japan's aggregate imbalance, but because Japan's aggregate imbalance with the United States should strengthen the U.S. bargaining position with regard to sectoral issues. And whether the United States should be concerned about the sectoral composition of its production should be a question of intense interest now, since the current U.S. trade deficit is likely to have an impact on the sectoral makeup of production in the United States long after the aggregate imbalance subsides.

Japan's Distorting Policies

Though anecdotal evidence abounds concerning the alleged height of Japan's trade barriers, quantitative support for this claim is harder to come by. Indeed, with one exception, the econometric studies reviewed by McCulloch reject the notion that the trade patterns of Japan are more distorted than those of other countries. These studies avoid attempts to actually measure existing trade barriers, choosing instead to infer the existence of trade restrictions from the unexplained portion of standard trade equations applied to the trade of various countries. For example, Saxonhouse (1983), pooling data for 109 commodities across countries and time, relates each country's trade flows to its factor endowments and looks for country-specific fixed effects in each commodity equation. His econometric evidence suggests a relatively minor role for Japan-specific fixed effects, a result interpreted as indicating the absence of uncommonly high barriers to trade in Japan.

While such studies are certainly useful, their interpretation becomes more clouded if a country's trade barriers are thought to be related to its factor endowments (as in, for example, Magee and Young 1987). If this is the case, much of the effect of trade barriers may already be captured in the equation's coefficients on factor endowments, and testing for an additional country-specific fixed effects may yield little in the way of information on uncommonly high trade restrictions. This is not to say that these studies are not valuable, but I would have more confidence in their conclusions if other approaches to analyzing relative distortions yielded broadly similar results.

Having said this, I mention briefly the results of a project undertaken by Alan Deardorff, Robert Stern, and myself on the distortions introduced by Japanese tariff and nontariff barriers (see Staiger, Deardorff, and Stern 1987). We estimated the distortionary effects of existing tariff and nontariff barriers in Japan and in the United States by simulating trade flows in the absence of trade barriers using the Michigan Computational Model of World Production and Trade. Several available estimates of existing trade restrictions in Japan and the United States were used alternatively in an attempt to acknowledge the inevitable inaccuracy of any one measure, and the results reported below were robust to these various measures. Taking the simulated changes in trade patterns that would arise if existing protection were dropped, we calculated the factor content of these changes and provided a theoretical argument for why relative changes in the factor content of trade should be related to changes in relative factor prices. Our results, then, concern the distortions in relative factor prices brought about by Japanese policy as compared to the distortions associated with U.S. policy, and can be summarized in three points:

- Comparing the effects of each country's trade policy on its own factor markets, Japanese policy is more distortionary than U.S. policy.
- Comparing the effects of each country's trade policy country by country, Japanese policy is again more distortionary than U.S. policy. In particular, Japanese tariff and nontariff barriers distort U.S. factor markets to a larger degree than do the trade policies of the United States itself.
- In Japan, farm workers are the biggest relative gainers from existing protection, while in the United States, operatives and craftsmen are

the biggest relative gainers, and farmers the biggest relative losers, from existing protection.

These results support the conclusion that Japan's trade policy may indeed have uncommonly high distortionary effects on U.S. factor markets, and that the United States–Japan sectoral issues may be a legitimate source of friction. But equally important is the point that, according to our results, Japanese trade policy actually has a favorable effect on workers in the U.S. manufacturing sector relative to other factors in the U.S. economy: as such, the recent decline in the U.S. manufacturing sector relative to other sectors is not attributable to the tariff and nontariff policies of Japan.

Sectoral Composition of Production

The concern over changes in the composition of U.S. production that have come about as the world becomes more integrated has often, though not exclusively, focused on the effects of Japanese policy in contributing to these changes. Such concerns have generated a great deal of scholarly interest in whether a country can gain by having, or having more of, a certain sector operating within its borders. As McCulloch points out, while theory raises this possibility, no clear evidence exists on whether such concerns are in fact well founded. Yet the answer to this question takes on an added importance now if, as seems likely, many of the changes in sectoral market share brought about by the large U.S. trade imbalance will persist long into the future. This brings up the important question, noted by McCulloch, of whether the United States is too cautious in its pursuit of trade policy, and the possibility that by waiting for "clear evidence," further delays in reversing present trends may leave the United States at a permanent disadvantage.

Here I suggest that the United States would not be overly cautious in continuing to wait for further and better evidence before pursuing activist trade policies to affect the sectoral composition of U.S. output. While the recent trade/IO results have shown under a variety of circumstances that activist trade policies can in principle raise national welfare from its free trade level, they have also demonstrated how carefully such policies must be designed: the form of welfare-improving intervention will hinge on the characteristics of the industry considered, and trade policy must be determined on a case by case basis. Unfortunately, the kind of discretion and flexibility with which an institution pursuing such trade policies must be endowed is likely to undermine its ability to augment national welfare, both because of the institution's heightened risk of becoming the servant of special interest groups, and because of its likely inability to credibly pursue the optimal trade policies that rationalize its existence. As such, even if there exist good reasons to be concerned about the changes in sectoral composition of national output brought about by the U.S. trade imbalance, it is not at all clear what, if anything, should be done.

References

Magee, S. P., and L. Young. 1987. Endogenous protection in the United States, 1900–1984. In R. M. Stern, ed., *U.S. trade policies in a changing world economy*. Cambridge, Mass.: MIT Press.
Saxonhouse, G. R. 1983. The micro- and macroeconomics of foreign sales to Japan. In W. R. Cline, ed., *Trade policy in the 1980s*. Cambridge, Mass.: MIT Press.
Staiger, R. W., A. V. Deardorff, and R. M. Stern. 1988. The effects of protection on the factor content of Japanese and American foreign trade. *Review of Economics and Statistics*. Forthcoming.

Comment   Peter A. Petri

Rachel McCulloch's treatment of the "Japan problem" is comprehensive, balanced, and analytically rigorous—a welcome addition to the growing and often frustrating body of literature in this area. Refreshingly, the chapter has no ax to grind—say, against recalcitrant Japanese bureaucrats or impotent American exporters—and no simple solutions to offer. The present crisis is attributed to macroeconomic forces, and in particular to the U.S. tax cut and the decline in the rate of investment in Japan. There is no promise of an early resolution, since the underlying macroeconomic imbalances call for difficult-to-swing changes in the levels of absorption in the United States and Japan.

Since this conference brings together sophisticated trade specialists, it is appropriate that the chapter begins by asking Is there really a Japan problem? McCulloch never explicitly answers this question, but the reader is left with the impression that there is no *economic* problem, in the sense that economic events are roughly in line with the (sometimes ex post) predictions of theory. In turn, the root of the *political* problem—the large U.S. bilateral deficit—is the result of temporary macroeconomic forces rather than other potential factors such as technological rivalry, nontariff barriers, or cultural differences. Even with the caveats surrounding the required macroeconomic adjustments, this is an optimistic message: after a few years of macroeconomic adjust-

Peter A. Petri is associate professor of economics at Brandeis University.

ments, Japan-bashing may become nothing more than an unpleasant memory.

Unfortunately, the opposite case is also reasonable. United States–Japan trade may always tend to be politicized—creating continuing friction that tends to flash into crisis in the appropriate macroeconomic context. This more pessimistic view rests on the argument that certain characteristics of the United States–Japan economic relationship make it unusually prone to political intervention, regardless of the economic logic of actual trade and capital flows. Thus, there is a *political economy* Japan problem—a persistent, undesirable interaction between economic variables and political behavior. The economic structure of the relationship just does not seem conducive to political peace and leads to chronic pressure for government management of bilateral trade.

Since McCulloch's chapter concentrates on purely economic issues, it is perhaps useful to focus these comments explicitly on the political economy perspective. Why is there so much conflict between the United States and Japan when in fact the United States runs a larger trade deficit (relative to GNP) with Canada and several other countries? Why was there sharp conflict as early as the late 1960s, well before the spectacular macroeconomic imbalances of the 1980s? Why is such a large proportion of bilateral trade (in textiles, steel, automobiles, chemicals, and semiconductors) managed by either one or both governments? The answers to these questions must be sought in the scale and structure of United States–Japan trade.

To begin with, the bilateral trading relationship is inherently imbalanced. The United States has run a bilateral trade deficit with Japan since 1965, and the ratio of U.S. exports to Japan to U.S. imports from Japan was already below .6 in the early 1970s. The export/import ratio hovered in the .5–.6 range until 1983, when it began a decline toward today's 0.32. Detailed analysis of the specialization patterns of the two countries (e.g., Petri 1984, chap. 5) suggests that a substantial U.S. bilateral deficit would emerge even when both countries' overall trade is balanced. There is nothing surprising or even significant about a bilateral deficit—except for its political economy implications.

A large bilateral deficit tends to tip political scales toward bilateral protection. In the case of balanced trade, the weight of intense protectionist interests (import-competing producers) is counterbalanced by that of intense trading interests (export producers) and to a lesser extent by that of diffuse trading interests (consumers). In the case of highly imbalanced trade, however, the absence of intense trading interests (the exporters' lobby) leaves the overall political balance vulnerable to protection. At present, domestic producer support for free bilateral trade is very thin and is not adequately replaced by direct Japanese lobbying efforts. (Incidentally, the declining importance of exports in *overall* U.S. trade has also contributed to a general increase in protectionist pressures.)

Imbalanced trade not only makes protection more likely, but also less risky. With imbalanced trade, the deficit country has the advantage of an asymmetric threat. In principle, U.S. discriminatory trade action against Japan could be subject to multilateral retaliation under GATT rules. In practice this is extremely unlikely, and U.S. policymakers will seldom look beyond Japan's relatively modest direct counterthreats.

Other structural features of United States–Japan trade exacerbate the problem. U.S. imports from Japan are dominated by politically important industries such as automobiles and semiconductors, and earlier, textiles and steel; research on the determinants of protection has shown that these large, concentrated industries are more apt to win protection than smaller, more competitive industries such as footwear (Lavergne 1983). In addition, the sectoral impact of imports from Japan is unusually intense because of their scale and high product concentration.

Finally, imports from Japan are more visible and protection-prone than other imports because they often consist of products that the United States did not previously import or perhaps even exported. In this context, Japanese exports displace primarily U.S. products rather than the products of other exporters and raise troubling implications for long-term competitiveness. Often, the industries affected have (or are thought to have) steep learning curves and concentrated global markets. Thus, requests for trade action against Japan are increasingly based on long-term strategic grounds—along lines that are now also attracting theoretical support from the industrial organization approach to trade policy.

There is no doubt that trade conflict will moderate if and when the present macroeconomic imbalances diminish. But some of the factors cited will continue to operate, and I suspect it is too early to declare the Japan problem dead. For the foreseeable future, governments are likely to remain deeply involved in managing this major bilateral trade flow.

Let me conclude with some observations about the macroeconomics. The prospects for an early reduction of current account imbalances may be better than argued in the chapter. *In Japan,* the decline in domestic investment rates is largely over, while savings rates are continuing to fall. The boom in Japanese asset prices has created a great deal of new wealth, especially when evaluated in foreign prices. Consumption levels are beginning to adjust to this new equation, as evidenced by burgeoning sales of German luxury cars, Korean knitwear, and U.S. vacations. *In the U.S.,* it is customary for new administrations to adopt fiscally conservative policies early in their term, and some fiscal tightening is likely in 1989. Private spending reductions could also follow; households and firms have been accumulating debt for several years now in an unusually favorable interest rate environment. Indeed, recent exchange rate changes suggest that investors are already anticipating a partial reversal of present capital flows.[1]

The trade effects of these macroeconomic adjustments are complex and interesting. It is possible, as I have argued elsewhere, that over the next few years the Japanese market will become the leading absorber of the growth of world trade, much as the U.S. market absorbed such growth in the early 1980s. Even this does not necessarily mean dramatically higher imports from the United States: Japan's most rapidly growing imports now are labor-intensive manufactures from East Asia and luxury goods from Europe. It is also possible, however, that U.S. imports will stop growing without compensating import growth from any other country. This is the scenario for global recession.

In either case, as Japanese firms accelerate their efforts to replace lost markets, they will compete aggressively with U.S. firms in sophisticated machinery, electronics, and services. In the end, the United States and Japan are close competitors in production with similar tastes in demand—a combination that simultaneously breeds vigorous trade and keen conflict.

References

Lavergne, Real. 1983. *The political economy of U.S. tariffs.* New York: Academic Press.

Petri, P. A. 1984. *Modeling Japanese-American trade: A study of asymmetric interdependence.* Cambridge: Harvard University Press.

1. One interpretation of the decline in the dollar and the rise of the yen is that investors' willingness to invest in U.S. assets has already sharply declined. This is not inconsistent with the fact that foreigners continue to finance an essentially unchanged (as of mid-1987) U.S. current account deficit. For the most part, the financing is now coming from official sources. But even private investors will provide capital if they believe that the dollar exchange rate is now so low that it can be expected to appreciate (or at least not fall further) as the trade adjustments proceed.

11   The Political Economy of Protectionism: Tariffs and Retaliation in the Timber Industry

Joseph P. Kalt

11.1   Introduction

11.1.1   A Brief Military History

The United States is in the middle of a trade war—or at least a skirmish—with its largest trading partner and one of its closest allies. The most important battle of this conflict is being fought over lumber. The first confrontation came in June 1986 when President Reagan imposed ad valorem duties of up to 35 percent on imports of wooden shakes and shingles, which are primarily supplied by Canada.[1] The Canadians retaliated almost immediately with duties on a hodgepodge of imports from the United States, including Christmas trees, computers, semiconductors, and books.

The shakes and shingles industry is relatively small, with annual U.S. sales of only $80 million and Canadian imports of $50 million per year. On October 16, 1986, however, the U.S. Department of Commerce issued a preliminary finding that Canada was subsidizing its softwood (construction) lumber imports at the rate of 15 percent of their value. This finding followed an initial determination by the International Trade Commission (ITC) that U.S. lumber producers were being materially harmed by Canadian imports. This set the stage for the United States to impose a 15 percent countervailing duty on issuance of a final Commerce Department finding of subsidy (due December 30) and a final ITC determination of material injury (due by February 1987). Pending these expected final determinations, importers

Joseph P. Kalt is professor of political economy at the Kennedy School of Government, Harvard University.

of Canadian lumber were required to post bonds equivalent to 15 percent of the value of their shipments (subject to refund should the United
States eventually drop its countervailing duty action).

The softwood lumber industry is important to both countries. Sales
in the United States total approximately $10 billion per year, and Ca-
nadian imports amount to $3 billion per year. In Canada, softwood
lumber is a $5 billion per year industry and is larger than metals,
agriculture, fisheries, and autos combined. Lumber accounts for approximately 4 percent of both Canadian GNP and Canadian exports
to the United States. Canadian imports hold roughly 30 percent of the
U.S. market and provide over 99 percent of the foreign lumber supplied
to the United States.

A week prior to the October 16 announcement of the U.S. softwood
lumber decision, Canada's minister for international trade had called
U.S. producers' lobbying for tariff protection "total harassment" and
explicitly warned of retaliation.[2] On November 7, with support from
liberals and conservatives in Parliament, the Canadian government imposed a 67 percent countervailing duty on U.S. corn exports to Canada.
Within two weeks, as tensions over the U.S. lumber duty mounted,
the U.S. secretary of state (then embroiled in the Iran-Contra scandal)
was in Ottawa attempting to find grounds for U.S. backtracking on the
lumber duty. With the 15 percent U.S. duty scheduled to become permanent on December 30, Canadian and U.S. negotiators reached an
agreement on December 31 that implemented a 15 percent Canadian
export duty in exchange for the U.S. lumber industry dropping its duty
action. As of 1987, the corn retaliation remained in place.

In terms of the size of the import sector and the anticipated domestic
price effects, the U.S. lumber duty was the largest countervailing/
antidumping action that the country has ever taken against a specific
trading partner under the terms of GATT. The Canadian corn retaliation
represented the first countervailing duty ever imposed on the United
States and one of the few times Canada has imposed such a duty on
any nation. Within Canada, the eventual lumber export tax has been
assailed by the timber industry as "bizarre" and "sickening,"[3] and
opposition parties had urged the Mulroney government to reject any
negotiated settlement and to mount its opposition to U.S. protectionist
measures through U.S. and international judicial proceedings. The negotiated settlement, they argue, puts Canada in a defensive posture
and establishes precedents that leave "any major Canadian export . . .
subject to this kind of action by the United States."[4] The Mulroney
government, meanwhile, defends itself on the grounds that U.S. domestic political pressures could not possibly have been deflected by
Canada, and that it is better that Canada collect the revenues from a
lumber duty than have the revenues flow to the United States. But

even Canada's trade minister laments that "today it's lumber—tomorrow it could be any number of issues. This is not the way to conduct business between the world's largest trading partners. There must be a better way."[5]

Interestingly, the timber trade war is taking place in the middle of high-level negotiations aimed at reaching a general free trade arrangement between the United States and Canada. The future and direction of the free trade negotiations, however, have been threatened by the lumber controversies. Public support in Canada for an agreement has declined markedly over the last year, as opinion polls show rising distrust of U.S. motives and promises, declining faith in the abilities of Canadian negotiators, and a general waning of the faith that free trade will improve the Canadian economy. In the face of these sentiments, even Prime Minister Mulroney has noted (specifically within the context of the lumber affair) that it is "extremely difficult for anyone, including Canadians, to be friends with the Americans."[6]

11.1.2   Can the United States Win a Trade War?

It goes without saying that there is much concern or hope, depending on one's viewpoint, that protectionist "sentiments" are on the rise in the United States and that a major change in the direction of U.S. trade policy may be in the offing. I suspect that among economists the protectionist trends afoot are viewed with apprehension. New theoretical developments and a certain amount of playing to the public's heightened nationalistic predilections may have softened the profession's traditional, if not downright doctrinaire, preaching of free trade, but most economists appear to continue to worry that protection that leads to cycles of confrontation and retaliation is nationally and globally harmful.

The U.S.-Canadian rift over lumber trade provides a potentially revealing example of one of the paths that the nascent changes in trade policy can take. On the face of it, the circumstances of the timber trade war do not appear extraordinary. The U.S. industry has been in the employment and output doldrums for a number of years; prospects for sharp improvement are not particularly encouraging; and import market shares have been on the rise. On the Canadian side, the lumber industry is an important industry in the economy—overwhelming, in fact, to certain regions of the country. It is unrealistic to think that Canada would not respond in some substantive way to attempts to limit its access to export markets.

The political origins and economic consequences of the timber trade war are the focus of this study. The former appear to lie in a combination of a well-organized and forceful group of beneficiaries (that is, U.S. lumber producers) and a serendipitous timing of congressional pressures on the White House. The outcome, to date, of the timber trade war has, indeed, been an improvement in the lot of domestic producers, as they have realized a rise in the price of lumber. From the broader perspective of nationalistic aggregate welfare, the United States appears to have started, but ultimately lost, the war. What began as a large-country, monopsony tariff directed against Canada has become a large-country, monopoly tariff directed against the United States.

11.2   The U.S. Countervailing Duty Decision

U.S. restrictive action against the importation of softwood lumber from Canada originated with a 1982 petition to the Department of Commerce and the International Trade Commission. This petition was filed by the Coalition for Fair Lumber Imports (CFLI), a lobbying association of 350 U.S. forest products companies and each of the eight major lumber and timber trade associations. The Coalition requested that the United States impose countervailing duties against Canadian softwood imports under the terms of the (amended) Tariff Act of 1930. The Coalition argued that countervailing duties were warranted because Canadian federal and provincial governments were subsidizing the production of softwood lumber, and subsidized production was materially injuring U.S. lumber producers.

The 1982 case ended in May 1983 when the Department of Commerce failed to rule in favor of the U.S. lumber industry. In essence, the Commerce Department found that there was ample evidence that Canadian governmental policy was subsidizing lumber production through below-market pricing of trees sold by public forest authorities, but that these subsidies were "generally available" and not specifically targeted at lumber producers. In the view of the Department of Commerce, this lack of specificity disqualified the Canadian subsidies as actionable under the countervailing duties provisions of the 1930 Tariff Act.

A reading of the record of the 1982 case leaves the very strong impression that the Commerce Department (or, more realistically, the White House) was squirming to find a technicality under which it could reject the Coalition's petition. Under the "general availability" criterion, the Commerce Department found that below-market-price trees were available to a number of parties beyond construction lumber producers, including manufacturers of pulp and paper, plywood and veneer, furniture, turpentine, and food additives. Within months of the lumber decision, however, the Commerce Department was enunciating a "dominant use" standard in order to provide protection to the domestic steel industry, which was requesting countervailing duties against imports of Brazilian steel made with subsidized iron ore (which has uses, albeit minor, beyond steel production). Under this standard, a subsidy could be generally available (in other words, to sectors other than the export industry of concern), but still qualify for countervailing duties, if the dominant user of the subsidized inputs if found to materially injure U.S. competitors. In the case of Canadian softwood trees, the lumber industry is by far the dominant user.

The broadening of the qualifications for countervailing duties prompted the Coalition for Fair Lumber Imports, with strong support from a number of members of the House and Senate, to again petition for protection. The resulting 1986 petition found the Commerce Department boxed in by the new precedent of its "dominant use" standard and the strong possibility that a negative decision would be overridden by federal legislation. The White House, in deciding whether to back the adoption of a countervailing duty, faced this second constraint as well as the fact that five Republican senators from major lumber-producing states (Washington, Oregon, Idaho, Georgia, and Alabama) were facing reelection challenges. Thus, with virtually the same substantive record before it (and, if anything, a slightly improved domestic industry), the Commerce Department reversed its 1983 decision and determined that purported Canadian lumber subsidies did meet the requirements of the Tariff Act.

11.2.1 The Case before the ITC and the Commerce Department

The basic substantive argument of the U.S. lumber industry before the Department of Commerce is succinctly summarized in table 11.1. Over 95 percent of Canadian softwood timber lands are publicly owned, compared to only 28 percent in the United States. The various Canadian governmental authorities sell the rights to remove trees from public forests to private logging companies (including lumber producers). The price at which the right to remove a tree is sold is known as the

Table 11.1   U.S. and Canadian Stumpage Prices

	United States	Canada	Canada as % U.S.
1977	$96.41	$10.16	10.5%
1978	$118.76	$21.59	18.2%
1979	$134.37	$30.96	23.0%
1980	$122.16	$27.48	22.5%
1981	$140.98	$12.09	8.6%
1982	$93.57	$10.57	11.3%
1983	$105.99	$11.63	11.0%
1984	$104.16	$11.84	11.4%

Source: U.S. ITC 1985.
Note: US$/per 1000 board feet (mbf).

"stumpage price." In most Canadian provinces, stumpage fees are based on mechanistic (if not totally arbitrary) formulas that work back from a selected end-market value, subtracting administratively determined forest-to-market costs to arrive at a value of trees on the stump. By contrast, rights to harvest timber on U.S. public lands are sold through a bidding process (with problems of its own) that is designed to recover full market value.

As indicated in table 11.1, the Canadian and U.S. systems for determining stumpage prices produce dramatically different results. U.S. prices are commonly many times higher than Canadian prices, and this holds even after adjustments for quality, transportation differentials, and production costs. This evidence that Canadian stumpage policy results in much lower Canadian stumpage prices has formed the central argument for protection before the ITC, the Commerce Department, Congress and, most recently, U.S.-Canadian negotiators.[7]

Evidence of the type presented in table 11.1 has been employed by interested parties to establish the existence of a Canadian lumber subsidy. ITC standards, however, require that any purported subsidy must be shown to cause material injury to domestic producers before countervailing duties may be imposed. The standards of "material injury" are problematic for the ITC. Economic criteria might be quick to equate "injury" with reduced profitability. Virtually any industry facing import competition will satisfy this criterion. The patterns of ITC cases, however, suggest that "material injury" commonly is interpreted as giving protection a bailout role. The criteria for determining the extent to which an industry is in need of protection under this definition of material injury, as revealed by ITC practice, include the existence of negative profits, declining employment, plant closings, and declining prices.

It is not sufficient (at least not according to the ITC's legislative mandate) that an industry seeking countervailing protection be able to show that it is experiencing hard times. The industry must demonstrate that it is materially injured by reason of the subsidized imports. To determine whether subsidized imports are the cause of material injury to a petitioning industry, the ITC's reports reveal that it explicitly examines such factors as the depth of any foreign sector subsidies, offsetting U.S. subsidies, exchange rates, macroeconomic growth and other general economic conditions, foreign-domestic price differentials, and the market share of imports.

The Coalition for Fair Lumber Imports emphasized four primary pieces of evidence regarding the extent and cause of the lumber industry's distress in its 1986 case before the ITC: (1) the market share of Canadian imports had risen steadily over the last decade (table 11.2); (2) sawmill capacity (and associated employment) in the United States

Table 11.2   **Imports, Exchange Rates, and Prices**

	Canadian Share of U.S. Lumber Consumption	Real Exchange Rate (US$/Can$; 77 = 100)	Real U.S. Lumber Prices (1984$/mbf)
1975	18.7%		
1976	21.9%		
1977	25.3%	100.0	$302.81
1978	27.6%	94.7	$323.81
1979	27.3%	93.6	$343.66
1980	28.1%	93.2	$295.97
1981	28.6%	91.9	$276.27
1982	29.2%	92.8	$204.06
1983	30.1%	94.9	$202.17
1984	30.7%	91.7	$214.87
1985	33.2%	89.8[a]	
1986	33.0%[a]		

Sources: U.S. ITC 1985; Coalition for Fair Lumber Imports 1986b.
[a]Estimated.

had declined over 1977–82, with only minor recovery since the end of the early-1980s recession (fig. 11.1); (3) profitability in the 1980s had deteriorated sharply (fig. 11.2); and (4) despite some recovery in demand since the early 1980s (fig. 11.1), real U.S. lumber prices showed little improvement and remained far below historic highs (table 11.2). This last point was played particularly hard by the Coalition. It provided the tactically important argument that "something is not right" with the workings of supply and demand and, by implication, the free trade views of neoclassical economists, since recovering demand did not pull up prices; the "something" that was not "right" was Canadian stumpage policy (Coalition 1986b). This argument was eventually endorsed by the ITC.

The ITC (U.S. ITC 1985) examined a number of indicators of relative competitiveness, but these showed little evidence of a strong Canadian advantage. As shown in table 11.3, the Canadians reveal a moderate advantage in unit labor costs, owing to higher productivity (that is, Canadian hourly wages actually exceed U.S. wages). Effective Canadian tax rates, however, are higher than U.S. rates in the lumber industry, and average total costs of U.S. and Canadian lumber production hardly differ at all.

This last observation is a reflection of the efficiency of the Canadian log market. That is, it might be thought that low Canadian stumpage prices should show up as low Canadian lumber prices. But the stumpage price is the price of removing a log from its forest, and, once removed,

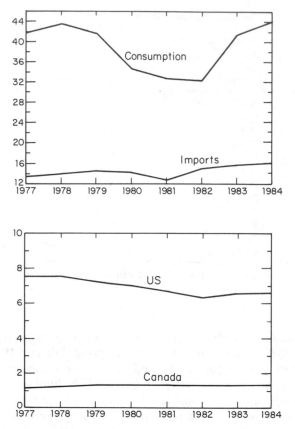

Fig. 11.1   Softwood lumber consumption and imports (billions of board feet) and number of sawmill establishments (1000s).

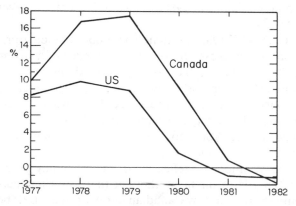

Fig. 11.2   Lumber industry return on assets.

Table 11.3   **Determinants of Production Costs in the Softwood Lumber Industry**

	Average Total Cost (US$ per mbf)		Unit Labor Cost (US$ per mbf)	
	U.S.	Canada	U.S.	Canada
1977	$180	$162	$67	$56
1978			$69	$61
1979	$278	$193	$73	$65
1980			$77	$67
1981	$240	$188	$79	$74
1982	$204	$206	$86	$78
1983	$221	$207	$85	$71
1984	$213	$205	$81	$65

	Average Hourly Wage (US$)		Labor Productivity (board feet/year)	
	U.S.	Canada	U.S.	Canada
1977	$5.14	$6.76	208,405	292,276
1978	$5.79	$6.75	206,718	285,679
1979	$6.07	$7.29	199,399	277,892
1980	$6.36	$8.15	185,418	285,207
1981	$6.80	8.79	185,061	269,209
1982	$8.27	$9.60	206,719	299,478
1983	$8.77	$9.98	243,640	365,979
1984	$9.26	$10.24	239,200	382,814

	Effective Tax Rates	
	U.S.	Canada
1977	26.4%	40.6%
1978	24.4%	36.1%
1979	21.6%	36.8%
1980	33.1%	29.4%
1981		23.1%

Source: U.S. ITC 1985.

logs are marketed by logging firms on the open market to Canadian lumber producers. Market-clearing log prices paid by lumber producers are roughly uniform, after accounting for quality differentials and transportation costs (FTC 1986). Canadian prohibitions on log (as opposed to lumber) exports do keep in-Canada log prices to lumber mills somewhat lower than U.S. prices, although differences turn out to be minor (U.S. ITC 1985; FTC 1986).

Thus, the vehicle by which the Canadian stumpage system could subsidize lumber exports is *not* through direct subsidization of lumber production. Rather, Canadian stumpage policy is alleged to subsidize lumber exports by subsidizing Canadian loggers, resulting in increased timber production turned into increased output from the Canadian lumber industry (Coalition 1986b). In the absence of the prohibition on Canadian log exports, an increase in Canadian timber production would tend to depress log prices evenly throughout North America—to the benefit of both Canadian and U.S. lumber mills. In the presence of restrictions on log exports, however, log prices tend to be levelized through an expansion of the Canadian sellers of log *products* (such as lumber). The result is that more of North America's sawmill capacity comes to be located in Canada than would otherwise be the case—to the displeasure of the U.S. Coalition.

11.2.2   The Economics of the ITC's Decision

Upon perusal of the kind of information available to the ITC and shown in tables 11.1–11.3 and figures 11.1–11.2, it is tempting to try to apply a more rigorous analysis to see if, in fact, Canadian stumpage prices (table 11.1) are the cause of the upward trend in the market share of imports (table 11.2), the soft prices in the North American lumber market (table 11.2), or depressed industry profitability. Do the data indicate changes in Canadian stumpage that correspond to changes in Canadian lumber export performance or lumber price levels? And what other explanations (such as exchange rate movements and recession) are there for the relative performance of the U.S. and Canadian lumber industries? These are, of course, the kinds of analyses that we might hope the ITC would perform in a systematic (for instance, econometric) fashion. However, there is a much more fundamental issue regarding the effects of below-market stumpage pricing in Canada.

The Federal Trade Commission, in its legal role as a guardian of consumer interests and in its de facto role as a proponent of free international trade, intervened in the 1982 and 1986 lumber proceeding before the ITC (FTC 1986). In its challenge to the Coalition's request for tariff protection, the FTC argues that the Canadian stumpage subsidy is entirely inframarginal; it has no effect on the level of forest harvest and, hence, no effect on Canadian lumber output. With appropriate references to Adam Smith, David Ricardo, Paul Samuelson, and Joan Robinson, the FTC asserts that

> the stumpage fee represents that portion of the trees' value, or economic rent, that is captured by the landowner. By definition, an economic rent does not affect the quantity of a factor supplied. Characterization of stumpage fees as part of economic rent rather than a cost that affects the quantity supplied follows from the fact that the

[Canadian] government, which decides how much land will be made available for logging, would make the land available for harvesting and loggers would harvest the logs regardless of where the stumpage fee is set, so long as it is within the range between zero and the amount by which the value of the logs exceeds the cost of harvesting them. (FTC 1986, 22–23)

The FTC's interpretation of the Canadian below-market stumpage prices as gifts of rent to loggers is founded on two observations. First, the stumpage prices do not even come close to clearing the market and are far exceeded by the market-clearing prices received on resale by loggers. That is, once cut, Canadian logs fetch prices that leave logging firms with unit revenues that exceed logging expenses and stumpage charges. Second, and most fundamentally, Canadian harvest (or "cut") levels on public lands are set administratively without reference to the stumpage price. By law, Canadian public cut levels are set (as they are on U.S. public lands) according to fundamentally noneconomic, biological criteria dealing with the physical sustainable yield, the age of the trees, and the species mix of the forest. Although specifics vary from province to province, the Canadian procedure for establishing a cut level begins with official determination of how much acreage to be allotted to tree harvesting and when to allocate that acreage to loggers. The right to remove timber from cuttable acreage is determined by an administrative process that awards long-term cut licenses to selected logging firms without charge and on the basis of explicitly noneconomic criteria. The licensee then submits a cut plan requiring approval on the basis of its conformation with sound logging practice. Loggers are permitted flexibility to vary their efforts at any point in time as market price and cost conditions vary, subject to the overall cut limit over the full term of the license. The stumpage price the licensee is charged on the removal of timber is determined through an administrative formula that arrives at the stumpage value as a net-back from the administratively calculated log value (FTC 1986).

In short, the Canadian cut of timber is not determined by reference to the price that public authorities receive for timber. Formally, the supply response of the Canadian cut to the stumpage price is zero. This conclusion leads directly to the FTC position that the Canadian stumpage system has no adverse effect on the U.S. lumber industry. The FTC's conclusion is based, however, on a combination of a priori economic theory and a reading of the literal content of Canadian cut policies. The FTC notes that there is an alternative hypothesis regarding the responsiveness of Canadian timber supply to the below-market stumpage system: "The Canadian stumpage fee systems could lead to an increase in the quantity of timber harvested if the timber companies successfully lobbied the Canadian federal or provincial governments to expand the quantity of cutting permitted *because the increased economic rents they would earn by cutting additional trees at the low stumpage fee*" (FTC 1986, 30–31, n. 38; emphasis in original). If true, this hypothesis provides support to the Coalition's assertions that U.S. lumber companies have been harmed by Canadian stumpage practices.

To test whether the Canadian supply of timber is responsive to the stumpage subsidy, we might directly estimate the supply of Canadian logs as

(1) $$Q_c^s = Q_c^s (P, SUBSIDY, X_c),$$

where Q_c^s is Canadian timber production, P is the price received for cut logs, $SUBSIDY$ is the stumpage subsidy, and X_c represents Canadian input cost and productivity variables (such as labor costs). The view of Canadian stumpage subsidies as entirely inframarginal implies that the effect of $SUBSIDY$ on Q_c^s is zero, while the U.S. lumber industry's assertion is that this effect is positive.

In reacting to the possibility that Canadian timber supply responds positively to stumpage subsidies, the FTC puts forth the possibility that the Canadian stumpage system might even discourage supply. The FTC argues that the noncompetitive process of license awards makes the Canadian system particularly likely to allocate harvesting to inefficient firms for whom some market-cuttable tracts are unprofitable. Raising stumpage fees worsens the fate of such firms and may cause a reduction in cut.

The FTC further notes that the arbitrary Canadian stumpage system may typically produce inframarginal rents, but it can also lead to the overpricing of some tracts of cuttable land for which market-determined levels of Ricardian rent are less than the stumpage fees. Such lands will go unharvested under the Canadian system; in effect, a rise in stumpage has no impact on tracts for which the stumpage fee is less than the associated Ricardian rent, but pushes some tracts and their supply out of the market. Both of these hypotheses amount to the observation that the Canadian stumpage system can reduce supply if and when fees are raised above market levels on particular tracts of forest, but should be entirely inframarginal when set below market levels.

The Canadian logging activity described in equation (1) is plausibly determined by the simultaneous action of supply and demand for timber. The indigenous Canadian demand for timber can be expressed as

(2) $$Q_c^d = Q_c^d (P, Z_c),$$

where Z_c represents determinants of timber demand, such as housing starts or aggregate income. Of course, Canadian timber markets are linked through trade in forest products to international markets. This really means U.S. markets, as transocean shipping costs effectively limit broader trade; only about 5 percent of North American timber output leaves the continent and most of these exports are specialty and high-grade products. Thus, there are corresponding supply and demand schedules for the U.S. that, together with equations (1) and (2), describe the market for timber in which Canadian loggers find themselves. Using u subscripts to denote the United States, this market can be described by equation (1) and the residual demand left over for Canadian suppliers after U.S. loggers have put their output on the market.[8] This demand is

$$(3) \qquad Q_{c,u}^d = Q_c^d + Q_u^d - Q_u^s = Q_{c,u}^d \,(P,X_u,Z_c,Z_u),$$

with s and d continuing to signify supply and demand.

Expressions (1) and (3) now constitute a two-equation system that we can estimate with available (albeit limited) data.[9] I have collected data for the six Canadian logging regions that produce all but a minute amount of the country's timber (Coastal B.C., Interior B.C., the Prairie Provinces, Quebec, Ontario, and the Maritime Provinces) over 1977–84. These data provide 48 sample points on prices (P) of logs (in real US$/ mbf), annual harvest levels (Q_c^s), and stumpage prices. *SUBSIDY* is measured by the difference between the price received by loggers and the stumpage fee.[10] To capture determinants of the cost of logging in Canada (X_c), we have data on industry labor costs and productivity.[11] Corresponding measures are used to capture X_u for the United States. The demand determinants reflected in Z_c and Z_u are measured by housing starts per year. The supply schedule in equation (1) is estimated using the pooled data and utilizing two-stage least squares, instrumental variables techniques that allow the separation of supply factors from demand influences on Canadian timber prices and quantities.

The estimated Canadian timber supply function is shown in table 11.4. A log-log (no pun intended, just lucky) specification is employed and produces elasticities of supply with respect to the indicated variables. My econometric "fishing" was restricted to the endogeneity/ exogeneity of *SUBSIDY* and labor productivity, and the inclusion/ exclusion of the lagged value of the dependent variable (Q_c^s). Results were not sensitive to these choices, including the magnitude and sign of the effect of *SUBSIDY*. Although confidence is weak, the elasticity of Canadian timber supply with respect to the price received by loggers appears to be of the same magnitude that others have reported when estimating U.S. supply functions (e.g., Adams, McCarl, and Homayounfarrokh 1986). It appears that the data allow the detection, with fairly good confidence, of the supply effects of costs and productivity factors.

Table 11.4 indicates that the elasticity of Canadian timber supply with respect to official stumpage prices has a point estimate of -0.13. There is moderate confidence suggested for this result, but I believe

Table 11.4   Does the Canadian Stumpage System Subsidize Lumber Exports?

The Canadian Timber Supply Function

Variable	Expected Sign	Elasticity	2-Tail Signif.
Stumpage subsidy	+ (Lobbying for +Q)	−0.13	0.27
	0	(−1.13)	
	(Inframarginal rents)		
Price	+	+0.23	0.46
		(.75)	
Labor Costs/HR	−	−2.03	0.04
		(−2.09)	
Labor Productivity	+	+0.68	0.003
		(3.14)	
Intercepts			0.10−0.00

Notes: Standard error = 0.11; F-statistic = 307.14; D.W. = 1.84; and number of observations = 48.

the most that can really be said is that the approach and data employed here have produced no evidence that the Canadian system of stumpage subsidies results in an increase in Canadian timber supply. In this negative sense, my results are supportive of the view that the ITC incorrectly ruled that the Canadian timber pricing system constituted an export subsidy to the lumber industry that warranted countervailing U.S. duties.

This is not to say that, had the ITC seen table 11.4 (or understood the FTC's argument about inframarginalism), it would have ruled any differently. My reading of the record of the case is that the ITCs decision turned on a combination of (1) evidence that, for whatever reason, the U.S. lumber industry finds itself in poor condition, and (2) irresistible domestic, election-year political forces. Indeed, from the Administration's point of view, it must have seemed far preferable to have protection for the lumber industry emanate from the Commerce Department and the ITC, rather than from congressional legislation. The former leaves the Administration in control of both the level of duties and negotiations with the Canadians regarding remedial measures.

11.3   The Welfare Consequences of Protection

Even if there were compelling evidence that the Canadian stumpage system for timber effectively subsidized the expansion of the Canadian lumber industry, the existence of a subsidy, by itself, would provide little economic justification for tariff protection of the U.S. lumber industry. Indeed, taking the sum of consumers' and producers' surplus as our yardstick of aggregate national welfare, the ITC might be instructed to send a note of gratitude to the Canadians, rather than impose a tariff against them. If Canada would like to tax other sectors of its economy (through resource diversion into timber and lumber production) to subsidize the production of goods for which the United States is a large net consumer, the United States benefits.

This (neo)classic response to the importation of products subsidized by foreign governments, of course, needs to be qualified. For example, were Canadian lumber subsidies part of a predatory strategy to drive the U.S. industry under in anticipation of a subsequent exercise of monopoly power, the United States might appropriately respond with protective tariffs. Successful predation, however, has as its first requirement the ability of the predator to drive its victim's capital out of production and to keep that capital out of production. This is hard to imagine in the timber or lumber industries. In the former, the basic capital stock on which production is based just keeps on growing if taken out of production, and the lumber industry's mills are extremely long-lived and highly specific to lumber production.[12] At any rate, figure 11.1 indicates that capital has been (re)entering the U.S. industry since the bottom of the early-1980s recession.

Other, nonpredatory justifications for countervailing against a subsidy to Canadian shipments of lumber are also difficult to defend. The Canadian industry is quite competitively structured and hardly presents an oligopolistic front to the United States. The lumber industry, in general, is low on the list of industries likely to produce beneficial technological spillovers if protected against subsidized imports. Strategic, national defense justifications for protecting an indigenous softwood (construction) lumber industry are equally unconvincing, since the probability of a military interdiction that cuts off supplies from Canada seems so farfetched. In fact, the Coalition for Fair Lumber Imports is notable, if not commendable, among lobbyists seeking protection for its *not* waving the national security banner.

11.3.1 The United States as an Import Monopsonist

If there is a nationalistic (that is, national welfare) justification for tariffs on imported lumber, it lies in the observation that the United States is a large-country importer of softwood products. As noted above, North America is virtually a closed market. The United States annually buys more than 60 percent of Canadian lumber production, and other outlets for Canada are subject to very high transportation costs and tend to be restricted to specialty products. Moreover, the elasticities of Canadian lumber supply, both for total production and exports, are quite low.[13] In short, Canada's very large neighbor to the south is its primary market, and the economics of forestry and milling are such that production levels are not especially sensitive to price. Policies such as U.S. import duties have the potential of depressing lumber and timber prices in Canada, and the country is an easy target for monopsonistic U.S. trade policies that improve the U.S. terms of trade—unless it can credibly retaliate.

Canada has, however, considerable scope for defending itself against an aggressive, monopsonistic United States. Canada is, for all intents and purposes, the sole foreign supplier of lumber to a country with a very inelastic demand.[14] In 1984, for example, the United States imported 12.995 billion board feet of softwood lumber. Fully 99.6 percent (12.947 billion board feet) of this total came from Canada.

The current trade wars in the timber industry, then, are being played out in a setting in which both trading partners have significant market power. Each might like to exercise its respective ability to act as a price maker, but the danger that a move away from the traditional free trade equilibrium will force the other country to exercise its market power is very real.

The stakes that the United States and Canada face, if not the game-theoretic optimal strategies each could play, can be quantified through the application of existing information on supply and demand responses in the lumber industry. From the U.S. perspective, an import duty on lumber from Canada has the potential of depressing the price of Canadian imports. Domestic producers stand to gain as the duty-inclusive price of imports is driven up. U.S. lumber consumers may not be pleased by having to pay higher prices, but the U.S. Treasury can collect the tariff wedge between U.S. and Canadian lumber prices. Depending on the height of the duty relative to the optimal monopsony tariff, the gains to U.S. producers and the Treasury can outweigh the losses of domestic consumers, and in that sense raise aggregate national welfare.

To estimate winners' gains and losers' losses from U.S. lumber duties, I have parameterized a simple three-sector model of North American lumber trade, employing the estimates of supply and demand elasticities provided by researchers who have specialized in modeling lumber markets. This model is used to simulate alternative tariff policies and measure the associated incidence and welfare effects. There are two supply sectors to be captured: the U.S. supply (Q_u^s) and the supply of imports from Canada (Q_c^i). These supplies must be priced to clear the U.S. market, given U.S. demand for lumber (Q_u^d). The two supply schedules and one demand schedule are taken to have constant elasticity functional forms over the relevant range, such that $Q = \alpha P^\epsilon$ where ϵ represents the elasticity.[15] When a duty of t percent is imposed on imports, the import supply schedule as perceived by the United States becomes:

$$Q_c^i = \alpha_i [(1 + t)P^i]^{\epsilon^i}$$

where P^i refers to the duty-exclusive delivered price of Canadian lumber and $P = (1 + t)p^i$. Solution of $Q_u^s + Q_c^i = Q_u^d$ for P then yields equilibrium prices and quantities. The model's results are clearly partial equilibrium results in the sense that no feedback effects to the macroeconomy or close substitutes and complements are calculated.

The elasticity of U.S. lumber supply is taken to have a value of .42, which is the three-region weighted (1985 quantities) average of supply elasticities reported by Adams, McCarl, and Homayounfarrokh (1986). Domestic demand elasticity is set at −.15, which accords with estimates reported by Spelter (1985) and Adams, McCarl, and Homayounfarrokh (1986). The most important of the elasticity values is the value for the elasticity of import supply from Canada. This elasticity fundamentally determines the extent of any U.S. monopsony power vis-à-vis Canada. This elasticity reflects both the elasticity of Canadian demand and the elasticity of Canadian supply:

(4) $\epsilon^i = \epsilon_c^s(Q_c^s/Q_c^i) - \epsilon_c^d(1 - Q_c^s/Q_c^i).$

Adams, McCarl, and Homayounfarrokh (1986) estimate a value of .917 for ϵ^i and this value is employed here. This is close to the estimate of 0.89 reported by Boyd and Krutilla (1987). While an import supply elasticity of less than one may seem small, it also accords with direct calculation of equation (4). Employing 1984 values for the quantities in equation (4), assuming that Canadian consumers have the same demand elasticity as U.S. consumers, and taking a value of $\epsilon_c^s = .23$ from table 11.4 produces an import supply elasticity of approximately 0.9. Any value in this range suggests a very high degree of monopsony power for the United States.

The Effects of a 15 Percent Countervailing Duty

Under the foregoing parameterizations, table 11.5 reports the calculated incidence and welfare effects of a 15 percent U.S. countervailing

Table 11.5   **Welfare Consequences of a 15 Percent U.S. Lumber Duty (millions of 1986 dollars)**

	Gains	Losses
U.S. lumber producers (labor, capital, land)	$416.8	
U.S. lumber users (intermediate and final)		$556.9
U.S. government (tariff revenues)	$340.5	
Net U.S.	$200.4	
Net Canada		$223.0
Net U.S. and Canada		$22.5

duty on Canadian lumber imports. Table 11.6 shows the corresponding price and quantity impacts on the North American lumber market. In each table, it is assumed that Canada does not respond with retaliation of any form. A 15 percent duty raises domestic lumber prices (by approximately 5 percent). Through the monopsony effect, however, the duty also depresses Canadian lumber prices. U.S. lumber producers are unambiguously better off—by an estimated $400 million per year. The U.S. Treasury also realizes a gain from tariff revenues totaling $340 million annually. These benefits are in contrast to the negative effects of a 15 percent duty on U.S. lumber consumers. Consumers suffer a burden of over $550 million per year.

The gains of U.S. lumber producers and the Treasury are large enough to more than offset consumers' losses. In this sense, a 15 percent duty raises national welfare. The duty effectively transfers some of the rents that otherwise accrue to Canadian lumber producers to U.S. producers and to U.S. governmental revenue collections. As a result, Canada in its role as a net producer of lumber is worse off. Canadian losses are on the order of $220 million (US$) per year. The $20 million excess of Canadian losses over U.S. gains is the deadweight "world" loss as a result of the exercise of U.S. monopsony in the international lumber market.

The "Optimal" Tariff

If the United States benefits, on net, from a 15 percent lumber duty, how far could it push the duty and still see rising benefits? How high is the optimal tariff? This question is addressed in tables 11.7 and 11.8. *Assuming no Canadian policy response,* table 11.8 indicates that the optimal duty is roughly 50 percent. A duty of this magnitude has very large impacts on the lumber market. The optimal duty would drive domestic lumber prices up sharply, severely depress Canadian prices, cut imports by close to 40 percent, and raise domestic production by 10 percent.

Table 11.6   Market Effects of a 15 Percent U.S. Timber Duty (1986 dollars)

	% Change from No Tariff	Price/Quantity Impact
Tariff	15	$29/mbf
Change in U.S. Price	5	$13/mbf
Change in Canadian price	−9	−$18/mbf
Change in U.S. production	2	698mmbf
Change in imports	−8	−1026mmbf
Change in U.S. consumption	−1	−328mmbf

Table 11.7   **Welfare Consequences of an "Optimal" U.S. Lumber Tariff (millions of 1986 dollars)**

	Gains	Losses
U.S. lumber producers (labor, capital, land)	$2,249.0	
U.S. lumber users (intermediate and final)		$2,910.2
U.S. government (tariff revenues)	$1,119.9	
Net U.S.	$458.7	
Net Canada		$890.0
Net U.S. and Canada		$431.2

The optimal, unopposed tariff would be a great boon to domestic lumber producers, who would realize a gain of over $2.2 billion per year. Similarly, the Treasury would see tariff revenues of more than $1.1 billion. These gains are in contrast to the $3 billion loss that would be experienced by domestic consumers. This burden would manifest itself in higher home construction costs and higher prices of homes, apartments, and commercial buildings. The gains of U.S. lumber producers and revenue collectors from an optimal tariff would outweigh the losses of consumers, by the definition of optimal. The net gain to the nation would be on the order of $450 million per year.

An optimal tariff would hit Canada extremely hard. As indicated in table 11.7, Canada would suffer a loss of almost $900 million per year. For an economy of the size of Canada's, this sum is hardly trivial and could be expected to engender a vociferous response designed to exploit Canada's monopoly power. The net international deadweight loss of $430 million, however, would presumably go unnoticed by anyone.

As previously discussed, the central parameter determining the degree of U.S. monopsony power in the lumber market is the elasticity of import supply. Not only is there the usual statistical uncertainty

Table 11.8   **Market Effects of an "Optimal" U.S. Lumber Tariff (1986 dollars)**

	% Change from No Tariff	Price/Quantity Impact
Tariff	53	$140/mbf
Change in U.S. price	26	$65/mbf
Change in Canadian price	−41	−$85/mbf
Change in U.S. production	10	3408mbf
Change in imports	−38	−4929mbf
Change in U.S. consumption	−3	−1521mbf

about this parameter, but an optimal tariff as large as indicated by table 11.8 would severely depress Canadian lumber prices. This could be expected to open up very significant trans-Pacific and trans-Atlantic trade for the Canadians, and would effectively move the United States into a much more elastic portion of the Canadian import supply function. To provide some indication of the sensitivity of welfare implications to the import supply elasticity, figure 11.3 graphs the net national U.S. welfare gains from an optimal tariff over alternative values of the import supply elasticity (again assuming no policy response by Canada). Cutting the import supply elasticity to .5 would imply an increase in U.S. monopsony power, and the net gain from an optimal tariff would exceed $700 million annually. Doubling the initial value of the import supply elasticity to 1.8 cuts the optimal tariff; the associated net welfare gains would be less than $200 million per year.

11.3.2   Canada as an Export Monopolist

Optimal duties approaching 50 percent are primarily of academic interest. The vehement response of the Canadians to the October actions in support of a 15 percent import duty provides an indication of the intolerance that would meet an even higher duty—and that would invalidate the calculations in tables 11.7 and 11.8. Moreover, the U.S. political and administrative process provides no indication that it con-

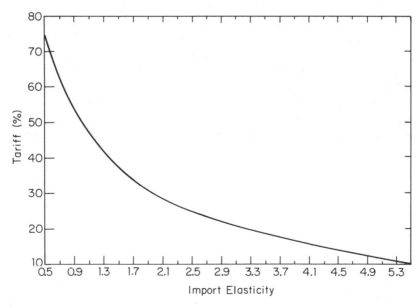

Fig. 11.3   Optimal U.S. timber tariff.

siders an optimal duty within the realm of possibility. The U.S. lumber industry's most aggressive demands have been in the range of 25–28 percent.

More relevant than the matter of an optimal tariff is whether the kinds of distributional payoffs to the domestic lumber industry and/or the associated net national impacts of the magnitudes shown in table 11.5 were worth putting the United States' broader relationships with Canada at risk of significant deterioration. The end result, after all, is that the negotiations regarding a general free trade agreement have been set back, and the December 30, 1986 lumber accords have left the United States subject to a monopolistic Canadian export tariff.

Table 11.9 shows estimates of the incidence and welfare effects of the Canadian 15 percent export duty, relative to the previous free trade regime.[16] The Canadian export duty raises delivered lumber prices in the United States and depresses prices in Canada. In fact, news reports out of the timber- and lumber-producing regions of Canada are already reporting output and employment cutbacks, as well as the attendant public outcry against the Canadian government for agreeing to the export duty. The export duty, however, permits Canada to exercise its monopoly power vis-à-vis the United States—although it is apparently no consolation that the resulting monopoly rents accrue to the Canadian treasury rather than to the Canadian timber and lumber industries. On net, Canada appears to gain roughly $120 million per year from the 15 percent lumber export duty.

The U.S. lumber industry cares little if its prices are raised by a U.S. import tariff or an equivalent Canadian export tariff (table 11.9). (In fact, this observation probably carries the heart of the political economy of the timber trade war.) U.S. lumber consumers are equally indifferent to the reason the prices they face are going up. At the national level, the

Table 11.9   **Welfare Consequences of a 15 Percent Canadian Export Duty (millions of 1986 dollars)**

	Gains	Losses
U.S. lumber producers (labor, capital, land)	$416.8	
U.S. lumber users (intermediate and final)		$556.9
U.S. government (tariff revenues)	$0.0	
Net U.S.		$140.1
Net Canada	$117.6	
Net U.S. and Canada		$22.5

primary economic difference between the countervailing duty and the ultimate Canadian export tax that has been adopted is found in which government gets to collect the tariff revenues. The move from a U.S. import duty to a Canadian export duty has caused a transfer from the U.S. Treasury to the Canadian treasury. Relative to the pre-October free trade regime, the United States now finds itself $140 million per year worse off. From a national perspective, the war has not gone well.

11.4 Conclusion

11.4.1 Observations on the Conduct of U.S.-Canadian Trade Relations

What began in October 1986 as a monopsonistic action against Canada has ended with a breakdown of free trade in lumber and the imposition of a monopoly tariff against the United States. While the economic logic of this is troubling, the political rationale does not seem hard to fathom. The U.S. lumber industry appears to have pulled off a classic case of industry capture of the political process.

It is fashionable to criticize simple industry "capture" theories of economic policy-making (e.g., Kalt and Zupan 1984), and in some sense it would be nice if there were a more complicated and less traditional story to tell here. In this case, however, the capture theory holds considerable appeal: the U.S. lumber industry was able to organize itself into a highly effective lobby group that was able to organize virtually all timber and lumber producers, suppress free-rider factionalism, produce technical legal and analytic submissions to the relevant administrative agency, and enlist particularly important congressional support in its appeals to the White House, the Commerce Department, and the ITC. In Washington, Oregon, Idaho, Georgia, and Alabama, the November elections for the U.S. Senate provided the catalyst that forced the political process to focus on the lumber industry. The finding, three weeks prior to the elections, that Canada was subsidizing lumber production and was subject to countervailing duties may have angered the Canadians, but within two months a negotiated settlement was reached that left the U.S. lumber industry and Canada better off than if no intervention had occurred. This helped the Administration preserve, or at least partially salvage, its relations with Canada while supplying the benefits to the domestic sector that put forth the most compelling political demand. In classic Stigler-Olson fashion (that is, more concentrated groups are more effective at political organization), the U.S. consumers of lumber products were so diffuse and faced such low per capita stakes relative to lumber producers that they had (and continue to have) little ability to block moves to raise the prices they pay.

From the Canadian perspective, the prospect of a countervailing duty imposed by the United States created sharp strategic choices: fight the ITC and Commerce Department findings through the courts or negotiate a settlement. The former path suggests a strategy designed to convince the United States of Canadian toughness in opposing monopsonistic U.S. tariffs, but why take this stand? The negotiated settlement, after all, offered the prospect of a net gain for Canada—a victory in the timber trade war. To imply, however, that the Canadians adopted the negotiations approach because they were pursuing the Net Canada entry in table 11.7 is to beg the question of why the Canadian political process would be driven less by capturing private interests and more by considerations of net national economic welfare than is the policy process in the United States. The Canadian lumber and timber industries would appear to be no less powerful relative to consumers than their counterparts in the United States, and they have not benefited from the timber trade war. The reality seems to be that Canada really was put in a defensive posture when the United States launched its import duty, and the negotiated settlement was explicitly justified internally in Canada by the argument that, if there is going to be a duty on lumber, it is better that Canada collect the sizable tariff revenues than let these monies accrue to the U.S. government.

It remains to be seen whether the timber trade war is completely over. If it is rekindled, the impetus will come from Canada. Only within Canada is there significant, continuing unrest and distress over the current state of affairs. Layoffs have begun in the Canadian timber and lumber industries, and nationalistic sentiments have been piqued by a sense of having been put on the defensive by the United States. The global solution may still ride on the fate of ongoing attempts to establish a general free trade agreement. The lumber incident, however, has probably reduced the prospects of a broad agreement. In the United States the lumber and timber industries now have vested interests in opposing a return toward free trade, and in Canada mistrust of the United States runs high.

11.4.2   Observations on the Conduct of Protectionist U.S. Trade Policies

The U.S.-Canadian lumber dispute forcefully demonstrates that the realms in which trade wars are fought are not solely the economic marketplaces. The outcome of the lumber dispute has hinged significantly on broader geopolitical, foreign policy concerns. For, at the core, the outcome of the timber trade war refllects a combination of (1) the domestic political necessity of transferring wealth to the U.S. forest products industry, while (2) trying to keep the Canadians "happy." The essence of the negotiated settlement of December 1986 (and table 11.9) is that to accomplish the former, the United States had to raise the amount it pays for the latter—by $117.6 million per year (table 11.9).

This interpretation of the timber trade war explains why the U.S. political system ended up at table 11.9—a Canadian monopoly export tariff—rather than a table 11.5—a U.S. monopsony import tariff. If the path to protection for the U.S. industry was a U.S. import duty, Canada was going to be harmed—table 11.5. The prospect of direct economic harm, as well as the fueling of Canadian nationalism, was demonstrably going to reduce the supply of an important ally's cooperation in the conduct of U.S. foreign policy. As Prime Minister Mulroney noted (threatened?), it is "extremely difficult for anyone . . . to be friends with the Americans."

This kind of Canadian response was unacceptable to the White House and, especially, to the State Department. But if protection had to be delivered, the congressional, legislative route to protection for the U.S. lumber and timber industries was the *least* appealing course: it would be extremely difficult and time-consuming to repeal tariff legislation and replace it with a policy that transferred wealth back to Canada. The alternative result of a temporary U.S. duty replaced by a negotiated Canadian export tariff was far more appealing, the Net U.S. loss of $140.1 million per year from table 11.9 is the price the nation has paid to satisfy the domestic political demands of the timber and lumber industries while ensuring continued Canadian cooperation and allegiance in the conduct of foreign policy. This sum really is a net loss for the United States: the country now pays a higher price to Canada for no more, and probably less, Canadian contribution to U.S. foreign policy.

The path of protectionism that this case reveals is sobering. It is not a picture of the United States engaged in strategic moves to improve the national welfare. It is not even a picture of the United States and its trading partners engaging in mutually destructive rounds of economic retaliation. Rather, it is a picture of the United States pushed into protectionist measures by powerful domestic political interests and then, through the foreign policy branches of government, having to find ways to quickly halt the resulting trade war and appease the affected foreign nations.[17] The United States must act in this way because, as the dominant member of its alliances, it is forced to bear the brunt of the responsibility for maintaining those alliances. Thus, this case suggests that, at least when it affects allies, protectionism can raise the cost and inhibit the conduct of foreign economic and political policy.

Notes

The author would like to thank David Butler and Eric Press for their valuable research assistance. The author has also benefited from comments by workshop participants at the Canadian Studies Conference (Duke University), the Conference on Trade Issues (National Bureau of Economic Research), the Hoover Institution, and the Energy and Environmental Policy Center (Harvard University). Special thanks are due Robert Baldwin, Henry Lee, Arye Hillman, Irwin Stelzer, and Raymond Vernon for their detailed remarks.

1. The shakes and shingles duties arose out of a section 201 case before the International Trade Commission. Section 201 cases allow for import protection of a domestic industry when the ITC is satisfied that imports have been shown "to be a substantial cause of serious injury." This criterion makes no reference to unfair trading practices by foreign competitors and is generally regarded as outside the intent of GATT provisions for countervailing duties.

2. *New York Times,* October 9, 1986.

3. *New York Times,* January 1, 1987.

4. Ibid.

5. *New York Times,* October 17, 1986.

6. *MacClean's,* January 5, 1987, 38.

7. The coalition's filings before the ITC predictably include a list of additional Canadian subsidies that allegedly harm U.S. lumber producers. This list includes preferential tax treatment, loan guarantee programs, and public reforestation programs. At least the first of these does not appear to be substantiated by the data (see table 11.3), and reading the coalition's discussion of these other subsidies, it is hard to resist the impression that the list of U.S. preferential programs for the forestry industry could be made to seem as extensive as the Canadian list.

8. After adjustment for transport costs and exchange rates. This formulation assumes that the process of log-price equalization through trade in log products works within the period of observation (one year in the data used below). Available data require this approach.

9. The basic limitation is disaggregated stumpage fees that can be matched to appropriate measures of logging output. All data employed here are from U.S. ITC 1985.

10. Data that would permit a more accurate accounting for the market-clearing stumpage price and the actual price are not available on a comparable basis.

11. The latter, in particular, may be endogenous since its measurement involves Q_c^s. Results reported below treat labor productivity as an endogenous variable. Results are not sensitive to this.

12. The human capital in the lumber industry is not particularly high skilled, with low-skill labor dominating the work force (see, e.g., the wages in table 11.3). It is also notable for its unwillingness to relocate.

13. See, for example, Adams and Haynes 1981; Adams, McCarl, and Homayounfarrokh 1986; and Boyd and Krutilla 1987.

14. Adams, McCarl, and Homayounfarrokh 1986, for example, estimates the elasticity of U.S. lumber demand to be in the range of $-.15$ to $-.17$.

15. The α's are explicitly calculated by parameterization of ϵ and insertion of actual values of Q and P.

16. The price and quantity effects are as indicated in table 11.8.

17. The United States–Japan dispute over Japanese auto imports followed the same general course: U.S. quota restrictions were superseded by Japanese voluntary export restraints that leave the rents from trade restriction in Japan.

References

Adams, Darius M., and Richard Haynes. 1981. U.S.-Canadian lumber trade: The effects of restrictions. In Roger A. Sedjo, ed., *Issues in U.S. international forest products trade*. Research Paper R-32. Washington D.C.: Resources for the Future.

Adams, Darius M., Bruce A. McCarl, and Lalehrokh Homayounfarrokh. 1986. The role of exchange rates in Canadian-U.S. lumber trade. Center for International Trade in Forest Products, College of Forest Resources, University of Washington, Seattle.

Boyd, R., and K. Krutilla. 1987. The welfare implications of U.S. trade restrictions against the Canadian softwood lumber industry: A spatial equilibrium analysis. *Canadian Journal of Economics* 20(1):17–35.

Coalition for Fair Lumber Imports. 1986a. *Lumber fact book: The facts, issues and policies behind the Canada/U.S. lumber trade problems*. Washington, D.C.

———. 1986b. *Petition for the imposition of countervailing duties pursuant to the Tariff Act of 1930, as amended, in the matter of: Certain Softwood Lumber Products from Canada*. Vol. 1. Washington, D.C.

Federal Trade Commission. 1983. *Prehearing brief by the Federal Trade Commission in the matter of: Certain Softwood Lumber Products from Canada, countervailing duty proceeding*. USITC.

———. 1986. *Post-conference brief of the Federal Trade Commission in the matter of: Certain Softwood Lumber Products from Canada*. No. 701-TA-274 (Preliminary). USITC.

Kalt, J. P., and M. A. Zupan. 1984. Capture and ideology in the economic theory of politics. *American Economic Review* 74 (June): 279–300.

Spelter, H. 1985. A product diffusion approach to modeling softwood lumber demand. *Forest Science* 31(3):685–700.

U.S. International Trade Commission. 1982. *Determination of the commission in investigation no. 701-TA-197 (preliminary) under section 703 (a) of the Tariff Act of 1930, together with the information obtained in the investigation, softwood lumber into the U.S.* USITC Publication 1320.

———. 1985. *Report to the president on investigation no. 332-210 under section 332 of the Tariff Act of 1980, conditions relating to the importation of softwood lumber into the U.S.* USITC Publication 1765.

Comment   Arye L. Hillman

Joseph Kalt has presented us with a most interesting case study of the political economy of protection. Kalt's study confirms the appropri-

Arye L. Hillman is professor of economics in the Department of Economics and Business Administration, Bar-Ilan University, Israel.

ateness of the political-influence models of protection in explaining the formulation of international trade policy and reveals how approaches to the determination of trade policy that presume a benevolent government pursuing efficiency objectives assume motivations for intervention that tend to be of little importance in the political arena wherein trade policy decisions are made. A particularly interesting aspect of the study is the revelation that whereas initially pleas for protection went unheeded, once the loophole had been found that provided a legal basis for protection, competition arose between the executive and legislative branches of government to become the provider of protection. This competition is clearly understood in political economy terms. Given that protection could now be provided, both the executive and legislative branches of government sought to reap the benefits attendant on being the agents dispensing increases in rents to the residual claimants in the domestic import-competing industry. Presumably the transaction is not one way; protection is provided against an offsetting return. The political competition was to designate the beneficiary of the return.

The economic theory underlying political-support-maximizing choice of trade policy is based on the principle that policymakers trade off the political costs and benefits of intervention; the costs are the loss of political support from the losers from intervention and the benefits are the gains via the political support from the beneficiaries. Kalt shows us that complex linkages can underlie this cost/benefit calculation. The United States instigated protection for the domestic lumber industry. But such protection in the form of an import tariff has associated political costs that either are absent or at least can be diminished if the same protection were seen to be the consequence of a trade-restricting policy by a foreign government, in this case, Canada. Hence, if one asks why the U.S. government insisted that the Canadians impose an export tax to replace the U.S. import duty, thereby transferring $220 million of revenue annually to Canada, the answer can only be that the political benefits to the United States of casting Canada as the interventionist government were at least equal to the present value of the revenue stream.

Of course, the ITC's position was that intervention in this case corrected for a market distortion rather than created one. Kalt's econometrics confirm that the assignment of rights to Canadian trees is a story about rents rather than subsidies. Rent-seeking activities of Canadian loggers could have evoked an output response, but Kalt's estimates indicate that the supply of Canadian logs is determined administratively, and thus, from an economic perspective, inelastically with respect to the price of logs. Thus the ITC's reasoning went the wrong way around: the difference between the payments made for logs in Canada and the United States does not affect Canadian output of logs, but administratively determined Canadian output establishes the value of the residual rents available to the recipients of the rights to fell Canadian trees.

Thus, rents are assigned in Canada via rights to trees, presumably to individuals who are adept rent-seekers. And a restriction of Canadian lumber exports increases the rents available in the U.S. lumber industry. The list of gainers, not taking into account more complex general equilibrium interdependencies, consists of the claimants to rents in the U.S. lumber industry, the Canadian federal government as the recipient of the revenue from the export tax, and Canadian consumers who presumably benefit from lower domestic lumber prices via the output-substitution effect of the export tariff on domestic Canadian producers' market allocation decisions; one must infer that the gainers also include the U.S. government, which initiated the interventionist process in the first place. Missing from this list are U.S. consumers of lumber, whose loss from intervention Kalt quantifies, and the Canadian logging industry.

The absence of the Canadian logging industry from the list of gainers from intervention is somewhat of a puzzle. After all, the Canadian loggers appear sufficiently politically astute and well organized to be the beneficiaries of the substantial rents from below-market-price access to Canadian trees. But enter a new set of actors: the Canadian provincial authorities who assign the right to log and thereby allocate the rents from logging. The Canadian export tax on lumber therefore effected a transfer from the beneficiaries of administrative allocation decisions made by the provinces to the Canadian federal government. The Canadian provinces lost and the Canadian federal government gained via discretionary assignment of rents and revenues.

There is one final step in tracing through the transfer of rents. The Canadian federal government has announced that revenue from the export tax is to be transferred to the provincial authorities, who, we recall, exercise the discretion to determine the assignment of rents from access to trees. Thus, somewhat circuitously, the Canadian provincial authorities have secured a share of the rents accruing from Canadian timber production. Of course, the provincial authorities could directly secure access to these rents if they could directly sell the right to trees. But the right to trees is "given away" at prices below market value. The export tax permits the Canadian provincial authorities to secure natural resource rents that otherwise are allocated via the interaction between provincial officials and loggers.

We have not been told how the Canadian federal government, the Canadian provincial authorities, and Canadian loggers decide on the mechanism for sharing Canadian natural resource timber rents. Nor do we know the sharing rule for the monopoly rents from restriction of Canadian supply. However, the Canadian rent recipients together have more rents to share subsequent to the intervention, because of the exercise of monopoly power. Taking the Canadian rent recipients into consideration, the list of losers from the United States–Canada lumber intervention reduces to one—domestic U.S. consumers. And this is what the political economy approach to explaining government intervention would predict. The diffused domestic U.S. consumers of the import-competing goods are the source of the rents for the more cohesive U.S. and Canadian industry-specific interests and for the Canadian authorities. "Rational ignorance" or perhaps "rational apathy" of the U.S. consumer facilitates this outcome.

Joseph Kalt is to be complimented for unraveling all of this for us, and for showing us how good applied economic theory and econometrics can be put to use to demonstrate that even though governments may frame their interventionist motives in efficiency terms, considerations of political support and income distribution, and not efficiency, more often explain governments' interventionist decisions. Indeed, in this case, since both governments appear to have gained, Kalt has shown us how international economic policy can well be collusive. The U.S. government can claim that it had no choice but to react to the Canadian "subsidy"; the Canadian federal government can claim that given the options it was presented by the U.S. government, it had no choice but to implement the export tax transferring the revenue to Canada for discretionary spending. And the Canadian provincial authorities, who also appear to be ultimate beneficiaries of the rent transfers, can claim to have been passive agents throughout the entire affair.

Kalt computes estimates of the Harberger efficiency costs of government intervention. But to these costs of intervention one could add the value of the real resources expended in contesting the rents created and assigned at government discretion. Direct computation of the cost of rent-seeking activity is not possible in this instance because we are not in a position to observe the various rent-seeking outlays that have been made. However, we are able to observe the values of the rents assigned and transfers made as the consequence of intervention, and procedures (for example, reviewed in Hillman 1988) can be proposed for inferring the value of the resources expended in a rent-seeking quest from the observed value of the rent being contested. The addition of the real resource cost of rent-seeking activity would result in an increase over the estimates of social loss based on Harberger efficiency costs alone.

Finally, a straightforward application of a basic theorem from the theory of international trade demonstrates a difficulty with the initial basis of the U.S. timber industry's claim of "unfairness" in international trade practices. The U.S. timber industry complained that it was "unfair" that it did not have access to "cheap" Canadian lumber because of the Canadian government's ban on the export of logs. However, the factor-price equalization theorem suggests that in a free trade equilibrium there would be no difference in price between Canadian and U.S. lumber, notwithstanding the Canadian export ban on logs. Kalt reports labor costs in the Canadian and U.S. timber industries to be more or less the same. Given a common technological coefficient on log/lumber, the price of logs is then equalized internationally if there is free trade in lumber. The complaint of the U.S. timber producers was therefore presumably not that they were denied access in the free trade equilibrium to "cheap" Canadian logs but that they were barred from access to competition for the rents associated with the assignments of rights to Canadian trees. The United States–Canada lumber intervention then proceeded to provide compensating rents for the U.S. domestic industry, and indeed it would appear there are gains all around, except for U.S. consumers.

References

Hillman, A. L. 1988. *The political economy of protection.* In the series, Fundamentals of pure and applied economics. New York: Harwood Academic Publishers.

Contributors

James E. Anderson
Department of Economics
Boston College
Chestnut Hill, MA 02167

Richard Baldwin
Graduate School of Business
Columbia University
611 Uris Hall
New York, NY 10027

Robert E. Baldwin
Department of Economics
University of Wisconsin
Madison, WI 53706

Magnus Blomström
Stockholm School of Economics
P.O. Box 6501
113 83 Stockholm
Sweden

Harry P. Bowen
Graduate School of Business
New York University
100 Trinity Place
New York, NY 10012

Drusilla K. Brown
Department of Economics
Tufts University
Medford, MA 02155

Avinash K. Dixit
Department of Economics
Princeton University
Princeton, NJ 08544

Robert C. Feenstra
Department of Economics
University of California
Davis, CA 95616

Richard K. Green
Department of Economics
University of Wisconsin
Madison, WI 53706

Gene M. Grossman
Woodrow Wilson School
Princeton University
Princeton, NJ 08544

Richard Harris
Department of Economics
Queen's University
Kingston, Ontario KTL 3N6
Canada

Arye L. Hillman
Department of Economics
Bar-Ilan University
52 100 Ramat-Gan
Israel

Joseph P. Kalt
John F. Kennedy School of
  Government
Harvard University
79 Kennedy Street
Cambridge, MA 02138

Kala Krishna
Department of Economics
Harvard University
Littauer 215
Cambridge, MA 02138

Paul Krugman
Department of Economics
Massachusetts Institute of
  Technology
E52-383A
Cambridge, MA 02139

Ksenia Kulchycky
Department of Economics
University of Pennsylvania
3718 Locust Walk
Philadelphia, PA 19104

Val Eugene Lambson
Department of Economics
University of Wisconsin
Madison, WI 53706

Edward E. Leamer
Department of Economics
University of California, Los
  Angeles
405 Hilgard Avenue
Los Angeles, CA 90024

James Levinsohn
Department of Economics
University of Michigan
Ann Arbor, MI 48109

Robert E. Lipsey
National Bureau of Economic
  Research
269 Mercer Street
8th floor
New York, NY 10003

Rachel McCulloch
Department of Finance
Brandeis University
Waltham, MA 02254

Catherine L. Mann
Room S-9035
The World Bank
1818 H Street, N.W.
Washington, DC 20433

Steven J. Matusz
Department of Economics
Michigan State University
East Lansing, MI 48824

John Mutti
Department of Economics
Grinnell College
P.O. Box 805
Grinnell, IA 50112

Peter A. Petri
Department of Economics
Brandeis University
Waltham, MA 02254

Raymond Riezman
Department of Economics
University of Iowa
Iowa City, IA 52242

Dani Rodrik
John F. Kennedy School of
  Government
Harvard University
79 Kennedy Street
Cambridge, MA 02138

Robert W. Staiger
Department of Economics
Stanford University
Stanford, CA 94305

Robert M. Stern
Institute of Public Policy Studies
University of Michigan
Lorch Hall
Ann Arbor, MI 48109

Marie Thursby
Department of Economics
Purdue University
West Lafayette, IN 47907

Beth V. Yarbrough
Department of Economics
Amherst College
Amherst, MA 01002

Author Index

Subject Index